BRITAIN'S HABITATS

A field guide to the wildlife habitats of Great Britain & Ireland

Sophie Lake, Durwyn Liley, Robert Still & Andy Swash

WILD Guides

PRINCETON
press.princeton.edu

This book is dedicated to the memory of John Underhill-Day, friend, colleague and mentor for 20 years.

Published by Princeton University Press, 41 William Street, Princeton, New Jersey 08540
In the United Kingdom: Princeton University Press, 6 Oxford Street, Woodstock, Oxfordshire OX20 1TR
press.princeton.edu

Requests for permission to reproduce material from this work should be sent to Permissions, Princeton University Press

First published 2015
Second Edition 2020

British Library Cataloging-in-Publication Data is available

Library of Congress Control Number 2020943984
ISBN 978-0-691-20359-1
Ebook ISBN 978-0-691-21179-4

Production and design by **WILD**Guides Ltd., Old Basing, Hampshire UK.

Printed in Italy

10 9 8 7 6 5 4 3 2 1

CONTENTS

The Broad Habitat Groups

Woodlands

Scrub

Heathlands

Grasslands

Mountains

Rocky Habitats

Wetlands

Freshwaters

Other Habitats

Coastal Habitats

Foreword

The variety of wildlife habitats in Britain and Ireland is truly astonishing. Ranging from dynamic coastal habitats to remote rocky mountains, from ancient woodlands and flower-rich grasslands to upland peat bogs and lowland heathlands, the list goes on and on – to the extent that there are now 65 different habitat types described in this second edition of **WILD***Guides*' excellent *Britain's Habitats*.

In these islands we have an astonishing record in terms of support for nature conservation –reflected, for example, in around 10% of the UK population being members of an environmental charity. Not only that, but we have protected species legislation and conservation programmes and national networks of protected sites with resources to support their management, which are the envy of the world. Despite this, each generation is experiencing an increasingly impoverished natural world, one where once-widespread plants, animals and fungi are now heading for extinction, and many habitats appear to be deteriorating inexorably. We are still going backwards on biodiversity, with the *2019 State of Nature* report revealing that over the last 10 years, more species are decreasing (44%) in the UK than are increasing (36%). But it is not only species abundance that is of concern, because species distribution is also heading in the wrong direction, having fallen by 5% since 1970 for a suite of 6,554 terrestrial and freshwater indicator species.

Despite the amazing efforts of so many people and organizations for the best part of a hundred years, it is clear that our traditional approach to nature conservation has not been sufficient to reverse the decline in biodiversity. Goodness knows where we would be without these efforts, but quite simply they have not been enough. We need something more besides – not instead of, but in addition – that enables dynamism to be restored and allows the development of functional natural systems. That something is rewilding – *the large-scale, long-term restoration of natural processes to the point where nature is allowed to take care of itself.*

Longhorn Cattle and Tamworth Pigs in mixed habitats at Knepp Wildland.

A key principle of rewilding is to be non-prescriptive, especially with regard to species outcomes, but it is still important to embark on the rewilding journey with a good understanding of the habitats that are expected to develop both during the transition and in the longer term. As this book explains, very few of the habitats in Britain and Ireland are in fact near-natural – those that are, being confined to unstable cliffs, inaccessible ravines and ledges, and shifting foreshores, where natural processes are able to continue more or less unhindered. Most of our wildlife habitats are semi-natural, maintained in their current state through human intervention such as tree clearance or grazing. Patterns of land use that have continued in one form or another for thousands of years have created a cultural landscape in which human action has replicated the disturbance and flux that key species and natural processes would in many cases have created. Now, however, with human influence so predominant, the remains of this cultural landscape are no longer sufficient to support our precious wildlife.

This superb book is a celebration of the habitats that we know and love – the jewels in the crown of our special sites. It shows us how rich and diverse our habitats can be. It also highlights how much of our landscape is taken up with intensive arable land, improved grassland or other degraded habitats. It provides an insight into the natural processes that shape habitats and how unfettering these could restore dynamism and connectivity in the landscape, helping to reverse the devastating wildlife losses we have presided over for too long. *Britain's Habitats* provides us with a wealth of evidence, not only for countering the scourge of 'shifting baseline syndrome' in our attitudes to managing the countryside and urban green space, but also for making genuine strides in mitigating the impacts of climate change and reversing biodiversity decline. I commend it to anyone with an interest in our many and varied habitats, and in the future wellbeing of our natural environment.

Alastair Driver

Prof Alastair Driver
Rewilding Britain

Introduction

Habitats are the places where plants and animals live. They are characterized by distinctive combinations of plant and animal communities and their physical environment. This makes it possible to identify individual types of habitat, which is useful in understanding where different species are likely to be found and what their needs are – crucial information for protecting wildlife. Habitats are also valued in their own right as the diverse products of interactions between plants and animals and their environment. For this reason, nature conservation legislation affords protection to habitat types as well as to species.

It is fairly easy to separate habitats into broad categories such as woodland, heathland, grassland, wetland and freshwater and many people are familiar with these terms. Yet within each of these categories there is a wide variety of different habitat types. These habitat types have been classified under a range of different systems (see *page 35*) that have been designed for a variety of purposes, and are in some cases very technical. This book provides a clear description of each of the wildlife habitats that are likely to be encountered in Britain and Ireland, enabling them to be recognized with confidence. For each habitat type, information is provided on its distribution and extent in Britain and Ireland, its ecology, origins and the way it has developed, and the conservation issues. These 'habitat accounts' also indicate the key features and species to look out for and the best times of year to visit.

Although most habitats can be recognized quite readily, it is important to remember that they are variable – the habitat types described in this book are perhaps best considered as nodes on a continuum, with many variations and transitions. These transitions (sometimes called 'ecotones') may support species typical of both habitats as well as other species that are adapted to the transitional conditions – this can make them particularly rewarding to investigate. Sometimes habitats occur in easily distinguishable and often extensive patches with clear boundaries, but in other instances the transition is much more gradual and there is no distinct boundary. In some environments, or under particular management regimes, a variety of different habitat types and transitions between them can be found together in a distinctive combination which can, itself, be considered as a unique habitat. For example, Soft Cliff often contains a mosaic of grassland, wetland and scrub habitats, and Wood Pasture is a combination of woodland and grassland.

Some habitats will not fit easily into any one of the accounts given in this book – they they might be transitional between different habitats, a fine-scale mosaic of habitats or a particular local expression of a habitat. For example, this site in Connemara supports a curious patchwork of Machair and Lowland Dry Heath.

ABOVE: **Frenchman's Creek, Helford River, Cornwall**. Here the boundary between the different habitats types (**Mudflat** and **Woodland**) is clearly defined. BELOW: In this view of the **Lake District** several different habitat types can be seen, including ❶ **Scree**, ❷ **Rocky Slope**, ❸ **Upland Acid Grassland**, ❹ **Bracken**, ❺ **Mixed Scrub** and ❻ **Upland Oak Wood**. Individual habitat patches are straightforward to identify, but the edges are in some cases transitional, with one habitat type blending into another.

TYPES OF HABITAT

When trying to decide on a name for a habitat there is an impressive array of terms to choose from. Although some are broad and overarching (*e.g.* 'freshwaters'), others are very precise (*e.g.* 'Hard oligo-mesotrophic waters with benthic vegetation of *Chara* spp.'). The titles given to the habitat types included in this book err towards the more specific end of the spectrum as these are generally more informative. Full accounts are given for 65 main habitat types that fall within the broad habitat categories of woodlands, scrub, heathlands, grasslands, mountains, rocky habitats, wetlands, freshwaters, coastal habitats and 'other habitats', the latter being a catch-all for anything that did not fit comfortably elsewhere. Summary accounts are provided for a further nine rare habitats (five types of heathland and four types of freshwater lake).

Although most of the habitats covered in this book are recognized as UK Priority Habitats (see *Habitat Classification*, page 35), even if their names may vary slightly, there are a few exceptions. This is either because, although not considered a priority for nature conservation, it is still a distinctive semi-natural habitat of some interest for wildlife (*e.g.* Upland Rush Pasture), or because it is in some way considered to be unique (*e.g.* Atlantic Hazel Wood). In order to provide a more logical classification from the point of view of identifying habitats in the field, some habitats have not been included within the same broad category that applies to UK Priority Habitats. For example, Calaminarian Grassland and Purple Moor-grass and Rush Pasture are within the grassland section of this book, although they are considered under 'inland rock' and 'fen, marsh and swamp' respectively as part of the UK Priority Habitat classification system. In addition, for ease of reference, most mountain habitats have been grouped together.

The map opposite (together with the other habitat introduction maps) is derived from satellite imagery. The data are from the CORINE land cover, which is overseen by the European Environment Agency. The minimum size used in the map data is 25 ha, so parcels of habitat smaller than this are not recorded. The pie-chart summarises the data shown in the map.

Relative areas of the different broad habitat categories

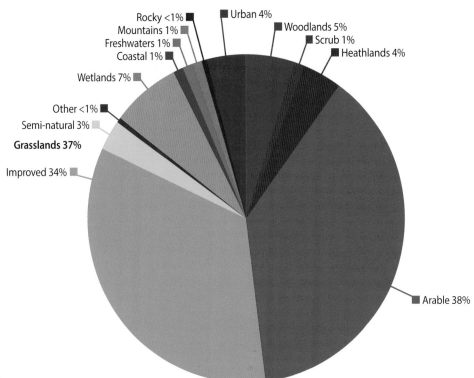

The Habitats of Britain and Ireland

KEY

■ Woodlands	*page 40*	■ Rocky Habitats	*page 218*
■ Scrub	*page 100*	■ Wetlands	*page 234*
■ Heathlands	*page 120*	■ Freshwaters	*page 270*
■ Grasslands	*page 152*	■ Coastal Habitats	*page 316*
■ Mountains	*page 198*	■ Other Habitats	*page 364*

WOODLANDS

pages 40–99

Woodland habitats are those dominated by trees. They include our most structurally diverse and natural-seeming habitats, although almost all are a product of the long-term interaction between people and nature.

Lowland Mixed Oak and Ash Wood
page 52

Lowland Dry Oak and Birch Wood
page 57

Beech Wood
page 60

Yew Wood
page 63

Wet Woodland
page 66

Wood Pasture
page 72

Upland Oak Wood
page 78

Upland Mixed Ash Wood
page 83

Caledonian Forest
page 86

Atlantic Hazel Wood
page 91

Upland Birch Wood
page 94

Coniferous Plantation
page 97

SCRUB

pages 100–119

Scrub includes habitats dominated by shrub species. Hedgerow and Bracken are included within this category, as they are in many ways ecologically similar.

Mixed Scrub
page 108

Bracken
page 117

Hedgerow
page 111

HEATHLANDS

pages 120–151

Heathland includes open habitats dominated by dwarf-shrubs such as heathers, Bilberry and Crowberry. Most is semi-natural, a consequence of traditional agricultural practices carried out on poor soils.

Lowland Dry Heath
page 130

Lowland Wet Heath
page 140

Upland Dry Heath
page 143

Upland Wet Heath
page 149

GRASSLANDS
pages 152–197

Grassland habitats are those dominated by grasses and herbs. Some meadows are enclosed as fields, other grasslands form open landscapes, particularly in the uplands and on downland. Most would eventually revert to woodland without management.

Lowland Calcareous Grassland
page 162

Lowland Dry Acid Grassland
page 168

Lowland Meadow and Pasture
page 171

Upland Calcareous Grassland
page 183

Upland Acid Grassland
page 192

Northern Hay Meadow
page 186

Calaminarian Grassland
page 195

Upland Rush Pasture
page 189

Coastal and Floodplain Grazing Marsh
page 177

Purple Moor-grass and Rush Pasture
page 174

MOUNTAINS

pages 198–217

Mountain habitats are found above about 700 m and are primarily influenced by environmental conditions; they are some of our most natural habitats.

Montane Dwarf-shrub Heath
page 204

High Montane Heath and Snow-bed
page 208

Mountain Ledge
page 212

Montane Scrub
page 215

16

ROCKY HABITATS

pages 218–233

Rocky habitats are exposed vegetated rock. Although very typical of mountains, they are also found in the uplands, and even at sea level (although this category does not include maritime cliffs).

Rocky Slopes
page 224

Scree
page 227

Limestone Pavement
page 230

WETLANDS

pages 234–269

Wetlands are a very diverse group of habitats predominantly influenced by the presence of freshwater. Most are transitional, but some have reached an equilibrium due to the wet nature of our climate or ongoing management.

Blanket Bog
page 244

Raised Bog
page 249

Upland Spring and Flush
page 252

Lowland Fen
page 256

Valley Mire
page 260

Reedbed
page 265

FRESHWATER

pages 270–315

Freshwater habitats include rivers, lakes, streams, ponds and canals; all have open water, which can be either standing or flowing.

Nutrient-rich (Eutrophic) Lake
page 282

Upland Lake, Loch and Tarn
page 285

Peat-stained (Dystrophic) Waters
page 288

Turlough and Fluctuating Mere
page 291

Other types of Lake
page 294

Pond
page 298

Ditch
page 301

Canal
page 304

Fast-flowing River and Stream
page 307

Sluggish River and Stream
page 310

Chalk River and Stream
page 313

19

COASTAL HABITATS

Coastal habitats include muddy, sandy and rocky shoreline habitats from the intertidal zone to the point inland where the maritime influence is no longer overriding.

Mudflat and Sandflat
page 326

Saltmarsh
page 329

Sand Dune
page 332

Machair
page 338

Coastal Vegetated Shingle
page 342

Saline Lagoon
page 348

Rocky Shore
page 352

Soft Cliff
page 355

Hard Cliff and Cliff Slope
page 358

OTHER HABITATS

pages 364–381

Other habitats include those that are most strongly influenced by humans but can nevertheless still be rich in species, particularly Garden, Brownfield and Arable.

Arable
page 368

Brownfield
page 372

Traditional Orchard
page 375

Garden
page 378

FACTORS INFLUENCING HABITATS

The habitats that are evident today owe their origins to a complex range of factors, including geology, geography, topography, climate and the influence of humans. Although we tend to think of habitats as stable in character, as fixed endpoints resulting from past interactions between the above factors, this is not necessarily the case. Habitats in Britain and Ireland will continue to evolve and, as we move further into the Anthropocene, are likely to be increasingly influenced by human activities and their unintended consequences (such as climate change and mass species extinction). On the plus side, developing approaches to conservation, particularly habitat restoration and creation, may also result in different types of habitats, and it is important to keep an open mind about these too.

Geology and soils

Britain and Ireland have an incredibly varied geology, which is reflected in a great diversity of habitats – unusual in such a relatively small area. The bedrock is fundamental in shaping the landscape and habitats present, although in some places its influence is softened by superficial deposits. These are derived through weathering (over geological time scales) or are transported by the wind (as in the case of Sand Dune and Machair), or by glaciers and their melt-waters. Such glacial drift covers much of Britain and Ireland, excluding the south of England. Soil nutrient status and acidity/alkalinity are also key factors in determining the type of habitats present. In some cases, soils can also disguise the character of the bedrock, but the two are usually closely related as soils are derived from weathered rock. The decomposition of vegetation, leaching (whereby soluble substances are carried down through the soil by rainwater and become unobtainable to plants) and climate also influence the soil. On well-drained soils that developed under woodland, leaching is not a strong factor, and the soil, known as brown earth, contains plenty of organic matter incorporated by the activities of earthworms. In colder and wetter climates, leaching is more pronounced, leading to nutrient-poor soils. Where waterlogging occurs, anaerobic gleys form; these are widespread in the uplands where they support moorland habitats. Waterlogging can also lead to the formation of peat and wetland habitats. On limestone, the strongly calcareous influence of the bedrock is too pronounced to be leached out and thin, slightly alkaline, free-draining soils (known as rendzinas) support distinctive calcareous grassland habitats.

Rock type

LEFT: **Igneous** rocks such as granite and basalt are formed from molten magma and are usually very hard. They include both volcanic rock (formed by eruptions) and intrusive rock, which is formed deep in the earth's crust. Patchily distributed, these rocks are slow to erode and form the hard cliffs of Lundy and Strumble Head, Snowdon, parts of the Lake District, Arthur's Seat in Edinburgh, the highest peaks in Scotland and the tors of Dartmoor. CENTRE: **Sedimentary** rocks dominate across most of England and much of Wales and central Ireland. They are ancient sediments laid down by rivers or on the sea bed, and include limestone, sandstone and shale. RIGHT: **Metamorphic** rocks are secondary rocks, generated from either igneous or sedimentary rocks through heat and/or pressure, deep within the earth's crust. Limestone metamorphoses into marble, and shale into schist or slate. Metamorphic rocks dominate in the Highlands of Scotland, Tyrone, Londonderry and Donegal.

The Geology of Britain and Ireland

Numbers refer to
the locations
illustrated overleaf.

KEY

SEDIMENTARY ROCKS

Eocene, Oligocene, Pliocene and marine Pleistocene
Cretaceous
Jurassic
Triassic
Permian
Carboniferous
Devonian
Silurian
Ordovician
Cambrian
Late Precambrian

METAMORPHIC ROCKS

Lower Palaeozoic and Proterozoic
Early Precambrian

IGNEOUS ROCKS

Intrusive
Volcanic

Cul Mor, Assynt. These dramatic peaks are relics of a great sheet of Precambrian sandstone laid down on top of ancient metamorphic gneiss well over 2,000 million years old. Much of the landscape is characterized by Upland Wet Heath and Blanket Bog, with mountain habitats found on the peaks.

Meall nan Tarmachan, near Ben Lawers, Perthshire. Rock formed from sands, muds and limestones deposited in an ancient sea *c.* 600 million years ago was subsequently subjected to intense heat and pressure. The resulting metamorphic schists are renowned for their Upland Calcareous Grassland and mountain habitats.

Breckland, Norfolk, is a gently rolling chalk landscape that has been overlain with wind-blown sands of glacial origins and supports stripes and patchworks of Lowland Dry Acid Grassland and Lowland Calcareous Grassland.

Woolbeding Common, West Sussex, overlies Greensand, a type of greenish sandstone laid down in the Cretaceous period. The area supports Lowland Dry Heath, Lowland Wet Heath and Wood Pasture, and secondary woodland including Lowland Dry Oak and Birch Wood.

Stonehill Down, Purbeck. This quarry was used to excavate chalk, a soft limestone formed during the Cretaceous (<100 million years ago) when this area was bathed in a warm, shallow sea. It supports Lowland Calcareous Grassland with Ash-dominated Lowland Mixed Oak and Ash Wood on the northern flank.

Igneous granite outcrops such as **Haytor on Dartmoor, Devon** are distinctive landmarks formed of hard rocks created around 300 million years ago. They are surrounded by heathland and grassland habitats with Blanket Bog.

Exmoor, Somerset/Devon. The relief is gentle compared to that of the Breacon Beacons (similarly formed of Old Red sandstone) as the glaciers did not reach this far south in the Pleistocene. Exmoor is characterized by Upland Dry Heath, Upland Wet Heath, Blanket Bog and Upland Oak Wood.

The Burren, Co. Clare, has extensive exposures of Carboniferous limestone, which formed as sediments in a tropical sea from approximately 350 million years ago, and supports Limestone Pavement, calcareous grasslands and a form of Atlantic Hazel Wood.

The Lake District hills are geologically varied and are composed of differently aged rocks, including volcanic rocks; sedimentary sandstones, siltstones, mudstones and limestone; and granite. They support a variety of upland habitats.

Climate, topography and geography

Britain and Ireland have an oceanic climate with relatively small differences between the summer and winter temperatures. The moderating influence of the Atlantic Ocean means that the climate is much milder than that of other places at comparable latitudes (*i.e.* those receiving a similar amount of solar radiation, such as Mongolia), and this shapes the habitats present. However, the climate varies across Britain and Ireland and this is reflected in the types of habitat that can be found in different areas. Oceanic western woodlands receive five times as much rainfall as their south-eastern counterparts, and are characterized by the abundance and diversity of moisture-loving mosses and liverworts (bryophytes). The wind-whipped Hebrides support unique coastal grassland heavily influenced by blown sand. Vast areas of the cool, wet north are blanketed in peatland habitats, while the continental climate of Breckland in East Anglia supports steppe-like grasslands and parched limestone grassland in the south can support Mediterranean plants.

This map shows upland areas of Britain and Ireland defined by climate, soils and altitude. Habitats change in character at about 300 m above sea level, although in more exposed situations the transition can be much lower. Temperature falls around 0·6°C for every 100 m increase in altitude, so only cold-tolerant species are found at higher altitudes. Topography can also accentuate climatic conditions and increase the variety of species and habitats found at different extremes. Corries on the glaciated north and east-facing slopes of mountains support rare montane habitats requiring moist, cool, sheltered conditions; in contrast, warm south-facing well-drained slopes in the south can support Mediterranean species near the limit of their range. The map shows the 300 m contour and the high mountains (the dots are peaks above 900 m). The hatching indicates approximate areas with upland characteristics based on the 300 m contour and extended to include areas with an upland environment (regardless of altitude). These areas are loosely based on those mapped by Averis *et al.* (see further information) and in the UK Countryside Survey.

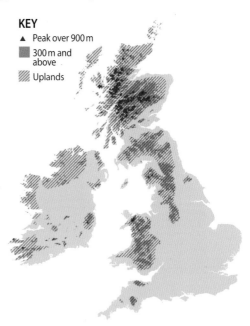

KEY

▲ Peak over 900 m

■ 300 m and above

▨ Uplands

LEFT: Rainfall averages 3,200 mm per year in the higher areas of the Lake District and feeds innumerable small streams. RIGHT: In Breckland, an average of 600 mm of rain falls per year and the drought-prone sandy soils support a sparse grassy sward.

Climate varies across Britain and Ireland according to latitude, the influence of the Atlantic Ocean and the prevailing south-westerly winds. Western areas are milder, wetter and windier, and show smaller differences in daily and seasonal temperatures. Eastern areas are drier with more extreme temperatures. The south of England can be influenced by the warm air mass from the continent, while northern Scotland is exposed to the polar air mass resulting in a 10–15 °C difference in temperature.

KEY

Mean January minimum temperature (°C)
1981–2011

7
5
4
3
2
1
0
−1
−2
−3
−4

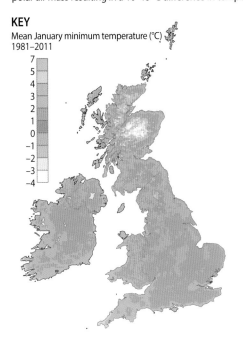

KEY

Mean August maximum temperature (°C)
1981–2011

25
23
21
19
17
15
13
11
9

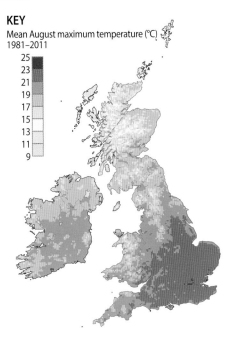

KEY

Mean Annual Rainfall (mm)
1981–2011

4,140
3,740
3,380
3,020
2,660
2,300
1,940
1,580
1,220
860
500

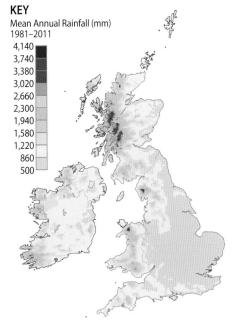

Climate change

The climate of Britain and Ireland has changed dramatically in the past and is changing rapidly now as a result of human activities. Current predictions suggest that all areas will get warmer, particularly in the summer, with temperature changes likely to be greatest in the south. Winter rainfall will increase and there will be an increase in extreme weather events such as droughts and flooding, and in sea-level rise. Habitats are likely to alter as climatic conditions become unsuitable for some existing species and new species for which conditions become suitable will arrive. Climate change may also exacerbate the impacts of other factors such as atmospheric pollution or pathogens. Habitats have adapted to changes in the past but the scale of change and the degree of fragmentation of many habitats makes climate change one of the biggest challenges for conservation today. Action is needed to increase the resilience of habitats by reducing other pressures, by improving habitat management and by providing the space and functional connectivity to enable habitats and species to respond.

Humans

Humans have had a profound impact on the habitats of Britain and Ireland since adopting a settled agricultural existence in the Neolithic period, when the process of woodland clearance became widespread. Seven thousand years later the area of woodland had been reduced by more than 95%. During the intervening millennia, open semi-natural habitats came to dominate the landscape as a consequence of agricultural and associated practices. The relative amounts of semi-natural habitat fluctuated through the ages, but it was when these practices began to change radically in the second half of the 20th century that a staggering proportion of habitats was lost to agricultural intensification, afforestation and development. Although habitat destruction has now slowed significantly (but not ceased), habitats are continuing to deteriorate due, for example, to pollution, inappropriate management, the effects of habitat fragmentation and climate change. However, deliberate re-creation and restoration is taking place. Recently, interest and experiments in rewilding – the concept of allowing natural processes (often involving free-ranging livestock) to shape habitats – has been growing rapidly. This approach has huge potential for restoring wildlife-rich habitats on degraded land. The dynamism of such systems may result in a more flexible approach to habitat-based conservation in the future.

Timeline of Key Events (extinction dates approximate for Britain and/or Ireland)

YEAR		EVENT
	108000	Start of Devensian/Midlandian Glacial period (ice covers much of Ireland and Britain, north of a line from South Wales to The Wash)
	24800	**Modern people arrive in Britain and Ireland (a peninsula of Eurasia)**
	10000	Early Holocene, temperate climate establishes, around 60% woodland cover. Ireland separated from Britain. **Woolly Mammoth and Woolly Rhinoceros extinct**
	9500	Climate warms at end of Devensian/Midlandian Glacial period; tundra-type vegetation; **significant movement of people into Britain**
	8000	**Movement of people into Ireland**
	7000	Scots Pine arrives in north-west Scotland
BCE	6000	Britain separated from European mainland. **Tarpan (wild horse) extinct**
	5000	Warmer, more oceanic climate; rain-fed bogs start to form
	4000	Woodland reaches fullest extent
	3000	**Woodland clearance starts by Neolithic peoples using stone axes and ring-barking. First evidence of coppicing; Stonehenge and Newgrange built**
	1500	**First field systems in permanent clearings**
	1000	**Aurochs and Eurasian Elk extinct in Britain and Ireland**
	500	**Copper mined; use of metal tools expands woodland clearings, heathlands become established**
CE	1000	*See opposite*
	2000	

YEAR		EVENT
	43	**Start of Roman Britain, roads, drainage (*e.g.* Fens). and woodland cover reduced to 15%. Dalmatian Pelican extinct**
	500	BRITISH HUMAN POPULATION 1·5 MILLION
	1600	**Reindeer extinct**
	1086	**Normans: 15% of England wooded; medieval open-field farming; Rabbit introduced**
	1349	**Black Death, widespread abandonment of agricultural land**
	1564	**First canal (Exeter)**
	1600	**Beaver extinct**
	1614	BRITISH HUMAN POPULATION 4 MILLION
	1621	**Wolf extinct**
	1637	**Start of major drainage works in Fens**
CE	1707	**Jethro Tull invents seed drill; agricultural revolution about to start**
	1760	**Industrial revolution, increase in use of fossil fuels, atmospheric pollution**
	1761	**Enclosure Acts: loss of open field systems in Ireland and England**
	1792	**'Year of the Sheep': Highland Clearances in Scotland**
	1832	**Great Bustard extinct**
	1845	**Irish Potato Famine; Irish population falls by 50%**
	1850	**Start of Roman Britain, roads, drainage (*e.g.* Fens)**
	1919	Woodland cover < 5%; coniferous afforestion starts
	1950	Agricultural intensification starts, resulting in the destruction or neglect of much natural habitat
	1958	The River Thames declared 'biologically dead' where it flows through London
	2000	Habitat decline slowing after English lowland meadow declined by 97%, lowland heathland by 80%, Raised Bog by 94% and 45% of Scotland's Blanket Bog was afforested in 20th century; BRITISH HUMAN POPULATION 58·6 MILLION
	2009	**Beaver reintroduction trial commenced in Scotland**
	2010	125 fish species recorded in the River Thames
	2015	Rewilding Britain launched, indicating increased momentum for habitat change and expansion through restoration of natural processes
	2019	2019 UK State of Nature report finds 15% of assessed species are in danger of extinction. 72% of land is managed for agriculture, 13% woodland cover
	2020	**White-tailed Eagle reintroduced to the Isle of Wight**

Lazy beds between Clare Island harbour and Portnakilly, Ireland. Lazy beds are a ridge and furrow farming system that can still be seen in parts of western Scotland and Ireland. In these areas seaweed is often applied as a fertilizer and the beds are used to grow potatoes. The field systems in much of Britain would have resembled lazy beds during the post-Roman period in the 5th and 6th centuries.

Natural change – succession

Succession is the sequential change in the species present in a given place over time. The process of succession is referred to frequently in this book as it is the key natural mechanism through which changes occur, both within and between habitat types. Succession is a result of the adaptations of species to specific environments, and the way in which species change their environment.

Primary succession starts on bare ground that is colonized by pioneer species adapted to cope with exposed conditions and low levels of nutrients. Which species these are depends on the nature of the substrate – for example, lichens and mosses are primary colonizers of bare rock (*e.g.* Scree), and specialist flowering plants are colonizers of bare sand (*e.g.* pioneer Sand Dune). These species gradually change the environment, increasing the organic content of the substrate and its capacity to hold water, and in some cases stabilizing the substrate and allowing it to 'build' (*e.g.* Saltmarsh and Sand Dune). These changes result in other, more vigorous species being able to colonize, which often outcompete the previous species and, in turn, change the environment. This may allow longer-lived species such as shrubs to become established and these eventually give way to trees. However, the succession need not stop here, as in particularly wet situations bog-mosses can start the process of peat formation. Where conditions become too wet for trees to become established, bog may develop. The process of change continues until an equilibrium (often called a climax community) is reached where there is no further potential for new species to colonize, or until disturbance events or environmental change disrupt or reset the successional process. Most habitats in Britain and Ireland are maintained at a particular stage in their successional pathway by human activities (such as livestock grazing). This is called a 'plagioclimax'.

Secondary succession occurs when an existing community is disturbed (*e.g.* by natural tree fall or by tree-felling in woodland) and the process is set back to an earlier stage (*e.g.* grassland or heathland). The pathway that succession takes is not random, but is influenced by a variety of factors such as climate and seed source, and the degree of the disturbance involved – and it can happen at any scale. Disturbance events that cause a reversion to bare ground, and subsequent succession, are a key element in many habitats, and lead to the development of a diversity of vegetation types and structures that are suitable for a range of different species, for example in Lowland Dry Heath (*page 130*) or Soft Cliff (see *page 355*).

A range of successional stages can often be observed together in the landscape. This can be in situations where secondary succession is patchy or is at different stages with a given area, or where primary succession is resulting in an environmental gradient (*e.g.* in accreting Sand Dune or Saltmarsh).

Reedbed

Woodland

Upper Saltmarsh

Pioneer Saltmarsh

Solway Firth, Dumfries and Galloway – successional stages from pioneer to upper Saltmarsh, Reedbed and woodland.

Succession over time presents a major challenge when the conservation aim is to maintain a particular successional stage but the activities that traditionally achieved this are no longer carried out. The photographs here illustrate the colonization of heathland by Scots Pine over a 14-year period.

Cerne Abbas, Dorset – a mosaic of successional stages is seen here with patches of Lowland Calcareous Grassland (LCG), Mixed Scrub and woodland intermingling on the hillslope.

Natural processes and the role of large animals

Together with storm events and the dynamism of watercourses, large herbivores such as Tarpan (wild horse), Aurochs (wild cattle) and deer once played a key role in disrupting the otherwise linear trajectory of succession. Their actions (grazing, browsing, trampling and debarking and breaking trees and scrub) are thought to have created shifting mosaics and transitions of open grassland, heathland and wetland with scrub and trees. This would have resulted in a huge diversity of niches for species dependent upon open conditions (such as those species currently confined to static open habitats maintained through conservation management today).

Other habitat architects were Beaver and Wild Boar. By creating bare ground, Wild Boar set back succession, exposed seedbanks and created regeneration opportunities for plants. Beaver shaped wetlands by coppicing trees to dam streams and create pools, again providing a range of microhabitats suitable for other species.

Predators such as Wolf and Eurasian Lynx probably also influenced habitats by creating a 'landscape of fear', in which herbivores avoided locations where they were at greater risk of predation (such as terrain where their escape would be impeded).

The absence of these free-ranging species, together with the taming of rivers and barricading of shorelines, means that the British and Irish landscapes have lost the crucial element of dynamism. Rewilding (see *page 36*) is increasingly being considered as an effective means of restoring such dynamism.

TOP: The scrubby grassland that has developed at **Knepp, East Sussex**, supports species that are in decline elsewhere, such as the Purple Emperor butterfly, Turtle Dove and Nightingale. BOTTOM: **Beaver**, River Otter, Devon. Beaver is a keystone species that can radically alter watercourses by coppicing bankside trees to create temporary dams that raise the water level around their lodges. This creates a variety of microhabitats, introduces woody debris into rivers, regulates water flow and improves water quality. There are now both free-ranging and contained Beaver populations in the UK.

At Knepp, East Sussex, **Old English longhorn cattle**, together with Exmoor ponies, Tamworth pigs and deer are part of a pioneering project using livestock to create a functioning ecosystem on ex-arable farmland.

HABITAT CLASSIFICATION

Several different systems are used to record or classify habitats in Britain and Ireland. These various systems have been devised for different purposes, for example to enable the legal protection of habitats or for survey purposes. The different systems can be initially confusing as they do not always correspond neatly. Some examples are illustrated here to show the complexity of the situation. The approach used in this book is straightforward, with habitat definitions largely similar to the UK Priority Habitats. To minimize potential confusion, the relationships between the most commonly used classification systems and the habitats described within this book are shown on *pages 382–396*, together with sources of further information.

Priority Habitats were identified in the UK as part of the UK Biodiversity Action Plan, the UK's response to the 1992 Convention on Biological Diversity. They are habitats considered to be under threat due to rarity or rate of decline, or for which the UK has particular international responsibility. They were placed within a framework of **Broad Habitat Types**. This Priority Habitat list is still used as the basis of much ongoing biodiversity work.

The Habitats Directive is European legislation that requires member states to designate, maintain, restore and protect sites to form a coherent network across Europe. Annex I of the Directive lists 189 habitat types (of which 79 occur in the UK and/or Ireland) considered to be rare or vulnerable in a European context. These are referred to as **Annex I habitats.** The habitat accounts in this book encompass all Annex I habitat types found in Britain and/or Ireland (with the exception of marine habitats). **CORINE Land Cover** is a European-level database of land cover based on satellite imagery (the name is derived from its full name Coordination of Information on the Environment) and uses a broader classification system, with 44 different habitat types recognized. The maps are derived from satellite imagery and use a minimum parcel size of 25 ha.

Saltmarsh (seen here on the Solway Firth) is a **UK Priority Habitat** and mapped as a single habitat type on the **Countryside Survey Land Cover Map** and the **CORINE Land Cover Map**. However, **Fossitt** (see *page 34*) differentiates between two saltmarsh categories (CM1 Lower Saltmarsh and CM2 Upper Saltmarsh; the image includes both types), and there are four **Annex I** saltmarsh habitat types that occur in Britain and Ireland (the Solway is designated for *Atlantic salt meadows (*Glauco-Puccinellietalia maritimae*).* The **NVC** describes 25 different saltmarsh vegetation communities within Great Britain, of which *SM13* Puccinellia maritima *saltmarsh* and *SM16* Festuca rubra *saltmarsh* can be seen in this photograph.

CORINE Land Cover data cover twelve European countries and are used to examine environmental change (such as the disappearance of wetlands, or agricultural intensification) across a wide area. The CORINE data cover the whole of the UK and Ireland, and are therefore used as the basis for many of the maps presented in this book. EUNIS (the European Nature Information System) is a successor to CORINE with classes that can be cross-matched to those used in the CORINE Land Cover Map.

Classification systems include the *Phase 1 Habitat Classification*, the *National Vegetation Classification* (**NVC**) and the *Irish Vegetation Classification* (**IVC**). **Phase 1** provides a standardized system for recording semi-natural vegetation and other wildlife habitats in the UK at a broad level through field surveys. The **NVC** is a far more detailed classification of the vegetation types (rather than habitat types) of Great Britain based on field surveys and covers 250 different plant communities. The **IVC** is a hierarchical vegetation scheme in which the upper three levels are based on physiognomy and ecology and the lower three levels are based on floristic data. It is an ongoing project and currently has 156 community types published online. In addition, the Joint Nature Conservation Committee has published a classification scheme for British rivers and lakes based on aquatic plant communities.

The *UK Habitat Classification* (**UKHab**) is a hierarchical system intended to replace Phase 1 that is compatible with all the above UK habitat classifications; it also takes into account the *European Nature Information System* (**EUNIS**), which provides data on habitats across Europe.

In Ireland, there is a standard scheme for describing habitats, often referred to as the *Fossitt Habitat Categories* after its author, Julie Fossitt. The scheme includes 11 broad habitat categories, split into 117 individual habitat types.

There are several national-level surveys of habitat extent. Within the UK, the *Countryside Survey* is a regularly repeated survey that has been running since 1978 and is designed to detect changes in the UK's countryside over time. There are two components to the survey: field surveys record data from a sample of 1 km squares, while the *Land Cover Map* uses satellite data to produce a digital map. These data cross-reference to Broad Habitat Types and Priority Habitats and provide estimates of the extent of a range of habitats. In Wales, this is supplemented by the *Habitat Survey of Wales* produced by the then Countryside Council for Wales (now Natural Resources Wales). In Scotland, the *Habitat Map of Scotland* (HabMos) provides a national repository for habitat and land-use data, and uses **EUNIS** and **Annex I** classifications. The estimates of the extent of each habitat presented in this book draw on these published data.

A diversity of habitats seen in **Morecambe Bay**, **Whitbarrow** and the **Pennines** from **Yewbarrow, Cumbria**, including ❶ Upland Calcareous Grassland, ❷ Upland Birch Wood, ❸ Scree, ❹ Yew Wood, ❺ Coastal and Floodplain Grazing Marsh, ❻ Raised Bog and ❼ Upland Acid Grassland.

Limestone Pavement (seen here on the Burren) can be classified in a variety of ways. **CORINE Land Cover** has a category for *Bare rock* and the **Countryside Survey Land Cover** for *Inland rock*. Limestone Pavement is categorized by **Fossitt** as *ER2 Exposed calcareous rock*. There is one relevant **Annex I** habitat – *Limestone pavements*, and three main **NVC** communities may apply (and possible overlaps with eight others). There is one relevant **Annex I** habitat – *Limestone pavements*. In Britain, three main **NVC** communities may be represented (with possible overlaps with eight others), while in Ireland two main **ICV** communities may be represented (with possible overlaps with at least three others). In the UK, Limestone Pavement falls within the **UK Priority Habitat** *Inland rock outcrop and scree habitats*.

Although Coastal and Floodplain Grazing Marsh (seen here in the Frome Valley in Dorset) is a **UK Priority Habitat**, there is no habitat type listed on **Annex I** to which it corresponds. **CORINE Land Cover** maps *Pastures*, and **Countryside Survey Land Cover** maps *Improved Grassland* and *Rough Grassland*, but both incorporate a much wider range of grassland habitats than just **Coastal and Floodplain Grazing Marsh**. Two **Fossitt** categories apply to the habitat: *GS4 Wet grassland* and *GA1 Improved agricultural grassland*. There are four main **NVC** communities that are relevant, and overlaps with a further 12 NVC types.

CONSERVATION OF HABITATS

Habitats have varying requirements and vulnerabilities. Today there is a multitude of different conservation organizations, including both statutory bodies and non-governmental organizations, working to protect habitats and species. They provide a considerable body of expertise about nature conservation combined with plenty of experience – species and habitat loss has been occurring for a long time! Once a case of protecting species, conservation now involves re-creating and restoring habitats, reintroducing species, lobbying and campaigning. However, despite the best efforts of the conservation sector, without which the habitats and species of Britain and Ireland would undoubtedly be much poorer today, 40% of Priority Habitats in the UK are still declining, and more than one in 10 of over 3,000 monitored species are at risk of extinction (and the status of only about 5% of terrestrial species is known, with much less known about marine species). On the flip side, 40% of species are increasing, including some seabirds and generalists such as Jackdaw and Woodpigeon. There have been some celebrated successes, such as the return of the Bittern, Red Kite and Large Blue butterfly, the expansion of Otter back into most of our major waterways, the return of wildlife to the Thames, and the re-creation of nearly 2,500 ha of lowland heathland. Nevertheless, our wildlife is in a state of flux and we are still losing more than we are gaining.

Faced with the apparently inexorable decline of habitats and species, the conservation movement has tended to look back to a time when these particular habitats and species were more abundant. In the desperate struggle to save vanishing species and fragments of habitat, there has been limited opportunity in the past for looking forwards and searching for ways to create more space for nature. However, schemes for wildlife-friendly farming and a move towards landscape-scale conservation are now heading in this direction. There is a burgeoning interest in rewilding, which focusses on ecological processes and involves reducing deliberate human intervention and reintroducing missing species such as Beaver that play a key role in ecosystem dynamics. This is of particular interest in areas that are already denuded of wildlife, such as much farmland, but discussion is also growing about how the habitat of large areas of semi-natural countryside that are of relatively limited wildlife interest (*e.g.* upland rough grasslands) could be enriched. The urgent need to reduce carbon emissions and boost carbon capture have also led conservationists to examine the role that rewilded habitat can play in the face of the climate crisis. Changes in agricultural policy away from land-based subsides towards reward for the provision of public goods may prove to be a catalyst. Public debate around how the countryside is managed in the face of climate change and what is now widely recognized as the sixth mass extinction is growing. In an environment that is increasingly urbanized and impoverished, an interest in more 'naturalistic' habitats is developing, and the need to find ways of helping people to reconnect with nature is becoming a priority within the conservation movement.

How Habitats are Protected

Name	Aim	Legislation/convention	Number in the UK	Number in Ireland
International				
Special Areas of Conservation (SACs)	To maintain, restore and protect sites to form a coherent network across Europe of habitats that are rare or vulnerable in a European context (listed in Annex I)	The Habitats Directive (European)	652	423
Special Protection Areas (SPAs)	To protect sites classified as important for birds at a European level	Wild Birds Directive (European)	270	154
Ramsar Sites	To protect wetlands of international importance	Ramsar Convention (global)	148	45
UNESCO World Heritage Sites	To protect sites of outstanding cultural or natural importance to all humanity	Convention Concerning the Protection of the World Cultural and Natural Heritage (global)	3 (natural)	–
National				
Sites of Special Scientific Interest (SSSIs) and Areas of Special Scientific Interest (ASSIs)	To protect sites noted for their biological or geological interest	Wildlife and Countryside Act 1981 in England and Wales; Nature Conservation and Amenity Lands (Northern Ireland) Order 1985; Nature Conservation (Scotland) Act 2004	approx. 6,800	n/a
Natural Heritage Areas (NHAs)	To protect areas considered important for the habitats present or which hold species of plants and animals whose habitat needs protection	Wildlife (Amendment) Act 2000	n/a	148

More than one designation can apply to sites. **Strumble Head, Pembrokeshire**, falls within the Strumble Head - Llechdafad cliffs SSSI, the St David's/Ty Ddewi SAC and forms part of the Pembrokeshire Coast National Park. This headland supports Maritime Heath, Hard Cliff and Slope, and Rocky Shore, and is famous for passing seabirds and cetaceans.

Special Areas of Conservation (SACs) (shown here) are the key sites for natural and semi-natural habitats in Britain and Ireland. Together with **Special Protection Areas (SPAs)** they are commonly referred to as **Natura 2000** sites and are afforded strict legal protection. The selection criteria for individual sites (available from the JNCC and NWPS websites) are a useful source of information, often containing detailed descriptions of the vegetation and species present.

FURTHER INFORMATION

Vegetation of Britain and Ireland by Michael Proctor (New Naturalist Series, HarperCollins, 2013)

The Hidden Landscape. A Journey into the Geological Past by Richard Fortey (Pimlico, 1993)

An illustrated guide to British Upland Vegetation by Alison Averis *et al.* (Pelagic Publishing, 2014)

The illustrated History of the Countryside by Oliver Rackham (Weidenfeld & Nicolson, 2003)

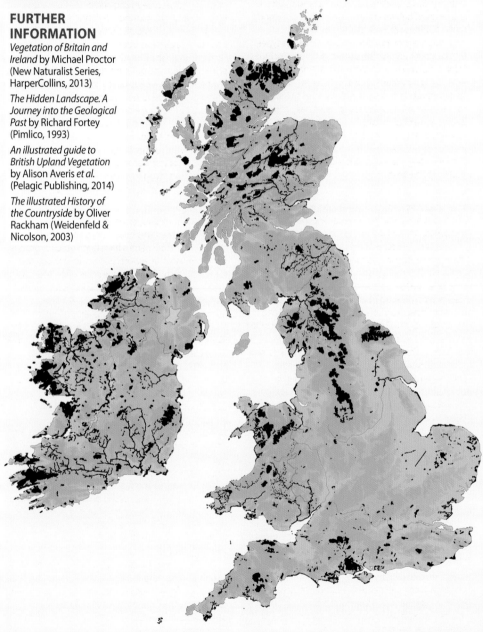

The Habitats

In this book, habitats are grouped under 10 sections: **Woodlands**, **Scrub**, **Heathlands**, **Grasslands**, **Mountains**, **Rocky Habitats**, **Wetlands**, **Freshwaters**, **Coastal Habitats** and **Other Habitats** (marine habitats are not covered). Each section has an introduction providing background information on the range of habitats found and themes common to the habitats within it. Within each section, accounts are provided for individual habitat types. Each account follows the same format and includes information on how to recognize the habitat, its ecology, any overlaps with similar habitats, its origins, its conservation and particular features to look out for (this section is expanded for especially complex or diverse habitats). Range maps are provided for all habitats, where appropriate. Each habitat account can be read on its own – it is not necessary to read the preceding accounts, although these will provide additional context.

Maps

The range maps have been derived from a variety of sources depending upon the data available. For the overall maps given in the introduction to each section, and for some of the individual habitat maps, it was possible to map the actual occurrence of the habitat(s) in question. In other cases, it was only possible to map the general distribution of the habitat by indicating in which 10 km grid squares it has been recorded. The maps are intended as a guide only. CORINE Land Cover data (which includes habitat patches of 25 ha and above) have been used for all the main habitat sections and for some individual habitats such as Coniferous Plantation. Data from the Annex I Habitat Reports that are compiled periodically and the Centre for Ecology and Hydrology Landcover data ('LCM 2015') have also been used (the full names of the relevant Annex I habitats can be found in the correspondence tables at the back of the book – codes are provided with the maps for brevity). These data are plotted according to 10 km grid cells that contain the habitat (the grid cells are aligned to a grid based on a European map projection rather than the British or Irish National Grid). Another source of data is the national inventories that are available for some habitats, including the Priority Habitat Inventory for England, the Habitat Map of Scotland (HabMoS) and the Terrestrial Phase I Habitat Survey of Wales and various others, including the Traditional Orchard Inventory and the Turlough Database. Data concerning canals and rivers are derived from OpenStreetMap (a crowd-sourced geographic dataset available online). For habitats that are specifically upland or lowland, the upland boundary shown earlier in the introduction has been used to separate the two. Sources for the map data and copyright information are given on *page 413*.

For each habitat, additional context on its distribution is given in a box below the map headed **Distribution and extent**. This also gives the area of each habitat type in England (Eng), Scotland (Sco), Wales (Wal), Northern Ireland (NI) and Ireland (Ire). Figures are indicative only and are not directly comparable as it has been necessary to use a wide range of sources. Given the different classification schemes used and different approaches to mapping, the extent figures have been derived wherever possible from the Annex I reporting (2019). In instances where the extent of a habitat type is not known the annotation 'n/k' is used. The reader is referred to the Annex I reports and relevant primary sources where further information is required. Where appropriate, an indication of the European distribution is given for habitats for which Britain and/or Ireland are of particular importance.

Species and habitat names

Common (English) species names have been used throughout this book. For consistency and accessibility, such names have been used for groups such as mosses, liverworts and some invertebrates for which scientific names are more often used. A list of the scientific names of all the species mentioned in the text is provided on *pages 401–406*. The nomenclature used for higher plants follows the *New Flora of The British Isles* (4th ed) by Clive Stace (C & M Floristics, 2019). For birds the names follow *The British List: a checklist of birds of Britain*, 8th ed. (*Ibis* 155: 635–676). In most other cases, the names used are those adopted by the relevant society of recording groups (Amphibian and Reptile Conservation Trust, Bees, Wasps and Ants Recording Society, British Bryological Society, British Dragonfly Society, British Lichen Society, British Phycological Society, Butterfly Conservation and The Mammal Society). The nomenclature used for the remaining groups follows the national checklists provided by the Natural History Museum. Species names are capitalized, unless more than one species of the same genus is referred to or the species is not identified to species level. For example, 'Sessile Oak' refers to that species, while 'oaks' refers to either (or both) Sessile and Pedunculate Oak.

Habitat names are capitalized where they refer to the habitats described individually in this book. Other broader habitats names are not. For example, 'Lowland Dry Heath' refers specifically to the habitat described on *page 130*, while 'heathland' refers to any heathland habitat.

WOODLANDS

ORIGINS

The development of woodland after the last glaciation has mostly been inferred from tree pollen preserved in wetland peat. Montane species of birch and willow and Common Juniper were the first tree species to colonize the tundra-like landscape left behind by the retreating ice around 12,000 years ago. They spread from small pockets of woodland that persisted in the unglaciated (although still very cold) southern extremity of England and from the European mainland (of which Britain and Ireland were still a part), and were then followed by other birches and Aspen and then by Scots Pine. As the climate became wetter and milder, the pinewoods retreated north and were followed by broadleaved species such as Hazel, Alder, oaks, elms and limes. Beech and Hornbeam were relative latecomers, arriving when climate became drier again about 6,000 years ago, and spreading as far as the Brecon Beacons in South Wales (their further spread may have been inhibited by the subsequent reduction in overall woodland cover rather than climatic factors). Beech, Hornbeam and Small-leaved Lime did not reach Ireland, presumably because they failed to cross the land bridge before it sank under the Irish Sea (several other characteristic woodland species did not make it either, including Hazel Dormouse, Roe Deer, Nightingale, Willow and Marsh Tits, woodpeckers, Pied Flycatcher and Purple Emperor and White Admiral butterflies, although Strawberry-tree, absent from the UK, did).

By the beginning of the Neolithic period (6,000 years ago), much of Britain supported woodland except for the Arctic-alpine tundra of areas like the Cairngorm plateau and the boggy northernmost tip of Scotland. Pine forest covered much of Scotland (and also Connemara in western Ireland), with birch dominant towards the far north. Oak–Hazel woodland covered lowland Scotland, most of northern England and Wales, parts of the West Country and the western tips of Ireland. Lime woods covered the English Midlands, East Anglia and much of southern England, with Hazel and elm woods in Cornwall, south-west Wales and much of Ireland. Willow and Alder carr covered wetland areas that were not bog. However, these woodlands did not form a continuous canopy but existed in a shifting equilibrium with other habitat types. The notion of a climax community of dense forest has been superseded in recent decades by the concept of a dynamic mosaic of woody and open habitats driven by the interactions between large herbivores and regenerating scrub and woodland.

Under the feudal system, land and trees were usually owned by Lord of the Manor, with villagers (commoners) having various rights to graze animals (including turning out pigs to eat acorns and beechmast in the autumn), and collect firewood.

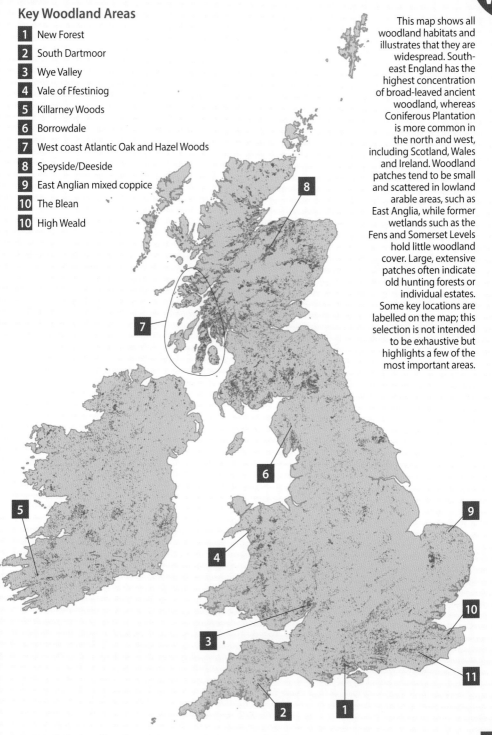

W

Key Woodland Areas

1. New Forest
2. South Dartmoor
3. Wye Valley
4. Vale of Ffestiniog
5. Killarney Woods
6. Borrowdale
7. West coast Atlantic Oak and Hazel Woods
8. Speyside/Deeside
9. East Anglian mixed coppice
10. The Blean
10. High Weald

This map shows all woodland habitats and illustrates that they are widespread. South-east England has the highest concentration of broad-leaved ancient woodland, whereas Coniferous Plantation is more common in the north and west, including Scotland, Wales and Ireland. Woodland patches tend to be small and scattered in lowland arable areas, such as East Anglia, while former wetlands such as the Fens and Somerset Levels hold little woodland cover. Large, extensive patches often indicate old hunting forests or individual estates. Some key locations are labelled on the map; this selection is not intended to be exhaustive but highlights a few of the most important areas.

41

LEFT: Despite a resurgence of interest in traditional woodland management techniques for cultural, historical and environmental reasons, the lack of such management still threatens the fauna and flora that developed under coppice regimes. RIGHT: A sapling is used as the return spring for the treadle in a pole lathe, which is known to have been used to turn green wood since at least Viking times and is now used by those with an interested in green woodworking.

Woodland had already been exploited by humans for wood and food, but human impacts increased markedly as settled agricultural lifestyles became prevalent in the Neolithic period and significant woodland clearance began on lighter, more fertile soils. Clearings were not permanent to begin with, and when cleared plots were abandoned they reverted to woodland. However, woodland clearance accelerated through the Bronze Age (4500–2500 years ago) with the development of metal tools, and a wetter and cooler climate stimulated the development of bogs in oceanic areas, preventing tree regeneration. By the end of the Iron Age (2,000 years ago, when the human population in Britain was over one million), 50% of woodland cover had gone. Tree composition also changed: the amount of elm had already decreased (possibly due to a pandemic elm disease), Small-leaved Lime decreased (possibly due to climatic changes and use as fodder for livestock) and there was a corresponding increase in Hazel. Secondary woodland spread after the end of the Roman period, but clearance began again in Saxon times, and by the Norman period (11th century, human population three million) only about 15% remained, by which time ownership of woodlands in much of Britain was defined under the feudal system and their use regulated. Norman management of Irish woods within their control was more exploitative, and some may have been completely felled and the timber exported. However in both countries coppice management was widespread. Deer parks and Royal Forests were also created at this time.

By the 14th century, woodland cover had declined to around 10% in Britain, and remained roughly at this level into the 19th century despite the vicissitudes of plague and famine – probably because the remaining woodland was by this time an integral part of local economies. The need for charcoal increased with the spread of the blast furnace in ironworks throughout the early 17th century, while the growth in merchant and naval shipbuilding in Britain around this time required timber and as a consequence the remaining woodlands were carefully managed. The replanting and selective weeding of less useful tree species then began to have a significant impact on the composition and structure of woods. The same demands for wood were felt in Ireland, which had a woodland cover of about 20% around this time. However, the English monarchy handed over large areas of land to non-Irish settlers, who cleared woodland to use as farmland. A large increase in the population saw further clearance in the 17th and 18th centuries and the woodland cover in Ireland is thought to have dropped as low as 2%, although planting was also encouraged during this time.

The development of the rail network in the 19th century meant that coal could be widely used. As a consequence, coppicing for firewood declined but woodlands were still cleared for cultivation. At the beginning of the 20th century woodland cover reached an all-time low of 5% in Britain and < 2% in Ireland. However, demand for home-grown timber increased during the First World War, and new planting (mostly coniferous) was undertaken on an unprecedented scale, mostly on infertile land but also within existing woodlands. Agricultural intensification from the 1950s saw further clearance of broad-leaved woodland, but around this time the rate of woodland loss became a concern, and the conservation movement started protecting ancient woodland sites. Woodland now covers around 10% of Ireland and 12% of the UK. A large proportion of this is coniferous plantation (75% in Ireland, 52% in the UK), although the area of broad-leaved woodland has also increased through planting and the expansion of secondary woodland. The area of semi-natural ancient woodland is tiny at 1·2% in the UK, while in Ireland, mapped ancient or long-established woodlands cover about 0·1% of the land area.

Legally binding carbon targets have increased recognition at policy level of the potential role of trees in carbon sequestration and may lead to the planting of tens of thousands of hectares with trees. This does not necessarily equate to tens of thousands of hectares of woodland, but if appropriate species and locations are chosen and natural regeneration allowed to play a role, it may expand the area of wildlife-rich woodland. Awareness is also increasing about the potential role of trees in the reduction of flood risk, which may lead to an increase in the extent of woodland in upper river catchments.

TYPES OF WOODLAND

Eleven types of semi-natural woodland are described in this book, as well as Coniferous Plantation. Woodland classification can be complex but in the UK the systems most commonly referred to are Peterken's stand types (which includes 12 main and 39 subsidiary types based on the presence of species of long-established trees), the National Vegetation Classification (based on samples of all vegetation present, which has over 50 woodland communities grouped under 18 main types) and the UK Priority Habitat types (nine types based on threat and vulnerability). In Ireland, woodland has been classified into seven semi-natural types and five highly modified types mainly according to vegetation characteristics. In this book, a pragmatic approach has been adopted based on the tree species present (linked to geology and climate) and conservation interest. The table on *page 45* summarizes the main features of each woodland habitat for which an account has been provided.

The woodland habitats described may be found on ancient woodland sites, and can be primary woodland, although all are likely to have been managed to a greater or lesser extent. Some occur as secondary woodland (*e.g.* birch wood that develops on heathland if grazing pressure is relaxed) or are naturally transient (*e.g.* willow carr, a type of Wet Woodland) and are likely to develop into other woodland types over time. Atlantic Hazel Wood, which is sometimes considered to be a coastal form of Upland Mixed Ash Wood or Upland Oak Wood (depending on the substrate), is described separately here as it is unique to Britain and Ireland and is of particular value for the suite of lower plants it supports. Yew Wood, often considered together with Beech Wood on chalk, is also given a separate section due to its distinctive

Looking east towards Farnham, Surrey from Farleigh Wallop, Hampshire – arable fields and settlements interrupt a mix of both managed and unmanaged Lowland Mixed Oak and Ash Wood, a scene that has remained relatively unchanged for centuries.

character. Although essentially a crop, Coniferous Plantation is included because it can support scarce or rare species or those associated with the habitat it replaced. Wood Pasture is anomalous as it is a product of a particular type of management used over a long time period. It is usually derived from Lowland Dry Oak and Birch Wood or Beech Wood but is very distinctive and of such conservation interest that it merits its own description. Traditional Orchards, which have some similarities to Wood Pasture, are covered in the Other Habitats section (*page 364*).

Climate and soil type are the key natural factors influencing the character and distribution of woodlands. Broadly speaking, oaks are the commonest dominant species in established woodland on more acid soils and on acid rocks. Ash is found on limestone and chalk and also on moist soils (and is the commonest woodland dominant in Ireland); Small-leaved Lime and Wych Elm also prefer more calcareous soils. Hazel is widely distributed and is found both as an understorey shrub and, on the Atlantic fringe, as a canopy species. Beech and Yew can tolerate thin, drought-prone soils and birches are pioneer woodland species found in a wide range of conditions. Alder grows on strongly flushed sites and in river floodplains and, like willows, grows readily in wetlands. Climatic factors are particularly evident in northern Scotland and Ireland, where high rainfall can inhibit tree growth (favouring bogs). Conditions in the Highlands are sufficiently harsh that species such as Scots Pine and birches, which would be out-competed in more favourable situations, can be dominant. In the west of Britain and Ireland, moist, oceanic conditions favour the growth of a rich suite of lower plants within woodlands. In southern England, species such as Field Maple, Beech and Hornbeam, which did not reach Scotland naturally, are found.

The character of most woodland is the product of thousands of years of often quite intense human management interacting with these natural factors. In many areas, woodland has been managed to favour particular species (*e.g.* oaks and Beech). Other species have been weeded out and key species planted. Elsewhere, planting has included non-native species (*e.g.* Sweet Chestnut and ornamentals such as Rhododendron). Non-native shrub species have often been planted as cover in woodlands used for pheasant-rearing. Sycamore is a component of many sites, particularly (but by no means exclusively) secondary woodland. It is thought to have been introduced in the Roman or Medieval period, possibly

Wildwood is used to refer to the natural woodland cover of Britain and Ireland before significant human impacts. If there are any remaining areas of wildwood that have never been significantly influenced by humans, they are likely to be small remnants in remote and inaccessible places such as ravines and perhaps small islands in lochs.

Semi-natural woodland has not been planted, but has experienced periods of more or less intense management that may have included coppicing, grazing, selective felling and planting.

Ancient woodland refers to sites where woodland is known to have been present since at least 1600 (1750 in Scotland), a date chosen because planting was not common before this. Some have been replanted but retain a ground flora typical of ancient woodland.

Primary Woodland is semi-natural ancient woodland that has never been cleared and replanted and so has physical continuity with the wildwood, even though it has been managed.

Secondary woodland develops by a natural process of succession on open habitats or arable land that is no longer managed. It takes woodland species a long time to colonize, and so many secondary woodlands lack specialist species. Secondary woodland can be ancient woodland if it colonized previously cleared land before 1600 (1750 in Scotland).

Plantation is artificially established woodland planted with the intention of obtaining a timber crop. Most plantations are coniferous and can be monocultures, although broadleaves are also planted. Many semi-natural woodlands include areas in which trees have been planted at some point.

The presence of a range of particular species is considered to indicate the likely ancient origins of woodland, although this varies according to the type of woodland (and the individual species are not necessarily confined to ancient woodland). Species include vascular plants (*e.g.* Moschatel, Ramsons, **Wood Anemone** (ABOVE), Pignut, Opposite-leaved Golden-saxifrage and Bluebell), a suite of epiphytic lichens, and trees such as Wild Service-tree and Small-leaved Lime.

HABITAT	DESCRIPTION
Lowland Mixed Oak and Ash Wood *page 52* | *page 399*	Mixed broadleaved woodland on relatively rich soils, usually with a history of coppice management. Includes classic lowland Bluebell woods.
Lowland Dry Oak and Birch Wood *page 57* | *page 399*	Oak and birch-dominated woods on dry, acid soils in heathland areas, often managed as high forest.
Beech Wood *page 60* | *page 398*	Beech-dominated high forest with a limited shrub and field layer found on a range of soils, famous for rare orchids and helleborines.
Yew Wood *page 63* | *page 400*	Yew-dominated woodland on chalk and Yew groves within Upland Mixed Ash Wood on limestone.
Wet Woodland *page 66* | *page 400*	Varied woodland of Alder, willows or birches found on wetlands, in river floodplains and strongly flushed situations. Includes bog woodland.
Wood Pasture *page 72* | *page 400*	Includes sites with a long-standing history of grazing that support veteran or ancient trees (usually Beech or oaks). Usually found on relatively infertile land, often common land, royal forests or deer parks. Rich in invertebrates and lichens. May once have been much more widespread as part of a dynamic wooded landscape.
Upland Oak Wood *page 78* | *page 400*	Upland woodland on more acidic soils, often supporting a diverse range of lower plants. Strong oak dominance is partly a consequence of management.
Upland Mixed Ash Wood *page 83* | *page 399*	Mixed woodland on calcareous outcrops in the uplands, often with a rich flora, naturally limited in extent.
Caledonian Forest *page 86* | *page 398*	Native pinewoods found only in the Highlands of Scotland.
Atlantic Hazel Wood *page 91* | *page 398*	Woodland with a natural Hazel canopy, rich in lower plants, confined to the Atlantic fringe.
Upland Birch Wood *page 94* | *page 399*	Widespread, dynamic woodland dominated by birches in the uplands. It is often transient.
Coniferous Plantation *page 97* | *page 399*	Plantations of pine, spruce and fir, usually found on nutrient-poor soils and particularly widespread in the uplands.

A selection of woodland leaves LEFT TO RIGHT: Alder, Ash, Beech, Silver Birch, Hazel, Pedunculate Oak, Yew.

to Scotland, although it did not become widespread until the 18th century. It is now considered an invasive species in some semi-natural woodland (although it has been argued that it may in fact be native as its pollen does not preserve well in peat and is not possible to separate from that of Field Maple).

This variety of human and natural influences contributes to the lack of conformity in woodland, much of which does not fit neatly into one category or another, particularly in the case of young secondary woodlands. The descriptions for the woodland types in this book should be treated as nodes on a continuum, rather than as self-contained woodland types.

THREATS AND ISSUES

Britain and Ireland are among the least wooded countries in Europe and the tiny amount of ancient woodland that remains is still under threat. Long-term monitoring of many woodland birds and a range of woodland butterflies has shown steep population declines, a stark reminder that all is not well within our woodlands.

Development pressure is particularly a problem in the south-east of England, and the irreplaceable nature of semi-natural woodland appears not to be fully understood or appreciated by decision-makers. Woodland wildlife is also threatened by changes in management. Traditional coppice management is no longer economically viable, and many woods are either neglected or managed for timber, both of which lead to structural changes and the lack of appropriate niches for species that flourished under traditional management. Many woodland habitats are fragmented into isolated patches and, as woodland species are generally not very mobile, local extinctions easily become permanent. A widespread increase in the deer population and, in the uplands, the number of livestock grazing woodlands (a traditional practice), is threatening regeneration within woods and 'fixing' the naturally dynamic boundaries of upland woodlands. Although disease and pests are a part of natural ecosystems and have always affected trees, the arrival of new species (e.g. through international trade in plants) to which trees have not had the opportunity to develop resistance can be far-reaching. Ash dieback (caused by the fungus *Hymenoscyphus fraxineus*) was first recorded in Britain and Ireland in 2012 and has since spread extensively. Climate change may increase vulnerability to pathogens. Projected increases in temperature, changes in rainfall seasonality and an increase in storm events are also likely to change the composition, structure and distribution of woodlands.

CULTURAL IMPORTANCE

Woodland is a much-loved feature of the landscape. For many people it provides a place for spiritual renewal and contemplation as well as fresh air and exercise, and of course the chance to see wildlife that is not encountered in the wider countryside. Stepping inside an ancient wood can be a welcome escape from the monotony of modern agriculture or the abrasive urban environment. The woodland boundary is often out of sight and out of mind; it is possible to be fully immersed in the structural complexity of a habitat that is three-dimensional at the human scale and where natural processes at least appear to predominate. The enduring nature of woodland can also engender a feeling of continuity with the past. Many woods are historical features in their own right, and have been documented for hundreds of years. Wood banks, old boundary pollards and coppice stools, charcoal hearths and other archaeological features all have a tale to tell about past lives and add to the historical value of woodland sites.

Woodlands are also valued as a source of traditional products such as locally produced charcoal and firewood, and Hazel for wattle hurdles and thatching spars – and the skills required for woodland crafts are valued in their own right. There is also interest in reinstating traditional coppice management to provide woodchip as a source of fuel. The rise of the forest school movement, which offers children hands-on learning experiences in an outdoor environment, is also raising the profile of woodlands among young people. The role of woodland in carbon sequestration and flood control is becoming increasingly apparent, although the lack of market value for these services provides little incentive to landowners to maintain or expand woodland.

CONSERVATION IMPORTANCE AND PROTECTION

Woodland includes some or our richest habitats and supports a huge range of species, many of which are rare or scarce. The varied geology and climate of Britain and Ireland had led to the development of a diverse range of woodland types, including ten Annex I habitats, of which half are priority features (*i.e.* considered

COMMON TREE FORMS

A veteran lime **stub** in the **Wye Valley, Gloucestershire**. Stubs are short pollards or high coppice stools.

Coppice – a multi-stemmed tree that has been cut at ground level and allowed to re-grow. Coppice stools can be hundreds of years old. Many woods, such as **Garston Wood in Dorset**, were traditionally managed as coppice with standards (*i.e.* coppice with well-spaced pollards or maiden trees). This periodically opened up the canopy and provided the edge habitat favoured by many woodland specialists. Coppicing was widespread, although the technique did not become widely practiced in Scotland until the 17th century.

A **phoenix** willow at **Salhouse, Norfolk**. Phoenix regeneration happens when a tree falls over and new shoots develop perpendicularly from the main trunk or branches.

A **maiden** oak at **Arne, Dorset**. A **standard** or maiden tree is one that has never been cut, coppiced or pollarded.

Recently **pollarded** willows at **Cricklade, Wiltshire**. Pollards are cut above animal grazing height to allow the regrowth to be harvested for wood or timber. Pollards are still found as standards within woods, on boundary banks, in hedgerows and along rivers, although many are no longer cut regularly.

to be particularly vulnerable and/or mainly restricted to Europe). However, only a small proportion of ancient woodland is legally protected (*e.g.* around 15% is designated as SSSI (see *page 37*) in the UK), and in the UK the conservation status of the majority of designated sites is deemed unfavourable, largely due to inappropriate forestry management, overgrazing (in the uplands particularly) and the presence of invasive non-native species. Much woodland is in private ownership, and conservation efforts often revolve around promoting appropriate management for conservation.

The area of some woodland types has increased in recent years and there are several key projects working to expand woodland, often for community benefits in addition to those for nature conservation. For example, in the English Midlands the National Forest is creating a multi-purpose forest landscape within 200 square miles of an ex-mining area. There is also increasing interest in reconnecting or buffering remaining areas of woodland to increase their resilience.

The value of continuing or reinstating coppice management on sites that have a history of such management is widely promoted, but there is also value in allowing abandoned coppice to revert to more 'naturalistic' high forest. Although this will not favour rare specialist butterflies requiring open conditions or encourage a high diversity of flowering plants, it will benefit decomposer species that require dead plant material and flourish in moist, sheltered conditions. Many species also depend on mature trees. For example, the abundance of leaf miners and spiders has been shown to increase with the age of coppice, and many moths are dependent upon mature canopies. However, most of these species are hard to see and even harder to identify, and therefore receive only limited recognition in the world of conservation. Coppicing is not appropriate in Atlantic woodlands with rich lower plant communities.

Stoborough, Dorset – secondary woodland is often afforded little if any protection, although some sites are recognized as being of importance at a county level. Secondary woodland is greatly valued as green space in both urban and rural settings and can provide a relatively robust location for recreation.

Banks and walls within woods often provide an indication of past use. **The Hudnalls,** in the **Wye Valley, Gloucestershire** was inhabited by squatters in the 18th century. Woodland recolonized cleared areas and old stone walls are all that now remains of the settlements. It has not been cut for 100 years and is now high forest (*i.e.* the trees are not pollarded or coppiced).

KEY FEATURES

Woodland is one of our most structurally diverse habitats types. There is generally a canopy layer, usually of taller tree species, a shrub layer of smaller trees and shrubs such as Rowan, Wild Cherry, Hazel, Wild Service-tree, willows and Guelder-rose, and a field layer of grasses, herbs, ferns, lichens, mosses and liverworts. The balance between these layers is determined by factors such as the amount of light penetrating the canopy and grazing pressure. Within this structure a wide range of microhabitats can be found. Key microhabitats to look out for are standing and fallen deadwood, ancient trees, wet areas and more open areas (included glades, rides and edges). Deadwood and leaf-litter are used by a huge diversity of organisms including fungi, bacteria and invertebrates – it is thought that around one third of woodland invertebrates require deadwood. These saproxylic species play a vital role in the woodland food chain by recycling nutrients. Many are too small to see with the naked eye or are out of sight, but look out for fungal fruiting bodies in a great variety of forms and macro-invertebrates such as Stag Beetle.

Ancient and veteran trees (see Wood Pasture, *page 72*) provide an important range of microhabitats, including deadwood habitat within living trees that is used by fungi and invertebrates. Ancient trees are also important for epiphytic lichens as their longevity provides the continuity of conditions needed for the development of a diverse flora. Wet areas provide excellent conditions for rotting wood and can support a different range of invertebrates. Glades, rides and scrubby woodland edges are important for species dependent upon sunny, sheltered conditions, including rare fritillary butterflies. Many woodland plants favour these more open conditions, and will be found flowering in recently coppiced areas or along ride edges. Shrubby species such as Hawthorn and Bramble provide good sources of nectar and pollen for invertebrates.

New Forest, Hampshire. Key woodland features include: ❶ veteran trees, ❷ dense leaf-litter, ❸ fallen deadwood, ❹ temporary pool.

W

FURTHER INFORMATION

Woodland Conservation and Management by George Peterken (Springer, 1993)

Woodlands by Oliver Rackham (HarperCollins, 2010)

Woodland Flowers by Keith Kirby (Bloomsbury publishing, 2020)

Atlantic Hazel Action Group – a group that aims to protect Scotland's unique Atlantic Hazel woodlands – sites.google.com/site/atlantichazelgroup/

Trees for Life – aims to restore functioning Caledonian Forest (and its missing wildlife such as Beaver and Lynx) to a swathe of Scotland – www.treesforlife.org.uk/

Ancient Tree Forum – provides information on the ecology, management and conservation of veteran trees – www.ancienttreeforum.co.uk

Hatfield Forest, Essex. Key woodland features include: **1** mature trees, **2** scrubby edges, **3** taller ground flora at edge of rides, **4** open rides.

Lowland Mixed Oak and Ash Wood page 399

Lowland Mixed Oak and Ash Wood encompasses a range of vegetation types resulting from long-term interactions between human activity, substrate and climate. While oaks and/or Ash are usually present, limes and Hornbeam can dominate the canopy (and are sometimes differentiated into separate woodland types). In many woods, Sycamore, suckering elms and Sweet Chestnut have colonized or been planted. Where the typical deep-brown earths are more acidic, Bluebell woods are found, with oaks and Hazel (also Holly, Rowan, Wild Cherry, Ash, and Yew) over Bracken, rambling Bramble and Honeysuckle, and an eye-catching ground flora of Bluebell, often with Wood Anemone. In more calcareous situations, the woods become more species-rich. Ash joins or replaces oak in the canopy, and Field Maple is characteristic. Lime-loving shrubs such as Dogwood, Spindle and Wayfaring-tree may be common, while Dog's Mercury tends to dominate a ground flora that may contain woodland rarities. Ferns include shield-ferns and Hart's-tongue, but they are not as prominent a feature as in Upland Mixed Ash Wood. In Ireland, Ash and Hazel tend to dominate this type of woodland, but without Field Maple.

Similar habitats

Lowland Mixed Oak and Ash Wood is replaced by other woodland types where the soil is very dry and limey, strongly acid and leached, or wet, but overlaps with these types where soils are deeper. Gradations to upland woodland types are common in the upland fringes or where the topography changes abruptly.

Old Hazel coppice with Bluebell ground flora at **Powerstock Common, Dorset**.

Origins and development

Enshrined in folklore as remnants of wildwood, these woods have in fact been shaped by human intervention over millennia. By the Middle Ages, coppicing (with or without standards) was almost universal. It finally ceased *c.* 1950, although by then many coppices had been overplanted or were already neglected. Subsequent clearance and replanting with non-native trees led to a 30–40% reduction in area, and the loss of hedgerows reduced connectivity between sites. More recently, planting and small-scale natural regeneration have increased the area of this woodland type.

Conservation

Traditional management is usually no longer economically viable and management for timber, or abandonment, has simplified the structure of woodlands, resulting in a closed canopy with few open patches. Overgrazing by deer often prevents regeneration. Many woods are surrounded by intensive agriculture, making them vulnerable to nitrogen pollution and reducing the amount of valuable edge habitat. Ash dieback could have a significant impact on nutrient cycling and species composition.

Massive declines in some woodland birds, moths and butterflies in recent decades indicate that appropriate conservation measures are urgently needed. To be sustainable, these need to re-integrate woodland management within local economics (*e.g.* through sensitive management for woodfuel). While the continuation or reinstatement of coppicing is generally favoured to maximize diversity, there is also a case to be made for allowing natural processes to function in non-intervention high forest. Allowing existing woodlands to spread beyond their current boundaries through natural colonization will increase resilience.

EXTENT IN KM^2	
Eng	700
Wal	266
Sco	280
NI	n/k
Ire	269

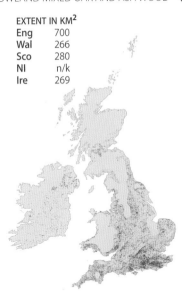

Distribution and extent

Scattered across the lowlands and very limited in Ireland. Map shows all lowland deciduous woodland in England, Wales and Northern Ireland so actual extent is less than shown. Extents are from different sources and approximate.

LEFT: **High forest** developed when coppiced woodland was overplanted with dense oak in the 19th century and from the growth of suckering elms and un-cut coppice in the 20th century. RIGHT: **A coppice coup** of recently cut Hazel with young oak standards. Rotational coppicing traditionally created a variety of open conditions that allowed a diversity of plants and invertebrates to persist.

What to look for

Look for glades, rides and woodland edges, as this is where many of the most interesting species will be found. Sheltered and well-lit, open areas provide structural variety including mature trees, scrub, tall herbs, short vegetation and bare ground; east–west rides are best as they receive most sunlight. Look for Spotted Flycatchers hunting from trees on the edges of clearings in the summer, and listen out for other summer migrants such as Garden Warbler and perhaps Nightingale in the scrub. Purple Hairstreaks tumble over the canopy top, and Silver-washed Fritillaries fly strongly along rides. In shorter vegetation, Common Dog-violet and Wild Strawberry provide food for the caterpillars of fritillary butterflies and Grizzled Skipper respectively. The nocturnal Hazel Dormouse is found in Lowland Mixed Oak and Ash Woods with dense undergrowth. Mature trees host hole-nesting birds such as woodpeckers, whose excavations are also used by roosting Noctule bats, while cracks behind peeling bark are preferred by Barbastelle bats. Dead and rotting wood are vital, and provide deadwood for invertebrates (*e.g.* Stag Beetle) and fungi (*e.g.* Chicken of the Woods, a distinctive bright orange-yellow tiered bracket fungus). Lowland Mixed Oak and Ash

1 **Hornbeam-dominated woods** are mostly confined to Kent, Sussex and East Anglia. Generally coppiced (for firewood), Hornbeam is also found with lime. **2** Lime woods are prominent in the Midlands and East Anglia and often found where there has been a long continuity of woodland cover. **3** **Solomon's-seal** – a distinctive plant of more calcareous woods with green-tipped white flowers and blue-black berries. The plant has a reputation for diverse healing properties when used medicinally. **4** Look for **Ramsons Hoverfly** in the spring where Ramsons are abundant.

1 Hazel Dormouse can be hard to see, but look out for empty nut shells with oblique tooth marks around the hole. Changes in woodland structure resulting in shadier conditions have favoured species of mature woodlands (*e.g.* **Speckled Wood, 2 Silver-washed Fritillary, 4 White Admiral,** and **Purple Hairstreak,** while species that favour clearings have declined severely (*e.g.* **Pearl-bordered Fritillary, Small Pearl-bordered Fritillary** and **3 Duke of Burgundy.**

Stag Beetle – the largest terrestrial insect in Europe; its larvae live for several years in rotting wood.

How to recognize

Small, contained by banks or ditches and often ancient, these woods are oases of wildlife amidst the sterile monotony of the lowland agricultural countryside. They are at their most vital in May when the canopy trees can still be easily differentiated by their colours. The air is pungent with Ramsons and alive with birdsong, and the intense hue of thousands of Bluebells can be captivating – for this woodland type includes the iconic Bluebell woods so central to our notion of British woodland.

In most woods traditional coppicing has been abandoned and high forest has grown up, which, although more naturalistic in appearance, is proving a challenge for many of the specialist inhabitants. However, open rides and glades can provide warm, well-lit and sheltered patches, while mature trees supply dead and rotting wood for beetles and fungi. Where coppicing is still practiced (usually on nature reserves), rare woodland butterflies and a spectacular spring flora can still be found. Many of these woods are quite close to urban centres, and can be much visited and loved for their beauty and the continuity they provide with the past.

Woodland is famed for its spring flora. Carpets of Bluebells can be breathtaking where the canopy is broken, accompanied by patches of Wood Anemone. The more calcareous sites are not so colourful but can be more species-rich, supporting plants such as Dog's Mercury, Pignut, Sanicle, Yellow Archangel, Bugle, Enchanter's-nightshade and Primrose (or Oxlip in East Anglia), with Moschatel and Opposite-leaved Golden-saxifrage in flushes around springs and moist places. Keep an eye open for more unusual plants such as Solomon's-seal, Herb-Paris and Greater Butterfly-orchid.

Did you know?

The average size of a Lowland Mixed Oak and Ash Wood is less than 20 ha. Lime woods are prominent in the Midlands and East Anglia and are often found where there has been long continuity of woodland cover.

When to visit

April–May for spring flora, late May–August for butterflies.

The Hudnalls in the Wye Valley is dominated by oaks, limes and Beech and is managed on a 'minimum intervention' basis with dead wood left in situ.

56

Lowland Dry Oak and Birch Wood page 399

Lowland Dry Oak and Birch Wood is found on gently undulating acid sands and gravels in the warm and dry south-east, and has a simple floristic composition. Pendunculate Oak is the most common oak, although Sessile Oak also occurs in places, becoming more common where the climate is wetter. Both Silver and Downy Birch are frequent, and although dense birch thickets suggests recent succession (*e.g.* from heathland), birches are also associated with canopy gaps and abandoned coppice. The shrub layer is mostly limited to Holly and Rowan that are able to persist in the shade of oaks and may in places reach the canopy. Wavy Hair-grass is characteristic of the field layer, and where Bracken is not too dominant species such as Heather, Broad Buckler-fern, Foxglove, Wood Sage and Heath Bedstraw are found. Bluebell is rare, and there is no showy display of spring flora. Bilberry and mosses are more frequent toward the northern limit of the habitat, and Bristle Bent replaces Wavy Hair-grass to the west. Taken in isolation, these woods are relatively species-poor, but many old stands include veteran trees important for their lichen, fungi and invertebrate assemblages, and other notable species are associated with patches of heathland or mire (peat-forming wetland).

EXTENT IN KM^2
Eng 45

Arne, Dorset – secondary birch woodland is a very common sight on southern heathlands, but in some cases contains a core of Lowland Dry Oak and Birch Woodland. It also often includes pine from nearby plantations. Dense, even-aged Silver Birch can regenerate rapidly within woods following disturbances such as felling.

Distribution and extent

Map shows broad distribution of the Annex I habitat (H9190). Only found in England.

57

Similar habitats

Lowland Dry Oak and Birch Wood intergrades with the more acid end of the spectrum of Beech Wood where both occur (*e.g.* the Chilterns and the New Forest) and often merges with open habitats and scrub. Many examples were historically managed as Wood Pasture. The lack of Hazel and the dominance of oaks differentiate it from Lowland Mixed Oak and Ash Wood, in which oaks tend to occur as sporadic pollards over Hazel.

Origins and development

Lowland Dry Oak and Birch Wood developed in areas once dominated by Small-leaved Lime after this species declined, perhaps as a consequence of increased livestock grazing during the Neolithic. By medieval times Lowland Dry Oak and Birch Wood was used as Wood Pasture, although coppice and high forest forms were also present. In the 18th century many coppices were planted with Sweet Chestnut.

Conservation

Lowland Dry Oak and Birch Wood suffers the threats common to most woodland habitats, particularly deer browsing (preventing regeneration), airborne pollution, and invasion by non-native species such as Rhododendron and Shallon. In heathland contexts, restoring heathland vegetation is often a priority over maintaining or enhancing Lowland Dry Oak and Birch Wood. However, where there is ancient woodland present, the woodland boundary may be allowed to expand.

1 **Common Cow-wheat** – an ancient woodland indicator species found on well-drained nutrient-poor soils. **2** **Fly Agaric** is an iconic species strongly associated with birch trees and forms a mycorrhizal partnership with the roots of the tree. **3** In the **New Forest**, Lowland Dry Oak and Birch Wood often merges with Beech Wood and heathland.

What to look for

Older stands can support birds such as Redstart. Look out for Common Cow-wheat, whose large seeds are distributed by ants.

How to recognize

Lowland Dry Oak and Birch Wood is an intrinsic component of some of the wilder landscapes of the southern English lowlands, where it intermingles with heathland, Scrub, mires and strips of Wet Woodland. It can also be found on patches of dry, sandy ground within other woodland types. Oaks are interspersed with birch groves and surrounded by deep swathes of Bracken (which are hard to walk through in summer) or heathy vegetation with soft tussocks of Wavy Hair-grass. Some Lowland Dry Oak and Birch Wood is ancient, and dark, knarled veteran oaks contrast with the pale trunks and slender branches of birches. However, much is young birch-dominated high forest that has recently colonized heathland.

When to visit

Summer–autumn for fungi; winter to explore when Bracken fronds are dead, making access easier.

TOP: **Dark Crimson Underwing** can sometimes be seen by day on oaks with sap runs. BOTTOM: **Staverton Park, Suffolk** – a classic Lowland Dry Oak and Birch Wood site previously managed as Wood Pasture. Veteran oak pollards are surrounded by large Holly trees that have grown up in the absence of grazing.

Beech Wood

Few woodland habitats are found on the same variety of substrates as Beech Wood. Calcareous Beech Wood (found on the Downs, Chilterns and Cotswolds) often includes some Ash or Sycamore in canopy gaps, while Yew and whitebeams may form a sub-canopy. Dog's Mercury is common, with Sanicle where steeper ground produces more open woodland. At the other end of the spectrum on acid sands and gravels (*e.g.* the High Weald, London Basin, New Forest), oaks join Beech in the canopy, and the heathy ground flora often merges into heathland. At intermediate sites on more neutral and waterlogged brown earths, Beech gains the greatest stature and is overwhelmingly dominant, with only Bramble and Holly frequently persisting in the understorey. These three types of Beech Wood often intergrade.

Beech is native to southern England and Wales. Its slow spread after the last glaciation meant that it had probably not reached its climatic limit before habitat fragmentation impeded its expansion northwards. However, Beech is now stretching existing notions of vegetation types by recolonizing sites where it was removed to favour Hazel coppice, by naturally colonizing sites outside of its historic range, and by invading vigorously from places where it has been introduced.

Similar habitats

Beech Wood is often found in intricate mosaics with other lowland woodland, grassland and heathland communities. Acidic stands that are managed as Wood Pasture are described more fully under that habitat.

New Forest, Hampshire. On some sites the Beech canopy can reach 30 metres: the soaring trunks and spaciousness are often likened to a cathedral.

Origins and development

Beech was slow to return after the last ice age, but gradually replaced limes in woodlands disturbed by cutting and pasturage. Existing stands have been strongly influenced by sylvicultural practices. While its low commercial value has meant that Beech Wood has suffered less from clearance than other woodland types, replanting with conifers and non-native species has nevertheless reduced its area.

Conservation

Deer and Grey Squirrel damage is currently impacting on the age structure and natural regeneration of Beech Wood, while pollution may be resulting in vegetation change. Beech is particularly susceptible to drought and storm damage, so the impacts of climate change are likely to be significant on thin soils in the south. However, conditions will become more suitable for this species farther north and west, where Beech may come to be seen as a valid component of semi-natural woodlands. Urban growth threatens sites where increased human activity results in trampling, disturbance and pollution. Conservation effort has focussed on restoring areas replanted with conifers, and promoting expansion on suitable sites. Within existing stands, allowing natural processes of recruitment and decay will maximize the structural diversity needed by invertebrates. Long-term planning is important to ensure continuity of veteran trees.

EXTENT IN KM²

Eng	170
Wal	34

Distribution and extent

Found on chalk and southern limestone, also acidic soils in the south-east. Map shows broad distribution of the Annex I habitats (H9120 and H9130).

LEFT: **Yellow Bird's-nest** – like the incredibly elusive **Ghost Orchid** also found in Beech Wood, this species lacks chlorophyll and gains its energy from a network of underground fungi. CENTRE: **Bird's-nest Orchid** is another non-photosythesizing plant and takes ten years to build up enough reserves to flower. RIGHT: The lack of undergrowth makes **Beech Woods** easy to places to explore, although the speciality helleborines, such as **Broad-leaved Helleborine** (CUTOUT), can be hard to find (except where caged against the depredations of herbivores).

What to look for

Beech Wood on chalk may support uncommon and rare species such as White, Narrow-lipped, Violet, Green-flowered, Red and Narrow-leaved Helleborines, Bird's-nest Orchid and Yellow Bird's-nest. Specialist invertebrates can be hard to find and identify, but look out for the Yellow-ringed Comb-horn, a striking black-and-yellow striped cranefly (below).

ABOVE: The **Yellow-ringed Comb-horn** breeds in rot holes in Beech trees. BOTTOM LEFT: **Beech mixed coppice and Wood Pasture** were once more common, but the removal of less favoured species and management for timber has resulted in Beech-dominated high-forest, which is now just old enough to be considered traditional. BOTTOM RIGHT: **White Helleborine** is able to colonize young Beech plantations.

How to recognize

Towering high forest on hill-top plateaux, hangers clinging to chalk slopes, and unruly mosaics of Beech and heathland all fall within this habitat. The dense shade created by Beech, together with intense root competition and slowly decaying leaves, limits the undergrowth and ground flora. The more calcareous sites can support rare and elusive saprophytic orchids. Beech Wood is also famed for its autumn fungi, including boletes, agarics and chanterelles, and where veteran trees grow adjacent to open habitats, they may be particularly rich in epiphytic lichens and rare deadwood invertebrates. These old pollards, with their fissured bark, hollow trunks and immense girth, impart a deep sense of history to woods where they are present. While Beech Wood can form a key part of some of our less intensively managed lowland landscapes, in many places is has been planted or is very actively managed.

When to visit

June–August for helleborines; summer–late autumn for fungi.

Yew Wood

page 400

Yew Wood develops where exposure and the dry, shallow soils of steep slopes discourage other woody species. In Yew Wood on south- and west-facing chalk slopes in southern England, Yew is overwhelmingly dominant, its dense evergreen shade excluding all but a scatter of whitebeams, Ash and Elder and sparse, patchy Dog's Mercury. These woods generally develop when a relaxation of grazing pressure on chalk grassland allows Common Juniper or Hawthorn scrub to grow. The scrub protects the more palatable but shade-tolerant Yew seedlings, which gradually shade out the scrub and out-live any faster growing species (*e.g.* Ash) that may colonize canopy gaps. Yew Wood is dynamic, and can spread, senesce and reinvade in a slow progression around coombes.

On the Carboniferous and magnesium limestone of northern England, Yew forms more diverse groves on steep rocky slopes, cliffs and in ravines. Ash and elms join Yew in the canopy, and the ground flora is an impoverished version of that of the surrounding Upland Mixed Ash Wood. The Yew Wood of the Killarney limestone pavements in Ireland includes Holly and Hazel with Ash where soils are deeper, and the rocks are thickly covered with bryophytes.

EXTENT IN KM²	
Eng	12
Wal	<1
Ire	1

Kingley Vale, West Sussex is the largest area of Yew woodland in Britain and is unusual in showing a full range of habitat structure and function.

Distribution and extent

Scattered throughout England and Ireland. Map shows broad distribution of the Annex I habitat (H91J0).

Similar habitats

Yew Wood forms transitions and mosaics with Lowland Calcareous Grassland and Mixed Scrub on chalk. In northern Britain it occurs in mosaics with Upland Mixed Ash Wood and Upland Oak Wood, whilst in the south it is also associated with Beech Wood.

Origins and development

On inaccessible limestone sites, Yew Wood may be primary woodland that has never wholly been cleared. On the southern chalklands it is mostly secondary, having colonized when grazing pressure on grassland has relaxed. Historically, Yew wood has been used for wood-turning and, more famously, for long bows, but rarely for timber production.

Yew bark, needles and seeds are toxic, but birds can ingest the berry (the fleshy 'aril' is edible), helping to disperse the seeds.

Conservation

Current threats are linked to limited ecological functionality. Browsing by deer limits natural regeneration, while afforestation of surrounding slopes prevents the small-scale migration once typical on chalk. This has resulted in relatively uniform stands. Air pollution may be a significant pressure on the structure and functioning of Yew Wood, and it may become geographically restricted due to the impact of climate change. Yew in tree nurseries has been affected by imported pathogens, but there is no evidence that these have spread to Yew Wood. Reducing deer pressure and releasing surrounding land from static management may allow natural processes to reassert themselves and reinvigorate many woods that are slowly deteriorating.

What to look for

The inconspicuous Triangle Spider, found on Yew and Box, spins a very characteristic triangular web from four radial threads, making up three sections of the normal orb. Locally, Box can be a significant part of the understorey, and has a distinctive smell.

Individual **Yew** trees may reach several hundred or even thousand years in age. Yew has an important role in ancient mythology and religion due to its longevity and powers of regeneration.

TOP: **Yewbarrow, Cumbria**. The Yew groves found on the Carboniferous limestone of northern England are sometimes considered to be part of the surrounding Upland Mixed Ash Wood, although they have a distinct character of their own. BOTTOM: In the nearly continuous semi-natural woodland of the Wye Valley, Herefordshire, where Yew either forms a dense canopy on rocky slopes or is scattered amongst other species. In spring, the dark needles contrast strikingly with the luminous spring colours of deciduous trees.

How to recognize

Yew Woods are only found on chalk escarpments, chalk coombes and steep limestone slopes and cliffs. They are easy to spot in the landscape as from a distance the dark, evergreen foliage of Yew stands out against surrounding vegetation (often calcareous grassland).

Inside Yew Wood, the contorted yet fluid forms of individual Yew trees are the prominent feature. Little else distracts the attention in these stark, species-poor woods; there is no real understorey, although the deadwood remains of Juniper Scrub that once protected the Yew seedlings may still scent the air. The ground is a soft carpet of slowly decomposing needles over bare rock and soil, with only a very patchy ground flora surviving in the dense shade.

When to visit

Year round.

Did you know?
Yew is considered to be the longest-living plant in Europe.

Wet Woodland

Wet Woodland includes willow and Alder carr, floodplain, hill and plateau Alder woods, and bog woodland. Carr is essentially a transient feature of peaty landscapes that develops as accumulating organic matter raises the soil surface above the water level, allowing scrub and trees to colonize. These dry the habitat out further and eventually more terrestrial woodland types become established. In some cases the trees are inhibited by the development of bog-mosses (fed by rainwater) so that a cyclical relationship between mire and carr develops. Willow carr is also very widespread in damp places on mineral soils, where it may gradually dry out and develop into other woodland types, although on exposed western coasts it can form a climax community.

Flood events and the slow meandering of rivers once made many Alder floodplain woodlands dynamic. However, natural processes have largely been curtailed by drainage and intensive land-use, with only a few significant areas remaining in un-drained floodplains in northern Scotland. In hilly country, Alder woods are also found on mineral soils along spring lines and in wet gullies, and can be quite species-rich, while plateau Alder woods develop where water seeps between boulder clay and capping sands or wind-blown sediment.

On some mires, a scattering of stunted Scots Pine or Downy Birch with the rich epiphytic flora of ancient woodlands is found; these are bog woodlands. Largely confined to Scotland, small patches are also found in the New Forest, on the Dorset heaths and in Ireland. A balance between the very slow tree growth and the development of the bog creates a stable habitat where the drainage patterns of the bog are unaltered by the trees. Little is known about this woodland type in Britain, although it is common in Scandinavia.

Studland, Dorset – In many cases carr is secondary, having colonized open vegetation in the last 100 years or so since traditional management such as grazing or cutting has ceased.

Similar habitats

Wet Woodland frequently occurs in mosaics with other woodland types and open habitats. In Alder woods, transitions to the wetter Ash-dominated end of Lowland Mixed Oak and Ash Wood are found, while Downy Birch carr is often transitional to Upland Birch Wood.

Origins and development

Wet Woodland first developed on open, wet habitats after the last glaciation, and has continued to colonize open habitats ever since. Where periodically disturbed (*e.g.* by flooding or coppicing), or where it forms stable transitions to dry woodland, Wet Woodland can persist, but it often succeeds to drier woodland types. Much carr is of recent origin, having developed on semi-natural open habitats. Although willow has been cropped for craft uses (such as basket making) and Alder coppices easily, Wet Woodland is hard to access and has little economic value compared to other woodland types. It has, therefore, suffered extensively from clearance and drainage for agriculture.

Conservation

Conserving a dynamic habitat in isolation within a static framework of intensive land-use presents challenges. Current threats include the lowering of the water-table through water abstraction and climate change, eutrophication, the clearance of newly established sites and invasion by vigorous non-native plants such as Himalayan Balsam. Much Wet Woodland is

EXTENT IN KM^2

Eng	26
Wal	32
Sco	55
NI	3
Ire	22

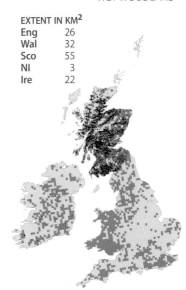

Distribution and extent

Map shows broad distribution of the Annex I habitats (H91EO and H91D0), with more detailed data for Scotland and Ireland.

ABOVE: **River Tay** – the largest areas of remaining floodplain Alder woodland are found along active river channels in Scotland, such as the Spey and the Tay.

ABOVE: **Insh Marshes, Speyside** – in some cases carr vegetation forms in the middle of mire such as this floodplain Transition Mire. BELOW: **River Bure, Norfolk** – where Wet Woodland develops at the water's edge, it provides shade and detritus for fish and aquatic invertebrates.

Carr woodland may form part of a successional series of habitats from open water to dry woodland. Here in **The Broads**, open water is fringed with swamp and Wet Woodland, but the succession stops abruptly at the boundary with agriculturally improved drier land.

successional and will particularly benefit from large, landscape-scale conservation projects that provide the space for habitats to change and develop. At the site scale, re-establishment of natural hydrological systems will allow dynamism within the habitat, creating microhabitats of varying structure suitable for a range of different species and helping to buffer the effects of climate change. Increased interest in using woodland to manage flooding and ameliorate poor water quality may lead to Wet Woodland creation and retention.

What to look for

The most extensive stands of carr are found in The Norfolk and Suffolk Broads and the Shropshire and Cheshire Meres and Mosses. These calcareous carrs can be quite species-rich, with scrub such as Buckthorn, Alder Buckthorn, Guelder-rose, Dogwood and Red Currant, and a ground flora of Meadowsweet, Greater Tussock-sedge, Royal Fern and Yellow Iris. A distinctive northern form with a low canopy of Bay Willow includes herbs such as Wood Stitchwort, Marsh Hawk's-beard and Angelica, and can support the rare Coralroot Orchid. Widespread, but also more common in the north, is a calcifuge community of Downy Birch growing over bog-mosses or Purple Moor-grass on the drier edges of mires.

Floodplain Alder woodlands of any size are harder to find. Isolated strips and patches can still be found in the loops and backwaters of meandering rivers and streams, and larger areas occur in remnant floodplains and shingle islands along active, braided river channels in Scotland. Look out for the scarce Black-poplar on river banks. The ground is usually dominated by ruderal species such as Common Nettle and Great Willowherb, fed with nutrients from river-borne silt. Drier Alder woods with Ash on slopes and plateaux tend to be more species-rich, with a flora including Wood Anemone and Creeping Buttercup.

Wet Woodland has few specialized animals but its humidity and the abundance of dead, rotten wood make it attractive to many species. Willow Tit prefers wet, scrubby woodland and excavates its nest holes in rotten wood. Siskin and Redpoll feed on Alder catkins and birch seed. Wetland trees, wet seepages and semi-submerged deadwood are home to a suit of invertebrates, some of them rare. Willows in particular support a rich assemblages of moths and other insects. Otter can use Wet Woodland for cover and breeding sites.

1 **Kingcombe, Dorset** – drier Alder woods can have a relatively species-rich ground flora. **2** **New Forest, Hampshire** – strips of floodplain Alder woodland can be found along winding streams where they are grazed by free-ranging livestock. **3** **Hoveton Great Broad, Norfolk** – accessible only by boat, this swamp Alder carr is floating on unstable mud and peat over medieval peat workings.

How to recognize

Thick vegetation and treacherously swampy ground make Wet Woodland difficult to access; such woods are often secretive places where few people venture and represent some of our most natural woodlands.

Many areas of Wet Woodland are vibrant places, still governed by successional processes, and made impenetrable by criss-crossing branches, fallen trunks, tangles of trailing creepers and dense undergrowth of shrubs, tall herbs, tussocky sedges and reeds. Fallen deadwood is abundant, often half-submerged in the many patches of standing water or flowing runnels. Others are frugal, sparse woods with a scattered, stunted canopy of just one tree species growing in a delicate balance with bog vegetation.

Floodplain woodland tends to be taller, often with large, multi-stemmed Alders, but intensive agriculture on fertile floodplains has left little room for woodland.

When to visit

Summer for drier conditions.

Did you know?
Submerged Alder does not rot, and was used to build crannogs (loch-dwellings) in the Iron Age.

1 **Siskin** is often seen feeding on Alder catkins. **2** **Upton Fen, Norfolk** – carr ground flora often reflects the flora of the preceding fen, and can include shade-tolerant species such as **Marsh Fern**. **3** **Morden Bog, Dorset** – this old-growth bog woodland of Downy Birch is located in the centre of a valley mire. **Greater Tussock-sedge** tussocks at least one metre in height are surrounded by peaty water.

Wood Pasture

page 400

Wood Pasture is an ecological structure rather than a specific vegetation type. Trees of different ages grow at varying densities in more or less open conditions, a function of light grazing. Grazing suppresses vigorous tree regeneration and the resulting semi-shade, together with the long-term presence of ancient trees, promotes a particularly rich epiphytic flora of lichens, mosses, liverworts and ferns, and an invertebrate fauna of deadwood specialists. Over the centuries, fluctuations in grazing pressure would have allowed the periodic recruitment of younger trees. However, both overgrazing and the cessation of grazing eventually result in the loss of Wood Pasture, either to closed-canopy woodland or to open heathland or grassland. The long life-span of veteran trees means that they can persist for many years amongst younger trees or conifers, but in such shaded conditions the diversity of species hosted by the veterans is greatly diminished and their vigour much reduced.

Wood Pasture is found from sea level right up to the tree line, often on nutrient-poor acidic soils that are unsuitable for cultivation, although it is by no means confined to these. Many well-known sites are in southern England but a few parklands are scattered throughout Wales and Northern Ireland. In Scotland, a continuum from closed-canopy woodland through grazed woodland to Wood Pasture is often seen.

Similar habitats

Wood Pasture is a particular expression of Lowland Dry Oak and Birch Wood and acid Beech Wood (parkland is also sometimes derived from Lowland Mixed Oak and Ash Wood).

The parkland of Windsor Great Park, Berkshire/Surrey holds the highest number of veteran trees in Britain and possibly Europe. Many UK invertebrates are known only from this site.

Origins and development

Wood Pasture may be derived from the post-glacial wildwoods, where fluctuations in the woodland canopy and the actions of wild herbivores created open areas. It developed through the complex interactions between human use (livestock grazing; collecting of leaf fodder, leaf-hay, firewood, timber and bark; and hunting) and natural processes. By medieval times such uses had become formalized under the system of common rights. Royal Forests and hunting parks were established, and included large areas of Wood Pasture. The subsequent decline of Royal Forests saw the loss of much Wood Pasture, although medieval parks were revived during the Tudor period in the 16th century, and again in the 18th century (when many were formally landscaped). The loss of Wood Pasture was exacerbated when communal grazing land was enclosed from the 17th century onwards and by conversion to plantation during the Napoleonic Wars at the beginning of the 19th century and again after the Second World War. In the uplands, a balance between grazing and regeneration was maintained until the agricultural revolution of the late 18th/early 19th centuries, when woods were enclosed or were grazed more heavily as year-round sheep pasture.

Conservation

A surge of interest in veteran trees in the late 20th century has resulted in efforts to manage and reinvigorate lapsed Wood Pasture. These efforts have focussed on how to renew and extend existing areas through appropriate grazing and the sensitive management of veteran trees. The full biodiversity benefits of extending Wood Pasture will be a long time coming, but such

EXTENT IN KM^2

Eng	578
Wal	n/k
Sco	105
NI	11
Ire	n/k

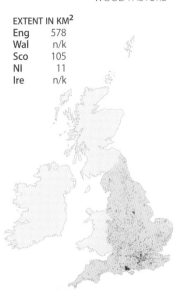

Distribution and extent

Scattered across Britain, scarce in Ireland. The New Forest is a particularly important location and. overall, Britain holds a significant proportion of the north-west European resource. Map shows only the distribution in England.

Borrowdale, Lake District – pollards were still cropped for livestock fodder within living memory. These Ash trees have been re-pollarded by the National Trust.

The diverse nature of a veteran tree
A veteran tree (FACING PAGE) can be defined as one that is of interest biologically, culturally or aesthetically because of its age, size or condition. Age depends upon the species – oaks might reach a millennium and Yews pre-date Christianity, but a veteran birch may be just a few decades old. Individual veterans are often named, well-loved, and enshrined in legends and stories. For example, the Fortingall Yew is said to have shaded the play of Pontius Pilate as a child. These trees speak to our souls, and their tenacity, the complexity of their ecology and the richness of the species they support is truly awesome. However, our veteran trees are a legacy from the past that we are failing to renew.

areas make good stepping stones between fragmented patches of woodland and open habitat in the shorter term. A long-term view is required, such as the 500-year management plan the Corporation of London has developed for Burnham Beeches in Buckinghamshire.

Wood Pasture is considered to have a low vulnerability to climate change. However, veteran trees may be impacted by drought and increased storm frequency and are particularly vulnerable in Wood Pasture settings. Allowing recruitment and 'veteranizing' young trees will be important in maintaining the continuity of dead and decaying wood features.

What to look for

The ground flora of Wood Pasture tends to be quite species-poor, although it can include grassland, heathland and woodland species, including fungi such as waxcaps (see *page 156*). Of the trees, oaks and Beech are the most frequent, but Ash, Hornbeam, Holly, elms, Alder, birches and, in Scotland, Scots Pine are all common. Parkland can also include planted non-natives such as Turkey Oak and Cedar-of-Lebanon. However, the overriding wildlife interest of Wood Pasture lies in the myriad species associated with veteran trees. Many of these trees have been pollarded in the past, extending their lifespans. However, such management is not a prerequisite since open-grown trees, with large, spreading canopies and horizontal branches, are also of great value.

As trees gradually age, their limbs die back, fungi hollow out the dead heartwood, and bark becomes craggy and loose. Nevertheless, they can still last for centuries, and this continuity is important for the sedentary species that colonize them. Fungi decompose standing and fallen deadwood, releasing nutrients for other fungi and feeding invertebrates. Mosses, liverworts and ferns colonize damp hollows, and lichens, fungi and algae grow on the bark, providing habitats for invertebrates in their turn. Beetles and flies use deadwood, sap runs, lightning strikes and old wounds, and are themselves prey for other invertebrates, birds

Staverton, Suffolk was once a medieval deer park. The thick Bracken growing under these venerable pollards shows that this area is no longer grazed.

Snag where
limb has
broken

Rot hole

Damp holes
colonized
by bryophytes

Deadwood

Bracket fungus

Swollen base

Epping Forest, Essex holds over 50,000 pollarded trees, including Hornbeam (TOP) and Beech (BOTTOM). Grazing has been reintroduced, using innovative 'invisible fencing'.

and bats. Some birds excavate nest holes in softened wood, and others use crevices for breeding, as do bats. The open canopy of trees also favours foliage-living invertebrates, while others depend on the micorrhizal fungi associated with tree roots, or with dung. Groups of veteran trees provide a greater range of microhabitats and support a more diverse fauna and flora than single trees.

1 The **New Forest**, Hampshire contains the largest area of Wood Pasture in NW Europe. It is one of very few sites that are known to have a continuous history of grazing since the medieval period. Light grazing helps to maintain the diversity of grassland species and creates a varied vegetation structure, including regenerating scrub and trees. **2** The classical Wood Pasture landscape holds wide appeal, and many people are drawn to veteran trees because of their character and links with the past. **3** **Southern Bracket Fungus** is widespread, particularly on old Beech trees. The brackets themselves can survive many years.

How to recognize

Veteran trees (see *page 75*) are the defining feature of this habitat. Often knarled, contorted into fabulous shapes and encrusted in lichens and fungi, they are scattered with other trees and scrub in a serene, savannah-like landscape.

Wood Pasture on former Royal Forests and wooded common is often extensive. Ancient, open-grown trees are interspersed with thickets of scrub and younger trees and they often merge into a mosaic of woodland and heathland or grassland.

Upland Wood Pasture may be associated with remnant ravine or cliff woodland, and often contains ruined sheilings (a hut, or collection of huts) or drove roads.

Wood Pasture found in old deer parks is usually more confined, with fences or banks demarcating an abrupt transition to farmland. In wooded commons it often has a more irregular boundary. All types are deeply cultural landscapes of historical interest, legacies of a multi-purpose tradition of land-use long since abandoned.

When to visit

Year-round for veteran trees and lichens.

Upland Oak Wood

page 400

Upland Oak Wood is widespread in the uplands on soils that range from strongly to mildly acidic. Sessile Oak is generally the dominant canopy species but Pedunculate Oak and hybrids of the two are more common in some locations (such as east Scotland and Dartmoor). Other canopy species include birches, Rowan, Hazel and some Holly, with occasional Ash and Alder in flushed areas or boggy hollows. In old coppices the diversity of canopy species is particularly low, a result of weeding in the 19th century; some Upland Oak Wood is in fact plantation, dating from the same period. These woodlands are often grazed, resulting in a mossy, grassy field layer, and limiting the regeneration of woody species. Dense patches of even-aged birch can sometimes be found, indicating a past reduction in grazing pressure that resulted in canopy gaps being 'infilled'. Both birches and Rowan may become more common – an increase in wind-blown oaks is a likely consequence of climate change.

On loch islands and in enclosed areas a lack of grazing is immediately apparent in the more complex understorey and a lush field layer with Great Wood-rush and Bilberry. The composition of the field layer is also influenced by the soil type: Heather and Wavy Hair-grass give way to Sweet Vernal-grass, Creeping Soft-grass and small herbs such as Wood-sorrel and Common Dog-violet on less acidic soils. Bluebells are common in more oceanic situations, replaced in the colder, drier east by Wood Anemone and Chickweed-wintergreen. Bracken is common, particularly over deeper soils; other ferns typically include Hard Fern and Common Polypody, joined in shady ravines by Lemon-scented Fern and Oak Fern, among others. Bryophytes and lichens are a defining feature of the different vegetation communities present and are particularly abundant and diverse in the west.

Upland Oak Wood, such as this streamside wood in **Snowdonia**, is often found clothing steep valley sites where diffcult terrain discouraged conversion to agricultural use.

Similar habitats

Oak tends to give way to birch upslope in northern Scotland until Upland Birch Wood becomes dominant. Downslope it often grades into Upland Mixed Ash Wood or Alder or birch-dominated Wet Woodland. In coastal locations (particularly Argyll), Atlantic Hazel Wood is found over a similar field layer. Where a long history of grazing has resulted in very open, grassy woodland and associated veteran trees, Upland Oak Wood is considered as Wood Pasture.

Origins and development

Most of the original Upland Oak Wood was destroyed in prehistory, and the fragmented remaining patches were exploited for timber and managed as coppice to provide tanning bark and charcoal used in iron smelting (mid-18th–mid-19th centuries). They were also used for sheltered grazing. Sheep pasturage increased markedly from the mid-18th century, and in recent decades deer browsing has added significantly to the grazing pressure. During the second half of the 20th century, clearance and thinning for conifer plantation, combined with conversion to rough grazing, reduced the area of Upland Oak Wood by nearly 40%. However, more recently, designation and initiatives to protect this habitat mean that it is likely to be increasing through both planting and natural regeneration.

EXTENT IN KM^2

Eng	200
Wal	480
Sco	226
NI	10
Ire	n/k

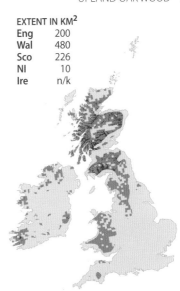

Distribution and extent

Locally extensive on the western and northern upland fringes. Map shows the broad distribution of the Annex I habitat (H91A0), with darker shading showing actual distribution for Scotland and Ireland only.

Erraid, Ross of Mull – exposed coastal oak woodland is often stunted.

Conservation

Encouraging the remaining islands of Upland Oak Wood to expand is a priority. Encouraging the remaining islands of Upland Oak Wood to expand is a priority. Promoting natural recolonization and planting seeds of local provenance will buffer and link existing sites, allowing marooned specialist species to expand their range. Targeting expansion in north-facing locations and along spring lines will help protect the more oceanic fern, bryophyte and fungus communities that will be most vulnerable to climate warming. Within existing Upland Oak Wood, non-intervention is generally the best approach, except where threatening exotics or conifers need to be removed and where, in the absence of natural predators, deer management is needed to ensure natural regeneration is not suppressed. Seasonal low-intensity grazing is often advocated in order to prevent a thick ground flora developing and shading out lower plants where these have become limited in extent. Coppicing, although favourable for spring flowers and some warmth-seeking insects, does not allow the development of rich epiphytic communities.

What to look for

Four characteristic summer migrant birds to listen for and look out for in the spring are Redstart, Pied Flycatcher, Tree Pipit and Wood Warbler. Mammals are less likely to be seen but Pine Marten (Scotland only), Red Squirrel (in the north), Badger and Polecat are all found in Upland Oak Wood. In sheltered woodlands in north-west Scotland look for Chequered Skipper in sunny clearings and rides. Pearl-bordered Fritillary is another scarce butterfly that may be present, and more common butterflies may include Speckled Wood, Silver-washed Fritillary and White Admiral.

A wide range of lower plants are favoured by the moist, clean air. Lichens include dangling beard lichens, leafy protruding lungworts and creeping and crustose species of the Parmelion community. Look out for the distinctive lichen Common Tree Lungwort (see Atlantic Hazel Wood, *page 91*), which is an indicator of ancient woodland, and other rarer species. Some of the more conspicuous mosses include the golden-green fingers of Neat Feather-moss; dark green, thyme-like Swan-necked Thyme-moss; and the bright, fern-like Common Tamarisk-moss; and inside the moist woodland interior rare woodland species can be found.

LEFT: The Parmelion lichen community occurs on trees with very acid bark, and includes creeping grey leafy-lobed lichens and cudbear lichens that are sometimes likened to splats of porridge (arrowed). RIGHT: **Loch a' Mhuilinn, Sutherland** – oceanic Upland Oak Woods with particularly rich lower plant floras, including many of our rarest bryophytes, are temperate rainforests.

1 **Snowdonia** – although often remote and wild in feel, almost all Upland Oak Wood has been used by humans for generations. Look for areas on cliffs or ravines to find possible unfelled remnants of wildwood. **2** **Dart Valley, Devon** – Upland Oak Wood is often found along rivers and stream. Look for filmy ferns such as **3** **Tunbridge Filmy-fern** on humid mats of bryophytes on boulders. **4** **Redstart** typically nest around the edges of woods or near clearings. **5** **Pied Flycatcher** is associated with open Upland Oak Wood where the understorey is sparse. **6** Listen for the distinctive accelerating song of the **Wood Warbler**, which is sometimes likened to the sound of a spinning coin.

How to recognize

This is the cool, moist oak wood of the rugged upland fringes, often found where the underlying hard rock is broken into jumbled boulders. Oaks generally dominate the usually fairly open canopy and vary from well-grown singles to lower-growing, multi-stemmed old coppice or even, on the Atlantic coast, prostrate trees stunted by westerly gales. Downy Birch is also common, with Silver Birch in the east, and scattered Rowan and Hazel, all growing over a grassy or heathy field layer.

On the west coast in particular, the mild, wet climate and clean air promote the lush growth of myriad lower plants – both on the rocks and on the trunks and branches of the trees, where bryophytes form a background for large leafy-lobed lichens, small ferns and dripping beard lichens.

Archaeological remains (such as levelled charcoal hearths), boundary walls, pollards and evidence of previous management as coppice or Wood Pasture often add an historic element to the atmosphere of these woods.

When to visit

From mid-April for birds (easiest to see when the leaves are not quite out!); May–early June for butterflies; year-round for lichens, mosses and scenery.

Did you know?

The epiphytic lichen assemblages of oceanic Upland Oak Wood are among the richest in Europe.

1 Chequered Skipper occurs in damp grassland (the larval food plant is Purple Moor-grass) on the edge of woodland. The best time to see adults is at the end of May/early June. **2** Wistman's Wood, Dartmoor is famed for its gnarled, twisted trees and epiphytic flora. Photo evidence shows that the wood has spread and the trees gained in height since the late 19th century. **3** Borrowdale, Cumbria – the structure/canopy species diversity of some Upland Oak Woods is limited because they were planted or other species were weeded out. These woods may become more diverse over time.

Upland Mixed Ash Wood

page 399

The species composition of Upland Mixed Ash Wood varies from north to south, and also locally according to slope, aspect and the degree of moisture. In the north, characteristic species include Rowan, Hazel, Downy Birch, oaks and Bird Cherry, while in the south, Small-leaved Lime, Field Maple, Wych Elm and Beech (which is probably native in South Wales and the Lower Wye Valley) are common. Sycamore is frequent and although native to this woodland type on the continent, is an introduced species.

The light shade and calcareous substrate of Upland Mixed Ash Wood mean that it is typically species-rich. Un-grazed woods can be carpeted with Ramsons or Dog's Mercury, together with less common species such as Lily-of-the-valley, Solomon's-seal and Herb-Paris and, in the north, Wood Crane's-bill, Globeflower, Marsh Hawk's-beard and Lady's-mantle. Where grazed, the ground flora tends to be grassy with Bracken and thick mosses covering the rocks. In the oceanic climate of north-west Scotland and southern Ireland, epiphytic bryophytes and ferns are particularly abundant, creating a characteristic winter greenness, while lichens can include the distinctive Lobarion communities found in other Atlantic woodland types. Upland Mixed Ash Wood has a rich invertebrate fauna, and is particularly important for specialists of flushes and for molluscs (which require calcium for their shells). Dead elms are a frequent sight and are good for insects that require decaying wood.

EXTENT IN KM²	
Eng	75
Wal	30
Sco	131
NI	3
Ire	n/k

Upland Ash Wood is often found as one of several components, such as here at **Glasdrum Wood, Argyll and Bute**, which also supports Upland Oak Wood. Glasdrum means 'grey ridge', which may be a reference to the grey bark of Ash trees.

Distribution and extent

Found mainly on limestone in the north and west. Map shows broad distribution of the Annex I habitat (H9180), with more detailed data for Scotland.

Similar habitats

Upland Mixed Ash Wood can merge with other woodland types due to irregular topography and soil conditions. Where grazed, it can form mosaics with limestone grassland or pavement communities.

Origins and development

Ash spread rapidly after the last glaciation, reaching its current range around 6,500 years ago and Upland Mixed Ash Wood probably represents the last vestiges of a more widespread climax vegetation type on calcareous soils in cool, sub-montane areas. Clearance, and more latterly overgrazing, quarrying and replanting with non-native trees have greatly reduced its extent, although the required substrate has always been more fragmented than for other upland woodland types. Many woods were coppiced for timber and firewood and often had oak standards. Young groves of single-stemmed Ash are now found in some woods where preferential management for oaks reduced the amount of Ash in the past.

Conservation

Upland Mixed Ash Wood often forms part of pastoral farming systems and grazing by deer and livestock continues to constrain regeneration, reduce structural diversity within woods and limit the field layer. Light grazing regimes can maintain some open patches. Coppicing is not recommended where there are rich lichen and bryophyte floras. Ash dieback is likely to significantly impact on this habitat. Over 1,000 species are associated with Ash, and of these around 100 are either highly associated with, or only occur on, Ash. Bryophytes, fungi, invertebrates and lichens, many of which are already of conservation concern, are thought to be at greatest risk of declining. Research suggests that no one tree species would make a suitable replacement for Ash. Which species replace Ash will be partly determined by climate change, but Aspen, Alder, Rowan and Small-leaved Lime should be encouraged and Sycamore retained where appropriate.

What to look for

Rarities include Dark-red Helleborine, Jacob's-ladder, Large-leaved Lime and rare whitebeams. Oceanic epiphytic lichen and bryophyte communities can be particularly rich.

LEFT: Ravine woodland near **Cowgill, Yorkshire Dales** – such woods can provide oases of wildlife in barren upland landscapes. RIGHT: **Lily-of-the-valley** is frequently found in Upland Mixed Ash Wood, but also on Limestone Pavement, in some lowland woods and as a garden escape.

How to recognize

Although often small or fragmented, Upland Mixed Ash Wood can be particularly beautiful, with a rich diversity of plant and invertebrate species under characteristically dappled shade. Found in the upland fringes of pastoral landscapes, it is largely confined to rocky limestone outcrops, crags and ravines or in irregular patches on flushed slopes of riverbanks, where the elegant form of Ash can be picked out from a medley of other species.

Upland Mixed Ash Wood can also be found hidden away in valley heads and on hillsides forming smaller zones and patches within other woodland types, with which it intergrades.

Ash regenerates readily in the absence of grazing and woods often include old boundaries, pollards, limekilns and quarries that have been subsumed by younger trees.

When to visit

Late spring–summer for flora.

Did you know?

A related woodland type (missing in Britain but still found in Scandinavia) of Ash, birches, willows and Bird Cherry over a tall-herb field layer is probably the origin of the distinctive Northern Hay Meadow flora.

1 **Scar Close, North Yorkshire** – open patches are important in Upland Mixed Ash Wood, supporting grassland species not found under the canopy. **2** **Rassal Ashwood, Wester Ross** – in the cool oceanic climate of northern Scotland, Upland Mixed Ash Wood can be found almost at sea level, and often supports rich epiphytic communities. Rassal is the most northerly sizeable Ash wood in Britain, probably at its climatic limit. **3** **Colt Park Wood, North Yorkshire** – wooded Limestone Pavement is uncommon, but provides an intriguing insight into how unmodified open limestone landscapes may have looked in the past.

Caledonian Forest is the only indigenous pine forest in Britain and Ireland, and is restricted to Scotland. It is found on infertile, acid soils from valley bottoms up to about 650 m; in most places the natural tree line is depressed by the effects of grazing rather than climate. Regeneration – or rather the lack of it – is a key factor in shaping the forest. Where browsing pressure is not too high, the forest regenerates readily, with young trees blurring the interface with heathland. Sparser forest with older, larger trees may be a product of selective thinning as well as grazing. Charismatic older trees with deep crowns growing in more open conditions ('Granny Pines') can also be relics of previous forest where regeneration was suppressed by browsing deer. Areas of dense young pines with high crowns result from planting, natural regeneration following felling, fire or changes in management. Species composition varies between regions, with Scots Pine dominating in the cold, dry east, while more humid, milder conditions in the west are more favourable for birches, Rowan, Holly and Hazel. Sessile Oak is found in the north-east.

Similar habitats

This distinctive habitat merges with other upland woodland habitats and with wetlands and heathlands. It can be hard to distinguish relatively natural Caledonian Forest, which has regenerated following felling or fire or in old stands, from planted areas.

Beinn Eighe, looking across Loch Maree – above the altitude that this photograph was taken, the pines largely give way to Upland Birch Wood.

Origins and development

Following the last glaciation, Common Juniper, willows and, later, Scots Pine colonized the Highlands of Scotland, and by 4,000 years ago some 1·5 million hectares of pine-dominated mixed woodland had developed. Felling and climate cooling during the Neolithic period started an ongoing decline. This increased from the 17th century onwards until only isolated remnants were left, largely in the more inaccessible upper glens. The removal of crofters and subsequent management of Red Deer for sport shooting led to a spurt of regeneration, although this was then contained by increased sheep-grazing. In the 20th century, reforestation programmes were initiated.

Conservation

The area of Caledonian Forest is limited by grazing animals, while the quality of existing forest is influenced by past and present sylvicultural practices. In the north-central Highlands, the Trees for Life project (see *page 51*) aims to restore significant areas to natural forest and eventually reintroduce its missing species: Beaver, Eurasian Lynx, Wolf and Wild Boar. Restoration involves planting as well as facilitating natural regeneration by fencing out Red Deer and livestock. At Abernethy, the RSPB plan to increase the forest by 2,000–3,000 ha through natural regeneration, using light grazing to optimise conditions for key species. Some areas, such as Abernethy, are managed primarily for their wildlife interest, but in others, such as Glenmore, commercial timber management is more of a priority. Recreational access is often an important factor influencing management.

EXTENT IN KM²
Sco   803

Distribution and extent

Confined to the Scottish Highlands. Map shows broad distribution of the Annex I habitat (H91C0); darker shading indicates actual locations.

Forest Lodge, Abernethy – thick field layer vegetation of Bilberry, Heather and abundant mosses can include species such as Cowberry, Wavy Hair-grass, and **Small Cow-wheat** (INSET).

1 Abernethy, Inverness-shire – old-growth forest is characterized by a range of tree ages and shapes and standing deadwood (left), plantation and regeneration in felled areas is more uniform (right). **2** The **Bumblebee Robberfly** is a large and dramatic fly – look for it on fallen pine trees and stumps, where it sits ready to ambush other insects. **3** **Green Shield-moss** is an endangered species known from just 13 sites (most of which are in Caledonian Forest). It is a deadwood specialist that mostly grows on boughs bigger than 20 cm diameter. Unlike most other mosses its leaves are invisible. **4** **Crested Tit** – endemic to Europe with an endemic subspecies in Scotland, this bird is strongly associated with Caledonian Forest and is often seen in or around old trees.
BELOW: View across Caledonian Forest in **Rothiemurchus** with the Cairngorm massif in the background.

LEFT: **Pine Marten** – an omnivorous species that eats a range of fruit and caterpillars, as well as small mammals, Capercaillie chicks and Red Squirrels. It is most easily seen at dedicated feeding stations and bird feeders.
RIGHT: **Capercaillie** – the world's largest grouse became extinct in Britain over 200 years ago, but was reintroduced in 1837. Bilberry is an important food source.

What to look for

Caledonian Forest supports relatively few species (and often at low density) compared with more fertile lowland woodlands, but many of those that do occur are absent or very rare elsewhere in Britain and Ireland. Red Squirrel, Wild Cat and Pine Marten are closely associated with Caledonian Forest, but were more widespread in the past. Pine Marten and Wild Cat were heavily persecuted and Red Squirrel has disappeared from much of England due to disease and competition from Grey Squirrel – Caledonian Forest has provided sanctuary for these species. While a chance encounter with either predator is unlikely, the knowledge that they are still present adds to the wild feel of the habitat. Red squirrels are still relatively common and can be easily seen at sites such as Abernethy or Rothiemurchus.

Key bird species include Crested Tit, Capercaillie and crossbills. Crested Tit nests in holes in standing dead trees and can occur in pine plantations, but is found at higher density within Caledonian Forest. It is found in forests in Easter Ross, Glen Affric, Strathspey and the Moray Firth coast. Capercaillie occurs mostly south of the Great Glen and prefers old forest with a dense understorey. Crossbills prefer large, broad-crowned and isolated trees and three species breed in Caledonian forest (Common, Scottish and Parrot Crossbills). Notoriously hard to separate, the species differ in their calls and morphology (particularly bill shape). The Scottish Crossbill is Britain's only endemic bird species.

With a bit of luck (and persistence) some unusual flowering plants can be found among the Heather and Bilberry. Creeping Lady's-tresses, Twinflower and One-flowered Wintergreen all have white or very pale flowers. Mosses are abundant and Glittering Wood-moss is particularly characteristic and very common. Tooth fungi are mainly associated with Caledonian Forest, Orange Tooth and Blue Tooth fungi being restricted to native pinewoods.

Caledonian Forest is also important for hoverflies, flies and beetles, including a number of species with very restricted distributions. Many of the important species, such as the Bumblebee Robberfly, are saproxylic, relying on dead pine wood. There are also up to seven species of wood ant that occur in Caledonian Forest, including the Narrow-headed Ant which has its stronghold around Loch Morlich in the Cairngorms. This rare ant can only persist in areas with an open understorey.

1 **One-flowered Wintergreen** occurs in both old-growth forest and pine plantations. 2 **Twinflower** is a boreal species predominantly associated with old Caledonian Forest and is confined to approximately 50 sites in Scotland, mainly in drier woods in the east. 3 **Rothiemurchus, Inverness-shire** – a typical transition between forest and heathland.

How to recognize

Caledonian Forest has a feeling of wildness and expanse that is rare in Britain and Ireland. It is easily identified by its geographic location (the central and north-east Grampian Mountains and northern and western Highlands) and characteristic species.

Scots Pine forms an open canopy with birches and Rowan above a richer layering of shrubby Common Juniper, Heather, Bell Heather and Bilberry. In places it grows more densely over a diminished shrub and field layer.

Many of the remnant areas are vast (*e.g.* Abernethy Forest is 28 km^2) and show natural functions such as intact transitions to other habitat types and natural regeneration. This, together with the apparent lack of human intervention, contributes to a pervading sense of naturalness in the landscape.

When to visit

Year-round for characteristic birds, July–August for rare plants and Heather in bloom.

Did you know?

Caledonia, the Roman name for Scotland, is derived from the early celtic word "caleto" meaning hard or strong. Caledonian Forest is often considered one of the last real wildernesses in Britain.

Atlantic Hazel Wood

page 398

Hazel's natural growth form is that of a multi-stemmed shrub and the longevity of an individual 'tree' is not therefore limited by the lifespan of a single trunk. As a consequence, in places where exposure and thin soils prevent other woody species from establishing themselves, Atlantic Hazel Wood can persist indefinitely. Single-stemmed 'trees', the product of extensive grazing, are found in heavily grazed woodlands and Wood Pasture. In some places Hazel rings are evident. These are created when satellite stools grow up around a 'mother' plant that is eventually shaded out and leaves a circle of clones behind. It is conjectured that some of these trees may be many hundreds of years old, providing stable conditions for epiphytes to flourish.

Variations in the underlying substrate are reflected in the ground flora, which typically includes woodland spring flowers such as Primrose, Wood Anemone, Bluebell, Common Dog-violet and Wood-sorrel, together with ferns and bryophytes. The flora is richest on limestone substrates, where it is comparable to that of Upland Mixed Ash Wood. Leafy lichens are also present, and include the 'Lobarion' community of large, lobed species, smaller, more adpressed species, and those with a jelly-like consistency.

EXTENT UNKNOWN

Similar habitats

The ground flora tends to be the same as either Upland Oak Wood or Upland Mixed Ash Wood, depending on the substrate. Canopy transitions are found where deeper soils or less exposed situations allow other species to overtop Hazel, which can remain a part of the understorey.

Origins and development

Older by far than Upland Oak Wood, and even some Caledonian Forest, these woods are thought to be a survivor of the pioneer

Isle of Eigg, Hebrides. The impenetrably dense canopy of exposed Atlantic Hazel Wood.

Distribution and extent

Found on the western seaboard of Scotland between Knapdale and Sutherland, also some sites in western Ireland. Extent unknown. Considered unique to Britain and Ireland. Pale shading shows approximate area within which the habitat occurs; darker shading indicates Hazel woodland.

Hazel woods that colonized Britain and Ireland after the last glaciation. Protected from livestock grazing and felling because they occur on rough ground and because Hazel can regenerate, they have had a continuous presence for over 10,000 years. During this time it is likely that some woods have been selectively cut (although entire stools were not generally cut-over) and used for pasturage, particularly to shelter livestock. Where the Hazel growth is impenetrably low and dense, it is hard to imagine these woods have ever been used. Current threats include coppicing and overgrazing, which reduce suitability for lower plants, destroy the internal structure and in the case of grazing, prevent regeneration.

Conservation

Atlantic Hazel Woods do not fit into the National Vegetation Classification of British plant communities, nor are they currently recognized by the European Habitats Directive. Few sites fall within protected areas, and the habitat does not easily fit the criteria of current management grants. To ensure its conservation, greater recognition is needed of the ancient origins of this habitat and its unique lower plants. Light seasonal grazing is recommended to help create and maintain small glades. Areas of Hazel without the distinctive lower plant communities of the ancient sites are widespread and have value as potential future habitat, allowing linkage and expansion of current sites.

1 The moss **Dwarf Neckera**; the lichens **2** *Pyrenula occidentalis*, **3** **Golden Specklebelly**, **4** **Common Tree Lungwort** and **5** *Arthonia cinnabarina*; **6** **Octopus Suckers** – a jelly lichen.

How to recognize

Also known as Celtic rainforest, these ancient woods are strange and magical places.

Always close to the sea and on steep or rocky ground, Atlantic Hazel Wood can form self-contained stands, or may be part of other woodland. The low canopy of Hazel filters out the light, making them shady and cool even in summer. The regular, abundant rainfall and moist sea-mists, together with an equable, mild climate allow incredibly rich assemblages of oceanic mosses, liverworts and lichens to flourish, including species that occur nowhere else in the world. Mosses carpet the ground and creep up trunks. In exposed places, the smooth bark of young stems appears pale, mottled with patches of crustose lichens.

Deeper in, large leafy-lobed lichens emerge from thick moss on older branches whose fissured bark traps moisture. Sometimes these heavy stems lean out or are wrenched over in storms, creating a canopy gap that is rapidly filled with young whips sprouting from the base of the stool, and allowing the wood to perpetuate.

When to visit

Year-round for lichen interest.

Did you know?
20 species of crustose lichen are confined to Atlantic woodlands

1 The rubbery orange fingers of the fungus **Hazel Gloves** only occurs in ancient Atlantic Hazel Wood.
2 **Assynt, Sutherland** – light grazing has created a grassy field layer, but has not prevented regeneration of Hazel shoots.
3 **Cathir Chomáin, Co. Clare** – large areas of pioneer Atlantic Hazel Wood have developed on the limestones of Co. Clare and Co. Fermanagh as a result of farming changes. They included more ancient core areas, but mostly lack the species-richness of old-growth areas.

Upland Birch Wood

page 399

Upland Birch Woodland is characterized by the predominance of birch in the canopy. Both species may be present, although the tougher Downy Birch tends to replace Silver Birch in wetter, more exposed locations. Other trees can include Rowan, willows and Hazel. In exposed locations, the conditions are often too harsh for oaks and Ash, although in some cases the preponderence of birch may have been exggerated by the removal of these species for timber. In the cool and windy north-west Highlands, a shrubby form of Downy Birch reaches no more than 1m in height. In the north and east Highlands, both species form almost pure stands, with the presence of a little Common Juniper and Scots Pine hinting at a past continuum with Caledonian Forest. In other places, birch dominance can be a result of selective felling for timber. In northern England and Wales, where there is little remaining woodland at high altitudes, birch woods are scarce, tending only to occur in patches within other woodland types or, more rarely, as wet, valley bottom woodlands with an understorey of bog-mosses and Purple Moor-grass (see Wet Woodland, *page 66*). Downy Birch stands are considered a part of upland oak woodland in Ireland.

Birches are pioneers, their small, wind-blown seeds allowing them to colonize open areas quickly. As birches are short-lived and easily shaded out by other species, Upland Birch Wood tends gradually to move across the landscape as older stands either senesce and revert to moorland or succeed to other woodland types, and new stands develop on open ground. Newer woods tend to be relatively species-poor and even-aged, occurring where a temporary relaxation of grazing pressure results in a pulse of regeneration, leading to even-aged stands of trees.

Like Atlantic Oak Wood and Atlantic Hazel Wood, the Upland Birch Wood of the Atlantic fringe can support rich lichen and bryophyte communities, including many rarities.

Similar habitats

Upland Birch Wood is closely related to other upland woodlands types, and can often be seen as a cyclical stage within these.

Origins and development

Birch colonized rapidly following the last glaciation and persisted where harsh conditions prevented other tree species from flourishing (*e.g.* in the north of Scotland and possibly on McGillycuddy's Reeks and the Wicklow Mountains in Ireland). The extent of Upland Birch Wood often fluctuated in a slowly changing mosaic of other woodland types, heathland and wetland, and they were generally not as intensively managed as other woodland types. However, their dynamic nature is now often constrained by land management practices (overgrazing and burning) that prevent regeneration and result in isolated and sometimes moribund stands. In the second half of the 20th century, overgrazing and replanting with non-native species led to significant losses, but planting under grant schemes and restructuring of conifer plantations may be reversing this trend.

Conservation

Upland Birch Wood is currently used for shelter and grazing for livestock, with some wood extraction for firewood. Overgrazing of woodland and adjacent habitats needs to be reduced to allow Upland Birch Wood move, change and regenerate. A strategic approach is needed to join new areas to existing stands, to allow cohesive forest ecosystems to develop, and to conserve genetic diversity across its range. Climate change may reduce longevity and affect regeneration.

EXTENT UNKNOWN

Distribution and extent

Widely distributed in the uplands, especially in Scotland. Map shows a detailed distribution for Scotland but data are more approximate for other areas. Around 150–250 km² are probably ancient, but much more is secondary woodland.

LEFT: **Assynt, Sutherland** – Birch Wood often forms mosaics with other habitats, including Upland Dry Heath as seen in this stream gorge. RIGHT: **Borrowdale, Cumbria** – oak woodland gives way to birch on the upper slopes.

What to look for

Boreal plants including Chickweed-wintergreen and Globeflower; stands of Aspen (which can support rare and scarce insects) in Upland Birch Wood in the Highlands; Pearl-bordered Fritillary.

How to recognize

Upland Birch Wood cloaks large swathes of the uplands (particularly in Scotland) where infertile, poorly drained soils are challenging for other species.

Birch woods often have a transient feel. They are generally open and grassy, quite even-aged, and dotted with glades, rocky outcrops and damp hollows. They can range from a scattering of individual trees over heathy vegetation to more established woods with dense thickets, mature trees and veterans that have changed the flora beneath them to grass and just a few herbs such as Wood-sorrel and Tormentil.

Although the flora is generally quite limited, inaccessible ledges in damp, base-rich ravines can support tall herbs. Upland Birch Wood provides habitat for typical upland woodland birds, and as birch wood rots rapidly, it provides excellent habitat for a great diversity of invertebrates and for fungi.

When to visit

Late spring/early summer for butterflies and flowers.

Did you know?

In the past, birch was used for firewood and for making small tools, herbal remedies and a fermented drink.

1 Pearl-bordered Fritillary can be seen in clearings where there are abundant violets (the larval food plant) and nectar sources, but populations can die out when clearings become overgrown. **2** The Kentish Glory occurs in open birch woodland (with young trees) and is now restricted to Upland Birch Wood in north-east Scotland (it historically occurred in England, where it was last recorded in 1970). **3** Yewbarrow, Cumbria – Upland Birch Wood is intrinsically transient, although individual woods are known to have persisted for hundreds of years. **4** Chickweed-wintergreen – although not species-rich, Upland Birch Wood provides habitats for flowering plants typical of northern Britain.

Coniferous Plantation

page 399

The wildlife of Coniferous Plantation reflects the type of
semi-natural habitat that was afforested or replanted (usually
heathland, bog and less profitable woodland types), and the age
and structure of the plantation. In dense plantations, deep shade
and needle-litter can inhibit plant growth, but where light can
penetrate along rides or in thinned areas, Bracken or heathland
species can develop. In plantations within broad-leaved
woodland, an impoverished woodland flora can persist.

Large sites that are a complex matrix of different plantation
stages and open habitats may support more species than the open
habitat would alone, as they can include woodland species that
do not inhabit the open habitat (*e.g.* bats such as Brown Long-
eared Bat or Noctule that roost in mature trees). Within woodland
sites, conifer-loving species benefit, and plantations have
extended the range of some species (*e.g.* Firecrest and Crossbill
in England). Early growth stages may support high densities
of birds that favour scrub, such as warblers, and young pine is
particularly important for Black Grouse, but the lack of structure
inhibits many woodland birds.

EXTENT IN KM²

Eng	2,971
Wal	1,616
Sco	10,270
NI	737
Ire	5,020

Similar habitats

Larger sites usually contain patches of semi-natural habitat
including mires, heathland, secondary woodland and ancient
woodland. Coastal sites can include Sand Dune.

Dentdale, Cumbria – uniform blocks of dense conifers jar the eye in
upland landscapes but can (when young) support species such as
Small Pearl-bordered Fritillary and Black Grouse.

Distribution and extent

Widespread in the uplands. Pale
shading indicates the broad
distribution of the two relevant Annex
I habitats (H8110 and H8120); darker
shading (not for England) shows actual
locations.

Origins and development

Large-scale coniferous afforestation started after the First World War, when woodland cover in Britain had reduced to 5% and in Ireland to less than 2%. In 1919, the Forestry Commission (now Forestry England (FE)) was formed to set up strategic reserves of timber, and extensive areas where poor soil fertility had precluded agriculture (mainly heaths and mires) were afforested. State afforestation commenced in Ireland in the 1920s. By the 1920s, large areas such as the New Forest, Thetford Forest and Kielder Forest were afforested, and planting moved into the uplands. Scotland now contains the largest sites and greatest area of Coniferous Plantation. In the 1980s, vast areas of natural peatlands in the Flow Country in northern Scotland were afforested due to tax breaks and forestry grants. Nature Conservation now forms part of FE's remit, and some areas are being restored to their former important habitats.

Conservation

While Coniferous Plantations can support a diversity of wildlife, their overall conservation value is generally less than that of the semi-natural habitat they replaced, and restoration projects are now underway to restore areas of heathland, mire and broadleaved

1 The increase in conifer plantations since the 1930s has enabled the **Pine Hawk-moth** to spread northwards in England. The main larval food plant is Scots Pine. **2** **Bentley Wood, Wiltshire** – clearings within plantations on woodland sites can support rare butterflies such as Pearl-bordered Fritillary and Duke of Burgundy. **3** **Holkham, Norfolk** – Scots Pine was planted in the late 19th century to stabilize the sand dunes. Rare fungi have been recorded here, together with uncommon plants such as Yellow Bird's-nest and Creeping Lady's-tresses.

woodland. The size of many plantations provides scope for creating habitat networks and rewilding in the landscape.

Where coniferous cover is retained, focus should be on providing rich edge habitats and a shifting mosaic of clearfell and young plantation, retaining old stands and managing watercourses sensitively. Recreation is increasingly part of the remit for state-owned sites, and a balance between such activities and maintaining and enhancing the wildlife interest can be difficult to achieve.

What to look for

Nightjar, Sand Lizard and Smooth Snake in southern heathland areas; Red Squirrel and Crossbill.

1 **Wareham Forest, Dorset** – the interface between Coniferous Plantation and heathland can support higher densities of Nightjar than heathland alone. **2** **Red Squirrel** – Coniferous Plantation in the north of England and Scotland remains a stronghold for Red Squirrel after the decline caused by the introduction of Grey Squirrel. Dense stands with continuous cover and a diversity of conifers to provide an ongoing food supply are important. **3** **Creeping Lady's-tresses** – a rare orchid found in pine woods in Scotland, Cumbria and East Anglia, which may have colonized naturally or been introduced with tree seedlings.

How to recognize

Plantations are easily identified. Our only indigenous coniferous tree – Scots Pine – is now only native to Scotland and dark, geometric blocks of uniformly aged trees planted in straight lines with little by way of shrub or field layer do not look any more natural than a field of wheat. However, many plantations (which can include pine, spruce and fir) are now managed more sympathetically than in the past.

Open ride-edges, firebreaks and clearfells can support natural vegetation, and animals including reptiles and Woodlark, while clearings in replanted woods may still support rare butterflies. Raptors including Goshawk and Osprey nest in tall pines, Crossbill and Red Squirrel forage for pine nuts and Red or Roe Deer may seek cover.

After dusk, plantations can be great places to see Nightjar, Long-eared Owl and bats, and big sites in particular offer superbly dark skies for star-gazing.

When to visit

Warm, still evenings May–August for Nightjar; year-round for Red Squirrel.

Did you know?

Beavers were reintroduced to Knapdale Forest in Argyll and Bute in 2009.

SCRUB

HABITAT	DESCRIPTION
Mixed Scrub *page 108* | *page 399*	Typically composed of thorny shrubs, this is a transitional habitat that develops on open areas in the absence of regular grazing or cutting and eventually succeeds to woodland.
Hedgerow *page 111* | *page 399*	Essentially a narrow strip of woodland edge habitat composed of scrub, trees and bulky herbs. Hedgerows can form wildlife corridors and are also of cultural signficance.
Bracken *page 117* | *page 399*	Comprises large swathes of the fern Bracken; generally considered as a conservation and agricultural challenge but in some circumstances provides wildilfe habitat.

ORIGINS

There has been much debate amongst ecologists as to how much scrub and open habitats existed in the 'natural' (pre-Neolithic) vegetation of Britain and Ireland. Scrub developed rapidly in some places after the last glaciation and was largely replaced by woodland, but the extent of the woodland canopy is questioned. Some argue that a shifting mosaic of scrub, woodland and open habitats was always present; there is certainly evidence that scrub has a long history in Britain and Ireland (*e.g.* Blackthorn has been found in pollen cores dating back at least 5,000 years ago and evidence of Blackthorn and Hawthorn has been found in Mesolithic deposits).

Scrub plants are pioneer woody species. They grow fast once established and do best where there is ample light, and as a consequence can colonize open habitat quite quickly. Scrub species also have a range of adaptions that enable them to respond rapidly to changing environments and colonize new areas (see below for some examples).

Near **Llanfachreth, Gwynedd** – in Welsh, *ffridd* (seen in this valley) refers to a complex mosaic of scrub, heath, Bracken and other habitats of uncultivated valley sides in the transition between upland and lowland. Often continuous, it can provide important habitat and corridors for fritillary butterflies and birds such as Whinchat.

Many shrubs have fleshy berries that are distributed in the droppings of a range of species, including birds such as thrushes. Seed fall is much heavier under trees and bushes where birds perch than in open grassland, but few seeds will germinate in dense shade. The highest density of new seedlings is therefore usually around the edges of scrub or under lone trees, so patches of scrub tend to spread outwards. Since huge numbers of berries are produced, some seeds are deposited in open grassland where they germinate readily and can form new scrub patches. Experiments involving planting Hawthorn seedlings in grassland have shown that those close to scrubby edges are less likely to be grazed down and have the highest probability of survival.

Scrub can expand rapidly in open habitats such as farmland, grassland or heathland as soon as they are less intensively grazed, cut or otherwise managed. Once established, scrub patches are rarely static, and scrub edges may fluctuate depending on grazing levels and conditions. Over time the canopy may close between bushes, and the vegetation of the surrounding habitat is shaded out and replaced by species such as Common Nettle and Cleavers. Tree species may become established as the scrub canopy becomes taller and thins a little and, after about 50 years or so, woodland will develop. The complete succession through to woodland does not always occur, and may be halted if disturbance, levels of exposure or lack of seeds limits tree regeneration.

Scrub is spreading onto grassland from the woodland edge after a reduction in grazing pressure.

TYPES OF SCRUB

Some scrub is dominated by a single species such as Bog-myrtle, Gorse, Sea-buckthorn or Shrubby Sea-blite, and is best considered as a component of the habitat within which it is found. Common Juniper can also form single-species stands of scrub, but is of particular conservation interest (see Juniper Scrub on *page 104*). In other cases, scrub is more varied, and can be treated as a habitat in its own right. **Mixed Scrub** is the common scrub of waste ground, abandoned farmland and grassland, and is typically found in the south and in the upland fringes. It is closely linked to grassland and woodland habitats but supports a distinctive suite of species. Mixed Scrub on calcareous grassland can be quite species-rich. **Hedgerow** is essentially linear scrub and forms a distinctive habitat of cultural importance. It can support unusual woodland-edge species. **Montane Scrub** is very rare and is unusual among scrub types in being a natural climax community; it is described further in the

Mature, established scrub has a limited ground flora.

Removal of mature scrub does not always mean a return to species-rich swards. Grassland seed banks are short-lived and impoverished swards can result from scrub clearance.

Adaptations of scrub species

Scrubby plants produce **high volumes of seeds**. Many, such as Bramble, produce berries that are dispersed by birds; Traveller's-joy (ABOVE) is wind-dispersed.

Once arching **stems** of Bramble **touch the ground** they **root and produce new shoots** and new plants develop. Some species, such as Blackthorn, spread by underground suckers.

Woody stems and spines (seen here on Hawthorn) are effective in deterring browsing animals.

Backwards-pointing thorns help the quick-growing stems of species such as Dog-rose to scramble over other plants.

Mountain Habitats section (*page 215*). **Bracken** is included here because, although not a shrub, it is forms a component of other habitats, can be transitional, and has some similar conservation issues.

THREATS AND ISSUES

Scrub has had a bad press – seen as something undesirable that needs to be tidied away. It is controlled on both farmland and on nature reserves, where it generally spreads at the expense of other, preferred (and often much rarer) habitats, which may not regenerate readily even if the scrub is removed. Similarly, farmland and roadside hedges are kept tightly trimmed to stop them from encroaching on fields and to minimize labour. In many upland areas, scrub has been lost through heavy grazing and that which remains is even-aged, tall and mature. However, scrub can be excellent for wildlife, and naturalists often gravitate towards the interface between scrub and open habitats. Fortunately, the value of scrub has become better appreciated in recent decades, and it is now established as an important component of semi-natural sites. This does not make it any easier to manage, as it is a dynamic habitat that needs space to move and deteriorates if fossilized in one place. The small size of many sites in the lowlands makes this a challenge, while difficulties in finding graziers for semi-natural sites means that scrub can overwhelm open habitats. In any case, grazing alone is unlikely to control scrub (unless it is at levels that are also likely to damage the open habitat), and in the past scrub was often cut for fuel and small timber. Cutting scrub is labour-intensive if carried out manually; done with machinery, it requires an all-or-nothing approach that can make it difficult to achieve a range of scrub types and ages.

CULTURAL IMPORTANCE

Scrub has always been an important part of the rural economy, providing fuel and wild foods. Even today many people still mark the seasons by making elderflower cordial, blackberry jam and sloe gin. Some scrub species have also played an important role in cultural traditions. Hawthorn (also called Whitethorn or May) is a symbol of May Day, and has a strong role in pagan beliefs. Hedgerows are particularly valued for what they tell us about the development of the landscape. Many are ancient, and follow boundaries established in the medieval period or even earlier. They are quick to grow and suitably impenetrable. The Old English name for Hawthorn is *haegporn* from *haga*, which means haw. The abundance of Hawthorn in hedges (it is the most frequently mentioned tree in Anglo-Saxon boundary charters) led to the name *haeg* or hedge for a boundary of Hawthorn.

CONSERVATION IMPORTANCE AND PROTECTION

Scrub occurs widely in SSSIs (although it is rarely a reason for their designation), around one quarter of the Special Areas of Conservation (SACs) in the UK are estimated to contain scrub habitats of nature conservation importance, and scrubby vegetation is a component of eleven different Priority Habitats in the UK. However, with the exception of Montane Scrub and Juniper Scrub, for which the UK has an international responsibility under the European Habitats Directive, scrub is rarely recognized in its own right. Its nature conservation interest generally lies in the species associated with it. These depend on particular characteristics, including patchiness and structural diversity, which are best achieved at large spatial scales.

FURTHER INFORMATION

Hedgelink – www.hedgelink.org.uk/

National Hedgelaying Society – www.hedgelaying.org.uk/

A Natural History of the Hedgerow: and ditches, dykes and dry stone walls by John Wright (Profile Books, 2017)

Juniper Scrub

Juniper is generally encountered as a component of the vegetation within other habitats. However, in some cases it forms a distinct association with other shrubs, shade-tolerant herbs, grazing-sensitive tall herbs, bryophytes and ferns (*e.g.* on chalk and Carboniferous limestone) and can also form a type of woodland (*e.g.* in the eastern Highlands). In these situations it is considered to be a habitat in its own right and one of European importance. Juniper can occur both as scattered individuals in other habitats and as a distinct association of its own. It was one of the first woody species to colonize Britain and Ireland after the last glaciation around 12,400 years ago and has a huge global distribution encompassing America, Europe and Asia. It occurs in a wide range of habitats, from sea level to 900 m, including Mixed Scrub, Calcareous Grassland, Lowland Dry Heath, Coastal Vegetated Shingle and Sand Dune (in north-east Scotland only), Limestone Pavement, Upland Dry Heath, Caledonian Forest, Montane Dwarf-shrub Heath and Montane Scrub.

Juniper occurs in a range of shapes and growth forms. There are two main subspecies: Common Juniper (the most frequent, found across Britain)

Key locations for Juniper Scrub

Cairngorms

Lake District

Cruit Island and Dawros Head

Upper Teesdale

Aston Rowant

Salisbury Plain

Juniper Scrub at **Noar Hill, Hampshire**, on chalk grassland.

and Dwarf Juniper (found on the Atlantic fringe of Ireland, in Scotland, Cumbria and North Wales). A third very rare subspecies is found in coastal heath in Pembrokeshire and on the Lizard in Cornwall. Many Common Juniper populations are isolated and genetic studies show a high degree of variability. Clusters of 50 or more plants are thought to be capable of recruitment and long-term survival without inbreeding, yet in many locations numbers are much lower than 50 and regeneration is very limited. After the bushes reach about 50 years of age the fruits they produce become increasingly sterile, so Common Juniper depends on regular recruitment of new seedlings. The seedlings require bare ground to germinate, but are very vulnerable to grazing. The outbreak of myxomatosis was the last time there was significant recruitment of seedlings in southern populations, many of which are no longer fertile.

Particularly large numbers of invertebrates are specific to Common Juniper and a high proportion of them are Red Data Book species. These include a range of moths (including the Juniper Carpet), gall midges and mites. Common Juniper also provides winter cover for Black Grouse in the uplands.

1 Well-developed Common Juniper 'woodland' is associated with Bilberry, Heather, Wood-sorrel, Heath Bedstraw, the distinctive branched mosses Common Tamarisk-moss and Glittering Wood-moss, and sometimes Chickweed-wintergreen (**Rothiemurchus, Speyside**). **2** Prostrate Common Juniper on rocky outcrops in Blanket Bog in **Roundstone Bog, Connemara**. In Scotland, Common Juniper can occur where the canopy of Caledonian Forest is absent. **3** Juniper Scrub at **Burnham Beeches, Buckinghamshire**, on acid soil.

Scrub species that form an integral part of other habitats:

1 **Bog-myrtle** suckers and forms dense patches in wet heathland and mires where there is some movement of groundwater. Several moth larvae feed on Bog-myrtle, including the day-flying Argent and Sable. **2** **Gorse** and Western Gorse are very common on light, well-drained soils and can provide breeding habitat for Dartford Warbler, Stonechat, Linnet and Yellowhammer. A number of scarce invertebrates are also reliant on gorse. **3** **Sea-buckthorn** spreads by rhizomes and layering, and can form dense thickets. Widespread in the late-glacial period, it is now only native on fixed dunes along the east coast of Britain. However, it is often used as an amenity shrub and become widely distributed, and can be problematic. **4** **Shrubby Sea-blite** grows on upper Saltmarsh, on shingle drift lines (seen here) and more rarely behind sea walls in Coastal Grazing Marsh in East Anglia, south-east England and Dorset.

KEY FEATURES

Scrub is important for a range of individual species that often require quite specific conditions. For example, Nightingale prefers dense scrub patches that include open ground; Dingy Mocha (a moth) seeks out isolated young willows on the edge of heathland, and Barberry Carpet (another moth) requires Barberry bushes with young, vigorous growth. Structural diversity within a wider mosaic of other habitats is often key in ensuring suitable niches are available for a variety of species, and the interface between scrub and open habitats is of particular importance.

There are not many words in English to describe different types of scrub, so ecologists have borrowed terms from elsewhere. *Saum* refers to the fringe of taller herbs and grasses around the edge of scrub patches, and can support rare plants and invertebrates. *Mantel* is the woodland edge zone supporting woody plants such as wild roses, Brambles and thorns. In North Wales the term *ffridd* refers to unenclosed land in the transition between upland and lowland, while in South Wales it refers to enclosed land, with the term *coedcae* being used to describe similar unenclosed areas.

In the image *below*, Mixed Scrub at the interface between Lowland Calcareous Grassland and Arable contains a number of key features. Flowering Hawthorn provides an important nectar source for invertebrates. Bramble creates a warm, sheltered microclimate (used here by Duke of Burgundy butterfly) and will also provide nectar after the Hawthorn flowers have dropped. Sheltered, bare ground in open, sunny areas provides an important habitat for insects. Young scrub is regenerating, creating structural diversity and ensuring the continuity of the scrub habitat while protecting plants from grazing animals. Thicker scrub near the boundary shelters the site from wind (helping to create a warm microclimate), provides nesting habitat for birds, forms a wildlife corridor and may also buffer the sensitive semi-natural grassland from spray drift from the adjacent field. An open-grown, mature tree provides different habitats for tree-dependent species compared with one found in a shaded woodland setting.

Mixed Scrub on Lowland Calcareous Grassland, **Cerne Abbas, Dorset**. Key features include: ❶ flowering scrub, ❷ sheltered, open bare ground, ❸ Bramble, ❹ mature open-grown tree, ❺ regenerating scrub, ❻ thick, mature scrub.

Mixed Scrub

Mixed Scrub is variable and depends on the soil characteristics and location.
Hawthorn and Bramble scrub is the commonest type, typically occurring with Ivy
on well-drained soils that are mildly acidic to calcareous. Blackthorn is also common
and on the coast can persist in a natural climax community. Elder is often found where
disturbance has created local nutrient enrichment. On acidic soils gorse is frequent, while
a suite of lime-loving species, including Dogwood, Wild Privet, Wayfaring-tree, Guelder-rose,
Spindle and Buckthorn and (rarely) Box, is found on calcareous soils, often with climbers such as
Traveller's-joy and Black Bryony sprawling over the canopy.

   Mixed scrub is a successional habitat that develops between open herbaceous vegetation and woodland,
and each stage is accompanied by changes in light and nutrient levels, and soil moisture. Initially the field
layer is that of the preceding habitat, but as the canopy closes the ground flora changes and is eventually lost.
Later, as the canopy becomes taller but thins, woodland species such as Ash and Sycamore can colonize and
eventually woodland becomes established.

   The dynamic boundary between scrub and open vegetation is the most important component for
wildlife. The scrub edge provides structure, shelter, fruits and seeds, and may protect grassland plants from
grazing and trampling, while the herbaceous vegetation allows light to penetrate and supplies nectar for
invertebrates. This interface may support a range of plants and invertebrates not found in either habitat on its
own. Scrub within ancient woodland, Wood Pasture and Calcareous Grassland can be particularly rich.

Similar habitats

Hedgerow supports similar vegetation but is linear and subject to a very specific management regime. Mixed
Scrub can occur with and alongside many other habitats and may conceal features such as ponds.

Bentley Wood, Wiltshire – this woodland clearing with Hawthorn and Bramble scrub supports a range of
butterflies, including Duke of Burgundy and Pearl-bordered Fritillary.

Origins and development

In a few circumstances (*e.g.* eroding and slumping cliffs, screes or quarries) Mixed Scrub can be entirely natural, forming part of a primary succession. However, it is generally part of secondary succession, occurring after grazing has been relaxed on grassland or heathland or on abandoned arable land. Unless the succession is arrested by some form of disturbance or particularly harsh conditions (or seed sources are sparse), the scrub will succeed to woodland within 50 years or so.

The decline in Rabbit numbers due to myxomatosis in the 1950s, combined with a general reduction in grazing, resulted in an increase in scrub on semi-natural open habitats in lowland areas. By contrast, in upland hill farming areas, decades of intensive grazing has resulted in scrub habitats becoming scarcer.

Conservation

The most valuable areas of scrub are dynamic and shift and change over time; the largest number of species will occur where there is a range of successional stages. Rotational scrub cutting is generally required to maintain structural diversity, while grazing is often used on the surrounding habitat to help prevent excessive scrub encroachment.

Distribution and extent

Widespread, occuring in many small patches and therefore difficult to map and record systematically. Map based on CORINE satellite data and only shows patches of 25 ha or more, so does not reflect complete distribution.

LEFT: **Noar Hill, Hampshire** – some scrub control and rotational management is required if a species-rich mosaic of grassland and scrub is to be maintained. RIGHT: **Port Eynon, Gower** – dense Mixed Scrub on limestone outcrops including Ivy, whitebeams, gorse, Blackthorn and Elder.

What to look for

Endemic whitebeams on shrubby limestone outcrops in the west of Britain; rare plants such as Bastard Balm, Purple Gromwell, also rare orchids (*e.g.* Fly, Man, Military, Monkey and Lady Orchid) on base-rich *saum* (see *page 107*); Black Hairstreak (Blackthorn in the Midlands). Listen for Nightingale, Whitethroat, Lesser Whitethroat, Willow Warbler, Garden Warbler and, in the uplands, Whinchat and Redstart.

How to recognize

Typical Mixed Scrub of thorny shrubs such as Hawthorn, Blackthorn and Bramble and other species occurring along woodland edges, roadsides and railway embankments, on abandoned agricultural land, commons, grasslands and heaths, in quarries, and on the coast.

Particularly eye-catching in the spring, when Blackthorn is one of the first plants to flower, and provides an early nectar source for invertebrates. At this time of year it can be alive with bird song, while later in the summer bush-crickets creak and rasp from tall herbage.

The best scrub for wildlife has a diverse range of species with a complex canopy structure and plenty of gaps and edges and transitions to short vegetation.

When to visit

Spring for Nightingale and other breeding birds; summer for plants and invertebrates at the scrub/grassland interface; spring and autumn for migrant birds near the coast.

It is worth searching scrub on calcareous soils for rarer species – **1 Purple Gromwell** is found in open coastal scrub (in addition to woodland edges); **2** the generally dark-coloured flowers of **Fly Orchid** (which attract male *Argogorytes* wasps) can be hard to see among scrub, but this is one of its typical habitats. **3 Dancing Ledge, Dorset** – Blackthorn can withstand wind-exposure better than Hawthorn and on cliff tops can form natural climax vegetation. Such areas provide important shelter for migrant birds in the spring and autumn. The abrupt edge (arrowed) is created by grazing. Farther west along the Dorset coast, high densities of Hazel Dormouse have been found in coastal scrub. **4** Hawthorn scrub at **Lodge Hill, Kent**. This site, an old army training camp, has been the subject of high-profile campaigns to protect it from housing development. It is rich in scrub and was designated as a SSSI for Nightingales in 2013

Hedgerow

Hedgerow is essentially woodland edge habitat, without the wood. The combination of woody structure and more open conditions provides many nesting, roosting and feeding opportunities for wildlife. Hedges can also act as wildlife corridors between isolated patches of woodland and scrub. However, their linear nature means they have a lot of edge, and land management practices adjacent to hedgerows have a disproportionately strong influence. Many hedges are affected by agricultural spray-drift (leading to loss of species through nutrient enrichment and damage from pesticides) in addition to unsympathetic management.

Traditional management involves hedge-laying (bending partially cut stems over at an angle and weaving them between stakes to provide a stock-proof barrier), which is repeated when the hedge becomes gappy at the base or stems are 5–10 cm in diameter and 2·5–5·0 m in height. This rejuvenates the hedge, retains deadwood (often kept to provide initial protection from livestock) and allows it to grow tall over a broad, thick base. Hedge-laying is labour-intensive and has largely been abandoned in favour of annual mechanized trimming, which creates more homogenous hedges with limited structural variation. Repeated severe cutting can also cause hedges to die back.

Ancient hedgerows are often the most species-rich, and the presence of certain plant species can be used to identify older hedges, particularly Field Maple (in the UK), Dogwood, Hazel and Spindle, which are relatively poor colonizers and are rarely planted. Ancient hedges also often include giant coppice stools or old pollarded trees.

An irregular patchwork of small fields bounded by hedgerows (near **Cahersiveen, Co. Kerry**). The commonest field enclosures in Ireland are earth banks topped with scrub.

EXTENT IN KM
Eng 420,000
Wal 54,000
Sco 21,000
NI 113,648
Ire 300,000

Distribution and extent

Map shows arable land and pastures where Hedgerow may be present. Species-rich hedges are found particularly in south-west England and South Wales. UK figures are estimates from the 2007 Countryside Survey; Ireland also an estimate.

Similar habitats

Hedgerows include similar species to woodland edges and scrub, but are linear features subject to regular cutting or laying. Unmanaged hedgerows can develop into shaws (thin strips of woodland found on field boundaries, often adjacent to a road), although shaws may also be woodland remnants.

Origins and development

Many hedgerows were planted but some have more natural origins as relics of woodland that has long since disappeared. Some West Country hedge-banks date from the Bronze Age and many hedges are medieval, planted to mark ownership boundaries, retain livestock and provide shelter. Some of these hedges have a distinctive 'S'-shape, a result of the need for space where a plough could be turned. During the enclosure of common land in the 18th and 19th centuries, an estimated 200,000 miles of hedge were planted in England, particularly in the Midlands. These are often dominated by Hawthorn and tend to be straight, sometimes cutting through other landscape features. After the 1950s, the fortunes of hedgerows declined as agricultural intensification resulted in tens of thousands of miles of hedgerows being removed, damaged by brutal trimming and spray-drift or simply neglected.

TOP: A sunken lane near **Swanage, Dorset**, bordered by a flower-rich hedgebank with standard trees.
BOTTOM: Small fields with hedges and woodland at **Cwm Onnau**, above Crickhowell, Powys.

Conservation

Much attention has been focussed on how best to manage hedgerows for wildlife. Left unmanaged, they turn into lines of trees and lose the structure and variety that is so important. However, tight annual trimming is damaging, and can result in patchy hedges with little body. Periodic hedge-laying or coppicing is considered best, followed by some trimming to encourage a dense structure to develop before the hedge is allowed to grow up ready for laying or coppicing again. Late winter is the best time to manage hedges, so that berries are retained for as long as possible throughout the winter but the bird nesting season is avoided. Encouraging sensitive harvesting for woodfuel, and increasing the awareness of the role that hedges play in reducing soil erosion and water run-off, could help protect the habitat.

1 **Sedbergh, Cumbria** – a recently laid Ash hedge. There are over 30 different styles of hedge-laying around the UK. Studies have shown that laid hedges support the largest numbers of invertebrates. **2** **Rackenford, Devon** – a relic hedge-bank that has developed into a line of Beech trees. Beech hedge-banks are a particular feature of north Devon. **3** **Bluebell** and **4** **Greater Stitchwort** growing in a hedge margin in Purbeck, Dorset. Herbaceous vegetation growing alongside and within hedges provides a rich nectar source for invertebrates and a welcome splash of colour along roadsides.

What to look for

Hedges that are good for wildlife provide nesting sites, song posts, roosting sites, foraging habitat and corridors for movement. Some 600 plant, 1,500 insect, 65 bird and 20 mammal species have been recorded in hedgerows. In addition to the suite of ancient hedgerow shrubs, keep a look out for veteran trees (including Black-poplar), Plymouth Pear (restricted to a few hedgerows in the south-west) and the endemic Devon Whitebeam (which is found in south-east Ireland as well as in Devon). An endemic herb, Purple Ramping-fumitory, is particularly associated with hedge-banks.

Hedgerows are good places to look for invertebrates. Bramble, Honeysuckle and thorn blossom provide nectar and pollen for a range of insects, some of which depend on Ivy flowers in autumn. Many beetle species can occur in the litter and tussocky vegetation at the base of hedges, including Stag Beetle, while hedgerow ditches adjacent to hedgerows are good for caddisflies. Bumblebees nest in hedgerows and use hedges as guides to their foraging sites. White-letter Hairstreak breeds on elm suckers, and also feeds on aphid honeydew on Field Maple. Look for Small Tortoiseshell and Red Admiral butterflies around hedgerow nettles, and Orange-tip on Garlic Mustard. The Barberry Carpet moth is occasionally disturbed from its foodplant (Barberry) during the day.

TOP: **Guelder-rose** is a widespread and attractive shrub found in hedges on neutral and calcareous soils. Look for the distinctive white flowers in May–June.
BOTTOM: The dense wood of **Spindle** was, as its name suggests, traditionally used for spindles. The berries are poisonous to humans but are eaten by a range of birds.

Near **Port Isaac, north Cornwall** – Cornish hedges comprise an earthen bank and stone-faced sides with or without shrubby vegetation.

Hedgerows provide nest sites for a range of birds including **1** **Whitethroat**, a widespread summer migrant, and **2** **Yellowhammer**, which often nests in the base of shrubby hedges with vegetated ditches and uncultivated margins. Hedgerows, which provide shelter and plenty of flowering plants, are excellent habitat for butterflies such as **3** **Red Admiral**. **4** **Brown Hairstreak** – rare and relatively secretive, its caterpillars feed mainly on Blackthorn in hedgerows; annual cutting is disastrous as the eggs overwinter on young twigs. **5** The **Hazel Dormouse** weaves summer nests of stripped bark (often Honeysuckle) about the size of a grapefruit for breeding. Hedgerows can be an important habitat for this species and also provide links between woodland and scrub patches along which it can disperse. They also provide fruit, nuts and insects – the perfect diet for omnivorous **6** **Bank Voles**.

Most bird species prefer tall hedges with many trees, although Whitethroat, Linnet and Yellowhammer are also found in shorter hedges. Uncommon species associated with hedges include Cirl Bunting, Turtle Dove and Tree Sparrow. Hazel Dormouse is famously found in hedges but Bank Vole is more common, and Harvest Mouse may also be seen. At dusk look out for bats – Serotine follows hedges to foraging areas, and species such as Greater Horseshoe Bat and Natterer's Bat glean insects from hedgerows.

How to recognize

Hedges are very variable, depending on local tradition and how they are managed. They are found lining green lanes, tracks and roads, encircling woods and dividing fields, and can be growing from earth or stone banks or along ditches. They may be tightly trimmed, traditionally laid or tall and rambling.

The best hedges are tall and broad at the base and support woody species such as Field Maple, Hawthorn, Spindle, Wayfaring-tree, Wild Service-tree and Blackthorn intertwined with Honeysuckle and Bramble and occasionally overtopped by mature standard trees. They can be thickly bordered with tall herbaceous vegetation, include wayside species such as Cow Parsley, Garlic Mustard and Hedge Woundwort, or may have a woodland flora of Bluebell, Primrose and Lesser Celandine. Many stony hedge-banks are rich in lichens, bryophytes and ferns.

Thick hedges can resound with birdsong in the spring, while in the summer they can be buzzing with insects. Even quite thin, over-trimmed strips of Hawthorn can support Whitethroat and Dunnock.

When to visit

Spring and summer for breeding birds and flowers; autumn for berries (for people and wildlife!); winter is a good time to look for Hazel Dormouse nests.

Did you know?
Hooper's rule of thumb that the number of tree and shrub species in a 30-yard length of hedge equates to the age of the hedge in centuries is generally true in many areas.

TOP: **Grey Partridge** – widespread but now uncommon, this species prefers open fields with uncultivated margins bordered by hedgerows, particularly those with grass litter at the base, where they nest. Declines since the 1950s have been attributed to increased pesticide and herbicide use, predation and removal of hedgerows. BOTTOM: A thick hedge with standard trees adjacent to an arable field margin.

Bracken

Bracken is the most common (and largest) fern in Britain and Ireland. It occurs within 36 different National Vegetation Classification communities, a reflection of the range of habitats in which it can be found. It favours dry, acid soils (up to around 450 m), and can spread at a rate of one metre per year by underground rhizomes. It regenerates from spores only on relatively bare ground, such as after burning. Livestock grazing increases the dominance of Bracken by reducing competitors, although cattle in particular can reduce its vigour through trampling.

Bracken produces plant toxins that, together with its shady canopy and deep litter, inhibit the growth of other plant species. Dense stands of Bracken often hold little wildlife interest, although a woodland flora is sometimes found (particularly on the coast) and Wild Gladiolus (restricted to the New Forest) only occurs under Bracken. A range of invertebrates feed on Bracken, including some rare sawflies, flies and moths, and it is linked to some of our most threatened and rapidly declining butterflies: High Brown Fritillary and Pearl-bordered Fritillary are virtually restricted to Bracken and Dark-green Fritillary and Small Pearl-bordered Fritillary may also be associated with it. Bracken is also a favoured habitat of the Sheep Tick.

EXTENT IN KM^2
Eng 91,100
Wal 62,700
Sco 131,500
NI 2,600
Ire n/k

Glen Creran, Argyll and Bute – an extensive area of Bracken within a large woodland clearing.

Distribution and extent

Widespread across Britain and Ireland. The map is indicative and shows areas of Scotland and Wales where continuous swathes of Bracken have been mapped. In addition, the map includes heathland habitats, transitional scrub and Coniferous Plantation (all mapped from satellite imagery) where Bracken may be a major component.

Similar habitats

Bracken is considered as a habitat type in its own right where it occurs in continuous swathes. Patchy or scattered Bracken is common in a range of other habitat types of which it is considered a part.

Origins and development

Bracken is often perceived to be spreading and its dominance is a management challenge at some sites. However, Bracken spores found in cores taken for pollen analysis show that the species has a long history in the landscape. In many cores Bracken peaks are associated with the loss of woodland cover at least 2,000 years ago. The amount of Bracken declined at some locations during the 14th century, coinciding with agricultural abandonment linked to the Black Death and a period with a colder climate. Current levels are perhaps, therefore, not exceptional, but historically Bracken was a valued resource (used for bedding, thatch and potash for soap and glass) and widely harvested, which would have helped contain its spread.

Bracken sometimes allows plants to grow that otherwise require a woodland canopy – in this case **Bluebell**.

Conservation

Bracken is not considered as a Priority Habitat for conservation and in many situations conservationists seek to control its spread or reduce the area present. It spreads at the expense of other habitats and can be problematic in other ways – its spores have been implicated as a carcinogen, it harbours sheep ticks and it can damage archaeological features. Bracken can be managed by spraying, cutting or bruising, but such treatments have to be maintained to be successful. On hill slopes, areas where Bracken has been eradicated can be vulnerable to erosion, or may be colonized by species such as Common Nettle. Woodland reversion may, in the long term, be a better solution for such locations.

   Although ineffective in controlling large patches of established Bracken, grazing is ideal on butterfly sites, where the paths and trampled areas created by livestock provide sunny patches that are ideal for violets – the foodplant for many fritillaries. Mosaics of Bracken and grassland with abundant violets and open areas are optimal for butterflies but can be difficult to maintain.

What to look for

Basking Adder; Whinchat and other breeding birds (uplands); Wild Gladiolus (New Forest); several species of fritillary butterfly.

Rhossili Downs, Gower – in August, Bracken forms conspicuous bright green patches in the landscape.

How to recognize

Bracken can cloak hillsides, form dense stands within woodland, and cover large patches of lowland grassland and heathland. Although it generally occurs within other habitats, extensive patches can be considered a habitat in their own right.

The bright green, tight-curled fronds emerge in late spring once the frosts have passed and grow quickly; by midsummer Bracken can form a closed canopy, often over head-height and impenetrable. It also has a distinctive smell at this time of year that is intensified by sunshine and is sometimes likened to almonds. In the autumn it dies right back, leaving rusty-brown fronds that litter the ground in winter.

When to visit

Look for fritillaries in the spring and summer: Pearl-bordered from late April–end of June, Small Pearl-bordered in June–July, High Brown and Dark-green mid-June–mid-August. Bracken can form a colourful part of the landscape in the autumn.

Did you know?
Bracken is one of the most widely distributed plants in the world, occurring in every continent apart from Antarctica.

1 **Common Dog-violet** can grow under Bracken and is the main food plant for caterpillars of several fritillary butterflies. **2** **Dark-green Fritillary** is found in a range of grassy habitats including acid grassland with Bracken.
3 **Small Pearl-bordered Fritillary** is widespread and locally common in woodland clearings and moorland.
4 **High Brown Fritillary**, together with Pearl-bordered Fritillary, favours warm, dry slopes. To raise their body temperature, the caterpillars bask on dead Bracken stems.

HEATHLANDS

HABITAT	DESCRIPTION
Lowland Dry Heath *page 130 | page 393*	Generally dominated by Heather, Bell Heather and gorse on sandy or gravelly soils, and largely confined to the warmer south. It includes a subset of distinctive types including Shingle, Dune, Maritime, Breckland and Limestone Heaths.
Lowland Wet Heath *page 140 | page 393*	Found above enclosed agricultural land but below the montane zone (between around 300–700 m) on thin peat and well-drained mineral soils that support species such as Bilberry and Crowberry in addition to Heather.
Upland Dry Heath *page 143 | page 393*	Found on thin peat or mineral soils with impeded drainage and characterized by Cross-leaved Heath, Heather and Purple Moor-grass, usually forming a continuum with Lowland Dry Heath.
Upland Wet Heath *page 149 | page 393*	Less heathery in appearance than Upland Dry Heath; found within the same altitudinal zone in more waterlogged conditions that are nonetheless too dry for peat formation and the development of Blanket Bog.

ORIGINS

Heathlands are semi-natural habitats that developed on relatively nutrient-poor and acidic soils as a result of forest clearance that in some cases may have started at least 5,000 years ago. Combined with subsequent use of the land for livestock grazing, the removal of trees contributed to a reduction in soil fertility and increase in acidity. This enabled heathland vegetation, which perhaps previously existed in clearings and under sparse canopies, to expand. Many current heathlands date from the Bronze Age, some 3,000 years ago, although in the uplands of Ireland and the Scottish Highlands transitions occurred much later. Heathland and woodland existed in a dynamic state, fluctuating according to the scale of human activity. In southern England, its coverage was probably greatest in the medieval period.

Unsuitable for cultivation, heathland became part of a farming system that integrated the use of infertile parts of the landscape with that of tilled areas. However, from the mid-19th century, changes in

The Lizard, Cornwall – The Lizard, Cornwall, supports four heather species that can be found in close proximity: Cornish Heath, Bell Heather, Heather (all seen here) and Cross-leaved Heath.

H

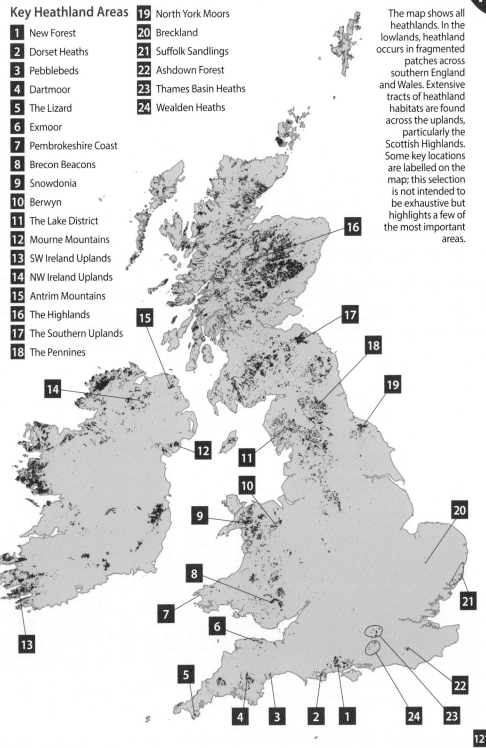

Key Heathland Areas

1	New Forest
2	Dorset Heaths
3	Pebblebeds
4	Dartmoor
5	The Lizard
6	Exmoor
7	Pembrokeshire Coast
8	Brecon Beacons
9	Snowdonia
10	Berwyn
11	The Lake District
12	Mourne Mountains
13	SW Ireland Uplands
14	NW Ireland Uplands
15	Antrim Mountains
16	The Highlands
17	The Southern Uplands
18	The Pennines
19	North York Moors
20	Breckland
21	Suffolk Sandlings
22	Ashdown Forest
23	Thames Basin Heaths
24	Wealden Heaths

The map shows all heathlands. In the lowlands, heathland occurs in fragmented patches across southern England and Wales. Extensive tracts of heathland habitats are found across the uplands, particularly the Scottish Highlands. Some key locations are labelled on the map; this selection is not intended to be exhaustive but highlights a few of the most important areas.

land management led to the breakdown of the more traditional, extensive systems that had evolved over centuries. In the lowlands, about 85% of the heathland in existence in 1800 was lost. Developments in farming techniques meant that heathlands were fertilized and cultivated. Many of those that survived were afforested, set aside for military training or built on (even into the 1980s). Small fragments that remained fell out of use, and natural succession (aided by the proximity of coniferous plantations) led to the development of secondary pine and birch wood. In the uplands, the change from mixed farming to sheep rearing from the mid-18th century saw a change in the way heathland was grazed and, in the Highlands, led to the brutal restructuring of local communities which had played a fundamental role in maintaining the cultural landscape. The rise of shooting estates in the 19th century meant that management priorities shifted; burning became widespread and increasing grazing pressure converted heathland to grassland. In the 20th century, huge areas were engulfed by forestry plantations.

TYPES OF HEATHLAND

Heathland is found from sea level up to about 1,000 m in both dry and periodically waterlogged situations, giving way to bog (see Wetlands, *page 234*) where waterlogging increases. Essentially, it occurs where nutrient-poor, acidic conditions favour the growth of dwarf-shrubs, particularly Heather, Bell Heather, Cross-leaved Heath, Dwarf Gorse and Bilberry, and where grazing or burning prevents the development of scrub and woodland. At high altitudes where conditions are too exposed for woodland (around 600–700 m, but variable), heathland communities are natural, and these are considered in the Mountain Habitats section (see *page 198*). The low-nutrient status and early-successional stage of heathland vegetation is reflected in the relatively low number of plant species it supports – but despite this, wide variation is seen throughout Britain and Ireland. Four heathland habitats are described within this section, but transitions and variations occur. **Lowland Dry Heath** (*page 130*) encompasses the dry heaths of southern England and Wales (including humid-heath). Some other types of Lowland Dry Heath are described in this section, including Maritime Heath, which is also found in Scotland and Ireland, and the peculiar heathland mosaics of Breckland. **Upland Dry Heath** (*page 143*), which is widespread throughout the uplands, supports different vegetation communities from Lowland Dry Heath and, like Lowland Wet Heath, faces quite different pressures and issues, particularly those concerning grouse moors. **Lowland Wet Heath** (*page 140*) is differentiated from **Upland Wet Heath** (*page 149*) as although it supports similar vegetation, it faces different management and conservation issues and the two types can support different specialist species. Heathland rarely occurs in isolation and, particularly in the uplands where it is far more extensive, it usually occurs within a mosaic of other habitat types, including Blanket Bog, Upland Acid Grassland and upland woodland habitats. In the lowlands, heathland often occurs with Valley Mire, Lowland Dry Acid Grassland and secondary woodland. Fifteen heathland vegetation communities and their sub-communities are described in the UK National Vegetation Classification.

THREATS AND ISSUES

Surviving lowland heathland is, in most cases, divorced from the agricultural practices and economics of the surrounding countryside, and this presents a challenge for conservation management. The functionality of the cultural landscape has essentially been lost, and modern conservation organizations are left trying to replicate historical grazing, cutting and burning regimes, often on relatively small areas of land, in an attempt to safeguard the remaining populations of heathland species. In other cases, heathland is surrounded by, or close to, urban conurbations, and provides much-needed green space. However, proximity to urban centres can pose problems, including increased risk of fire, eutrophication from dog waste, dumping, disturbance to birds and predation by cats. Often local residents have strong feelings about their local heathland, and wish to see it managed in a particular way or left to its own devices.

The situation in the uplands is different, as extensive tracts of open heathland have been maintained, and are still grazed as part of agricultural systems, even where the primary use is game shooting and deer hunting. Past subsidies, based on the number of livestock, encouraged high stocking rates, and many areas are heavily grazed and in some cases this grazing has converted heathland to grassland. Changes in the way subsidies are allocated has reduced this stress, but many areas remain very heavily grazed. There is increasing interest in expanding the area of semi-natural woodland in the uplands, as it is recognized that to restore functionality and safeguard species, bigger, connected areas of wood are needed. In many cases this will be at the expense of moorland habitats, including heathland.

The origins of the word **heath** lie in the old English word for untilled land, and heathland has long been regarded as wasteland, much to its detriment. Today the word heath usually refers to land dominated by dwarf shrubs such as Heather, but also encompasses similar low-growing and nutrient-poor vegetation that may be dominated by lichens and grasses. **Moorland** is generally used to refer to open upland landscapes beyond the limit of agricultural improvement and enclosures but below the climatic tree line. Moorland can include Upland Dry Heath, Upland Wet Heath, Upland Acid Grassland, Upland Calcareous Grassland and Blanket Bog. The derivation of the word is unclear, although it may stem from an Old English word meaning morass or swamp, and perhaps its use in the uplands is related to the low fertility of the habitats. Locally, moorland is also referred to as fell, wold, or simply 'the hill'. There is more moorland in Britain and Ireland than anywhere else in the world.

ABOVE: Lowland heathland at **Godlingston, Dorset**. BELOW: Steep, glaciated slopes of the **Lake District**, showing upland heathland alongside other upland communities.

CULTURAL IMPORTANCE

Heathland is particularly valued as a cultural landscape, one that has evolved through the long-term interactions between people and nature. Some of the evidence of human presence can still be seen today, including prehistoric worked flints and Bronze Age burial mounts. More recent boundary banks, enclosures and other features all indicate a time when heathland was used more intensively than it is today and played an intrinsic role in agricultural livelihoods. Farming encompassed both arable land close to dwellings and more extensive areas of heathland farther afield, which were often common land. Heaths were used by local people for grazing livestock (including animals used for farm work), turf was cut for fuel, gorse for livestock fodder and to use in bread ovens, Bracken for livestock bedding and Heather for thatch. In some areas, such as East Anglia, the management of arable land and heathland was further integrated through manuring. Animals that grazed on the heaths during the day were folded on arable land during the night so that their dung could fertilize the fields. Research into similar practices in Denmark suggests that around ten hectares of heathland was needed to provide manure for one hectare of arable land. Heathland burning was also practiced to provide a flush of new young growth for the livestock.

The large size of many upland heaths may provide some resilience to climate change, but this is not the case for lowland heaths, which are often fragmented and isolated. The increased risk of fire will need contingency measures in both situations and a shift in species composition in favour of grasses is expected regardless of altitudinal differences. Further changes in composition are likely in wet heaths, with the loss of wetter vegetation communities. However, there may be an increase in warmth-loving species such as Smooth Snake, Sand Lizard and Dartford Warbler. Resilience needs to be built by creating functional networks and by reducing pressure from recreation in the lowlands and from overgrazing and burning in the uplands.

Today, lowland heathland provides extensive tracts of open countryside that are not intensively farmed. Both upland and lowland heathland are valued for the recreational opportunities and sense of wilderness they provide.

Several hardy pony breeds are native to the mountains and moorlands of Britain and Ireland (in the sense that they were bred here – wild horses became extinct after the last glaciation). They are often seen leading a semi-feral existence in unenclosed heathland in places such as Dartmoor, Exmoor, the New Forest and parts of Wales, although all are owned. These animals are well adapted to surviving in heathland habitats, and are often now used for conservation grazing.

CONSERVATION IMPORTANCE AND PROTECTION

Heathlands are not intrinsically species-rich habitats, but are greatly valued for the specialist species they support, many of which are rare and largely confined to heathland. In the lowlands these can include reptiles

TOP: Furze cutters c.1890, **Dorset Heaths**. BOTTOM: Intensive management is required to maintain heathlands today, here conducted by the RSPB.

(such as Sand Lizard and Smooth Snake), birds (such as Nightjar and Dartford Warbler) and many invertebrates at the northern edge of their range. Particular suites of plant species are also associated with heathland microhabitats in the lowlands. Upland heathland can support Red Grouse, Black Grouse, Hen Harrier, Merlin, Mountain Hare and some globally rare plant communities, including one rich in rare liverworts and mosses. Oceanic heathland is confined to north-west Europe, and over 20% is found in Britain and Ireland.

A substantial area of heathland is protected through designation as SSSI (or equivalent) or SAC (four Annex I habitats cover most of the heathland types found in Britain and Ireland). However, in the UK heathland is considered to be in a worse condition than any other habitat category. In the lowlands this is largely due to lack of appropriate management, leading to scrub and Bracken encroachment; in the uplands it is due to overgrazing and burning leading to a loss of species and structural diversity. Fortunately, a considerable proportion is believed to be improving. Substantial funding has been put into conserving lowland heathland in the 21st century, but ongoing effort is required to ensure that heathland communities are sustained following restoration efforts. Conservation of upland heathland is mainly being addressed through agri-environment schemes, but it is not known how long it may take before a significant improvement in its condition can be detected.

1 Cannock Chase is the most extensive area of lowland heathland in the Midlands. The site is unusual in that the vegetation is intermediate between lowland sites in southern England and more northern/upland sites, supporting Bilberry, Cowberry and Crowberry. **2** Modern cultural links between heathlands and local communities are more likely to be through daily dog walks than people's livelihoods. **3** **The Lizard, Cornwall.** In the past trackway species were found in areas with heavy poaching by livestock or cart ruts; now conservationists deliberately create localized rutted/poached areas with machinery in the winter. **4** **Exmoor Pony** – one of the hardy native breeds that is able to withstand the challenges of grazing on heathland.

Heather

The life-cycle of Heather involves four stages. Individual plants can take 13–50 years to go through the cycle, depending on the characteristics of the location, including soil, climate and management.

Pioneer – up to about 6 years from seedling to bush, vertical growth.

Building – up to about 15 years old, dense lateral growth.

Mature – up to about 25 years old, growth slowing, centre opening.

Degenerate – central branches collapse, allowing seedlings and other species to grow.

There are nine native heather species found in Britain and Ireland, three of which are widespread.

Species	Distribution	Habitat types	Flowers
Heather	Widespread	Dry and wet heaths (also bogs)	Jul–Sep
Cross-leaved Heath	Widespread	Wet heath (also bogs)	Jun–Sep
Bell Heather	Widespread	Dry heaths	Jul–Sep
Dorset Heath	Dorset, S. Devon, Cornwall and Connemara	Wet heath	Jun–Sep
Blue Heath	Central Scotland, rare	Rocky upland heath with prolonged snow-lie	Jun–Jul
St Dabeoc's Heath	Connemara and Galway	Dry heaths	Jul–Sep
Mackay's Heath	Connemara and Donegal	Wet heath (also bogs)	Aug–Sep
Cornish Heath	Cornwall, Fermanagh	Dry and wet heaths	Jul–Aug
Irish Heath	Galway and Mayo, rare	Wet heath (also bogs)	Mar–May

Heather

Cross-leaved Heath

Dorset Heath

St Dabeoc's Heath

Cornish Heath

Bell Heather

Blue Heath

Mackay's Heath

Irish Heath

KEY FEATURES

Structural diversity is important in heathland. The most wildlife-rich examples include a range of structural features from open, bare ground through different stages of heather growth to patches of dense gorse and scattered trees. Bare sand, particularly on south-facing slopes is used by insects for basking, hunting and nesting, and sandy slopes and sand cliffs are particularly good for solitary bees and wasps. In the lowlands, Sand Lizards lay their eggs in warm, bare sand, often on the edge of tracks, trying a range of locations until they find one with the perfect degree of humidity. Also in the lowlands, a suite of plants is associated with very open, damp, compacted ground, such as that found in puddles and wheel ruts along wet heathland tracks. These include Allseed, Yellow Centaury, Chaffweed and, on the Lizard in Cornwall, Three-lobed Crowfoot and Pygmy Rush. Marsh Clubmoss is also found on bare, winter-wet ground.

Heather structure depends on age (see *page 126*) and different growth stages are suitable for different species. For example, Silver-studded Blue caterpillars require the soft shoots of pioneer or building heather; so does Red Grouse, which also requires taller heather nearby for shelter. Mature heather supports the largest diversity of invertebrates, and reptiles bask amongst degenerate heather, which provides shelter and pockets of warm, open ground; Nightjar also often nests in degenerate heather.

A variety of other vegetation structures adds to the overall diversity of heathlands. For example, gorse bushes provide habitat for web-spinning spiders and, even in winter, are a source of invertebrate prey for birds such as Dartford Warbler, which shelter in dense young bushes (and also nest in gorse). Peripheral woodland increases the overall diversity of invertebrates. In the south, the interface between woodland and heathland is often used by Nightjar, and scattered trees are frequently used as song posts by this species, as well as Woodlark. In the uplands, woodland and heathland mosaics provide habitat for Black Grouse. Flowery verges are an important source of nectar and pollen for insects when the heathers are not in flower, and patches of short Lowland Acid Grassland boost the overall botanical diversity and are used for foraging by species such as Woodlark.

Heathland pools are important features for species such as bladderworts and often support a range of dragonflies and damselflies, and shallow, poached edges can support rare plants such as Pillwort and Pennyroyal.

Glenfeshie, Inverness-shire. Key features in this transitional landscape include: ❶ stunted pines indicating that the natural tree line would be higher than the apparent tree line created by afforestation, ❷ bare ground along track, ❸ scattered trees creating a transition between woodland and heathland, ❹ regenerating woodland, a result of a concerted effort to control deer.

FURTHER INFORMATION

Heaths and Moorlands. Cultural Landscapes. Thompson, D.B.A., Hester, A.J. & Usher, M.B. eds. (HMSO, 1995)

Heathlands. A Natural History. Webb, N. (Collins New Naturalist, 1986)

Dunwich Heath, Suffolk. Key heathland features include: **1** bare ground, **2** thin, lichen-rich swards on mineral soil, **3** sand cliff, **4** scattered trees, **5** interface with woodland.

Hartland Moor, Dorset. Key heathland features include: **1** warm, south-facing slope, **2** trackway, **3** heathland pool with shallow margins, **4** dry knoll with mature heather, **5** gorse scrub, **6** acid grassland.

Lowland Dry Heath varies according to climate, soil, drainage, altitude and historical management (grazing and burning). It typically occurs on infertile and free-draining acid sands, gravels and other superficial deposits from sea level up to about 300 m. The dry, eastern heaths of Breckland and the Suffolk Sandlings tend to be species-poor, and are dominated by grasses and Heather, with Gorse along roads and tracks joined by Bracken in disturbed places. Bell Heather and Dwarf Gorse are common in the slightly wetter climate of the Wealden heaths, Ashdown Forest, the Thames Basin and the New Forest heaths. In the more oceanic west, Dwarf Gorse is replaced by Western Gorse, and Bristle Bent and Purple Moor-grass become common, the latter increasing where drainage is impeded. Some distinctive variants are described in the section *Some different types of Lowland Dry Heath* (*pages 135–139*).

Lowland Dry Heath is a dynamic habitat and is reliant upon some form of disturbance – usually grazing or burning – to remain open. Natural succession would otherwise lead to the development of scrub and pine and birch woodland. However, much of the diversity of heathland is determined by its structural variation, and the extent and nature of associated scrub. The presence of open areas and patches of tall herbs and grasses are also important. Bracken, gorse or other scrub are frequent on heaths, but extensive patches can indicate where natural succession is leading to the development of scrub and woodland communities, which conservation management aims to prevent. Brambles, nettles and lush green grass are signs of nutrient enrichment.

Similar habitats

On wetter ground, Lowland Dry Heath can grade into Lowland Wet Heath and Valley Mire (which are distinguished by the presence of Cross-leaved Heath, Deergrass and wetland species including bog-mosses). It also grades into Lowland Dry Birch and Oak Wood or birch-dominated secondary woodland. Some areas show characteristics intermediate between lowland and upland heaths, often with Bilberry (*e.g.* Cannock Chase and moorland fringes in the south-west peninsula).

Coombe Heath, Arne, Dorset. Young pines trees are cleared regularly from this heath (*e.g.* during Christmas 'Pull-a-Pine' events – a new heathland tradition), but a few mature trees are retained to provide suitable perches for Nightjar.

Origins and development

The origins of Lowland Dry Heath lie in forest clearance and management extending back to the Bronze Age or even the Mesolithic period. Heaths were maintained as open habitat through a diverse range of activities, which included livestock grazing accompanied by burning and the use of cut Bracken for livestock bedding, heather turves for fuel and gorse for bread ovens. Perceived as wasteland, huge areas of heathland were agriculturally improved, afforested or subject to urban development. Declines started before 1800, but escalated in the second half of the 20th century. During this time many patches developed into secondary woodland as the realities of agricultural economics resulted in the removal of grazing animals.

Conservation

Extensive livestock grazing is usually the preferred management, together with some burning and cutting and rotational scrub management. Removal of top soil (scraping) to remove nutrients is also an option but care needs to be taken to preserve archaeological features that have often been preserved on undisturbed heaths. On restoration sites, there can be public opposition to tree-felling and scrub-clearance, which are initially unattractive and can seem counter-intuitive to visitors. The challenge is to reintegrate heathland management into local economies (*e.g.* through extensive grazing and technological advances in biofuel production) and to help people move away from a perception of heathland as empty wasteland.

What to look for

The density of wildlife may be quite low, but Lowland Dry Heath supports a host of rare and specialist species, particularly invertebrates and reptiles. Continuous, even-aged Heather is poor

EXTENT IN KM^2

Eng	580
Wal	88
Sco	189
NI	58
Ire	n/k

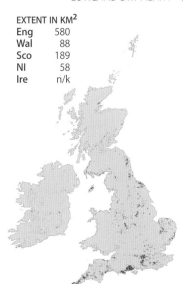

Distribution and extent

Scattered across the lowlands. Map shows broad distribution of the Annex I habitat (H4030) in the lowlands; darker shading indicates actual locations. Figures for extent are dated (from 2008 UK Biodiversity Action Plan) and will be overestimates as they include Lowland Wet Heath. Globally limited to the Atlantic fringe of Europe (from Norway to Portugal).

LEFT: **Canford Heath, Dorset** – one of the few remaining fragments of the extensive Poole Basin heaths that once covered what is now Bournemouth and Poole. The last major losses to development occurred just before SSSI designation. It now suffers from urban pressures. RIGHT: **Sutton Heath, Suffolk** – the dry Sandlings heaths of the Suffolk coast are by tradition sheep-grazed. Some sites are a mosaic of heathland and Lowland Dry Acid Grassland similar to those in nearby Breckland.

1 **Great Ovens, Dorset** – a range in structure from bare ground to scrub is important to accommodate the needs of a diversity of species. **2** **Sand Lizard** – look along path edges and on stumps that catch the sun in spring when the green coloration is brightest. Sand Lizards also occur in some sand dune systems. **3** **Smooth Snake** – found almost exclusively on lowland heath, it is largely restricted to Dorset and Hampshire, with small populations in other southern counties, and is hard to see. **4** **Nightjar** – listen at dusk between May and August for churring, "*quip*"s and the distinctive wing clap. It is present on all major southern England heaths, in southern Ireland and north into Scotland.

1 **Beewolf** – the adults feed on nectar and pollen, but catch and paralyse honey bees to feed their larvae.
2 **Heath Tiger Beetle** – a specialist of open bare ground, their larvae live in funnel-like pits that help them to catch ants and other prey. Adults chase prey over the surface. **3** **Mottled Bee-fly** – this rare and declining species is thought to parasitize the **Heath Sand Wasp** (**4**), which in turn relies upon moth caterpillars that are captured and placed in burrows to provide a larder for the offspring. **5** **Hartland Moor, Dorset**. Bell Heather and Heather mingle with Dwarf Gorse and Bristle Bent.

in species, so look for variation, including edges, damp hollows, banks, old diggings, patches of scrub and bare sand. Bare ground is especially important for many insects and for reptiles – look for sandy patches that catch the sun and are not too churned up by feet or wheels. Rare invertebrates that are hard to see include the Purbeck Mason-wasp and Ladybird Spider; like many species they are on the edge of their range in the UK and are limited to a small number of sites. Green Tiger Beetle and day-flying moths such as Emperor Moth and Fox Moth are easier to see, and flowery verges and scrub edges are good places to look for nectar feeders.

Heathlands are a good place for look for reptiles (all six British species can be present) including Sand Lizard, which requires bare, sandy patches to lay eggs and mature vegetation for cover, and Smooth Snake, which needs sunny, mature heath. Heathlands also support internationally important populations of Nightjar, Woodlark and Dartford Warbler. Nightjar uses surrounding habitat, including gardens, for foraging, and will travel as far as 7 km to find good feeding sites. Nightjar density tends to be greatest where there is some tree cover, such as along the interface between open heath and forestry.

Heathlands support very distinctive vegetation but this includes few rare species. On the humid heaths of the south-west look out for Dorset Heath, which hybridizes readily with Cross-leaved Heath. On The Lizard in Cornwall, Cornish Heath grows over base-rich Serpentine rock with Common and Western Gorse and Bell Heather. St. Dabeoc's Heath can also be found on dry heath, mainly in Connemara in Ireland.

How to recognize

Lowland Dry Heath is an open habitat, characterized by low, shrubby vegetation of heather with scattered pine or birch trees and areas of gorse scrub. The prickly and scratchy vegetation can be impenetrably thick, or quite open and springy, but in either case there are usually plenty of tracks or livestock paths to follow.

In spring the vegetation is slow to come alive although Gorse flowers early and adds a splash of colour (and a faint scent of coconut). By summer, heaths come into their own; Bell Heather colours slopes a rosy purple, which then changes to lilac as Heather starts flowering in August. Summer sunshine brings the sound of popping gorse seed pods, the smell of warm pines and the buzz of insects, and on warm evenings Nightjar can be heard churring. The heathland colours last well into autumn, but by winter become muted; sites often have names that reflect their dour winter appearance such as Blackhill, Blackheath and Blackdown.

Many heaths occur in areas of high human population density and the wide open spaces are a marked contrast to the urban conurbations surrounding them.

When to visit

Reptiles are easiest to see in spring (adders emerge in February) when the air is still cool and they need to bask in the sun to warm up; summer is best for Nightjar and invertebrates; heathers flower from July.

Did you know?
More than 80% of the lowland heathland that once covered much of southern England has been lost since the 1800s, and the remainder is fragmented.

TOP: The resident **Dartford Warbler** is particularly susceptible to harsh winters and needs mature gorse for shelter.
BOTTOM: **Near Kynance, Cornwall** – gorse intermingled with Cornish Heath forms a characteristic heathland community limited to the Lizard in Cornwall.

Some different types of Lowland Dry Heath 1/3

Shingle Heath

Found on stabilized shingle either on the coast (see Coastal Vegetated Shingle, *page 342*) or in rivers, Shingle Heath usually supports a sparse community of grasses, lichens, small herbs and Heather. The term 'Shingle Heath' is often used rather loosely to describe a range of vegetation communities that can include lichen-rich acid grasslands (sometimes with Bell Heather) and more conventional heathland dominated by Heather or Crowberry, often with gorse. It is also used to describe some transitional lichen-rich grassland communities that occur on shingle but do not fall readily within the National Vegetation Classification, such as those with False Oat-grass, Sea Campion, Biting Stonecrop and a variety of *Cladonia* lichens. Coastal Shingle Heath tends to be limited to the largest shingle sites such as on the Solent (Browndown), Dungeness and Spey Bay, and is particularly well developed in the north where unique communities occur. Riverine Shingle Heath is even rarer, but examples are found in actively braiding river systems in Ceredigion and in central and northern Scotland. It can support unique lichen assemblages, including montane species.

Dungeness, Kent – scattered Heather plants growing in a short, lichen-rich sward on stabilized coastal shingle.

Some different types of Lowland Dry Heath

Dune Heath

Heath can develop on old, stabilized sand dunes including those where sand mixed with calcium from marine organisms (including shells) has become leached over hundreds of years. Leaching is particularly widespread in the north and west where conditions are wetter. Provided grazing pressure from Rabbits or livestock is not too heavy, Heather can become established on fixed acid dunes (with Bell Heather in more western situations) and may be quite dense, although the sward can still contain some dune plants such as Sand Sedge or even Marram. Crowberry also occurs, but is restricted to Scotland and the north-west coast of Ireland. Dune Heath is most common in Scotland, although Winterton in Norfolk and Studland in Dorset both support Dune Heath.

TOP: **Singing Sands at Kentra Bay, Ardnamurchan** – part of a rich array of coastal habitats including Mudflat and Sandflat, Saltmarsh and Maritime Heath; BOTTOM: **Studland, Dorset** – an acidic dune system with stable dunes supporting Heather, in places mingled with Marram.

Maritime Heath

On sea cliffs on the west coast of Britain and Ireland, and also the north and east coast of Scotland, Maritime Heath can be found on gently sloping land above maritime cliffs on suitable soils. The short vegetation is often wind-clipped and scorched by salt on the windward side of tussocks. It is quite species-rich, including plants such as Spring Squill, Sea Plantain and Buck's-horn Plantain, sometimes with Thrift and Sea Campion. Heather is the most common dwarf-shrub, but in places Crowberry or Bell Heather are co-dominant and, in Cornwall, Cornish Heath can extend some way into the vegetation. Some of the Cornish rarities also find their way into the Maritime Heath, including Chives, Fringed Rupturewort, Spring Sandwort and Twin-headed Clover, as wall as prostrate forms of Broom, greenweeds and Common Juniper. Autumn Ladies-tresses, Autumn Squill and Portland Spurge extend farther north, and Scottish Primrose is found in northern Scotland and on the Orkney Islands. Maritime Heath is generally maintained by a combination of grazing and exposure, but a climax community with maritime forms of Cock's-foot, Hairy Greenweed, and Kidney Vetch identified in Cornwall and Wales is thought to be rare.

TOP: **Near Claddaghduff, Connemara** – Crowberry, Bell Heather and Heather in a wind-clipped sward on an exposed headland; BOTTOM: **The Lizard, Cornwall** – tussocks of Western Gorse growing with Cornish Heath are scorched on their seaward side.

Some different types of Lowland Dry Heath

Breckland Heath

A unique mix of Lowland Dry Acid Grassland and
Lowland Calcareous Grassland with dwarf-shrub
heath has developed on the patchy, wind-blown
sands over chalk of the East Anglian Breckland.
These heaths experience a more continental climate,
with hotter summers and colder winters and lower
rainfall than the western heaths. As a result they
are more lichen-rich and include some continental
species such as Grey Hair-grass. The heathland and
grassland communities occur in close proximity due
to stone-striping (soil patterning caused by freeze-
thaw conditions at the end of the last glaciation) and
variations in the depth of the sand. In the past, heavy
Rabbit- and sheep-grazing meant that in places the
sand was mobile, and in the 17th century created
inland dunes (reportedly up to 20 yards in height)
which practically engulfed the village of Santon
Downham and blocked the river for several miles.
A remnant of inland dune can be seen at Wangford
Warren.

TOP: **Spanish Catchfly, Cranwich Camp, Norfolk.** A characteristic Breckland plant that requires disturbed soil for its seedlings to germinate. Its scent is strongest at night, attracting moths which then pollinate it. It has declined significantly due to agricultural intensification and afforestation; BOTTOM: **Wangford Warren, Suffolk** – the short sward contains Sand Sedge and the rare Grey Hair-grass, and several lichen species including reindeer lichens (*e.g. Cladonia arbuscula*), and a distinctive branched, shiny brown lichen *Cetraria aculeata*.

Limestone Heath

Limestone Heath occurs where thin superficial deposits of sand overlay limestone (including chalk), often on plateaux or the top of slopes. This sand, blown from the front of glaciers farther north and deposited on downland, allows species such as Heather to grow alongside lime-loving plants such as Common Milkwort, Dropwort and Salad Burnet. Once more widespread, many sites were lost under the plough, but natural leaching plus the accumulation of acidic humus (aided by a decrease in Rabbit grazing) has also led to increased acidification.

Limestone Heath tends to be found in relatively small patches where conditions are favourable for its development. In the south-west of England and Wales, it may be a relic of vegetation that developed on deeper, more acidic soils, which have since eroded – such a habitat cannot be recreated.

TOP: There are no species unique to Limestone Heath. The flora is a paradoxical mix of lime and acid-loving plants. Typical heathland species such as Sheep's Sorrel and Bell Heather are can be found with those characteristic of Lowland Calcareous Grassland such as **Dropwort**, Betony and Salad Burnet; BOTTOM: **Lullington Heath, East Sussex** – in the 1950s, myxomatosis decimated the Rabbit population that had previously maintained a short sward. Dartford Warbler and Stonechat and more recently Nightingale and Whitethroat, have colonized as the amount of scrub has increased.

Lowland Wet Heath occurs on seasonally waterlogged shallow peat and mineral soils where the degree of moisture favours the more shallow-rooted Cross-leaved Heath over Heather, which, although present, is generally sparser. Lowland Wet Heath shares many plant species with bogs, including some with an oceanic distribution such as Brown Beak-sedge and Marsh Clubmoss. More common species include Compact Bog-moss, Deergrass, Tormentil, Heath Spotted-orchid and Lousewort, while Round-leaved Sundew and White Beak-sedge are limited to wetter hollows. However, frequent uncontrolled burning, heavy grazing or drainage can impoverish the sward, leaving only Purple Moor-grass, Heather and Cross-leaved Heath. Conversely, a lack of burning or grazing can allow Downy Birch, Grey Willow and pine to colonize, often with a field layer of dense, tussocky Purple Moor-grass. Climate and substrate also influence the vegetation. In the Poole Basin and Cornwall, Dorset Heath can be locally abundant and on the Lizard, Cornish Heath contributes to a very localized plant community with Black Bog-rush, Purple Moor-grass, Western Gorse and Petty Whin.

The mosaics formed by Lowland Wet Heath with Valley Mire and Lowland Dry Heath are important for invertebrates and several rare and scarce species can be seen. For example, the Southern Damselfly, which needs base-rich runnels or streams that can be found in Lowland Wet Heath over clay substrates. The Purbeck Mason-wasp may visit damp heathland in search of moist clay with which to seal the entrance of its nest, and the Large Marsh Grasshopper may occur where Lowland Wet Heath and Valley Mire form a mosaic.

Similar habitats

Lowland Wet Heath grades into Valley Mire, but typical peat-forming mosses such as Papillose and Magellanic Bog-mosses are largely absent. Bell Heather and Western Gorse indicate transitions to Lowland Dry Heath, and Bristle Bent is characteristic of a humid variant found in the south and south-west.

Red Devon cattle on **Hartland Moor, Dorset**. The loss or decline of several characteristic Lowland Wet Heath and Valley Mire plants was attributed to the cessation of traditional grazing in Dorset; grazing has, however, been reinstated on many sites for conservation purposes.

EXTENT UNKNOWN

Distribution and extent

Found throughout lowland Britain and Ireland within heathland areas. Map shows broad distribution of Annex I wet heathland habitats (H4010 and H4020) in the lowlands; darker shading shows actual locations. In Europe it is restricted to the Atlantic fringe (from Scandinavia to Normandy), with 85% of the resource in Britain and Ireland.

When to visit

April–August depending on species for scarce plants, June–July for Silver-studded Blue and Southern Damselfly.

TOP: **Goonhilly Downs, Cornwall** – The Lizard holds a unique kind of Lowland Wet Heath dominated by Black Bog-rush with Cornish Heath. BOTTOM: **Stoborough Heath, Dorset** – Purple Moor-grass can dominate Lowland Wet Heath, usually where the soil is derived from a slightly more base-rich substrate, or is influenced by the flow of enriched groundwater.

Origins and development

Lowland Wet Heath develops where soils conditions are suitable within heathland landscapes. It has suffered similar losses to Lowland Dry Heath, but the habitat has also been degraded through changes in hydrology including groundwater extraction, pollution and drainage associated with agricultural improvement, forestry and housing developments.

Conservation

Lowland Wet Heath is usually managed as an integral part of a heathland complex. Free-ranging livestock are often used with other heathland management techniques such as rotational scrub cutting to maintain open, diverse swards.

What to look for

Silver-studded Blue in open, heathery swards; Southern Damselfly where there are runnels; a suite of scarce plants including Marsh Gentian, Brown Beak-sedge, Marsh Clubmoss and Petty Whin.

How to recognize

Look for Lowland Wet Heath in depressions, around pools and anywhere that drainage is a little impeded on heathlands. It often forms a narrow band between Lowland Dry Heath and Valley Mire, although in some places it can cover significant areas. Lowland Wet Heath is characterized by Cross-leaved Heath, which comes into flower earlier than other heathers, and its clustered rose-pink heads speckle the ground from June, enlivening the sward of Purple Moor-grass, Heather, Deergrass and cushion-like Compact Bog-moss.

The ground may squelch underfoot, but it is generally possible to walk through the short vegetation with relative ease, except in situations where Purple Moor-grass has become dominant and formed large tussocks, in places interspersed with Bog-myrtle.

When to visit

April–August depending on species for scarce plants, June–July for Silver-studded Blue and Southern Damselfly.

Did you know?

Female Silver-studded Blues only lay eggs where they detect suitable ant pheromones (the caterpillars are taken by ants into their nests and tended there).

1 Silver-studded Blue – look during June and July in areas with a short sward, such as along firebreaks. **2 Petty Whin** is hard to see except when it flowers in April; this woody species may persist for some time un-observed in un-grazed Purple Moor-grass dominated Lowland Wet Heath, flowering again when grazing resumes.
3 Marsh Gentian is typically found where there is some seasonal movement of surface water, it can flower (August–September) profusely following burning.

Upland Dry Heath

page 393

Upland Dry Heath is usually found between enclosed agricultural land and the montane zone (about 300–700 m), although in the harsh climate of northern Scotland it can occur right down to sea level. It grows on thin peat and mineral soils that are usually fairly well-drained but kept moist by rain, mist and snow. The vegetation is largely influenced by climate, altitude and management. Much of this habitat type is characterized by a deep canopy of young Heather and Bilberry, sometimes with Crowberry and Cowberry, overtopped by Wavy Hair-grass and growing out of thick mats of large leafy mosses and reindeer lichens. Bell Heather is found in more oceanic areas, and Bearberry in the boreal heaths of north-east Scotland. In south-west England, Western Gorse and Heather grow together and create a distinctive yellow and purple sward when in flower.

Upland Dry Heath is found within the woodland zone and falls midway on the successional spectrum between grassland and woodland. Succession to woodland is generally prevented by grazing and burning. Heavy grazing can eliminate Heather and Bilberry (resulting in acid grassland), while burning encourages the regeneration of Heather but eliminates other species.

EXTENT IN KM²

Eng	1,488
Wal	777
Sco	4,790
NI	168
Ire	1,230

Foel Cynwch, near **Llanfachreth, Gwynedd** – Heather, Bell Heather and Western Gorse

Distribution and extent

Widespread in the uplands. Britain holds a significant proportion of the global resource, which is restricted to north-west Europe. Map shows broad distribution of Annex I habitat (H4030) in the uplands; darker shading shows actual locations. Extent figures are over-estimates as they reflect the total area of Annex I habitat type H4030, which includes Lowland Dry Heath.

Similar habitats

An increase in Purple Moor-grass, Deergrass, Cross-leaved Heath, bog-mosses and Hare's-tail Cottongrass indicates transitions to Upland Wet Heath and, in wetter areas, Blanket Bog. Gradations to Montane Heath with prostrate and small dwarf-shrubs occurs at higher altitudes in mountainous areas.

Origins and development

Most Upland Dry Heath is a modified form of the understorey of woodland or scrub communities that were extensively cleared by people from the Neolithic period onwards. At high altitudes, some communities may be near-natural, but most are prevented from succeeding to woodland through livestock grazing and burning. The last 200 years have seen many changes. In the 19th century, heathland was lost through agricultural improvement and deteriorated with the rise of sheep ranching, shooting estates and associated heather burning. In the 20th century, huge areas were afforested, and loss and deterioration through agricultural improvement, heavy sheep and deer grazing and burning continued – 27% was lost in England and Wales during this period and about 80% of designated heath is currently in poor condition.

1 Near Balnakeil, Durness – here, Upland Dry Heath defies stereotypes by growing over limestone almost at sea level. The patterning is a result of severe wind-pruning.
Damp, oceanic heath in the west of Scotland and Ireland can support large, leafy liverworts such **Wood's Whipwort** (**2**) and **Bird's-foot Earwort** (**3**) in a community that is globally restricted to these areas and Norway. Known as the northern hepatic mat, this community extends into snow-beds in the montane zone and is susceptible to burning, particularly when followed by heavy grazing.

Conservation

In many cases, Upland Dry Heath is impoverished and modifications to grazing and burning practices are widely needed. Atmospheric pollution is an issue in the South Pennines, and may be contributing to the poverty of lower plant communities. Upland Dry Heath has high recreational value and activities such as mountain biking, off-road driving, skiing, fell walking and running can be damaging where they are not carefully managed.

Upland Dry Heath is valued as a cultural landscape, and unlike lowland heathland remains integrated into the economics of local communities through (subsidized) farming practices and management for game. However, an increasing awareness of the environmental and ecological cost of these land-use practices (including damage to peat and the persecution of raptors) and the need for better water catchment management and carbon storage and a growing interest in rewilding, are all factors that will contribute to the much-needed debate over the future of the British uplands.

Strath Nethy, Cairngorms. Upland Dry Heath on the slopes grades into Upland Wet Heath and Blanket Bog on flatter ground beside the burn.

What to look for

Upland Dry Heath vegetation is typically quite species-poor, but there are interesting variations to be seen. Look out for more oceanic heathland plant communities in the north-west (or on warm south-facing slopes in the north) with Bell Heather, moorland grasses, Wild Thyme and small herbs such as Fairy Flax and Selfheal, and, higher up, the distinctive Woolly Fringe-moss. In the cold climate of the east Highlands, stony soils support a more boreal heathland type, and the distinctive leathery, veined leaves of mat-forming Bearberry become apparent in gaps in the Heather canopy. Wherever there are richer brown earths or the underlying rock is more base-rich, more species-rich heath can be found with Intermediate Wintergreen, Common Bird's-foot-trefoil, Wood Anemone, Bitter-vetch and northern species such as Mountain Everlasting. Shady, steep north- or east-facing slopes often support damper heath with richly coloured carpets of bog-mosses. In places this damp heath includes rare oceanic liverworts and the tiny Wilson's Filmy-fern, which looks more like a moss than a fern.

Notable groups of species include upland birds and moorland invertebrates. Look out for Red Grouse (in open heather), Black Grouse (in habitat mosaics and moorland fringes) and Twite (moorland edges), as well as Merlin, Hen Harrier and Short-eared Owl (all of which nest in open heather but are often scarce or absent around grouse shooting estates due to illegal persecution). The invertebrate fauna is diverse, with up to 15% of British ground beetles, and 20% of British spiders found in areas with a range of moorland vegetation types and structures.

1 Grey Mountain Carpet (moth) is common and well distributed across the uplands; it is easily disturbed from rocks where it often rests. 2 **Mountain Hares** are native to the Highlands of Scotland, and were introduced to the Peak District in the 19th century. The Irish Hare is smaller and does not grow a white coat in winter. 3 The **Red Grouse** (an endemic subspecies of the European Willow Grouse) – listen for the distinctive *"go-back, go-back"* call, or the whirring of wings when a bird is disturbed from the ground.

How to recognize

Upland Dry Heath covers slopes and crags in the wild, open moorland and mountain landscapes of the British and Irish uplands.

From a distance, the low canopy of dark Heather and lush green Bilberry contrasts with the paler vegetation of upland grasslands and Blanket Bog. Vertebrates are few and far between in this bleak and windswept landscape, although the haunting calls of breeding Golden Plovers can be heard and the songs of Meadow Pipits and Skylarks over the associated grasslands are a constant presence in spring.

The rolling moors of the Southern Uplands, Pennines and North York Moors are managed heavily for grouse shooting and are often little more than monocultures of Heather, coloured a pretty purple in late summer, and striped and patched where they have been recently burnt to promote young growth for Red Grouse.

When to visit

Late summer for scenic beauty.

1 **Creag Meagaidh, Central Highlands** – with reduced grazing, and provided there is a nearby seed source, Upland Dry Heath gradually reverts to woodland. Here deer control and the deliberate removal of sheep is resulting in the development of Upland Birch Wood. **2** **An Creagan, near Balmoral** – Heather burning (also referred to as muirburn) is a widespread practice, particularly on grouse moors, and results in a distinctive patchwork of different aged Heather. Its impact on the structural and species diversity of heathland is dependent on rotation length, the amount of old degenerate heather retained, and the interaction with grazing. Larger areas are also burnt by sheep farmers to give an early bite. **3** **Near Carn Lochan na Beinne, Cairngorms** – rocky ground at about 700 m supporting Crowberry and Bearberry among low Heather.

Derwent Valley, Lake District – The darker vegetation on the steeper crags is Heather and Bilberry (INSET), while the paler green on less steep terrain indicates where intense grazing has converted heathland to acid grassland. Ring Ouzel can be found on the heathery crags.

Upland Wet Heath

Upland Wet Heath is found at moderate altitudes on shallow peats and acid mineral soils that are waterlogged for at least part of the year, but are too dry or too shallow for active peat formation. It generally occupies gently sloping hillsides where there is some movement of water, often above Blanket Bog but below the better drained steeper slopes where drier heath is found. These habitats often intermingle. Drier areas on mineral soils often support grasses, particularly Mat-grass and Wavy Hair-grass, while Heath Rush is common on shallow peats. Where the heath is slightly flushed with moving water, Carnation Sedge grows with other sedges and Round-leaved Sundew. Heather, Cross-leaved Heath, Purple Moor-grass and Deergrass are common throughout; reindeer lichens and Woolly Fringe-moss are more common in drier regions and bog-mosses in wetter conditions. In areas where it is heavily grazed, Upland Wet Heath can be characterized by Deergrass, Mat-grass and Heath Rush. There is a degree of overlap between the wetter moorland habitats.

EXTENT IN KM^2	
Eng	688
Wal	144
Sco	3,700
NI	583
Ire	1,599

Ardnamurchan, Argyll with dry heath in the foreground and wet heath in the distance, showing the distinctive warm glow of Deergrass.

Distribution and extent

Found in the western uplands. Map shows broad distribution of Annex I habitat (H4010) in the uplands; darker shading shows actual locations (no data for England). Extent figures are over-estimates as they include Lowland Wet Heath.

Similar habitats

It can sometimes be difficult to distinguish Upland Wet Heath from Upland Dry Heath or Blanket Bog at first glance, particularly as Heather and Purple Moor-grass may be present in each. However, Upland Wet Heath lacks the typical peat-forming species characteristic of Blanket Bog such as the pale greenish-ochre Papillose Bog-moss and Hare's-tail Cottongrass. Upland Dry Heath tends to have a thicker Heather canopy and usually lacks species such as Cross-leaved Heath, Bog Myrtle and Deergrass, although damper versions may contain bog-mosses.

Origins and development

Upland Wet Heath may have occurred in open, boggy areas within woodland, but most probably developed on shallow slopes on the waterlogged ground that resulted from tree clearance that began about 4,000 years ago. Much habitat has deteriorated through overgrazing, burning and drainage, while losses have been caused by afforestation and, more recently, the development of tracks and renewable energy infrastructure.

1 **Rothiemurchus, Speyside** – hollows within Caledonian Forest support Upland Wet Heath in a range of transitions to Upland Dry Heath. The rare montane ground beetle *Amara alpina* is associated with Upland Wet Heath in the Cairngorms and feeds on the seed heads of Deergrass. **2** **Scotch Argus** is found in Scotland around bog margins in sheltered Upland Wet Heath, which covers extensive tracts of land on relatively shallow lower slopes, such as at **3** **Beinn Eigh, Wester Ross.**

Conservation

Although some grazing is beneficial in promoting floristic diversity by preventing Heather or Purple Moor-grass from smothering smaller species and lower plants, a reduction in grazing levels would benefit many upland sites. Burning, which is often carried out in large patches to stimulate fresh growth for livestock, can damage lichens and bryophytes. Many upland woodlands are adjacent to Upland Wet Heath, and so woodland expansion is often likely to be to the detriment of Upland Wet Heath.

What to look for

Flushes with butterworts, sundews, White Beak-sedge and Many-stalked Spike-rush. Bog Asphodel adds colour from July. Look for Mackay's Heath in western Ireland.

1 White Beak-sedge and **2** Bog Asphodel indicate wetter conditions. **3** Twelve Pins (Na Beanna Beola), Connemara. Much of the landscape is clothed with Upland Wet Heath, with Blanket Bog on flatter areas.

GRASSLANDS

ORIGINS

Almost all grasslands in Britain and Ireland are semi-natural, a result of millennia of human activity that has favoured grassland over woodland and wetland, generally to provide animal fodder. However, this does not mean that grassland did not exist before the Neolithic period, when the clearance of woodland began. Pollen records suggest that tundra and tall-herb communities predominated over Britain and Ireland for a period at the end of the last glaciation. As woody species colonized, these communities were able to persist at high altitudes beyond the natural limit of tree growth, on exposed cliff slopes and shorelines, in dynamic river floodplains, and in glades within woodland maintained by large wild herbivores such as Aurochs. Tree clearance, drainage and grazing with domestic livestock allowed these communities to expand and adapt on suitable soils, and grassland became a key feature in the landscape from about 6,000 years ago. On more acid soils where these activities resulted in heathland, grassland sometimes developed subsequently as a result of heavy grazing and burning. Grassland has ebbed and flowed with changing human population pressure but remains a defining feature of the British and Irish countryside today.

The extent of almost all semi-natural habitats in Britain and Ireland has declined significantly, but the loss of lowland grassland has been particularly severe, with a 90% decline in the 20th century. Cultivation and re-seeding became widespread by the 18th century amongst wealthy landowners, but it was in the 1940s and 1950s that destruction escalated. Technological advances and the drive for increased national self-sufficiency in food led to the extensive use of new chemicals and grass varieties, increased intensity of cutting and grazing, and the use of incentives to encourage farmers to plough up meadows, pastures and downland. Conversely, in the uplands, subsidies encouraged high stocking rates, which adversely affected grasslands, but also increased the areas of Upland Acid Grassland at the expense of heather-dominated habitats.

Caeau Penglaneinon, Elan Valley, Radnorshire is a 'Coronation Meadow', one of a series of meadows selected as outstanding examples of species-rich grassland to be flagships for their county.

HABITAT	DESCRIPTION
Lowland Calcareous Grassland *page 162* | *page 391*	Species-rich, on limestone and chalk mainly in the southern lowlands, of particular interest for invertebrates.
Lowland Dry Acid Grassland *page 168* | *page 391*	Species-poor, but supports specialist species, part of heathland landscapes on dry acid soils.
Lowland Meadow and Pasture *page 171* | *page 391*	Rich in generalist species, highly fragmented and limited in extent on neutral soils. Meadow is cut for hay or silage, pasture is generally grazed throughout the year.
Purple Moor-grass and Rush Pasture *page 174* | *page 392*	Marshy grassland with specialist species found in the lowlands.
Coastal and Floodplain Grazing Marsh *page 177* | *page 391*	Seasonally flooded, mostly semi-improved, of interest for breeding and wintering waterfowl.
Upland Calcareous Grassland *page 183* | *page 392*	Species-rich, of naturally limited extent on limestone and other basic rocks in the uplands.
Northern Hay Meadow *page 186* | *page 391*	Species-rich, of very limited extent mainly in and near the Pennines.
Upland Rush Pasture *page 189* | *page 392*	Species-poor rough grazing, of interest for its bird fauna, widespread in the uplands margins.
Upland Acid Grassland *page 192* | *page 392*	Species-poor rough grazing, widespread and extensive in the uplands on siliceous rocks, of interest for breeding waders.
Calaminarian Grassland *page 195* | *page 391*	Supports specialist metalliferous species, widespread but very limited in extent.

Magdalen Hill Down, Hampshire – an area of species-rich chalk downland of particular note for its butterflies.

TYPES OF GRASSLAND

Estimates vary depending on definitions and survey techniques, but grassland probably covers around 40% of the land surface of the UK and over 60% of that of Ireland. In the UK, over half of this is permanent pasture, about 40% is rough grazing (*i.e.* semi-natural permanent pasture in the uplands). The remaining 10% is grass ley. Of the permanent pasture, the majority is improved or semi-improved (see box), with only a fraction remaining unimproved. Estimates for unimproved grassland are around 100,000 ha for England. To put this into perspective, the total area of grassland in England is over 4·5 million hectares.

There is a tiny amount of near-natural grassland in Britain and Ireland. It is found where climate, exposure, or changing environmental conditions naturally prevent woody species from becoming established (*e.g.* in montane situations, in exposed places, and where the substrate shifts such as in sand

Anthills (typically formed by Yellow Meadow-ant) indicate long-established semi-natural grassland. The ants (which farm underground aphids) create the mounds while excavating underground galleries where they care for their young. The mounds, which are warmed by the sun and act as storage heaters, support individual colonies that may be over 100 years old. They can be found on dry acid or calcareous grassland, and the fine material often supports different species of plants from the surrounding sward, including scarce species such as Nit-grass. Green Woodpeckers feed from anthills using their particularly long tongue. Anthills are also used by basking Common Lizard and by Common Field Grasshopper for egg-laying.

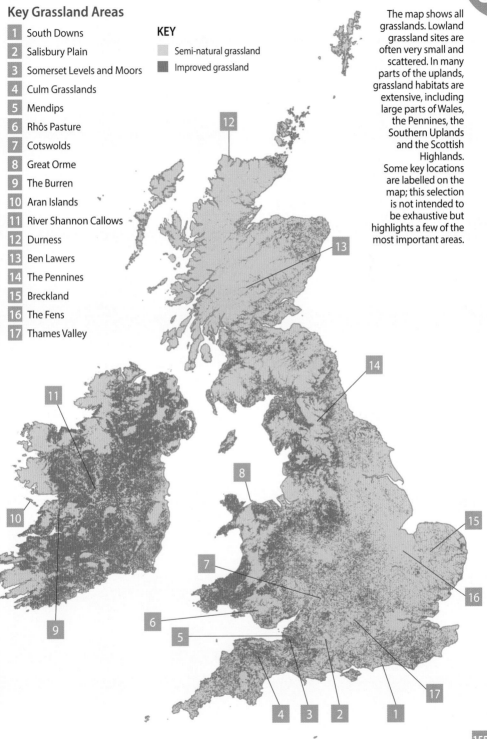

Key Grassland Areas

1. South Downs
2. Salisbury Plain
3. Somerset Levels and Moors
4. Culm Grasslands
5. Mendips
6. Rhôs Pasture
7. Cotswolds
8. Great Orme
9. The Burren
10. Aran Islands
11. River Shannon Callows
12. Durness
13. Ben Lawers
14. The Pennines
15. Breckland
16. The Fens
17. Thames Valley

KEY

Semi-natural grassland
Improved grassland

The map shows all grasslands. Lowland grassland sites are often very small and scattered. In many parts of the uplands, grassland habitats are extensive, including large parts of Wales, the Pennines, the Southern Uplands and the Scottish Highlands. Some key locations are labelled on the map; this selection is not intended to be exhaustive but highlights a few of the most important areas.

G

dune and shingle systems). The remainder of unimproved grassland is generally referred to as semi-natural because, without human intervention, successional processes would otherwise result in scrub and woodland developing (some types could revert to wetland habitats). Semi-natural grassland is generally found within agricultural systems, and much is either in protected areas or managed through agri-environment schemes.

Grassland is, by convention, divided into upland and lowland, with the 300 m contour taken as an approximate delimiter. This is because cooler, wetter and more exposed conditions in the uplands favour different species from those adapted to the generally warmer and drier conditions in the lowlands. However, as in all habitat types, transitions occur, and some 'upland' communities are found at sea level where conditions are harsh. The division also has practical relevance as the fate of lowland grassland has been different from that of the uplands, and a different approach to the conservation of each is needed.

Grassland can also be defined according to the pH of the substrate, and is often described as acid (*e.g.* on sands, gravels and siliceous rocks) or calcareous (on rocks rich in magnesium as well as different limestones). Both acid and calcareous grassland support specialist species, although calcareous swards tend to be significantly more species-rich. Some species are found in both. Grassland that supports species that are able to tolerate intermediate pH is called 'neutral' and is generally found on clays and loams. This type of grassland is also referred to as 'mesotrophic', as it is inherently more productive than acid or calcareous grassland.

Management is another key factor. Pastures are often grazed year-round, and are not cut. Meadows are shut off from livestock in the spring to allow vegetation to be harvested and stored for the winter – traditionally as hay but now more often as silage. Wet grasslands generally experience regular flooding, mostly in the winter, and in some cases this is actively managed. However, there is variation in how particular habitats are managed; for example, pastures can be cut for hay in some years and wet grasslands may be meadow or pasture. In some cases grassland has survived by accident, for example in churchyards and on road verges where it is also cut sporadically.

Semi-natural grassland in Britain and Ireland is very varied, a product of the diverse substrate, soil, topography, climate and land-use history of these islands. Ten types are described this chapter but these are, as always, nodes on a continuum, and transitional types are of no less interest.

Uffington White Horse, Oxfordshire – many archaeological features have been preserved in semi-natural grassland, including Bronze Age figures such as this and the Cerne Abbas Giant in Dorset, the origins of which are obscure.

Waxcap grasslands are particularly rich in fungi, although not necessarily in plant species, and are found in short, nutrient-poor swards across the spectrum from acidic to calcareous. The most striking species are the waxcaps, which can be white, pink, purple, yellow, orange or red, and colours in between. They generally have smooth glossy or sticky caps and thick, waxy gills. Fairy clubs, pinkgills and earthtongues are also characteristic of waxcap grasslands. The presence of particular species can be used as 'indicators' of the quality of a site. Waxcap grasslands occur principally in Europe, and are most extensive in Britain.

Some **semi-natural grassland** has become established relatively recently as a consequence of development, such as on railway cuttings and road embankments where the substrate has been exposed. It is sometimes reseeded with wildflowers, in this case Oxeye Daisy.

CONSERVATION IMPORTANCE AND PROTECTION

Semi-natural grassland supports distinctive communities of plants, fungi and invertebrates in particular, including species that are greatly valued for their attractiveness and rarity. For example, 206 of the UK BAP priority species are found in lowland semi-natural grasslands, and 41 in Upland Calcareous Grassland and Northern Hay Meadow. Although often celebrated as being species-rich (and it is wonderfully species-rich in comparison to the improved grassland that has so often replaced it), grassland is not intrinsically species-rich compared to woodland it generally replaced if all life-forms are taken into account. It is an early-successional habitat that lacks the complexity of later stages. However, it supports species for which those later stages are too enclosed, and which presumably would once have occurred in natural openings. Most woodland remnants are now too small, fragmented and constrained for such natural openings to occur, and species dependent upon open conditions are limited to semi-natural grassland and Wood Pasture. In Europe as a whole, around 50% of the endemic plant species are dependent on grassland.

European designation helps to protect six types of grassland in Britain and Ireland. This excludes Coastal and Floodplain Grazing Marsh, most Lowland Dry Acid Grassland, Upland Acid Grassland and Upland Rush Pasture, although the former is recognized as a Priority Habitat for conservation within the UK and all four can be found within Special Protection Areas (SPAs) notified for their internationally important breeding or wintering birds. Unusual or species-rich variants of Upland Acid Grassland are sometimes notified as SSSIs, but in general, together with Upland Rush Pasture, the impoverished sward is of less interest than that of the other moorland habitats such as Upland Dry Heath, Upland Wet Heath and Blanket Bog from which they are derived. There is growing interest in exploring how some of these impoverished habitats could be reinvigorated. The removal of heavy grazing pressure would result in an increase in dwarf-shrubs and eventually woodland (although given the distance to seed sources in many cases, this could take many years). In wetter situations some habitat would revert to Blanket Bog. Changes in the Common Agricultural Policy, which used to link subsidies directly to numbers of livestock, has seen a decline in grazing pressure, but about 75% of protected Upland Calcareous

FUTURE THREATS

Nitrogen deposition has affected the species diversity and composition of acid and calcareous grassland respectively. While major changes have probably already occurred, ongoing deposition may see further change.

Neglect of semi-natural lowland grassland has resulted in a decline in condition, and is a reflection of the poor economic returns from low-productivity grassland. Funding for conservation grazing is needed if this decline is to be reversed.

Climate change is likely to directly impact on semi-natural grasslands, although exactly how is still unclear. Changes in hydrology may result in wet grasslands becoming drier, and areas where the climate is suitable may be reduced for northern species such as Globeflower and Wood Crane's-bill.

Conservation branding is seen as a way to add value to produce from semi-natural grasslands. There is also some evidence to suggest that the quality of meat from semi-natural grassland is better than that from improved grassland. The importance of the botanical diversity of forage for cattle in terms of cheese flavour has already been established.

Silage being turned, prior to baling, on Coastal and Floodplain Grazing Marsh.

Grassland remains in poor condition largely due to overgrazing by sheep. On the whole, changes in management are likely to have more impact on dry grasslands than the direct effects of climate change. For wetter grassland types, both summer drought and prolonged winter flooding may result in changes in vegetation composition. All grassland types may be affected indirectly if climate-induced changes in agricultural economics put grazing regimes at risk or encourage intensification of low-input grasslands.

Information on how much grassland is designated is most readily available in England, where around 68% of semi-natural grassland is thought to be protected by SSSI notification. However, this proportion varies widely between grassland types, with, for example, a much great proportion of calcareous grassland protected than Purple Moor-grass and Rush Pasture. Designated sites are, on the whole, in better condition than undesignated sites, but their condition is deteriorating. In contrast, the condition of some non-SSSI semi-natural grassland has improved slightly, a consequence of agri-environment schemes and increasing expertise in grassland restoration. Species-rich grassland is still being lost (although the rate has slowed), and the ongoing declines in associated species are alarming: 22 butterfly species found on farmland saw a 37% decline between 1990 and 2009; declines in breeding Yellow Wagtails in Northern Hay Meadows accelerated through the 1990s; and populations of breeding waders continue to dwindle. A major change in policy is needed, so that the multi-faceted value of species-rich grassland is better appreciated and low-intensity management is better supported. The advent of ecosystem services valuation, does raise the profile of the environmental

TOP: **Common Rock-rose** is a small evergreen shrub typical of calcareous grassland that is widely distributed throughout Britain and Ireland. Flowering from June to September it is a food plant for several butterflies and moths, including Brown Argus, Green Hairstreak, Silver-studded Blue and the iridescent green day-flying moth Cistus Forester. MIDDLE: **Yellow-rattle** is widespread in dry neutral grassland and flowers from June to September. It is a hemi-parasite, tapping into the roots of grasses to obtain nutrients; this reduces their vigour and dominance in the sward, providing opportunities for other less robust species to become established. It can play a key role in grassland restoration. BOTTOM: **Pasqueflower** – an iconic species of calcareous grasslands in Britain, flowering during late April and early May. Its decline (due to agricultural improvement) has been long-term, and it is now restricted to a handful of sites.

benefits provided by grassland in terms of flood prevention, carbon storage and water purification, as well as the benefits to heath and well-being and contributions to tourism. It is, however, important not to lose sight of the intrinsic value of habitats.

CULTURAL IMPORTANCE

Wildlife-rich grassland is valued as a cultural landscape, a serendipitous product of thousands of years of human impacts on ecological processes. Once an intrinsic part of every farm, flower-rich grassland is deeply embedded within our culture and has recurred as a theme for artists and writers for centuries. Much loved for its sheer beauty in an increasingly monotonous countryside, such grassland is becoming increasingly scarce – it is unusual to come across any by chance and, for younger generations, uniform green fields are the norm in pastoral landscapes. There is the danger that some types will soon be limited to folk memory and literature unless declines in extent and quality are halted.

Semi-natural grasslands also have a range of historical management practices and traditions associated with them that are valued for their cultural significance. For example, in Wessex, flocks were shepherded on the chalk downland, then enclosed on arable land to fertilize it. From the 17th century, water meadows were an important part of the system, and had their own customs and skills linked with them. 'Drowned' or 'floated' using a system of channels, drains and sluices, usually in early spring, they were managed to provide an 'early bite' in the spring, and hay for the winter. The famous Lammas meadows of the Thames Valley were common land. Commoners drew lots for 'doles' marked with boundary stones from which hay had to be cut and carted away by Lammas Day in August.

Corfe Common, Dorset. In the lowlands, grasslands often only survived because multiple ownership or common rights made gaining consensus for 'improvement' difficult.

Fox Fritillary Meadow, Suffolk – open days on privately owned flower-rich grasslands are popular – an indication of the affection with which meadows are regarded, and of how difficult it can otherwise be to see them.

G

KEY FEATURES

Most key features of grassland are related to variation in the structure, microclimate or wetness of the habitat. Grazing animals (generally domestic livestock) are a crucial component of almost all grasslands. Grazing (or mowing) is essential for maintaining the floral species diversity and abundance, as it prevents bulky, competitive species and scrub from engulfing finer grasses and herbs. Appropriate grazing creates a diverse sward structure with a mosaic of short, tall and tussocky vegetation, as well as bare ground. This structural diversity is particularly important for invertebrates, whose requirements can be complex. For example, blue butterflies have a fascinating relationship with ants, secreting a sweet liquid that the ants feed on before taking the caterpillars into their nest under the misapprehension that they are ant grubs. The caterpillars eat the real grubs and hibernate in the nest until the following summer, safe from predators. The butterfly is therefore reliant upon the specific conditions required by the relevant 'host' ant species (usually very warm, short swards, typically on south-facing slopes). Bare patches can be particularly valuable for wildlife: a biodiversity audit in Breckland, East Anglia found that the presence of bare, disturbed ground was more important than habitat type in determining how many species were present on a site. Disturbed, short swards can provide ideal conditions for annual plants to regenerate from the seed bank (*e.g.* Lowland Acid Grassland species such as a suite of scarce and rare clovers and Annual Knawel. The dung produced by livestock is also important, as it attracts coprophagous beetles and flies. For example, the larvae of the rare Hornet Robberfly feed on dung beetle larvae.

Other key features are related to variations in the moisture content of soils. Anthills are an important feature of many grassland types as they provide particularly well-drained, warm microhabitats. They often support different plant species compared to the surrounding sward (*e.g.* Common Rock-rose and Wild Thyme and tiny plants such as Thyme-leaved Sandwort and Changing Forget-me-not). They also provide a source of food for Green Woodpecker and egg-laying sites for grasshoppers. Flushes in Northern Hay Meadow can support localized plant species such as Bird's-eye Primrose and Grass-of-

Fontmell Down, Dorset. Key grassland features on this Lowland Calcareous Grassland include: ❶ bare ground, ❷ tussocks, ❸ anthills, ❹ steep, south-facing slopes, ❺ livestock, ❻ scrub, ❼ bright green ('improved') grassland in valley bottom (poor for wildlife).

Parnassus. Moist areas (and animal dung) on Lowland Calcareous Grassland can sometimes attract clouds of butterflies (*e.g.* Small and Chalkhill Blues) in search of mineral salts.

Margins, ditches, and transitions to other habitat types are also key features that add to the diversity of grassland sites. The transition to Scrub is particularly important, as it provides a sheltered microclimate.

Hay meadow management

With the widespread development of efficient metal tools in the Iron Age, hay-making became a possibility. Dried herbage, rather than tree-forage, became the winter mainstay for livestock in Britain (although tree-lopping persisted into the 19th century) and meadows evolved. In Ireland, the milder climate meant that stock could be out-wintered more readily, and hay-making was not so ubiquitous.

In meadows, the livestock are excluded from around the beginning of May and moved to alternative pasture, often common land, downland or hill grazings. The mixed sward of grass and herbs is cut from about midsummer onwards, ideally after it sets seed. It is then left to dry in the field for three days or so. Historically, it was cut by a team of people with scythes and turned by hand. Nowadays the process is mechanized but is still time-consuming; the hay generally needs to be turned several times and 'rowed up' overnight. Hay-making is entirely dependent upon fair weather, and in a poor season can be delayed until September, although by this time the rank herbage can be difficult to dry properly. Traditionally, hay used to be stacked on tripods or built into haycocks to minimize the impact of dew or rainfall overnight. Now, it is more likely to be big-baled and wrapped for silage in inclement weather. After the crop has been removed, livestock are let back in to graze the regrowth (known as 'aftermath') and any uncut corners and margins. Grazing usually continues throughout the winter and, in the spring, farmyard manure and sometimes lime are applied to help maintain fertility.

Mechanization (and the widespread availability of plastic) has made silage-making comparatively easy, and it has now largely replaced hay-making. Silage is more nutritious than hay (although not suitable for horses). The grass is cut green, then fermented in anaerobic conditions, causing carbohydrates to be converted to acids that preserve the silage and improve digestibility. The grass can be cut earlier, does not need drying, and more than one cut can be taken in a year. Expensive equipment also requires greater returns, and artificial fertilizers are used to maximize the crop. Early and repeated cutting and fertilization greatly reduce the plant species diversity of the sward and can be devastating for birds and invertebrates.

Meadows. George Peterken (Bloomsbury Publishing, 2018)

Jewels beyond the plough, a celebration of Britain's Grassland. Richard Jefferson (Langford Press, 2012)

Floodplain Meadows – Beauty and Utility edited by Emma Rothero, Sophie Lake & David Gowing (NatureBureau, 2016)

Lowland Calcareous Grassland

page 391

Classic chalk grassland is mostly found in the warm and dry southern chalk country (Dorset, Wiltshire, the twin ridgeways of the North and South Downs and the Chilterns), where its character is determined by the climate, rather than the particularly type of limestone on which it occurs. Towards the cooler and wetter north it becomes increasingly limited to south-facing slopes. Famous for its incredible floristic richness (up to 40 or more species per square metre), it usually contains a mixture of fine-bladed grasses and small herbs such as Meadow Oat-grass, Quaking-grass, Wild Thyme, Small Scabious, Dropwort, Common Bird's-foot-trefoil, Salad Burnet and Yellow Feather-moss. Hawthorn and Blackthorn scrub is common, and Common Juniper thrives locally. The diversity of plants is mirrored by that of invertebrates, which favour the open, well-drained conditions of calcareous sites, particularly where there is a good diversity of structure within the vegetation.

In Breckland, the dry climate and lack of fertility of the wind-blown sands have shaped a chalk grassland that is more akin to the continental steppes. Frost-sorting (repeated freeze-thaw cycles that sort small stones according to size, resulting in patterned ground) following the last glaciation has formed a patchwork of grassland and heath. Distinctive smooth, grey-green patches indicate plentiful reindeer lichens, while close inspection of the broken turf of Sheep's-fescue, Wild Thyme and Mouse-ear-hawkweed reveals tiny spring-flowering annuals such as Parsley-piert, Thyme-leaved Sandwort, Early Forget-me-not and Little Mouse-ear.

In contrast, the oceanic climate of southern and western coastal fringes, where most hard limestone is found, favours species such as Carline Thistle, Yellow-wort, Black Medick, rock-roses and squills. On shattered, rocky outcrops conditions are often quite disturbed, and annuals such as Fern-grass and Early Gentian (which is endemic to the UK) are found. The Irish limestone grasslands of the Burren have more affinity with Upland Calcareous Grassland.

Noar Hill, Hampshire – chalk grassland is characterized by species such as Stemless Thistle, Horseshoe Vetch and Squinancywort, and can support rarities such as Chalk Milkwort, Bastard Toadflax, Chalk Eyebright and Common Juniper.

Similar habitats

Transitions occur with Mixed Scrub and Beech and Yew Woods in particular. In Breckland, chalk grassland is found with Lowland Dry Heath (*page 130*). Limestone Heath (*page 139*) includes plants characteristic of Lowland Calcareous Grassland.

Origins and development

Chalk and limestone grassland is the product of millennia of livestock grazing following woodland clearance that started in the Mesolithic, and may have focussed on the relatively sparse, well-drained woodland of limestone. Changing agricultural pressures meant that grassland was increasingly ploughed up from about 1700 onwards, although much remained until the mid-20th century, after which destruction accelerated. Now, of a habitat type that used to dominate whole landscapes, only scattered pockets are left on slopes too steep to plough or in areas whose military use precluded modern agricultural practices. Grassland on remaining sites has often succeeded to Mixed Scrub, partly due to the impact of myxomatosis on Rabbit populations. Outright habitat loss has mostly been stemmed, but there has been a notable decline in characteristic species in recent years.

EXTENT IN KM²

Eng	490
Wal	7
Sco	7
NI	9
Ire	14

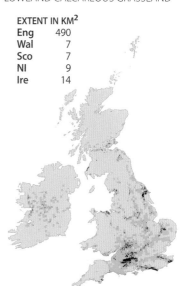

Distribution and extent

Largely confined to southern England, the north and south coast of Wales and central Ireland. Map shows the broad distribution of the Annex I habitat in pale green (H6210); darker shading shows actual locations, drawn from satellite data (LCM 2015) and other sources. Estimates for the extents are based on the Annex I reporting for H6210. Chalk grassland only occurs in north-west Europe and the UK holds a significant proportion; it is found from Dorset, through Wiltshire (Salisbury Plain) and Hampshire into the South Downs, the North Downs, East Anglia and north to the Yorkshire Wolds. Limestone grassland is found on the western and southern coastal strips, notably in Dorset, around Torbay in Devon, on the Burren, the Isle of Wight, the Gower and St. Orme's Head, as well as in the Mendips, the Cotswolds and the central plain of Ireland.

TOP: **Ballard Down, Dorset** – un-grazed chalk grassland on cliff slopes, kept short on the cliff top by exposure and the thin, friable soil, develops into a taller sward farther back and includes Nottingham Catchfly. BOTTOM: **The Manger, near Uffington, Wiltshire** – a dry chalk valley the rippled sides of which were created by retreating permafrost during the last glaciation.

Conservation

Conservation management generally aims to create a structurally diverse sward that includes short areas on south- and west-facing slopes. Low intensity sheep or cattle (also Rabbit) grazing is mostly preferred but, unfortunately, agricultural policies do not necessarily favour appropriate stocking rates. Fragmentation is a real concern and in some areas is being addressed through projects to re-create and reconnect sites – Lowland Calcareous Grassland may otherwise be facing extinction debt (the likely future loss of species as a consequence of past habitat loss). It is not yet clear how the impacts of climate change will manifest, but connecting more areas of habitat will increased the ability of species to respond.

Over 30 of Britain's butterfly species occur on chalk grassland, and at some sites still occur in great numbers. The blues are particularly associated with this habitat, with five species and many thousands of individuals flying at exceptional sites. Each of the key chalk grassland butterfly species has different habitat requirements, as summarized in the following table:

Species	Main Food Plant	Calcareous Grassland Preferences
Silver-spotted Skipper	Sheep's-fescue	Hot, sun-baked chalk grassland, short turf, often steep south-facing scarp
Lulworth Skipper	Tor Grass	Dense mature clumps of Tor-grass at least 20 cm tall
Small Blue	Kidney Vetch	Sheltered grassland with a mix of short turf and taller plants
Brown Argus	Common Rock-rose	Short vegetation on steep south-facing downs, banks or earthworks
Chalkhill Blue	Horseshoe Vetch	Short, open grassland
Adonis Blue	Horseshoe Vetch	Short, sun-baked turf
Large Blue	Thyme	Closely grazed grassland, warm (often south-facing)
Duke of Burgundy	Cowslips or Primroses	Warm pockets of grassland among scrub, medium sward height
Marsh Fritillary	Devil's-bit Scabious	Chalk grassland with a short-medium sward, often on south-facing slopes
Marbled White	Red Fescue	Tall, unimproved grassland

Eggardon Hill Fort, Dorset – the best habitat is often found where the ground is steep, well-drained and thin-soiled, such as on scarps and ancient earthworks. It can also develop in disused limestone quarries and chalk pits, on spoil heaps, road verges and railway cuttings.

CHALK GRASSLAND BLUE BUTTERFLIES FACNG PAGE, LEFT TO RIGHT: **Small Blue**, female; **Large Blue**, female; **Chalkhill Blue**, male. THIS PAGE, RIGHT: **Adonis Blue**, male.

LEFT: The flora of **Breckland** chalk grassland contains a high proportion of rarities, including Spanish Catchfly (shown here), Purple-stem Cat's-tail, Spiked Speedwell, and Maiden Pink. RIGHT: **Cressbrook Dale, Peak District** – Scrub is an integral part of most Lowland Calcareous Grassland, and is of particular importance to breeding birds and invertebrates, some of which are dependent upon scrub-edge microhabitats. Transitional scrubby vegetation can host uncommon and rare plants such as Bloody Crane's-bill or Lizard Orchid.

What to look for

The tremendous abundance of plant species in Lowland Calcareous Grassland is possibly due in part to the sparseness of the woodland that colonized the thin soils after the last glaciation, which perhaps allowed species requiring open conditions to persist. A long list of scarce and rare species may be found, many of which are particularly attractive or intriguing, such as Pasqueflower, Round-headed Rampion, Monkey Orchid and the spider orchids.

Bare areas and short swards on south-facing slopes are often excellent places to look for insects. Sites with good structural and botanical diversity are best for insects. Over-wintering species use taller tussocks for shelter, while butterflies, bees and hoverflies need flowering plants for nectar and pollen, and some craneflies rely on the leaf-litter underneath scrub. Still, sunny days are best for seeing invertebrates, but around July, a night-time visit might reveal Glow-worms; the flightless females of this beetle give off a soft yellowish-green light at night to attract a mate. Birds are more limited, but look out for Skylark, Corn Bunting, and in Breckland and at some Wiltshire sites, Stone-curlew. Keen bryologists may wish to look out for the very rare 'southern hepatic mat', an association of leafy liverworts and mosses including Tamarisk Scalewort, Bitter Scalewort and Rough Earwort, which is known from north- to west-facing slopes on a few English chalk and Welsh limestone grasslands.

Fertilized downland swards are of limited wildlife interest but easily identified as they contain far fewer species and include generalists such as Crested Dog's-tail, Yorkshire-fog and White Clover.

Although grasshoppers and crickets are common in this habitat, only the **Rufous Grasshopper** and Stripe-winged Grasshopper are considered to be characteristic of old, species-rich turf.

How to recognize

Typically found in open, rolling landscapes strongly influenced by the underlying limestone or chalk, Lowland Calcareous Grassland is easily identified from a distance by its soft, moss-green colour, which contrasts with the more strident, uniform green of nearby improved grassland. The sward appears more textured and has scrubby patches, and is typically found on steep slopes. In summer, the short, springy turf is alive with butterflies and the air is scented with aromatic herbs and alive with sound of grasshoppers and crickets. This rich diversity is on a small scale, and often merits getting down on hands and knees so that the more diminutive species are not missed.

Chalk grassland has an ancient feel, and is often found on prehistoric burial mounds, hill forts and trackways. Today, the notion of settled pastoralism evoked by chalk landscapes is often tempered by the close proximity of urban centres and the effects of cultural eutrophication. By comparison, the limestone sites of exposed coasts feel wilder, while the desolate flat grass-heaths of Breckland have their own special quality.

When to visit

April–August for flowering plants and invertebrates, depending on species (the extremely rare Fringed Gentian has been overlooked in the past because it flowers in the autumn).

Did you know?

Salisbury Plain is the largest area of chalk grassland in Europe. Extending to more than 21,000 ha, it contains over half the Lowland Calcareous Grassland in the UK.

Lowland Calcareous Grassland sites can be important for a wide diversity of orchids – **1** Burnt Orchid, **2** Frog Orchid, **3** Early Spider-orchid, **4** Bee Orchid, **5** Pyramidal Orchid, **6** Chalk Fragrant-orchid.

Lowland Dry Acid Grassland is found on acid soils derived from sandstone and igneous rocks, and on sands and gravels, and varies across the country according to climate and soil characteristics.

Sometimes called lichen-heath or grass-heath, parched acid grassland is found in Breckland, the Suffolk Sandlings, the New Forest, the Dorset heaths and the Wealden heaths. It is the most species-rich acid grassland type, containing up to 25 species per square metre, many of which are uncommon, including Mossy Stonecrop, Annual Knawel, Bur Medick, Clustered Clover and Smooth Cat's-ear. In the more humid south-west, parched acid grassland gives way to species-poor swards dominated by Bristle Bent, particularly where humid heathland has been burnt. In the moister north and west, the sward tends to be tighter and quite species-poor, although the border hills of Powys and Shropshire contain some species-rich examples. In Scotland, Lowland Dry Acid Grassland can occur on rock outcrops in the hills and on shingle river banks.

Lowland Dry Acid Grassland is important for specialist invertebrates. Dry sandy patches in particular support ground-dwelling and burrowing invertebrates such as solitary bees and wasps, and very rare species such as Field Cricket. Good habitat includes taller swards where flowering plants provide nectar and pollen and south-facing banks that provide warm nesting and basking areas. A little scrub adds to the range of niches; however, where grazing has ceased, encroaching Bracken and scrub can smother the distinctive grassland species.

Similar habitats

Often found in a mosaic with Lowland Dry Heath, transitional vegetation between the two is common. It can grade into wetter grassland types (look for Purple Moor-grass and Sharp-flowered Rush) and coastal grass (with Red Fescue, Buck's-horn Plantain and maritime species such as Thrift). In Breckland, abrupt transitions to chalk grassland create 'stone stripes' (see *page 166*).

Middebere and Stoborough Heath, Dorset – a patchwork of Heather and Lowland Dry Acid Grassland in an area that was cultivated briefly in the mid-20th century, and is now reverting to heathland (INSET). Cat's-ear, Sweet Vernal-grass and bent grasses characterize a lightly grazed sward in July. Earlier in the season, Suffocated Clover, Clustered Clover and Subterranean Clover can be seen on the track.

Origins and development

Lowland Dry Acid Grassland is an intrinsic part of heathland landscapes. From the Mesolithic onwards it developed where Lowland Dry Oak and Birch Wood was felled and heathers were excluded through heavy grazing, spasmodic cultivation or other disturbance. The relative proportions of heathland and grassland in extensive heathland landscapes have probably always fluctuated according to changes in agricultural economic and social pressures. However, the second half of the 20th century saw significant losses in both habitats through agricultural intensification and extensive use of what was considered to be unproductive land for afforestation and urban development.

Conservation

The area of Lowland Dry Acid Grassland is still reducing, and declines in butterflies and specialist plant species within extant grassland are ongoing (despite much of it being designated or managed as nature reserves). The decline in plant species-richness has been linked to increased acidification through atmospheric pollution. Efforts have been made to restore and expand the habitat, although it is unlikely to be prioritized over heathland. Generally used as pasture (but also found on golf courses and airfields), almost all Lowland Dry Acid Grassland needs grazing (or cutting) to maintain its distinctive flora and invertebrate fauna. Changing agricultural policies and economics have seen a decline in traditional grazing, resulting in scrub and Bracken encroachment. Conservation of this habitat depends on the restoration of functioning pastoral landscapes.

What to look for

In very early spring listen out for one of the loveliest sounds of the lowlands: the spiralling, liquid song of the Woodlark. The eerie whistling of the Stone-curlew is a sound peculiar to dawn and dusk on Breckland grass heaths. Characteristic butterflies

EXTENT IN KM^2

Eng	201
Wal	360
Sco	43
NI	7
Ire	n/k

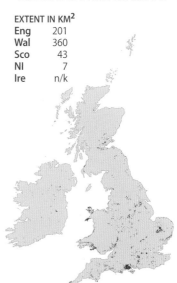

Distribution and extent

Scattered, mainly in England and Wales. The habitat occurs widely throughout north-western Europe; Britain may hold a significant proportion of European parched acid grassland. Pale shading indicates the broad distribution of the Annex I habitat (H2330, which is inland dunes and therefore very restricted); darker shading shows actual locations, drawn from various sources including satellite imagery (LCM 2015).

RIGHT: **East Wretham Heath, Norfolk** – many areas of Breckland were managed as Rabbit warrens from the 12th until the early 20th centuries. Rabbit grazing is encouraged as it can maintain the short, disturbed sward required by many Breckland specialities.

include Small Copper, Grayling and Green Hairstreak. In Breckland look out for a classic suite of rare species including Spiked Speedwell, Sand Catchfly and Perennial Knawel.

How to recognize

Short, dry grassland found within heathland landscapes is likely to be Lowland Dry Acid Grassland. It can be found along tracks and around outcrops on sites otherwise dominated by Heather, but also forms extensive areas in its own right. Also look out for it on commons, in ancient parkland, on coastal grasslands and stable shingle.

Lowland Dry Acid Grassland is characterized by a short, open sward of fine grasses, mosses and reindeer lichens scattered with tiny ephemeral annual plants such as Early Hair-grass, Shepherd's Cress, and Common Stork's-bill, and often forms transitions with heathland vegetation. In the spring it can take on a distinctive red sheen created by thousands of flowering stems of Sheep's Sorrel. In summer it burns off and by August the turf becomes brown and scrunches underfoot.

When to visit

March–April is best for Woodlark and Stone-curlew, April–July for a characteristic suite of plants (flowering times vary within this period).

1 **Brockenhurst, Hampshire** – in the New Forest, look out for dry 'lawns' kept tightly grazed by ponies. Such areas are worth searching for uncommon plants such as Hairy Bird's-foot-trefoil and Smooth Cat's-ear, and in the autumn and winter you might see the distinctive and rare Nail Fungus on pony dung. **2** **East Wretham Heath, Norfolk** – The characteristic red sheen of **Sheep's Sorrel** in flower. **3** Other species in the sward include **Early Hair-grass, Biting Stonecrop, Smooth Hawk's-beard, Common Whitlowgrass, Little Mouse-ear**, the reindeer lichens *Cladonia ciliata* and *C. portentosa*, and **Broom Fork-moss**.

Lowland Meadow and Pasture

page 391

Lowland Meadow and Pasture is generally found in moist conditions on deep neutral clay and loam soils. This habitat type includes flood meadows and water meadows that are found on the floodplains of large rivers (including the Shannon, Thames, Yorkshire Ouse, Trent and Severn), as well as on stream floodplains, and are periodically subject to inundation during the winter. On moist but not waterlogged soils, characteristic grasses include Red Fescue and Crested Dog's-tail, which are dependent upon adequate surface drainage during the growing season. Where the water-table remains high throughout the summer and around springs and seepages, Marsh-marigold and small sedges are typical. On more freely draining soils, clovers, buttercups, Yellow-rattle, Rough Hawkbit and Common Knapweed can form very herb-rich vegetation. Churchyards, road verges and railway embankments can also support this type of vegetation.

Lowland Meadow and Pasture provides habitat for a wide range of invertebrates, including butterflies, grasshoppers and Yellow Meadow Ant, and many support strong populations of common species. The abundance of nectar sources means that meadows can be important for threatened bumblebees, and associated features such as paths, banks, livestock dung and flushes add to the diversity of species present. However, only a handful of specialists are found. Corncrake, once a common denizen of hay

EXTENT IN KM²

Eng	16
Wal	<1
Sco	n/k
NI	n/k
Ire	2

Corfe Meadows, Dorset – old, undisturbed hay meadows can be very rich in herbs (up to 90% cover).

Distribution and extent

Widely but very sparsely distributed. Pale shading indicates the distribution of the Annex I habitat (H6510); darker shading shows actual locations, drawn from a range of sources (which may overestimate the extent, particularly for England). Extent figures drawn from the Annex I reporting for H6510.

meadows, has been banished by modern farming practices to the Hebrides (although reintroductions have now taken place).

Similar habitats

Lowland Meadow and Pasture can grade into Purple Moor-grass and Rush Pasture in wetter areas or into Lowland Acid or Calcareous Grassland (depending on the substrate) in drier areas.

Origins and development

The pre-Neolithic landscape probably contained clearing, glades and floodplains which supported the species that are now associated with Lowland Meadow and Pasture. These areas were expanded through forest clearance and drained where necessary. From the Iron Age onwards, grasslands were used for making hay (see *page 161*) and by the 13th century most floodplains were probably managed as meadows. However, since 1935, 97% of Lowland Meadow and Pasture has been lost, largely through agricultural improvement or gravel extraction, but also through neglect and unsuitable mowing regimes. A tiny fraction has survived, generally where older farmers resisted modern intensification, or where common rights or multiple ownerships thwarted change. The remaining habitat is now highly fragmented; most sites are under 10 ha and occur in isolation. Put together, the remaining lowland meadows would occupy an area 1/10th the size of Greater London. However, a slight increase was recorded in the first decade of the 21st century, thought to be due to re-creation projects.

Conservation

Early conservation legislation did little to protect Lowland Meadow and Pasture, perhaps because it was so enmeshed in the farmed landscape, and only about half of the remaining area is designated. A large proportion of sites is in private ownership, and conservation initiatives are focussing on disseminating information and advice to landowners.

1 **Itchen Stoke, Hampshire**, on the occasion of its first 're-floating'. Water meadows were irrigated from adjacent rivers and streams to encourage early grass growth in the spring. The practice peaked by 1800 but has now largely ceased, although a few sites have been restored and are 'drowned' annually. **2** **Martin's Meadow, Suffolk**. One of three ancient meadows known in Suffolk. A succession of species is seen, from Cowslip and Early-purple Orchid in spring to Meadow Saffron in late August. **3** **Adder's-tongue** – a small fern considered to be an indicator species for ancient meadows and pastures.

What to look for

Rare plants such as Fritillary, Meadow Saffron, Pepper-saxifrage, Dyer's Greenweed and Adder's-tongue can still be found on some sites. Large meadows can support breeding waders.

How to recognize

Lowland Meadow and Pasture is now mostly found tucked away in corners of farms that have for one reason or another escaped agricultural improvement. Meadows are allowed to grow tall and are then cut for hay, whereas pastures are grazed through the summer, but both support a similar assemblage of quite widely distributed species.

Situated on low-lying ground enclosed by hedges, Lowland Meadow and Pasture are bright with Dandelions and Cowslips in spring. By summer, these are overtopped with a medley of other flowers such as Oxeye Daisy, Great Burnet and Meadowsweet, and are busy with invertebrates. Pasture is not as showy as meadow in the summer, but can support large anthills or ancient features such as ridge and furrow or the remains of old settlements.

When to visit

April for Cowslip and Fritillary, June–July for hay meadows in flower.

Did you know?

'Ridge and furrow' topography created by traditional ploughing techniques is often considered to indicate grassland that may be of medieval origin, although in some cases it can date from as recently as the early 19th century.

1 **Clattinger Farm, Wiltshire** – flood meadows are found in river valleys. Often flooded in winter, they are used for grazing and hay cropping and include the iconic Lammas Fritillary meadows of the upper Thames. **2** **Meadow Crane's-bill** – a hay meadow species that has become increasingly restricted to roadsides because of changes in agricultural practices. **3** Wet meadows provide breeding habitat for **Yellow Wagtail**, which can often be seen feeding on insects around the feet of cattle.

Purple Moor-grass and Rush Pasture is found on moist peaty-mineral soils poor in nutrients on the better-drained margins of wetlands where it is not regularly flooded. In the south-west of England and Wales, north-west Ireland and locally in south-west Scotland, it is often found with heathy vegetation on more acid soils. In these areas, Compact Rush grows with Meadow Thistle, Tormentil and Cross-leaved Heath in a tussocky sward of Purple Moor-grass. A distinctive and particularly short form is found in the heavily pony-grazed lawns of the New Forest. In the north of England and Scotland, cold-sensitive species such as Meadow Thistle are replaced with Globeflower and Marsh Hawk's-beard. Where Purple Moor-grass and Rush Pasture is derived from Lowland Fen on more base-rich soils (*e.g.* in East Anglia, central Ireland), Purple Moor-grass is joined by rhizomatous rushes and sedges such as Blunt-flowered Rush and Lesser Pond-sedge; often mown, it is known as Fen Meadow. A rich sward with Devil's-bit Scabious, Ragged-Robin, Marsh-marigold and other herbs flourishes where the rush and sedge cover allows, sometimes overtopped by tall-herb fen species such as Wild Angelica and Meadowsweet.

Throughout the cool and wet west, acidic peats support a much more widespread type of rush pasture typified by abundant Soft Rush and/or Sharp-flowered Rush with species such as Greater Bird's-foot-trefoil and Marsh Bedstraw. This community is often found in patches where drainage is impeded within improved pasture, and is of limited interest for wildlife.

Similar habitats

This habitat can show similarities to wetlands, heathlands and drier grasslands. Fen Meadow is related to Lowland Fen but occurs on drained or drier soils where traditional management has created a species-rich sward.

Rackenford and Knowstone Moor, Devon – Purple Moor-grass can form distinctive tussocks where grazing levels are low. A patchwork of short swards and taller tussocks is ideal for Marsh Fritillary (butterfly).

Origins and development

Purple Moor-grass and Rush Pasture supports a distinctive vegetation type that was originally derived from wetland vegetation through grazing and/or annual mowing for livestock fodder and bedding, and can be ancient. Much Purple Moor-grass and Rush Pasture of conservation interest has been lost through agricultural improvement. Some of this loss is recent – almost 50% of Culm Grassland was destroyed in the last two decades of the 20th century.

Conservation

Britain and Ireland hold a significant proportion of the European resource of relatively species-rich Purple Moor-grass and Rush Pasture. Conservation effort it focussed on linking fragmented sites and reinstating appropriate grazing regimes, particularly where populations of Marsh Fritillary butterfly are present or nearby.

What to look for

Look out for butterflies (particularly Marsh Fritillary) and Narrow-bordered Bee-hawkmoth. Orchids can include Heath Spotted-orchid and Lesser Butterfly-orchid, and Whorled Caraway may be present. Other species to look for are breeding Curlew and Snipe, Common Frog and Grass Snake.

EXTENT IN KM^2

Eng	25
Wal	5
Sco	1
NI	35
Ire	6

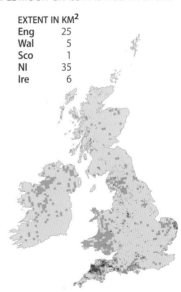

Distribution and extent

Widespread in the lowlands, particularly in the west; extending east in England where the soils are wetter. Pale shading indicates the broad distribution for the Annex I habitat (H6410); darker shading (all areas apart from Northern Ireland) shows actual locations.

Cefn Bryn, Gower – Purple Moor-grass and Rush Pasture forms transitions with Lowland Wet and Dry Heath on the Gower commons, where management includes grazing, Bracken control and mowing firebreaks.

1 Purple Moor-grass and Rush Pasture scattered with Heath Spotted-orchid. **2** Marsh Fritillary – the gregarious larvae, which feed on Devil's-bit Scabious, spin protective webs that are easily seen in late summer. Threatened across Europe, this species is restricted to Purple Moor-grass and Rush Pasture and Lowland Calcareous Grassland on chalk sites. **3** Heath Spotted-orchid and **4** Lesser Butterfly-orchid – in the more oceanic south-west, Atlantic species such as this, Lesser Skullcap, Ivy-leaved Bellflower and Wavy St. John's-wort (absent from Ireland) can be found. **5** Meadow thistle – a classic species of Purple Moor-grass and Rush Pasture.

How to recognize

Purple Moor-grass and Rush Pasture is a damp type of grassland found within the enclosed agricultural landscape, on unenclosed common land or as part of Lowland Fen. It is generally grazed and sometimes mown for hay.

Although not as colourful as Lowland Meadow and Pasture, it can be species-rich and has its own distinctive character. The thick, tussocky sward of rushes and coarse grasses can be specked yellow with Meadow Buttercup in the spring and purple a little later with Devil's-bit Scabious, Meadow Thistle, Water Mint, Selfheal and vetches – and may include scarce species such as Whorled Caraway. Some areas of Fen Meadow (*e.g.* in the East Anglian fens) support tall herbs such as Meadowsweet. In the west it is a key habitat for the threatened Marsh Fritillary butterfly.

When to visit

Late May–early July for Marsh Fritillary; summer for a suite of interesting plants.

Did you know?
Culm Grassland is the term given to Purple Moor-grass and Rush Pasture overlying the Culm Measures of north Devon and north-east Cornwall. Rhôs Pasture refers to similar vegetation in Wales, while the East Anglian fen meadows are sometimes known as Litter.

3

4

5

Coastal and Floodplain Grazing Marsh page 391

Coastal and Floodplain Grazing Marsh is grassland that is seasonally flooded or has a high water-table. It is dependent on hydrology, topography and management rather than vegetation or substrate type (which can be alluvial or peat soil). Grazing Marsh that is extensively flooded with shallow water (<50 cm) throughout the winter can support huge numbers of wintering wildfowl. The most diverse assemblages are found where there are a range of conditions suitable for dabbling, diving and grazing species. Marshes with a mixture of tussocky vegetation, short turf and long grass also provide good nesting habitat for a variety of waterfowl. Where the water-table remains within about 20 cm of the surface, it pushes invertebrates to the surface and the ground remains soft, ideal for probing waders (although areas under water for prolonged periods become deplete of invertebrate prey).

Almost all Grazing Marsh has experienced some degree of agricultural improvement and less than 5% of marshes in the UK are semi-natural. The sward is often species-poor, dominated by Perennial Rye-grass, Yorkshire-fog and rushes, although inundated areas can support characteristic communities with Creeping Bent, Marsh Foxtail, Floating Sweet-grass and Silverweed. The few remaining unimproved sites are often too small to support significant bird populations.

EXTENT IN KM^2

Eng	2,181
Wal	802
Sco	n/k
NI	200
Ire	n/k

Aldeburgh, Suffolk – shallow winter flooding provides ideal habitat for wintering waterfowl in the RSPB's North Warren reserve.

Distribution and extent

Found along the lower reaches of lowland rivers and on low-lying coasts. Map shows known locations (no data for Northern Ireland). Figures for extent are very approximate.

Similar habitats

Grazing Marsh often adjoins Lowland Fen and Reedbed but does not support extensive patches of tall-herbs and reeds. Saltmarsh, present just over the seawall on most coastal grazing marsh sites, supports very different vegetation. Purple Moor-grass and Rush Pasture tends to be on more sloping ground that does not experience regular flooding.

Origins and development

Most Grazing Marsh was created through the embankment and drainage of floodplain and coastal marshes from medieval times onwards. Embanked washlands were created for the purpose of floodwater storage, notably in the East Anglian Fens in the 17th century. Some floodplain marshes owe their existence to the ongoing management of water flow and ditch levels in otherwise well-drained floodplains, which allows water to be retained in the summer to provide drinking water, lush grazing swards and wet fences for livestock. Most grazing marshes are grazed, usually by cattle, and some are cut for hay or silage.

Conservation

Much of Britain and Ireland's grazing marsh has been lost in the past century, generally through drainage and conversion to cereal production. Remaining marshes are often too dry, too heavily grazed or cut too early/frequently to support significant populations of breeding waders; most species have declined severely in the last few decades. Conservation management focusses on providing a range of conditions and is dependent on the ability to regulate water levels and stocking densities. A more strategic approach to restoration is beginning to see wetland recreation in whole river catchments. In some places on the sinking east coast of England, marshland will be lost as sea defences are realigned, and some of its value is seen in its potential for the re-creation of other wetland types.

1 **River Ant and Ant Marshes, Norfolk** – a wetland landscape including embanked Floodplain Grazing Marsh, Reedbed and Lowland Fen. **2** **Wareham Marshes, Dorset** – floodplain grazing marsh in the valley of the River Frome. **3** **Tinker's Marsh, Walberswick, Suffolk** – light cattle-grazing has created a diverse sward structure and range of microhabitats.

1 Icelandic **Black-tailed Godwits** spend the winter in the UK and feed on mudflats. They switch to wet grassland as their food is depleted on the estuaries before returning to Iceland to breed. **2** **White-fronted Goose** – most grazing wildfowl prefer short grass (< 15 cm) and grazing can be managed to achieve this. **3** **Lapwing** is the breeding wader most commonly found on Coastal and Floodplain Grazing Marsh. It requires a short sward, and is less dependent upon wet conditions than other species. **4** Summer flooding can disrupt traditional management such as grazing and cutting for hay.

What to look for

During the winter months Grazing Marshes can draw spectacularly large flocks of waterfowl, many migrating from northern Europe, including Bewick's Swan, Whooper Swan, Teal, Bean Goose, Brent Goose, Wigeon, and Golden Plover. In the spring, several species of breeding wader can be seen: look for Lapwing tumbling overhead, listen out for the eerie drumming of snipe, and search for the scarce Black-tailed Godwit. Other scarce breeding species include the secretive Garganey (look in vegetation around pool edges), Spotted Crake and Yellow Wagtail (which favours cattle-grazed areas). Cranes occur in some east-coast sites, and their astonishing trumpeting calls can also be heard in the Somerset Levels and Moors, where they have been reintroduced. Floodwater provides protection from terrestrial predators, but not from birds of prey such as Marsh Harrier and Peregrine, which are drawn by the large numbers of waterfowl, while Barn Owl and Kestrel hunt for small mammals.

Although hundreds of plant and invertebrate species have been recorded from Grazing Marsh, the invertebrate and plant interest is mostly associated with ditches (see Ditch) rather than the grassland itself. However, Grazing Marsh supports a range of invertebrates including ground beetles, snails and the adult forms of many species (such as dragonflies) whose larval forms are aquatic. Dragonflies strongly associated with drainage ditches in Grazing Marsh are Scarce Emerald, Variable Damselfly, Norfolk Hawker, and Hairy Dragonfly (which can tolerate brackish conditions). Scarce plants such as Sea Clover, Slender Hare's-ear and Divided Sedge can be found on coastal sites where there is a brackish influence.

TOP: **Black-poplar** – Pollarded willows and Black-poplar, whose branches have a distinctive droopy shape, are characteristic features of floodplains. BOTTOM: **Cliffe Marshes, Kent** – a typically flat and expansive Coastal Grazing Marsh adjacent to the Thames.

How to recognize

Coastal and Floodplain Grazing Marsh is found on low-lying, wet ground in the valleys of slow-flowing rivers and along estuaries and on low-lying coasts. It is often behind sea walls where Saltmarsh has been 'reclaimed' from the sea and converted into pasture, or behind natural barriers such as sand dunes and in places, the sinuous curves of old saltmarsh creeks can still be visible. Earlier sea walls are found inland where coastal marshes have been progressively enlarged.

Ditches, seasonally wet hollows and pools can be teeming with invertebrates and rich in plants, far more so than the grassland, which has generally been agriculturally 'improved' and is, in itself, of little interest.

It is the birds that really define Grazing Marsh. In winter huge flocks of ducks, geese, and swans congregate on the wide, open expanses of flooded grazing marshes, while in the spring waders nest and probe in the damp grassland.

When to visit

October–March For wintering waterfowl, mid-March–June for breeding waders.

Did you know?

Of an estimated 1,200,000 ha of wet grassland (all types) found historically in England and Wales, only 300,000 survived until the 1930s, and only 100,000 ha now hold significant bird populations.

1 **Scarce Chaser** – found from May until early August in lowland floodplains and water meadows in southern England. Its habitat requirements include ditches with thick emergent vegetation and nearby scrub. **2** **Cuckooflower** – a distinctive spring flower often found in less improved Grazing Marsh. **3** **Mousetail** – a distinctive and scarce annual (flowering May–July) of seasonally flooded, poached gateways and ruts that persist on Grazing Marsh.

Holkham Freshmarsh, Norfolk is famous for wintering waterbirds. It was also the place where Spoonbills started breeding again in the UK, in 2010.

Upland Calcareous Grassland

page 392

Upland Calcareous Grassland occurs mainly on limestones and basic metamorphic schists, generally above about 300 m. High rainfall means that the soils are more leached than those of Lowland Calcareous Grassland and, as a consequence, some of the more exacting calcicoles of southern grasslands are absent, while those that favour more acidic conditions, such as Mat-grass, Tormentil and even a little Heather, are found. The total area of the habitat is less than the distribution of calcareous bed-rock would indicate, as its influence is often limited by deposits of boulder clay or thick glacial drift.

The vegetation varies according to soil characteristics, climate and altitude. On Carboniferous limestone (*e.g.* the Morecambe Bay area, the Craven Dales, Upper Teesdale, the Burren and the Dartry Mountains in Co. Sligo/Leitrim), Blue Moor-grass dominates in a short, species-rich sward that includes Limestone Bedstraw and Common Rock-rose. It is typically found on skeletal soils where there is no glacial drift obscuring the underlying limestone, and can include a number of rarities. On more mature, but still fairly base-rich soils covering large areas of hillsides, less calcicolous species (*e.g.* Common Bent, Selfheal, Harebell and Glittering Wood-moss) join Sheep's-fescue and Wild Thyme. Over about 600 m in the cool, wet climate of

EXTENT IN KM²	
Eng	3
Wal	1
Sco	46
NI	<1
Ire	6

Near **Slieve Carron, Co. Clare**. The dry calcareous grasslands of the Burren support Arctic-alpine species such as Spring Gentian and Mountain Avens, together with Mediterranean species like Hoary Rock-rose and Dense-flowered Orchid.

Distribution and extent

Scattered across the uplands. Pale shading indicates broad extent of the relevant Annex I habitats (H6210 and H6230); darker shading shows actual locations, drawn from various sources including satellite imagery (LCM 2015).

the Lake District and the Highlands (but lower in north-west Scotland), Alpine Lady's-mantle becomes abundant, often joined by Viviparous Fescue, Pill Sedge and Arctic-alpines. Species-rich swards found on more siliceous rocks, particularly in the western Highlands, are often considered with this habitat, and include tall mesotrophic herbs such as Wild Angelica, Wood Crane's-bill and Wood Avens.

Under the particular climatic conditions of the north of Scotland and the Burren, a procumbent dwarf shrub, Mountain Avens, dominates in a characteristic community with Glaucous Sedge, Sheep's-fescue, Fairy Flax, Ribwort Plantain, Sea Plantain and tufts of mosses. In places it is joined by other dwarf-shrubs such as Bearberry, Crowberry, Creeping Willow and Bell Heather. This community is found on strongly calcareous, skeletal soils and wind-blown shell sand from just above sea level to about 450 m; although found a low altitudes, it is sub-montane in character.

Similar habitats

Upland Calcareous Grassland often grades into more species-poor Upland Acid Grassland. At high altitudes the addition of Moss Campion and an array of rare Arctic-alpines indicate a montane dwarf-shrub community (see High Montane Heath and Snow-bed, *page 208*), and un-grazed swards can support typical Mountain Ledge species such as Wild Angelica.

Origins and development

Most Upland Calcareous Grassland types were derived through prehistoric clearance of woodland and subsequent livestock grazing. Mountain Avens heath is a surviving example of the type of vegetation that developed across Britain on base-rich, gravelly soils left behind as the ice retreated after the last glaciation, and was subsequently out-competed by more robust herbs, and then scrub and trees. It could probably persist naturally due to exposure and the harsh climate on the north coast of Scotland, but is dependent upon grazing in more sheltered areas.

Conservation

In common with most of the uplands, Upland Calcareous Grassland is usually heavily sheep-grazed, and many sites would benefit from a relaxation in grazing pressure. However, without grazing, most Upland Calcareous Grasslands would succeed to herb-rich Upland Mixed Ash Wood, with the loss of

TOP: **Yewbarrow, Cumbria** – swards of **Blue Moor-grass**, the shiny purple-blue panicles of which (BOTTOM) are conspicuous in April and May, are often on steep slopes under limestone crags, or among rocky outcrops.

characteristic species. Conservation grazing with hardy cattle is used in some key areas to achieve a balance. As Mountain Avens heath is more accessible than other types of Upland Calcareous Grassland, it has suffered more from conversion to improved pasture.

What to look for

Arctic-alpines and other plants to look out for include Spring Sandwort, Hoary Whitlowgrass, Alpine Forget-me-not, Alpine Pearlwort, Shrubby Cinquefoil, Spring Gentian, and Limestone Bedstraw. Look out for Bird's-eye Primrose, Scottish Asphodel and False Sedge in flushed areas. The invertebrate fauna is not as rich as that associated with Lowland Calcareous Grassland, but in June, keep an eye out for Northern Brown Argus (the larvae feed on Common Rock-rose). Skylark, Wheatear and Lapwing nest in Upland Calcareous Grassland.

This habitat type includes the famous Teesdale assemblage of plants that is found on metamorphosed 'sugar' limestone and comprises both Arctic-alpines (at only 350–353 m) and lowland species. It includes Teesdale Sandwort and Teesdale Violet (both unique to Teesdale), Spring Gentian (also found in the Burren), Hair Sedge, False Sedge, Scottish Asphodel, Alpine Bartsia (also found in the Highlands) and Dwarf Milkwort and Hoary Rock-rose (also found farther south).

How to recognize

Moist, dense and springy, or sparse and summer-parched over crumbly rock, Upland Calcareous Grassland comprises a sward of fine grasses such as Sheep's-fescue starred with Wild Thyme and other small herbs. In upland limestone country it is a key component of the landscape, but also occurs in patches around outcrops of basic rocks or flushed areas in siliceous landscapes. Since it is favoured by livestock, it is generally hard-grazed; so much so that in many places plants rarely flower and the short, green swards free of plant litter often stand out against the surrounding vegetation. Where grazing is less intense, its intrinsic species-richness becomes more apparent.

When to visit

May to July for flowering plants (a little earlier for Spring Gentian) before more parched swards burn off.

Did you know?
Genetic analysis of Fringed Sandwort from Ben Bulben in Co. Sligo has shown that the species survived the last glaciation in situ.

1 Balnakiel, Sutherland – Mountain Avens heath is now one of the rarest vegetation types in Britain and Ireland. It can contain many rarities, including Scottish Primrose, Arctic Sandwort and Dark-red Helleborine. **Mountain Avens** was so widespread towards the end of last glaciation that three time periods were named Dryas after its scientific name. **2 Ben Lawers, Perthshire.** In the cool, wet Highlands **Alpine Lady's-mantle** can become so abundant that the community is referred to as grass-heath rather than grassland. **3 Bird's-eye Primrose** at Ingleborough, North Yorkshire.

Northern Hay Meadow page 391

Northern Hay Meadow is found on brown earth soils in a cool, submontane climate on level or gently sloping sites between about 200 and 400 m where non-intensive hay meadow management has been carried out. Hay meadow vegetation can also be found along river banks and on road verges. A variety of grasses is found throughout, but none is dominant overall, and it is the abundance and diversity of herbs that is distinctive. Typical species include Sweet Vernal-grass, various lady's-mantles, Yellow-rattle, Water Avens and less common plants such as Melancholy Thistle and Globeflower. The mix of northern species (*e.g.* Wood Crane's-bill) and southern species (*e.g.* Great Burnet) is also distinctive. The best meadows support up to 120 species and around 30 species per square metre.

The flora has been shaped by the practice of hay-making and the associated grazing, liming and manuring of the sward. The regular removal of vegetation excludes more robust, coarse species that would out-compete the finer grasses and herbs. Applications of farmyard manure and lime offset the loss of nutrients and gradual leaching of the soils and maintain relatively fertile conditions. Variation between fields is common and is often due to differences in farming practices, particularly the timing of the hay cut. Although hay meadows provide abundant nectar for invertebrates, the radical change brought about by cutting is inimical to many species, and there is only a limited fauna adapted to the conditions. They can, however, provide nesting sites for birds such as Yellow Wagtail and Lapwing, and Snipe and Redshank can breed in damp flushes.

Similar habitats

The flora is similar to that found on calcareous mountain ledges, although these also contain Arctic-alpines, and some characteristic species are also found in the ground flora of Upland Mixed Ash Wood.

Northern Hay Meadow is a very characteristic feature of the Yorkshire Dales. In winter the meadows appear rather dull but in summer a yellow wash creeps gradually up each valley to the cooler valley head, where Meadow Buttercup comes into flower a little later than in the meadows farther down the valley.

Origins and development

Northern Hay Meadow vegetation is probably derived from the post-glacial tall-herb flora that survived in open woodland glades and which is still found on some mountain ledges. Following large-scale woodland clearance, grazing-tolerant versions of this vegetation type were able to expand, and by the Iron Age hay-making was underway. The importance of meadows in providing winter feed for livestock meant that many persisted in the landscape into the second half of the 20th century. Since then, severe losses and degradation have been as a consequence of increased use of artificial fertilizers, a switch to sheep-grazing in the winter, and conversion to silage-based systems in addition to ploughing and reseeding.

Conservation

Agri-environment schemes have targeted species-rich grassland, and have perhaps helped maintain existing meadows, but have had mixed success. Expertise in improving and re-creating flower-rich meadows (*e.g.* using seed collected and spread as 'green hay') is now well-developed and current initiatives are involving the wider community in hay meadow conservation through diverse projects, events and festivals.

EXTENT IN KM²

Eng	9
Sco	1

Distribution and extent

Found in upland valleys in northern England with outliers in Scotland. The floristic composition differs from that of equivalent mountain hay meadows in Europe. Map shows the broad distribution of the Annex I habitat (H6520); darker shading shows actual locations.

The pale sward of recently cut meadows can be picked out along the valley bottom in late July (ARROWED).

What to look for

Look for Bird's-eye Primrose and Grass-of-Parnassus in wet flushes. Orchids can include Early-purple Orchid, Common Spotted-orchid, Frog Orchid, Heath Fragrant-orchid, Common Twayblade and Small-white Orchid. Twite can sometimes be seen feeding on seed heads.

How to recognize

Northern Hay Meadow is found within a distinctive upland landscape of small fields enclosed by stone walls, each often with its own small stone barn. Typically found in the Yorkshire Dales and parts of Durham, Cumbria and Lancashire, it occurs in valley bottoms and on shallow valley slopes, giving way to permanent pasture then open fell above. It is at its best at midsummer, when the yellow sheen of buttercups gradually sweeps along the valley bottoms, reaching the upper meadows by late June. Close-up, the knee-high sward is made up of many different textures and colours, with deep red Common Sorrel, frothy white Pignut, and vivid blue splashes of Wood Crane's-bill. After hay-making, the muted green fields are geometrically patterned with lines left by mowers and balers, and it is no longer easy to distinguish flower-rich meadows from those that are species-poor due to agricultural intensification.

When to visit

June–July for flora.

Did you know?

The characteristic sweet scent of new hay comes from the coumarin found in Sweet Vernal-grass, which is widely used in perfumes, nowadays in synthesized form.

1 Uncut corners are important for invertebrates and plant species intolerant of cutting such as the **Giant Bellflower**. **2** **Wood Crane's-bill** – an iconic species of the Yorkshire Dales hay meadows. Its cup-shaped flowers are more upturned than those of the similar Meadow Crane's-bill. **3** **Dentdale, Cumbria** – a hay meadow prior to cutting. Hay is cut in the summer, often in July, and a run of dry days is required so that it can be dried on the fields.

Upland Rush Pasture

page 392

Upland Rush Pasture is found on soils kept permanently moist by ground or surface water in the upland fringes up to about 400 m. Farther north it is found at lower altitudes, and is common in the Inner Hebrides, but scarce in the Highlands. It usually comprises a grassy sward dotted with varying amounts of Soft Rush and (particularly in the west) Sharp-flowered Rush. Hard Rush is also found where the habitat occurs on limestone (*e.g.* the north Pennines and Craven Dales). Rushes can form separate tussocks or thick swards. The underlying grasses, which can be heavily grazed, include Yorkshire-fog, Creeping Bent, Red Fescue and Sweet Vernal-grass, and there is often a little Creeping Buttercup and other mesophytic herbs such as Common Sorrel and White Clover. On more acidic, peaty soils, Marsh Bedstraw may twine through the rushes. On drier soils, the grassy understorey can resemble Upland Acid Grassland or improved grassland.

Upland Rush Pasture is most notable for the distinctive suite of breeding waders it can support. Curlew, Redshank, Snipe, Lapwing and Oystercatcher all breed where there is a suitable mosaic of rushy tussocks and shorter grassier patches, but each species requires slightly different conditions: for esample, Snipe needs tall, rushy tussocks and damp ground; Lapwing is found in shorter swards and slightly drier conditions; while Redshank prefers short swards with tussocky areas for nesting.

EXTENT IN KM²	
Eng	3,760
Wal	1,373
Sco	9,030
NI	97
Ire	n/k

Gruinart, Islay – sheep grazing rush pasture at sea level.

Distribution and extent

Ubiquitous through the uplands. Map based on satellite data (CORINE) and shows pasture in the uplands, with additional areas in Scotland and Wales added. Extent figures are the combined area of Upland Rush Pasture and Upland Acid Grassland.

Similar habitats

Upland Rush Pasture is often found on the edge of the fells between improved pasture (or Northern Hay Meadow) on flatter ground in valley bottoms and Upland Acid Grassland above the limit of improved grazing. It supports some of the same vegetation types as its lowland counterpart, Purple Moor-grass and Rush Pasture.

Origins and development

Ultimately derived from woodland through clearance and then heavy grazing of the ensuing heathland, Upland Rush Pasture is dependent upon grazing. In many cases, Upland Rush Pasture has been converted through drainage to Upland Acid Grassland, and through subsequent liming and fertilizing to Perennial Rye-grass–Crested Dog's-tail swards. Agricultural intensification after the 1950s, and particularly increases in stocking densities, resulted in a significant decline in the populations of Lapwing, Curlew and Redshank, and the local loss of Snipe.

The stippled brown of rush clumps marks out ❶ Upland Rush Pasture mid-slope, with ❷ Northern Hay Meadow below and ❸ Upland Acid Grassland above.

Conservation

Conservation management of Upland Rush Pastures revolves around ensuring appropriate cover of rushes for breeding waders, usually using light cattle-grazing. Where rushes become too widespread, open areas needed for feeding are lost (and suitability for grazing animals, which maintain the sward, decreases) but where tussocks are very sparse, not enough cover is available for nesting. Swards are often topped in late July, after chicks have fledged, to help prevent the spread of rushes.

What to look for

In addition to breeding waders, look out for Little Owl, which sometimes breeds in stone barns. Merlin, associated with nearby heathland, can occasionally be seen hunting for pipits.

G

Upland Acid Grassland

page 392

Upland Acid Grassland varies between spongy swards of fine grasses rich in mosses and thick, tussocky vegetation of rushes or Purple Moor-grass. Usually found over sandstones, acid igneous rocks or superficial sands and gravels; the specific community type is generally determined by grazing pressure and soil type. On mildly acidic brown earths on the relatively well-drained lower slopes of hillsides, sheep-shorn swards of Sheep's-fescue and Common Bent grasses (or Bristle Bent in the south-west) are speckled with the tiny flowers of Tormentil and Heath Bedstraw, and are springy with branched mosses such as Cypress-leaved Plait-moss, Red-stemmed Heather-moss and Springy Turf-moss. On moist, peatier soils over shallow slopes and on degraded Blanket Bog, dense swards of wiry and unpalatable Mat-grass are widespread. Where the climate is cooler and the peat deeper, Mat-grass is replaced by looser swards of Heath Rush and Common Hair-cap moss, with bog-mosses in the wettest places. Patches of taller rushes are common where the soil is wet year-round. On the peaty hillsides of the western upland fringes, Purple Moor-grass covers huge areas; this vegetation can be quite boggy, and may include Upland Wet Heath species.

Similar habitats

This habitat is linked to the heathland and wetland communities from which it is derived, and may often show transitional characteristics where grazing pressure is reduced. Where soils become base-rich it can merge with forms of Upland Calcareous Grassland, distinguished by the presence of calcicoles such as Wild Thyme, Harebell, Fairy Flax and Quaking-grass.

View from **Knoutberry Hill, Yorkshire Dales** – for many years Cloudberries (known locally as Knoutberries) were missing from this eponymous hill. More recently, changes in grazing pressure have resulted in the widespread return of this species. Here the landscape is patterned with Upland Acid Grassland, Upland Rush Pasture, Blanket Bog and Coniferous Plantation. Upland Dry Heath persists on the railway cutting, and Heather is reappearing within the grassland sward.

Origins and development

Upland Acid Grassland is generally derived from heathland and mire through livestock grazing and often also burning and draining. The increasing predominance of sheep from the 18th century onwards resulted in an increase in the habitat, which continued with the promotion of high stocking rates through agricultural subsidies in the late 20th century. The loss of mixed grazing regimes saw further changes, with an increase in Matgrass (unpalatable to sheep but eaten by cattle). More recently a change in incentives has seen some decreases in stocking levels, and localized return of heathland species.

Conservation

This habitat is valued as part of a cultural landscape resulting from centuries of upland farming. However, with the exception of species-rich variants in flushed conditions, it is usually of less wildlife interest than the habitats it replaces, and is only protected where it falls within sites supporting other vegetation types of conservation interest. Given its ubiquity and impoverished nature, and the reliance on agricultural subsidies to support the upland farming practices that maintain it, there is increasing interest in modifying grazing and burning regimes to restore heathland or scrub and woodland.

EXTENT IN KM^2

Eng	3,760
Wal	1,373
Sco	9,030
NI	97
Ire	n/k

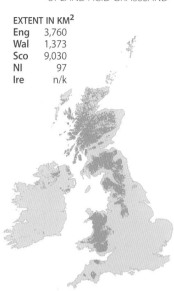

Distribution and extent

Ubiquitous through the uplands. Map derived from satellite data (Landcover) and with additional areas in Scotland and Wales added. Extent figures are the combined area of Upland Rush Pasture and Upland Acid Grassland.

LEFT: **Northern Glyders, Snowdonia** – Upland Acid Grassland covers huge areas of upland Wales, where grassheath mosaics are thought to indicate the impact on Upland Dry Heath of recent increases in sheep numbers.
RIGHT: Looking south-west from **Catbells, Cumbria** – Upland Acid Grassland forms vast areas of rough grazing in the Lake District, where it is much appreciated both as a key part of the landscape and for its amenity value.

What to look for

Species-rich flushes with Mountain Pansy and Grass-of-Parnassus; waxcap fungi on short swards; Mountain Ringlet in the Lake District and Highlands; sparse populations of breeding Curlew and Snipe in tussocky areas; Black Grouse (Wales, Pennines, Scotland) in mosaics with heathland and Mixed Scrub or Coniferous Plantation.

How to recognize

Great swathes of the hill-country of Britain and Ireland are dominated by rather dull Acid Grassland that nonetheless contributes to the overall diversity of the upland landscape.

Beyond the limit of inbye walls, the mossy tones of these unimproved swards contrast with the more luminous green of improved pasture below and (where these are still present) the browner tones of Blanket Bog or the more intense purple-brown of Heather above.

This is an impoverished habitat, but the wide open spaces are heart-lifting, and in summer there is the distinctive mossy, peaty tang of the uplands in the air, while the sound of Skylark and Meadow Pipit is never far away. In spring, the bubbling song of Curlew is still common.

When to visit

Early summer for waders, midsummer for Mountain Ringlet, autumn for waxcaps.

Did you know?

Although this is generally a habitat of limited conservation interest, you may find species such as Globeflower and Grass-of-Parnassus in flushed areas.

1 Whernside, Yorkshire Dales – Heath Rush and Common Hair-cap moss with patches of Hare's-tail Cottongrass in a sward that is transitional to Blanket Bog. **2 Rise Hill, Yorkshire Dales** – the pale sheen of Mat-grass contrasts with the brown Heather that is recolonizing the less-grazed steep slope following a reduction in overall grazing pressure. **3 Mountain Pansy,** which can be yellow or purple, is found in pastures across the uplands.

Calaminarian Grassland

page 391

The ecology of Calaminarian Grassland is driven by soil chemistry. High concentrations of toxic heavy metals (commonly lead, copper and zinc), usually as a consequence of mining, result in a sward that is often very sparse and quite species-poor. Discarded minerals such as fluorspar, calcite, and barites present in spoil heaps also influence the vegetation, and overall it can be quite varied within (and between) sites, occurring in a mosaic with other vegetation types associated with the parent rock. Zinc is the most challenging metal for plants, and is often present as a waste product at lead mines (*e.g.* in North Wales and the Pennines). Tin and copper mines also support this habitat (*e.g.* in Cornwall) and near-natural examples of this habitat type are found on skeletal soils rich in nickel, chromium and cobalt

A distinctive suite of metal-tolerant vascular plants is found in Calaminarian Grassland and can include Moonwort, Pyrenean Scurvygrass, Spring Sandwort and Alpine Pennycress. Some species, such as Thrift and Bladder Campion, have particular genetically adapted forms that occur in Calaminarian Grassland. Areas of bare ground offer suitable habitat for stress-tolerant lichens and liverworts, including Greater Copperwort and other rare threadworts. Widespread plants such as Sheep's-fescue, Harebell and Wild Thyme are common, while other less common species like Chalk Fragrant-orchid and Frog Orchid can benefit from the general paucity of plant minerals that prevents other more robust species from become established.

Similar habitats

Transitions tend to be fairly clearly demarcated, but occur with upland grasslands (particularly calcareous), heathland and some montane habitats.

Gang Mine, Derbyshire – the undulating topography of spoil heaps and old mine shafts is clearly visible.

EXTENT IN KM^2

Eng	2
Wal	1
Sco	1
Ire	<1

Distribution and extent

Widely distributed in diverse locations. Pale shading indicates the broad distribution of the Annex I habitat (H6130); darker shading shows actual locations (no data for Ireland or Wales). Approximately 29% of Europe's designated Calaminarian grasslands are in the UK.

Origins and development

Mines at Calaminarian Grassland sites often date back to Roman times, and many were subsequently more extensively exploited in the 19th century, meaning that much of the habitat is of recent origin. Natural sites may be far older, as the toxicity of the heavy metals tends to hold back succession, allowing a grassland sward to persist, and many are in any case grazed. In some places Calaminarian Grassland communities may have occurred naturally on rock that has since been quarried away, and now only persist on spoil heaps. In a handful of rivers, such as the Tyne and Allen in northern England, heavy metals from mine-washes have accumulated in exposed river shingle that supports Calaminarian Grassland species.

Conservation

Many Calaminarian Grassland sites have strong historical and cultural links that make each site unique, and management needs to be sensitive to the particular conditions and history at each location. Sites tend to be very small, often in a mosaic with other habitats, and this can lead to problems protecting them and ensuring appropriate management. Scrub control and grazing is used in some cases to prevent succession that would result in the loss of characteristic plant species. Threats include agricultural improvement and reworking for minerals.

What to look for

Scarce species to look out for include Northern Rock-cress and Forked Spleenwort. Northern sites support boreal species such as Arctic Sandwort and the endemic Shetland Mouse-ear. Lower plant enthusiasts will find a suite of rare and specialist species.

1 **Greenhurth Mine, Upper Teesdale** – bare ground often indicates areas where metal levels are high and it is difficult for plants to grow, but species such as **2** **Alpine Pennycress** can survive here. **3** **Cwmystwyth, Ceredigion** – spoil heaps, screes and rocky outcrops have been colonized by heavy-metal tolerant plants, including the rare Lead Moss. Mining waste has helped shape Shingle Heath on river gravel downstream.

How to recognize

Calaminarian Grassland is a strange habitat, where rare and specialized plants grow among spoil heaps and the derelict paraphernalia of mine-workings. It can be found in obviously post-industrail landscapes but also where old diggings have softened with time into gently undulating grassland.

It is always limited in extent, but sometimes sites follow distinct lines in the landscape (called rakes in the Peak District), reflecting the mineral veins where mining activity was focussed. In a few places, serpentine rock and mineral veins support near-natural Calaminarian Grassland, but this is very restricted in distribution, found mainly in the Scottish Highlands and Islands. Stable, exposed riverine sediments also support Calaminarian plant communities, although in some cases this is a result of mining activity within the catchment.

When to visit

Most of the speciality plants can be seen flowering between June and July.

Did you know?
Calaminarian Grassland is named after Zinc Violet Viola calaminaria, *which is characteristic of metalliferous soils in continental Europe.*

1 Glen Isla, Caenlochan – open serpentine debris on the plateau supports species such as **2** **Alpine Catchfly**. **3** **Spring Sandwort** is a good indicator of Calaminarian Grassland (although it also occurs in parched calcareous grassland); its local name in Derbyshire is 'leadwort'.

MOUNTAINS

HABITAT	DESCRIPTION
Montane Dwarf-shrub Heath *page 204	page 394*	Low growing heath of montane dwarf-shrubs such as Mountain Crowberry and Arctic Bearberry.
High Montane Heath and Snow-bed *page 208	page 394*	Moss, sedge and rush heath found on very exposed shoulders, plateaux and summits; mossy communities found under melting snow-beds.
Mountain Ledge *page 212	page 394*	Lush herb-rich vegetation protected from grazing on moist mountain ledges.
Montane Scrub *page 215	page 394*	Low-growing scrub of montane willows or Common Juniper found in un-grazed locations, often on mountain ledges. Also includes Dwarf Birch scrub that is found on blanket mire at lower altitudes.

Mountains are forced into being as the earth's surface shifts, and in Britain and Ireland are ancient stumps of a range once as huge as the Himalaya. Sculpted by numerous ice ages and constantly eroded and weathered, they are now patchily covered with a thin layer of hardy vegetation and sparsely inhabited by some of our rarest wildlife. Mountains are generally defined as peaks that extend at least 600 m above their surroundings, although some lower peaks are montane in character. They can occur as single, isolated peaks (such as Suilven in Assynt), but are more often found as part of a range (such as the Cairngorms). Above the natural limit of tree growth is the montane (or alpine) zone. This usually starts at around 600–700 m above sea level, although montane vegetation is found at lower altitudes in more exposed situations (*e.g.* from around 300 m in northern Scotland). Above 900 m, mountains support particularly specialized communities of plants and animals. There are around 300 such peaks in Britain and Ireland, the majority of which are in Scotland, with a handful in each of Ireland, North Wales and the English Lake District.

The distinctive peaks of **Inverpolly, Assynt** are formed of Torridian sandstone. A capping of hard Cambrian quartzite prevented them from being eroded down to the underlying Lewisian gneiss, one of the oldest rocks in the world that forms the cnoc and lochan landscape surrounding them.

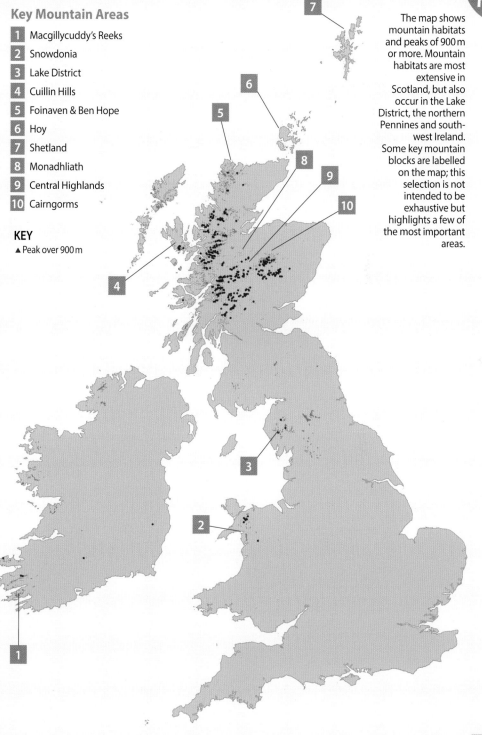

Key Mountain Areas

1 Macgillycuddy's Reeks
2 Snowdonia
3 Lake District
4 Cuillin Hills
5 Foinaven & Ben Hope
6 Hoy
7 Shetland
8 Monadhliath
9 Central Highlands
10 Cairngorms

KEY
▲ Peak over 900 m

The map shows mountain habitats and peaks of 900 m or more. Mountain habitats are most extensive in Scotland, but also occur in the Lake District, the northern Pennines and south-west Ireland. Some key mountain blocks are labelled on the map; this selection is not intended to be exhaustive but highlights a few of the most important areas.

M

M

The rolling, granite plateau of the **Cairngorms** (LEFT) contrasts with the steep-sided valleys, narrow ridges and shattered peaks of Moine schists in the **western Highlands** (RIGHT). Glacial action was more severe in the west where greater snowfall meant that glaciers were deeper and flowed more quickly.

ORIGINS

Our mountains have been shaped by immense geological forces over huge time periods. The oldest rocks are Lewisian gneiss and Torridian sandstone (around 3,000 million and 1,500 million years old respectively). These are found in Wester Ross and Sutherland in Scotland, which were once part of the ancient continent of Laurentia that included much of North America. When Laurentia collided with the European continental plate 300–400 million years ago, the Caledonide mountains were thrust up. The north and central Highlands are the worn down stumps of these mountains that stretched into North Wales and parts of northern and western Ireland. Volcanic activity resulted in vast areas of granite, which formed mountains such as the Cairngorms and those of Donegal. During the same period, the sediments of the ocean floor were uplifted and now form the Southern Uplands of Scotland and parts of Northern Ireland. In south-west Ireland, material eroded from the Caledonides built up into layers of sandstone, which were forced up into mountains some 250 million years ago when another collision of continents occurred. This collision also caused folding and faulting in the Pennines and created the granitic uplands of southern England. During the ice ages that followed, glaciers sculpted the landscape, carving out corries and scoring deep 'U'-shaped valleys.

The current interglacial started about 11,500 years ago. Open tundra-like vegetation spread from the unglaciated south and included arctic plants such as Mountain Avens, Crowberry and Dwarf Willow, with scattered Common Juniper and Dwarf Birch. A rich tall-herb community followed on the raw, lime-rich soils but gave way to woodland as tree species colonized. However, woodland was prevented by climatic conditions from ascending beyond about 800 m, a limit known as the tree-line. This limit has fluctuated with climatic variation, and is now considered to be at around 700 m. It is also dependent upon geography, occurring much lower in exposed northern or western situations (*e.g.* about 500 m in Ireland). Above the tree line tundra-like habitats were able to persist, but progressive leaching of the soils created more acidic conditions than were initially found, and the tall herb and scrub communities became restricted to calcareous rocks, whilst acid-loving dwarf-shrubs became widespread.

TYPES OF MOUNTAIN HABITAT

Montane habitats are generally found on peaks, ridges, high plateaux, boulder fields and steep-sided corrie walls. They are characterized by low-growing perennial woody dwarf-shrubs and dwarf-herbs with mosses and bryophytes, grasses, sedges and rushes, and can cover extensive areas. Shrubs and tall herbs are found on mountain ledges and moist, sheltered un-grazed areas, and are far more limited in extent and distribution. Rocky habitats that are too unstable or steep for a continuous cover of vegetation to become established and for soil to develop, are also very widespread and common on mountains – these are considered in detail in a separate section (see Rocky Habitats *page 218*). Montane forms of wetland habitats, particularly Upland Spring and Flush and Blanket Bog, and grassland habitats are also found on mountains (see Grasslands *page 152* and Wetlands *page 234*).

THREATS AND ISSUES

Montane habitats are vulnerable to climate change. They can only become more limited in extent as conditions warm, and it seems likely that some iconic mountain species, together with their lesser known associates, will be lost to Britain and Ireland. Identifying and protecting any refugia where the microclimate may remain suitable for Arctic-alpine species is a priority. Montane vegetation has also been affected by atmospheric pollution, which has particularly impacted on high-altitude moss-heath (mosses gain most of their nutrients from rain and the air, and deteriorate rapidly if nitrogen levels are too high). Overgrazing is having a significant impact on much mountain habitat, reducing the ability of more palatable plants to reproduce and maintain themselves, and impacting on vegetation structure. Recreational pressure can be an issue along popular paths and climbing routes.

IMPORTANCE

Mountains were considered as bleak, forbidding places by early travellers. However, they became more appreciated during the Romantic era in the first half of the 19th century and mountaineering took off at about the same time. Mountains are now greatly valued for a variety of reasons including the beauty of the landscape, the wildlife they support and the recreational opportunities they offer – evoking as they do a unique sense of wilderness.

CONSERVATION IMPORTANCE AND PROTECTION

The oceanic climate of Britain and Ireland, with its cool summers, mild winters and abundant rain and wind, makes our mountain habitats distinctive. They also occur at lower altitudes than elsewhere in Europe. Nationally, they are greatly valued as examples of climax or near-natural communities that are otherwise rare in Britain and Ireland, where almost all habitats have a long history of modification by humans. Botanical excursions to explore the mountain flora started in the 19th century, but mountain habitats were not among

A rare example of a natural tree-line at **Creag Fhiaclach in the Cairngorms**. In Britain and Ireland, natural transitions from woodland to montane vegetation are incredibly rare, as prehistoric tree clearance followed by a deterioration in the climate and a long history of grazing and burning has eliminated trees and scrub at altitudes where the transition might be expected to occur. Instead, a more subtle transition between upland heathland or grassland and montane communities is generally found.

Ingleborough, North Yorkshire (723 m). The mountains and high hills of the northern Pennines are formed of Carboniferous limestone, often capped with Millstone Grit – sedimentary rocks tough enough to stand proud of the surrounding landscape but also sculpted by glaciers. Although not usually considered to be mountains, the highest peaks of these hills support montane vegetation including rare Arctic-alpine species.

those first protected by the fledgling conservation movement, and some were initially protected by virtue of their association with other habitats, such as Caledonian Forest, rather than in their own right. However, many mountains are now protected as SSSIs or equivalent, and are designated as SACs for their alpine, boreal, and sub-arctic communities. Unfortunately, the majority of these sites are not currently considered to be in favourable condition for nature conservation, largely due to overgrazing. Projects to exclude sheep and deer from remnant patches of Montane Scrub and Mountain Ledge habitat have proved successful in reducing grazing damage, although regeneration remains an issue for scrub. The challenge facing conservationists is how to reduce grazing pressure over large areas to make montane habitats more robust in the face of climate change.

M

KEY FEATURES

Topography, altitude and climate are the main factors that shape the montane zone. The temperature drops by 0·6°C with every 100 m increase in altitude, so the growing season is shorter and snow lies longer higher up. Humidity increases too; as relatively warm, moist air rises up the windward side of a mountain it gradually cools until the moisture condenses, eventually falling as either rain or snow. Conditions on mountains are also windier because wind speed increases as air density decreases with height, particularly away from obstacles that can cause friction. These environmental gradients result in a marked vegetational zonation from upland heathland to Montane Dwarf-shrub Heath and then High Montane Heath. Although it is usually necessary to climb above about 700 m to find montane heath, in exposed locations this habitat can occur much lower (making it easier to reach). Exposed spurs, ridges, peaks and plateaux are key places to look for montane habitats. Other features to look for include north-facing or east-facing corries and hollows that may shelter late-lying snow-beds and their associated zoned vegetation communities.

Grazing is another important factor in the mountains – both Mountain Ledge vegetation and Montane Scrub are highly sensitive to grazing, and were probably more widespread on suitable substrates before the rise of sheep farming and deer estates. Anywhere out of reach of grazing animals, including steep slopes, is always worth investigating. However, the classic calcareous tall-herb ledge plant community is only found on basic rock in moist conditions and is unlikely to be encountered by chance. Similarly, Montane Scrub is, on the whole, so restricted in distribution that it is necessary to visit a known site to see this habitat type.

Above Loch Avon, Cairngorms. The head of the loch is around 700 m above sea level. Key features include: ❶ crags, with potential for alpine plants and breeding birds, ❷ late-lying snow patches on north-facing slope, ❸ boulders providing shelter for dwarf-shrubs, ❹ plateau supporting High Montane Heath, ❺ glacial moraine creating a varied topography and holding a small tarn, ❻ stream fed by snow-melt.

FURTHER INFORMATION

The Nature of The Cairngorms: Diversity in a Changing Environment edited by Philip Shaw & Des Thompson (The Stationery Office, 2006)

Hostile Habitats – Scotland's Mountain Environment edited by Mark Wrightam & Nick Kempe (Scottish Mountaineering Trust, 2019)

Mountain Flowers by Michael Scott (Bloomsbury Publishing, 2019)

Coire Ardair, Creag Meagaidh. Corries are often on north- or east-facing slopes. The shadier conditions of hollows on these slopes meant that snow accumulated and, over thousands of years, formed glacier ice. This scraped out the rock and deposited debris on the lip, enlarging the corrie (called cwm in Wales). When the ice melted, a tarn often formed in the bottom of the hollow. The moist, sheltered conditions and protection from grazing animals means that corrie walls can be hotspots for Arctic-alpine plants. They are also used for winter ice-climbing.

Montane Dwarf-shrub Heath is one of very few natural climax communities in Britain and Ireland, its structure and flora being determined almost entirely by climate and topography. It is generally found on stony, acidic and well-drained soils above the potential altitudinal limit of woodland at around 600 m (500 m in Ireland), but descends almost to sea level in the extreme north-west of Scotland. It is also found where glacial moraine breaks through Blanket Bog in exposed locations. Some plant communities that occur on only a few high peaks in the Highlands form the southernmost outposts of tundra vegetation. Others are more widespread across the Scottish uplands, with outliers in the Lake District, northern Pennines and North Wales. The transition from woodland to Montane Dwarf-shrub Heath has largely been eliminated by woodland clearance and subsequent grazing, but the transition from Montane to High Montane Heaths is generally intact.

Montane Heath vegetation is quite diverse, showing clear altitudinal gradients and variation between oceanic and continental conditions. For example, Heather gives way to Bilberry with increasing snow-lie and abundant lichens are characteristic of the drier eastern heaths, while Woolly Fringe-moss and a suite of rare Atlantic liverworts are found in the more oceanic west.

Similar habitats

Moorland habitats also hold similar species but Montane Dwarf-shrub Heath can be distinguished from these by the prostrate growth form of dwarf shrubs and the presence of Arctic-alpine species. High Montane Heath lacks abundant dwarf-shrubs.

Creag Meagaidh, central Highlands – wind-shorn Mountain Crowberry with patches of pale Woolly Fringe-moss and spikes of Fir Clubmoss between boulders on the mountain plateau at around 850 m.

Origins and development

Montane Heath is a natural (or near-natural) community maintained by harsh climatic conditions. Unlike most heaths it is not dependent upon some form of anthropogenic disturbance to prevent succession to other vegetation types, and is easily damaged by grazing and burning. In North Wales and northern England, a loss of lichen and bryophytes and corresponding increase in grasses has been attributed to nitrogen deposition and overgrazing.

Conservation

Montane Heath is greatly valued as one of a series of montane habitats that together form the most extensive areas of natural vegetation in Britain and Ireland. The factors that need addressing are mainly the systemic issues of pollution and climate change rather than local management issues, although a reduction in grazing and the prevention of burning would be beneficial. Montane Heath can also be affected by trampling, as walkers often favour the ridges and spurs that support this habitat.

What to look for

In the eastern Highlands, look out for small Arctic-alpines such as Mountain Crowberry, Bog Bilberry and Alpine and Fir Clubmosses in lichen-rich heath of prostrate Heather spiked with Stiff Sedge. Farther west, Dwarf Juniper, Alpine Bearberry and Trailing Azalea may be seen. On cold and wet rocky slopes and boulder fields in the west of Scotland, the Lake District and North Wales, where the weather systems create an extreme oceanic climate (mild and wet), a community found nowhere else in the world supports rare Atlantic bryophytes. In steep, shaded places on moist peaty soils, look for Cloudberry and Dwarf Cornel growing with large, branched mosses. This

EXTENT IN KM²

Eng	12
Wal	<1
Sco	410
NI	1
Ire	151

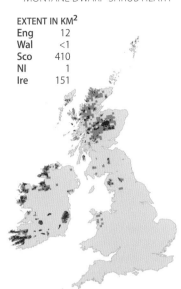

Distribution and extent

Found mainly in the Scottish Highlands, with examples in other northern and western uplands. Pale shading indicates broad distribution of the Annex I habitat (H4060); darker shading shows actual locations, drawn from a range of sources (no data for Wales). Similar habitat is found in Scandinavia, but oceanic bryophyte-rich versions are unique to Britain and Ireland.

LEFT: **Cul Mor, Assynt** – here, prostrate Heather forms a low sward with Bilberry, Fir Clubmoss and Woolly Fringe-moss on a stony plateau at about 600 m. RIGHT: In the north-west Highlands, **Dwarf Juniper** (a subspecies of Common Juniper) can form a continuous mat ('Juniper heath') that provides shelter for oceanic liverworts. It is very sensitive to fire, and may have once been more widespread, forming a continuum with more upright forms of Common Juniper in the east.

1 **Fir Clubmoss** growing in a short sward of Stiff Sedge, Bilberry and Viviparous Fescue. Clubmosses belong to the most ancient group of land plants. **2** **High Spy, Lake District** – transitional Heather-Bilberry heath at around 600 m showing prostrate growth forms but no Arctic-alpine species. **3** At close quarters, the tiny, gentle pink flowers of **Trailing Azalea** can speckle well-drained, exposed slopes. This woody plant can live for 50 years or more. **4** Male **Dotterel** are less brightly coloured than females, and have the job of incubation and chick rearing. Females sometimes leave the area and breed with a different male before returning to north Africa for the winter. **5** The distinctive leaf and five-petalled flower of **Cloudberry** is often found on upper slopes that face north-west or east and where snow lies relatively late into year. **6** **Ptarmigan** is seasonally camouflaged, moulting its snowy white feathers at the end of winter. It is thought that crows, attracted to the high tops by rubbish left behind by mountain walkers, are predating Ptarmigan chicks.

community is more widespread, and can be found as far south as the Cheviots and North Wales.

Montane Heath in Scotland provides habitat for Ptarmigan and Dotterel (which also nests on High Montane Heath). Ptarmigan breeds in montane habitats and is a year-round resident, moving down to the forest edge in particularly harsh weather. A distinctive croak is often heard long before the bird is seen exploding up from behind nearby rocks. A small population of Snow Bunting breeds in Britain, joined by Arctic breeders over the winter. Look for these tough songbirds searching for insects among mountain-top lichens. Dotterel is harder to see, but a few hundred still breed on high plateaux among montane mosses, feeding on craneflies and spiders. After the first snow-melt in spring, look out for Mountain Hare, when its white winter coat stands out against the dark background.

Montane invertebrates are restricted by the extremes of microclimate and the limited number of plant species. Characteristic species are highly adapted, and populations may be long-standing. Several are very rare, and there are probably undiscovered species. In the Cairngorms, look out for the striking red-and-black Scotch Burnet (June–July). This moth hides amongst vegetation in poor weather, but in sunshine it can be seen flying close to the ground among flowers such as Mountain Everlasting.

Beinn Eighe, Wester Ross, is known for some of the best examples of upland plant communities.

How to recognize

This is a distinctive habitat of high, exposed mountain spurs and ridges where strong winds sweep away the insulating blanket of snow and expose vegetation to fierce, prolonged frosts. Prostrate forms of Heather and Bilberry only a hand span high hug the ground, which can be thick with spongy reindeer lichens and mosses. In very exposed places wind erosion creates patches of bare ground and the vegetation forms in parallel strips aligned with the prevailing wind. Although the vegetation may change gradually and subtly as it reaches the montane zone, at this altitude the magnitude of the landscape, its vastness and silence, and the overriding power of nature, are awe-inspiring and unmistakable.

When to visit

Summer months for Arctic-alpine flora and breeding Dotterel, winter for Ptarmigan in its white plumage.

Did you know?
The impacts of climate change combined with atmospheric nitrogen deposition are likely to lead to a reduction in the range of Arctic-alpine species.

High montane communities are determined by altitude and topography and further shaped by climate. With increasing altitude the snow lies for longer and the growing season is shorter, dwarf-shrubs give way to grass-heath, moss-heath, sedge-heath and rush-heath, and ultimately to snow-bed communities reminiscent of arctic tundra.

On the high summits, blasted free of snow by freezing, desiccating winds in winter and scorched by sun in the summer, only a handful of well-adapted species can survive. In the oceanic west, moss-heath dominated by Woolly Fringe-moss covers large areas. In the colder, drier east and central Highlands, where most precipitation falls as snow, this moss-heath is replaced by sedge-heath. As the environment becomes more extreme over about 1,000 m, sparse rush-heath grows on loose gravel around rocks.

Where snow is caught in hollows and against the headwalls of north- and east-facing corries, snow-bed communities are found. The snow insulates the vegetation from the worst of the weather, but deeper snow cuts off light for all but a few weeks of the year. Flowering plants need about three months to grow, flower and set seed, so only mosses and liverworts can survive where the snow lasts longest. An extensive snow-bed will have several communities, from grass-heath under the early melting snow around the outside, to colourful patches of mosses and liverworts under late-melting snow in the centre.

Similar habitats

Transitions to Montane Dwarf-shrub Heath and upland grasslands occur at lower altitudes. Snow-beds can include Upland Spring and Flush and northern hepatic mat (see Upland Dry Heath, *page 143*) communities.

Cairngorm plateau – where water flow is impeded by frozen ground, saturated soil creeps gradually down the slope (solifluction), resulting in distinctive patterned mosaics of Three-cornered Rush (note the rills in the central hollow – see Upland Spring and Flush, *page 252*)

Origins and development

In most cases high montane vegetation types are natural climax communities maintained through harsh conditions. Those communities dependent upon snow-lie are particularly vulnerable to climate change, and snow patch longevity is already declining. Rush-heath is not dependent on snow-lie and may be more resilient. Snow-beds in particular are damaged by atmospheric depositions. The impacts of grazing can interact with pollution in damaging vulnerable species such as Woolly Fringe-moss and result in the impoverished montane vegetation typical of the Lake District and Snowdonia.

Conservation

Huge challenges are presented by the threat of climate change in particular, and iconic montane species are likely to become extinct in Britain and Ireland. A reduction in sheep and deer grazing and trampling would increase the resilience of High Montane Heath to atmospheric pollution and climate change.

What to look for

A suite of small and rare Arctic-alpine vascular plants, mosses and liverworts is found in High Montane Heaths and Snow-bed. On grass-heath look out for Alpine Clubmoss, Iceland Moss (a foliose lichen) and conspicuous cushions of the distinctive pale blue-grey liverwort Alpine Silverwort that indicate places where icy water trickles slowly from springs. In snow-beds look for rare rock-mosses, Dwarf Willow, Alpine Hair-grass, Starry Saxifrage and Dwarf Cudweed, as well as mossy carpets of Northern Haircap, Starke's Forkmoss and Bristly Fringe-moss and wrinkled, species-rich crusts of liverworts.

Most soils in the high montane zone are nutrient poor (being either based on acid rocks or strongly leached), but where soils are more base-rich or where frost heave has redistributed

EXTENT IN KM²

Eng	11
Wal	1
Sco	701
NI	1

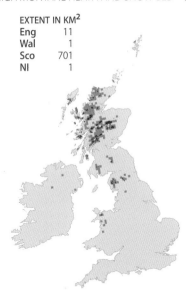

Distribution and extent

Largely confined to the Scottish Highlands, with outliers in the Lake District, north-west Wales and the north Pennines. Pale shading indicates the broad distribution of the Annex I habitats (H6150 and H6170), darker shading shows actual locations. Darker shading in England will include some Montane Dwarf Shrub Heath. Extent figures are the combined extents for H6150 and H6170

LEFT: **Beinn Eighe, Wester Ross** – a thick mat of Woolly Fringe-moss and other bryophytes spiked with Stiff Sedge and Viviparous Fescue carpets broad ridges. RIGHT: **Beinn Eighe, Wester Ross** – the location of snow-beds in winter can often be identified by the vegetation in summer. In this case, grass-heath and sedge-heath indicate an early melting snow-bed, with the pale Mat-grass sward giving way to Stiff Sedge and bryophytes where drainage is more impeded.

LEFT: **Cairngorm plateau** – extending for miles, tufty orange-brown tussocks of Three-leaved Rush are interspersed with stony ground and large crustose lichens and mosses or a little Bilberry and Dwarf Willow. RIGHT: **Snow Bunting** feed on craneflies that emerge after the spring snow-melt. They also forage for insects blown up by the breeze from lower down the hillside and caught on the surface of the snow. These insects also provide prey for spiders that migrate to snow-beds to feed on them.

nutrients within the soil, more species can be found. In such situations, look for Alpine Lady's-mantle and rarities such as Alpine Mouse-ear and Alpine Cinquefoil on grass-heath and dwarf-herbs such as Moss Campion, Cyphel, Alpine Bistort, Alpine Meadow-rue, Purple Saxifrage, Sibbaldia, and a suite of rare species on moss-heath. Unsurprisingly, many montane species are rare and some (*e.g.* Diapensia, Norwegian Mugwort, Curved Wood-rush, Drooping Saxifrage and Highland Saxifrage) are restricted to a few or single locations.

Invertebrates can sometimes be found in the low sward – look out for Mountain Ringlet basking on grass tussocks in sunny conditions and a strikingly marked wolf spider *Tricca alpigena* in Mat-grass and Woolly Fringe-moss. It is worth looking up from the vegetation underfoot too: montane habitats provide a great vantage point for spotting Golden Eagle and there is always the chance of seeing Dotterel.

MAIN IMAGE: **Creag Meagaidh, Central Highlands** – a bryophyte community revealed in early June as the snow melts.

BELOW: Bright apple-green patches of **Mountain Thread-moss** are visible from a distance, and indicate the presence of springs. INSET BELOW: **Mountain Ringlet** can be found on grassland from about 300 m up to the montane zone. It has a low, fluttering flight and is only active in sunny conditions, although it can be disturbed from the ground. Mountain Ringlets form discrete colonies, and can be seen in their hundreds at the best sites.

How to recognize

On the highest cols, shoulders and plateaux of mountains, the fierce winter wind scours away the snow, exposing the meagre vegetation to bitter and prolonged frosts. Only a sparse layer of brownish sedge and rush or silver-grey moss persists, patterned by frost-heave or solifluction and sometimes stretching for miles. In gullies, hollows and corries the wind carries the snow into deep drifts that remain well into the summer months, gradually melting to reveal a miniature community of mosses and liverworts where the snow was deepest. Incredibly rare and specialist species inhabit this stark landscape, and while challenging terrain and weather mean it is hard to reach, the remote beauty of one of Britain's wildest and most natural habitats makes the effort well worthwhile.

Did you know?

Some snow-bed communities are considered to be the last relics of genuine late-glacial vegetation.

When to visit

The summer months once most of the snow has melted.

Mountain Ledge

page 394

Mountain Ledge vegetation varies according to both substrate and altitude. On base-rich rocks, classic tall-herb vegetation of Wild Angelica, Meadowsweet, Roseroot, Water Avens, Wood Crane's-bill, Lady's Mantle and Marsh Hawk's-beard forms thick swards with Bilberry, Tufted Hair-grass and mountain sedges, and rushes over lush mosses. The tall vegetation precludes small Arctic-alpines, but larger species include Alpine Meadow-rue, Alpine Bistort, Mountain Sorrel, Alpine Saw-wort and Holly-fern.

Acid ledges with deep soils are dominated by Great Wood-rush and Bilberry. Ferns are abundant, typically Broad-buckler Fern with Hard Fern, Lemon-scented Fern and the delicate Oak and Beech Ferns. Starry Saxifrage may be present in wetter situations. Rowan and Aspen are sometime frequent in stands at lower altitudes. Rare species are found at higher altitudes, including montane willows such as Downy Willow, Dark-leaved Willow, Woolly Willow, Net-leaved Willow, and the very rare Alpine Blue-sow-thistle.

On skeletal soils where the base content is constantly replenished by the weathering of calcareous rocks, Mountain Avens can form extensive dark mats with cushion herbs such as Moss Campion and Cyphel; taller herbs such as Globeflower, Roseroot and Water Avens; and montane willows and saxifrages. This community supports lime-loving Arctic-alpines such as

BELOW: **Ben Lawers, Perthshire** is celebrated for its Mountain Ledge flora and Arctic-alpine rarities.

EXTENT IN KM^2

Eng	1
Wal	1
Sco	2
NI	<1
Ire	1

Distribution and extent

Found mainly in the Scottish Highlands. Pale green shading indicates the broad distribution of the habitat based on Annex I reporting, darker shading indicates known locations.

Alpine Milk-vetch, Alpine Saxifrage and Alpine Bartsia, together with Round-leaved Wintergreen, Grass-of-Parnassus and Mountain Everlasting.

Similar habitats

There is strong floristic continuity with Downy Willow Montane Scrub and, at lower altitudes, with the ground floras of some types of upland woodland and with Northern Hay Meadow. Transitions to grazed Upland Calcareous Grassland also occur.

Origins and development

Mountain Ledge vegetation is entirely natural. Although to some extent limited by geological and hydrological requirements, it was probably once more widespread at suitable altitudes, but has been reduced and fragmented by grazing, to which it is highly vulnerable. Evidence for this is seen in its presence on un-grazed loch islands, the tops of large boulders out of the reach of grazing animals, and lightly grazed slopes.

Conservation

Stands of Mountain Ledge vegetation in more accessible locations are usually overgrazed, and in some cases threatened by burning. The impact of grazing by feral goats is a particular issue in Snowdonia. Access to cliffs for recreation (climbing and ice-climbing) can damage vegetation. Fencing has been undertaken at some sites to relieve grazing pressure (*e.g.* at Cym Idwal in Wales and Ben Lawers and Caenlochan in the Highlands) and has resulted in the expansion of Mountain Ledge vegetation. Targeted reductions in grazing pressure elsewhere could result in further increases, and the aim should ultimately be the restoration of an intact transition from woodland through Montane Scrub to Mountain Ledge communities.

LEFT: **Yellow Saxifrage** is often found sprawling over wet rock. RIGHT: **Alpine Saxifrage** is a small species found on ledges where taller vegetation is absent.

What to look for

An outstanding array of northern meadow and Arctic-alpine plant species; Golden Eagle, White-tailed Eagle and Peregrine nesting on ledges.

Did you know?

Some of Britain's rarest plants survive on base-rich ledges at high altitude and include Alpine Woodsia, Yellow Oxytropis, Alpine Bartsia and Alpine Gentian.

1 **Combe Scar, Dentdale** – Great Wood-rush, Rosebay Willowherb, Foxglove, Broad Buckler-fern, Oak Fern, Wood Sage, Goldenrod and Orpine under a patchy canopy of Aspen and Rowan hint at the woodland that might have once been more prevalent. **2** **Roseroot** is a classic Mountain Ledge species; seen here in bud, its flowers are yellow when open. **3** **Yellow Oxytropis** is a very rare glacial relict found only on cliffs.

Montane Scrub

page 394

Tiny fragments of Arctic-alpine willow scrub are found on moist, north- or east-facing base-rich mountain ledges or un-grazed gravelly slopes next to streams where the winter snow lies for long periods. It is dependent upon snow cover for insulation against air frosts, and on inaccessible locations for protection from grazing animals. It currently occurs between about 650–900 m above sea level in the Highlands. The largest patch (at Caenlochan) is only half a hectare in extent. The most common species is Downy Willow, followed by Myrtle-leaved Willow. Mountain Willow is restricted to higher altitudes (concentrated in Breadalbane) and Woolly Willow is the rarest, found only on cliff ledges (notably at Caenlochan). Other more widespread species are also found (*e.g.* Eared Willow, Dark-leaved Willow, Tea-leaved Willow and Goat Willow), and Net-leaved Willow is sometimes found on ledges with Mountain Avens. Downy Willow also occurs in very small numbers on Helvellyn in the Lake District.

Alpine Juniper Scrub comprises short, upright Common Juniper scattered over Heather and dwarf shrubs without forming a continuous canopy. Its central location is the eastern Highlands, where it is locally frequent in the Cairngorms and can also form part of tree-line woods. Elsewhere it is found on cliff ledges.

Dwarf Birch is found scattered or in clumps on Blanket Bog and Upland Wet Heath at moderate altitudes, although it can reach 850 m in the western Highlands, particularly Ben Wyvis and Beinn Dearg. In grazing exclosures it can reach almost a

EXTENT IN KM^2
Eng   <1
Sco   <1

Montane Scrub of Common Juniper in the Cairngorms.

Distribution and extent

Highly fragmented and limited in extent, almost entirely restricted to the Scottish Highlands. Pale shading shows broad distribution of the Annex I habitat (H4080); darker shading shows actual locations in Scotland.

metre in height, but is usually shorter, at the same height as the surrounding vegetation. It is nationally scarce and populations are supressed by overgrazing and heather burning.

Similar habitats

Juniper Scrub (see *page 104*) is found in Caledonian Forest where the canopy has been removed, and more widely through the uplands where it colonizes heathland and calcareous grasslands. Dwarf Juniper, which can be hard to differentiate from prostrate Common Juniper, forms a Montane Heath community with Heather. The flora associated with willow scrub is often that of Mountain Ledge.

Origins and development

Scrub dominated Britain and Ireland for a brief period as the climate ameliorated immediately after the last glaciation. As tree species colonized up to their altitudinal limit (at around 800 m above sea level when tree cover was at its greatest extent, lower in Ireland and west Britain), Montane Scrub became restricted to a narrow altitudinal band just above the tree-line, where it probably formed an ecotone (transitional habitat) between forest and montane heath. Rather than a continuous band, it is likely to have formed patches in more sheltered hollows (Common Juniper) or on wetter, flushed ground and base-rich rock (willows). There is evidence that the area of scrub began to decrease in prehistory, and this decline has intensified over the last 200 years as deer and sheep have increased in numbers.

Conservation

Much Montane Scrub is in poor condition and shows limited functionality due to the small population sizes of its characteristic species and its isolation; tiny populations are also particularly threatened by stochastic

LEFT: **Ben Lawers, Perthshire – Woolly Willow** flourishing in an exclosure erected in 1980. Arctic-alpine willow scrub has probably always been limited by its exacting requirements, but is likely to have been more widespread in places where it is currently limited by grazing pressure. RIGHT: **Creag Fhiaclach, Cairngorms** (600 m) – Common Juniper occurs with knarled Scots Pine in an almost unique expression of natural tree-line vegetation virtually lost from Scotland today.

events (*e.g.* rock falls and landslips). The habitat is susceptible to grazing and burning and to climate change. Restoration projects are underway to conserve vulnerable populations and to allow complete natural successions from valley woodlands to open mountain tops (*e.g.* at Ben Lawers, Abernethy, Creag Meagaidh and Glen Affric). Efforts are concentrated on protection from heavy grazing and expansion of the habitat through planting where populations are too small or isolated for natural regeneration.

What to look for

Rare and scarce willows and their associated invertebrates, which include rare sawflies.

How to recognize

In a very few places in the Scottish Highlands upland woodland reaches the natural altitudinal tree line. Here, small, gnarled and twisted Scots Pines give way to a fringe of Common Juniper and then Heather and Bilberry heath. Where the trees do not grow up to their altitudinal limit, Common Juniper sometimes grows scattered over the heathland. Elsewhere, willows form a low canopy, sometimes only knee high, on inaccessible crags and un-grazed burnsides. At lower altitudes on damp, peaty slopes, Dwarf Birch peeps out from the surrounding vegetation. These are all Montane Scrub communities, tiny relics of a natural transition between forest and montane heath that is now largely absent. Remote and fragmented, the habitat is scattered across the Highlands, but it is hard to find and often inaccessible.

When to visit

Summer when willows and Dwarf Birch are in leaf, year-round for Common Juniper (conditions permitting).

Did you know?

One of the best sites for willow scrub is in the Grampian mountains at Corrie Seileach (which means corrie of the willows); it has been known to botanists for centuries.

1 **Dundreggan, Highland** – an unusually large Dwarf Birch with two **Downy Birch** behind. Dwarf Birch is found on gently sloping peatlands up to 800 m. **2** **Borrowdale, Lake District** – **Common Juniper** limited to a rock crevice on a heavily grazed hillside. **3** **Mountain Willow** may be more tolerant of grazing than other montane willows.

ROCKY HABITATS

HABITAT	DESCRIPTION
Rocky Slopes *page 224* | *page 395*	Cliffs, crags, outcrops and boulder fields, where crevices support sparse and scattered vegetation.
Scree *page 227* | *page 395*	Unstable slopes of broken rock that support pioneer species.
Limestone Pavement *page 230* | *page 395*	Horizontal sheets of bare, fissured limestone with a calcareous flora that flourishes within cracks between the slabs.

ORIGINS

Inland rocky habitats are generally widespread in the uplands where the bedrock has been exposed through glacial action and the erosion of weathered material. Limestone Pavement is also found at sea level, and in north-west Scotland, montane communities are found on rocky exposures near sea level. Caves, quarries and disused mine workings are also found in the lowlands.

The rock exposures of Britain and Ireland include rocks from almost all geological eras dating back early 3,000 million years. They can be divided into two main types, siliceous (acidic) and basic (alkaline), and this may be reflected in the plant communities they support. Siliceous rocks, those with a high silica content, include granite, gneiss, sandstone and quartzite and predominate in the upland landscape. Basic rocks are rich in calcium or magnesium and include limestone, calcareous-schists and some igneous rocks such as serpentine and basalt. They are more restricted in their extent, but tend to support a greater range of plant species.

TYPES OF ROCKY HABITATS

Rocky habitats include inland cliffs, crags, rocky outcrops, screes, boulder-fields, fell-fields, limestone pavements, caves and quarries, most of which typically support a sparse scattering of vegetation. Of these, habitat sections have been provided for three categories: **Rocky Slopes** (including cliffs, crags, rocky outcrops and some boulder-fields where these support crevice vegetation), **Scree** and **Limestone Pavement**.

Whernside, Yorkshire Dales. A barren fell-field of shattered rock lies above the tarns on an exposed shoulder of Whernside at about 650 m.

On cliffs and crags, vegetation is limited to crevices and narrow ledges (wider ledges supporting tall herbs or scrub are considered in the Mountain section under Mountain Ledge and Montane Scrub). Rocky outcrops on shallower slopes can also support grassland or heathland species, depending on the steepness and size of the outcrop. The term boulder-field is often used rather loosely to refer to both screes of larger boulders (also called block talus) and areas of boulders left behind by retreating glaciers. Fell-field is another term that is used variably. It is generally applied to gravelly or rocky areas on the most exposed mountain summits and high ridges that support very sparse vegetation. Fell-field vegetation is particularly well-developed in the western Highlands, Skye, Mull and Shetland. The sparse, scattered vegetation typical of fell-fields, bryophyte-dominated Scree and some crevice communities is not fully covered by the National Vegetation Classification.

Balnakeil, Sutherland. Rocky outcrops, cliff and pavement are found almost at sea level on Durness limestone where they support montane plants.

Limestone Pavement is somewhat different from the other habitats, occurring at lower altitudes in karst landscapes (*i.e.* open limestone landscapes where water movement is mostly under rather than on the surface). Caves are also formed by the dissolution of soluble rock, usually limestone. Caves in Britain and Ireland, which have been relatively recently glaciated, are much less species-rich than their continental counterparts, but support bacteria, algae, fungi, and invertebrates adapted to low light levels (including a blind spider). They also provide roost sites for four protected bat species. Quarries are an artificial rocky habitat that can support a rich flora, particularly on limestone sites, and some species, such as the Bee Orchid, appear to favour such areas. Quarries also provide nesting habitat for Peregrine and Raven, and, in North Wales, Chough. Some bat species, such as the Greater Horseshoe Bat, are very dependent on quarry workings for roosting sites.

Creag Meagaidh, Central Highlands. Exposed rock predominates in mountain landscapes.

THREATS AND ISSUES

Rocky habitats are some of the most natural found in Britain and Ireland. Often remote, difficult to access and of little agricultural value, they have not been shaped by human activities in the same way as most other habitats. However, the uplands are generally grazed, and only sheer cliffs and the rockiest screes and boulder-fields are out of the reach of grazing livestock and feral goats. Limestone Pavement, particularly in Britain, is heavily influenced by grazing, which limits plants to crevices and prevents succession to woodland. It has also suffered from quarrying. At higher altitudes montane communities will be affected by climate change, and nitrogen deposition and associated acidification related to the high precipitation rates in upland areas may be an issue. Recreational pressure is an issue at some more accessible sites where activities such as climbing, bouldering and hill-walking can threaten vulnerable plant populations and disturb breeding or roosting birds, or, in the case of caves, bats.

CULTURAL IMPORTANCE

The diversity of British and Irish geology has inspired generations of pioneering geologists, and features of particular significance are often revealed by rocky habitats. Caves also have a special role to play in our understanding and appreciation of the prehistoric fauna and Paleolithic people. The 33,000-year-old skeleton known as the Red Lady of Paviland found in a cave on the Gower coast is the oldest ceremonial burial discovered in west Europe, and a nearby cave holds a 14,000-year-old carved reindeer. Unsurprisingly many caves also have prominent roles in legends. High, rocky place that feel close to the sky may also have had spiritual importance to our ancestors. For example, it is speculated that the Iron Age ramparts and hut circles at 723 m above the sheer Ingleborough scarp in North Yorkshire had ritual significance. Rocky places are undeniably awe-inspiring and often capture people's imagination. A wealth of paintings and literature have been inspired by craggy mountains, waterfalls and caves, such as Turner's paintings of Ingleborough. The Limestone Pavement of the Burren has a particularly rich archaeological heritage with megalithic tombs, burial cairns, prehistoric farmsteads, and more recent historic structures recording 6,000 years of human occupation. Until recently, there was also an unusual tradition of winter-only cattle-grazing on the Burren.

CONSERVATION IMPORTANCE AND PROTECTION

Rocky habitats contribute to the overall biological diversity of the uplands and are natural habitats in what is generally a semi-natural landscape. Montane cliffs can support a suite of rare Arctic-alpine plants, and provide nesting places for Golden Eagle, Peregrine and Raven. Limestone Pavement supports a unique mix of rocky, woodland and calcareous grassland species, and is particularly well represented in Britain and Ireland. Caves and disused mine workings can support large populations of bats, including one of the biggest roosts in Europe.

Some upland and montane Rocky Slope and Scree, caves (without public access) and Limestone Pavement are included within Annex I of the Habitats Directive. Limestone Pavement can also be protected under the Wildlife and Countryside Act (1984).

King Arthur's Cave in the Wye Valley, Herefordshire. Excavations in the 19th century revealed the remains of Woolly Mammoth, Spotted Hyena and other extinct Pleistocene mammals. Current inhabitants include horseshoe bats.

Knockan Crag, Assynt – famously the inspiration for the geological debate that revealed how tectonic forces can move rocks sideways. Here the Moine Thrust fault is revealed, showing older Moine rocks (some of the oldest in the world) forced up on top of much younger Cambrian and Ordovician rocks.

KEY AREAS

Rocky Slope and Scree are widespread in the uplands, particularly in the Lake District, the Scottish Highlands, and the north-west and west coast of Ireland. The best areas for Limestone Pavement are the Burren in Ireland, the Morecambe Bay area, the Craven Dales and Ingleborough in northern England and Durness in north-west Scotland.

1 The famous **Poulnabrone** portal tomb on Limestone Pavement in the Burren, Co. Clare, is one of nearly 2,000 monuments recorded there to date. **2** **Cyphel** and **3** **Moss Campion** – species of rocky places are often cushion-forming and deep-rooted, and have small and rolled or hairy leaves to reduce the impacts of exposure and maximize water absorption and retention. **4** **Holly-fern** favours cool, moist positions on rocky ledges, in stabilized boulder scree and in deep grykes in Limestone Pavement.

KEY FEATURES

The nature of rocky habitats is primarily influenced by the chemistry of the underlying rock, the stability of the substrate, and altitude and aspect, all of which affect the availability of water, nutrients and shelter (including the shelter provided by snow). The harsh conditions presented by rocky habitats suit species with specific adaptations that would be out-competed in other environments. Key features are gullies, overhangs and seepages on north-facing cliffs that remain wet – these provide moist conditions for crevice plants in an environment that generally lacks water-retaining soil. Scree also retains moisture and provides protection from frost, but here plants must cope with the instability of the substrate (although some are able to regenerate from rhizomes if covered by rocks). Stability is therefore a key feature, and stable, bare rock can support bryophytes and lichens, while ledges provide a purchase for cushion-forming herbs such as Moss Campion and Cyphel, which have inrolled or narrow leaves that help prevent desiccation, and strong root systems.

In situations where the climate is mild enough for tree growth, the influence of grazing is pervasive, and key features are those that prevent access by grazing animals. Below the tree line, trees can grow on exposed rock, but often the only trees present in the upland landscape are those that have become established on rock faces out of the reach of grazing animals. Ash, Rowan, Hazel and Yew can grow on stabilized Scree, and on Dartmoor, Devon a handful of iconic Upland Oak Woods grow on slopes covered in granite blocks known as clitter. On Limestone Pavement, grazing often limits vegetation to the deep fissures.

At lower altitudes, particularly in south-west Britain, hedge banks and sunken lanes support a community rich in ferns, such as Polypody, with mosses and Navelwort.

Coire an-t Sneachda, Cairngorms, Aberdeenshire is a glaciated corrie. Key features include: ❶ a damp, north-facing headwall with ledges and crevices beyond the reach of livestock, ❷ areas of active, largely unvegetated Scree, ❸ boulder moraine in the valley floor, ❹ rocky outcrops on shallower slopes.

FURTHER INFORMATION

www.burrenbeo.com – about the Burren

Ingleborough: Landscape and History by David Johnson (Carnegie, 2008)

Buckland Beacon, Dartmoor. The unglaciated tors of Dartmoor are of great interest geologically. Tors also support up to 60 lichen species, as well as a number of ferns that are otherwise uncommon in southern England.

Rocky Slopes page 395

The plants of rock crevices and fissures ('chasmophytic vegetation') are unable to compete with more vigorous species in less challenging environments but, adapted to the stresses of drought, low nutrients, and poor shelter, they can persist in rocky habitats where there is little other competition. The vegetation tends to be sparse and scattered and is usually limited to more sheltered and humid situations. The suite of species present reflects the nature of the underlying rock. On acidic rocks, bryophytes include fringe-mosses and the vivid green rounded hummocks of Mougeot's Yoke-moss. Mountain crags shelter Arctic-alpines such as Alpine Speedwell, Highland Cudweed and Mountain Sorrel and, where snow lies late in high, sheltered corries, a fern snow-bed community characterized by Alpine Lady-fern occurs among boulders and on ledges.

Calcareous cliff communities are less widespread. Found at some celebrated sites such as Ben Lawers in the Scottish Highlands and Moor House in Upper Teesdale, they can support a rich flora when out of reach of grazing animals, particularly at higher altitudes. Frizzled Crisp-moss (which shrivels into contorted spirals when dry) and cushions of Moss Campion, Cyphel and Snow Pearlwort grow on narrow ledges, as do rarities such as Alpine Woodsia, Alpine Gentian and rare saxifrages. At lower altitudes, crevice species include Green Spleenwort and Brittle Bladder-fern, and Maidenhair Spleenwort and Wall-rue are typical of sunny crevices and are often found growing from mortar in stone walls in the more humid west of Britain and Ireland.

Similar habitats

At lower altitudes more continuous woodland may develop in gorges and on Limestone Pavement (*e.g.* in the Avon Gorge and on the Morecambe Bay pavements) and crags can support rare whitebeams (*e.g.* in the Brecon Beacons).

Origins and development

Cliff vegetation grows on rock features that were exposed or formed during and at the end of the last glacial period and is not dependent upon any form of human management. However, grazing by sheep and feral goats limits the distribution of plants to the most inaccessible sites and is endangering some species.

Conservation

Rocky slopes often support low numbers of individual species, making populations vulnerable. Climbing is of concern at some sites, particularly ice-climbing on north-facing, wet, vegetated slopes that are avoided in the summer. A reduction in grazing pressure would allow some species to spread from their current refugia, and increase their resilience to other stresses. Climate change is likely to alter the Arctic-alpine component of the flora.

What to look for

Golden Eagle favours inaccessible cliff ledges for its eyries, and Peregrine and Raven also nest on cliffs. Look out for scarce and rare Arctic-alpine flowering plants and ferns at high altitudes. The granite tors of Dartmoor in Devon are particularly good for lichens.

EXTENT IN KM^2

Eng	16
Wal	15
Sco	376
NI	1
Ire	19

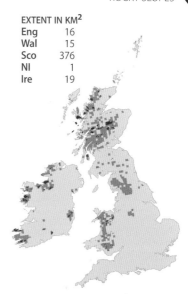

Distribution and extent

Found mainly in the Scottish Highlands. Pale green shading indicates the broad distribution of the habitat based on Annex I reporting; darker shading shows actual locations.

LEFT: **Northern Corries, Cairngorms** – mosses grow where water seeps continuously over the rock, and here provide niches for saxifrages to become established. RIGHT: **Near Seathwaite, Lake District** – at lower altitudes cracks in sheer cliffs can support Heather, and trees that are otherwise scarce in the grazed upland landscape, such as Rowan and Aspen, can also gain a foothold.

How to recognize

On cliffs, crags and rocky outcrops an attractive suite of mosses, liverworts, ferns and small herbs cling in crevices and spill down bare rock faces. Scattered plants find a home in fissures and on tiny ledges in the shelter of damp gullies and under overhangs dripping with water. Many of the more formidable cliffs are inaccessible (except to climbers) but some crags and smaller outcrops are quite easily explored on foot. A careful search (binoculars help) can reveal cushions of bryophytes, ferns sprouting from narrow cracks and, at higher altitudes, the intensely coloured flowers of small Arctic-alpines.

When to visit

Summer for flora.

Did you know?

The iconic Snowdon Lily, known from just six rocky sites in North Wales, has been identified as the first Arctic-alpine likely to go extinct in Britain as a consequence of climate change.

Rocky slopes can provide habitat for plants such as **1 Arctic Mouse-ear** and **2 Mountain Sorrel. 3 Oblong Woodsia** – this rare species of Rocky Slopes suffered serious declines due to 19th century plant collectors. Reintroduction projects have been more successful on Scree, from which it may have been eliminated through grazing and collecting.

Instability, lack of soil and significant temperature differences between day and night make Scree (also called talus) a challenging environment. However, the stones give some protection from frost and also retain moisture. Pioneer lichens are the first species to colonize, followed by bryophytes that can help to consolidate the loose rock. Parsley Fern is next to colonize, flourishing in more stable areas along the flanks and bottom edges of screes and behind boulders. Subsequent colonization by other species depends on the build-up of decomposing fern fronds, which are slowly incorporated with decaying mineral material into a raw soil.

Species composition is variable, and is initially probably a result of chance colonization, but fine grasses such as Wavy Hair-grass and Sheep's-fescue are frequent, together with Heath Bedstraw and Fir Clubmoss, and rhizomatous plants such as Bilberry and Bracken can gain a foothold around the peripheries. Calcareous Scree can support a wider range of species, including Limestone Fern and many other rarities. In the north-west Highlands, Woolly Fringe-moss forms extensive carpets over block Scree.

Scree is intrinsically unstable, and the successional process of vegetation development can be re-set at any time as the mobile surface layer shears away, leaving discrete patches of vegetation scattered across slopes. Patterns in the vegetation are formed

EXTENT IN KM^2	
Eng	37
Wal	4
Sco	602
NI	1
Ire	16

Knotts, Stonethwaite, Lake District – a typically fan-shaped scree spilling out from the bottom of a gully.

Distribution and extent

Widespread in the uplands. Pale shading indicates the broad distribution of the two relevant Annex I habitats (H8110 and H8120); darker shading (not for England) shows actual locations.

where plants persists in the shelter of boulders but are prevented from spreading laterally by moving rocks, which tend to build up on either side, leaving it in a slight depression. Scree vegetation usually only covers a few square metres, but in some situations can extend over hectares.

Similar habitats

Similar vegetation can be found on shattered rocks on mountain summits and in the crevices of boulders left by retreating glaciers (boulder fields).

Origins and development

Rock gradually disintegrates as a consequence of physical and chemical weathering. Rock falls, frost heave, avalanches and summer storm water all result in rocky material building up at the base of cliffs. Continued weathering and the addition of new material causes the rock to move downslope. The material varies in size from fine gravel brought by water to jumbles of bigger rocks from falls, and becomes sorted according to size as it flows down the slope, creating patches of evenly sized material. Larger rocks, which travel the furthest, tend to accumulate at the base of the scree. Over long time periods, Scree can consolidate and within the woodland zone would eventually support woodland, but this is generally prevented by livestock grazing and heather burning, and stable Scree tends to support heathland or grassland. Climatic conditions prevent succession at higher altitudes.

Conservation

Recreational activities (such as scree-running and hill-walking) impact on fragile vegetation and alter the structure of Scree, resulting in finer material sliding to the bottom of the slope. Atmospheric pollution may be preventing the establishment of fern communities in the southern Pennines. Screes are generally subject to the management practices of the surrounding land and a relaxation of livestock grazing and heather-burning would, in many cases, be beneficial in promoting the development of plant communities and allowing some natural succession to open woodland.

What to look for

Scree can support a rich fern flora, including Parsley Fern, Holly-fern, Limestone Fern, Oak Fern and Mountain Male-fern. The rare Arctic-alpine Alpine Lady-fern is characteristic of a snow-bed community occurring at high altitudes on block talus. Ring Ouzel and Wheatear nest in crevices. Look under stones for scarce invertebrates, including ground beetles, money and jumping spiders, and whorl snails.

LEFT: A sparse woodland cover of **Hazel** and **Yew** over limestone Scree in Cumbria. RIGHT: **Parsley Fern**, an early colonizer, growing on stabilized Scree.

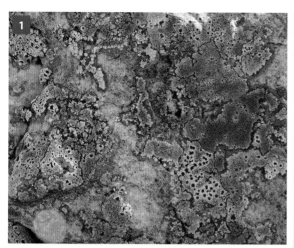

How to recognize

Scree is formed of drifts of broken rock that fan out on slopes beneath crags and the headwalls of corries in the uplands. From a distance, these smooth skirts of stone look completely bereft of life. At closer quarters, a scattering of vegetation becomes apparent, but the grey expanses of shifting rock still seem inhospitable. In late spring, as the ice melts, the clatter of falling rocks from the cliff above reminds the unwary that the process of scree formation is ongoing, while underfoot the rocks are unstable and easily dislodged. Around the margins and on more stable areas the fresh green of fern fronds catch the eye in summer. A closer look reveals crustose lichens and bryophytes, and screes in the montane zone can host a suite of small, rare Arctic-alpines.

When to visit

Late spring to summer for ferns and Arctic-alpine rarities.

Did you know?

The term scree comes from the Old Norse term for landslide, skriða

1 Crustose lichens are the first species to colonize. In the north-west Highlands, rocky habitats can support Atlantic bryophytes, such as the glossy **Donn's Notchwort** **2**, Juniper Prongwort and Bird's-foot Earwort (all species of the northern hepatic mat community).
3 The fresh, green fronds of **Scaly Male-fern**, another species found on Scree, stand out in the summer, and turn rusty-red as they die back in the winter.

Limestone Pavement page 395

Limestone Pavement is formed of exposures of Carboniferous limestone (*e.g.* the Burren, the Pennines and around Morecambe Bay) and Durness and Dalradian limestones (*e.g.* north-west Scotland). The exposed rock is scored by repeated fissures (known as grykes) that are usually 1–2 m deep, (although they have been recorded up to 6 m deep) and about 10 cm wide. The intervening blocks (clints) are washed clean of soil by rain. Their variable size and shape is a reflection of the composition and structure of the bedrock and the direction of the ice movements that exposed it. In some places the limestone is shattered, and chunks and chips lie scattered across the ground.

Limestone Pavement can have a very diverse flora, the result of the wide variety of microhabitats it creates. Thin, well-drained turf develops around clints on shattered Limestone Pavement and between terraces of pavement on hillsides, and supports species typical of Upland Calcareous Grassland (which sometimes shows a regular pattern of hummocks and dips where pavement is hidden under the turf). Shady, humid grykes, shallow pans and other solution features formed by the action of rainwater hold water and can be rich in ferns. Small rock fissures and cracks allow species typical of Rocky Slopes to take root. Overall, the vegetation of Limestone Pavement is strongly influenced by livestock grazing. Heavy grazing confines plants to grykes, but without grazing, scrub and trees can develop and shade out the specialist flora. Climate also plays a role in the variability of pavement flora, with montane species occurring at higher altitudes and in the north of Scotland.

Similar habitats

Limestone Pavement supporting long-established woodland is considered under Upland Mixed Ash Wood. Extensive areas of the Burren now support secondary Hazel scrub.

Origins and development

Limestone Pavement occurs where hard, horizontally bedded limestone was scoured or plucked (in the case of shattered pavement) by glacial action. Subsequent weathering by meltwater and rainwater along

Wild Boar Fell, Mallerstang, Cumbria – Limestone Pavement can occur in small patches within moorland where there are outcrops of limestone.

lines of weakness in the rock created grykes, although some larger grykes in smooth pavement are considered to have been formed during the Carboniferous, some 300 million years earlier. Rainwater percolating through woodland and soil became more acidic, furthering the development of solution features. Soils may then have washed into the grykes, sometimes vanishing into the subterranean drainage systems characteristic of limestone country. Human clearance of the woodland and subsequent grazing speeded up the process of exposure.

Conservation

Limestone Pavement generally forms part of agricultural systems and subsidies have promoted overgrazing. However, on the Burren, the traditional practice of winter grazing with hardy breeds of cattle has declined markedly, resulting in a recent increase in Hazel scrub. Light grazing is ideal, as it can prevent succession to closed woodland and maintain open areas without eliminating tall herbs.

What to look for

It is the combination of different floristic elements that makes the flora of Limestone Pavement so interesting. The humid microclimate and protection from grazing livestock provided by grykes is ideal for ferns, notably Limestone Fern, Rigid Buckler-fern, Green Spleenwort and (in Ireland) Maidenhair Fern, but also more widespread species such as Hard Shield-fern, Rustyback, Hart's-tongue and Male-fern. The shady conditions also suit woodland species (possibly relics of earlier woodland cover), and wherever a little soil has built up plants such as Wood Anemone, Primrose, Dog's Mercury and Lily-of-the-valley can be found. Look out also for plants associated with more open, calcareous conditions such as Burnet Rose, Bloody Crane's-bill,

EXTENT IN KM^2

Eng	20
Wal	1
Sco	3
NI	2
Ire	320

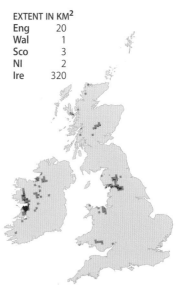

Distribution and extent

Widely distributed but limited in area. Pale shading indicates the broad distribution of the Annex I habitat (H8240); darker shading shows actual locations. Britain and Ireland holds a globally significant amount of Limestone Pavement and the Burren is a particularly important site.

LEFT: **Yewbarrow, Cumbria** – grazing promotes the growth of grasses (*e.g.* Blue Moor-grass and Sheep's-fescue) and, in this case, has created odd-shaped Yew. RIGHT: **Scar Close** on the flanks of **Ingleborough, North Yorkshire** has been protected from grazing since the mid-1970s and supports a rich and relatively tall flora of ferns and herbs together with Ash, Hazel and other tree species.

Limestone Bedstraw and Greater Knapweed.
The thin turf between terraces, amongst shattered
pavement and around pavements can be particularly
rich in calcareous grassland species. Leached soils
can support acidic heathland species, and the
bizarre juxtaposition of Heather and Tormentil with
calcareous species is a regular sight.

The botanical richness of Limestone Pavement is
its most obvious feature, but it also provides a variety
of niches for invertebrates. A specialist aquatic fauna
capable of withstanding desiccation is found in
solution hollows. Mossy and shaded clint tops support
scarce snails, rove beetles and woodlice. The Wall
Mason Bee (black, with metallic blue glints) needs full
sunlight, and collects pollen from Common Bird's-
foot-trefoil. On warm days butterflies can be abundant
– look out for the threatened High Brown and Pearl-
bordered Fritillaries as well as more common species.
Limestone Pavement is not particularly attractive to
birds, but Wheatear and Wren may nest in crevices
and holes, and Meadow Pipits are rarely far away. In
Ireland, the Burren is a stronghold for Pine Marten,
which is associated with Hazel scrub. Look for
Common Lizard basking on top of clints.

1 Cattle-grazing with a hardy breed such as this **Blue
Grey** on Whitbarrow in Cumbria is more suitable than
sheep-grazing in areas with Limestone Pavement.
2 **Hard Shield-fern** (*right*) and **Hart's-tongue**
(*arrowed*), two typical gryke species. **3** **The Burren,
Co. Clare** – most pavements are flat or gently sloping
but in karst landscapes such as the Burren they can be
terraced.

Did you know?

Hollows in the surface of clints collect rainwater, which gradually eats away at the limestone aided by acidic enzymes secreted by a blue-green algae. On the Burren, these solution hollows provide habitat for Mudwort, a rare annual.

How to recognize

Limestone Pavements are unique and unmistakable; strange, stony deserts where bare grey rock cut by deep fissures into striking geometric patterns can stretch to the horizon. Worn smooth and sculpted into swirled hollows and runnels, they are a testament to the power of millions of years of rainwater. On many pavements, any vegetation is closely cropped by livestock, but the deep, moist grykes can harbour a luxurious flora of ferns and there is sometimes a scattering of dwarfed and knarled trees and bushes. The richest sites support a beautiful flora of woodland species together with those of open, calcareous conditions. The smooth, stepping-stone like rocks combined with the possibility of rare species in the next gryke, make pavements inviting places to explore. Hollowed-out rock can ring underfoot, and the stone becomes warm to the touch in the slightest sunshine, although it can be slick with water in rainy weather.

When to visit

Late April (Spring Gentian) through to July/August (Bloody Crane's-bill) for flowering plants; ferns can still be seen into autumn.

1 **Southerscales, Ingleborough, North Yorkshire** – exposed conditions give little space for root growth and the lack of nutrients and water can result in dwarfed or even prostrate tree growth. **2** A wealth of orchids, including **Dark-red Helleborine** and other rare and scarce plants occur on Limestone Pavement; other specialities to look out for include Baneberry, Angular Solomon's-seal, Alpine Cinquefoil, Downy Currant, Bird's-foot Sedge and, in Ireland, Spring Gentian and Hoary Rock-rose. **3** **Spring Gentian** – an iconic plant of the Burren. The Burren supports 75% of the plant species found in Ireland and includes Mediterranean species as well as Arctic-alpines such as this gentian. **4** **Bloody Crane's-bill** is named after the deep red of its leaves in autumn. **5** **Limestone Fern** is particularly abundant on the Morecambe Bay pavements

WETLANDS

ORIGINS

Wetlands occur in a diversity of situations as a consequence of several different hydrological mechanisms, and most are peat-forming. Peat accumulates where conditions are too waterlogged for vegetation to decompose fully, which instead builds up into a layer of organic matter. This helps to retain moisture, raising the local water-table. Peat can reach several metres in depth, and in bogs isolates the vegetation from the more mineral-nutrient-rich groundwater. In contrast, fens still receive groundwater, for example in floodplains or open water transitions. Bog peat is of entirely vegetative origin, whereas fen peat tends to include a greater proportion of inorganic matter that has accumulated as silt in open water situations. Although it is often straightforward to identify the habitats present in a particular wetland (see *page 237* for a summary of habitat types described in this section), it is not always clear-cut where transitions occur. For example, areas that are predominantly Blanket Bog may also include wetland features associated with moving water; both Lowland Fen and Blanket Bog can include areas of Raised Bog; and Lowland Fen, Valley Mire and Raised Bog can all have patches of Quaking Bog.

Some wetlands are entirely natural while others have developed as a consequence of environmental changes created by humans. Some wetlands, such as Raised Bog and some Blanket Bog, are apparently relatively stable end-points in a successional trajectory that started with open water or bare rock after the last glaciation (or more recently, as in the case of the wetlands of the Norfolk and Suffolk Broads). Others, such as Reedbed and Lowland Fen, are inherently transitional and would generally develop into a different wetland type or woodland if left undisturbed.

Because of the constrained nature of lowland wetland habitats in particular, and perhaps also because of the overridingly dominant influence of anthropogenic factors, it is all too easy to lose sight of the natural dynamism of many wetlands in an attempt to safeguard the species typical of particular successional stages.

The Norfolk and Suffolk Broads are of particular interest in terms of hydrosere development as they demonstrate how it can be re-set by human activities. Peat originally developed in shallow valleys during the Atlantic Period, and eventually came to be dominated by carr (see Wet Woodland *page 66*). However, sea-level rise caused a return to open fen conditions and between the 12th and 14th centuries the area was extensively dug for peat. The dug areas subsequently re-flooded, creating the broads. Gradually, the open water silted up and swamp vegetation developed. Until the mid-20th century, many reed and sedge beds were cut, preventing succession to tall-herb fen and carr woodland, but recent decades have seen a rapid increase in the amount of carr.

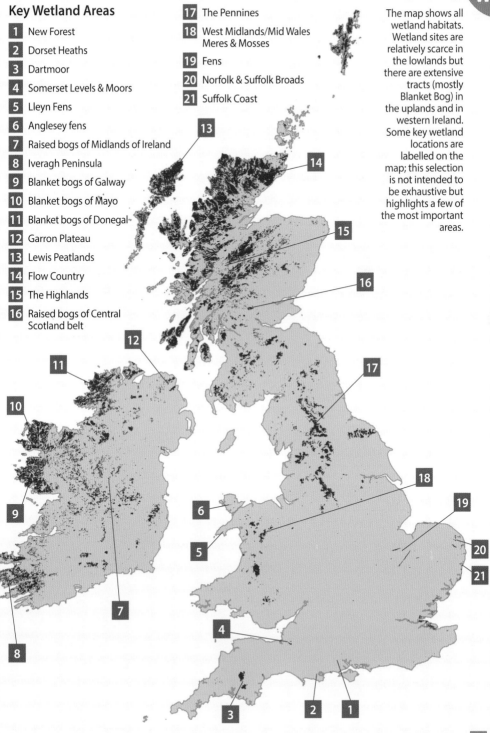

Key Wetland Areas

1 New Forest
2 Dorset Heaths
3 Dartmoor
4 Somerset Levels & Moors
5 Lleyn Fens
6 Anglesey fens
7 Raised bogs of Midlands of Ireland
8 Iveragh Peninsula
9 Blanket bogs of Galway
10 Blanket bogs of Mayo
11 Blanket bogs of Donegal
12 Garron Plateau
13 Lewis Peatlands
14 Flow Country
15 The Highlands
16 Raised bogs of Central Scotland belt

17 The Pennines
18 West Midlands/Mid Wales Meres & Mosses
19 Fens
20 Norfolk & Suffolk Broads
21 Suffolk Coast

The map shows all wetland habitats. Wetland sites are relatively scarce in the lowlands but there are extensive tracts (mostly Blanket Bog) in the uplands and in western Ireland. Some key wetland locations are labelled on the map; this selection is not intended to be exhaustive but highlights a few of the most important areas.

W

Wetland terminology Wetland terminology is notoriously confusing, largely because of the variability of wetlands and the lack of vernacular words to describe different conditions. Some frequently used key terms are defined here.

Ombrogenous	Wetlands formed on soil or rock through *paludification*, whereby water derived from precipitation is prevented from evaporating by a humid climate. They form peat and are hydrologically isolated from the landscape. Most are found in the wetter north and west.
Topogenous	Wetlands formed where the water-table reaches the surface in low-lying hollows or other places where landforms impede drainage. Waterlogging promotes the development of wetlands through the *terrestrialization* of shallow open waterbodies. They form peat.
Soligenous	Wetlands formed where the water-table reaches the surface in springs or seepages. They are found on slopes, and the ground surface is usually wet. They may or may not form peat, are most frequent in the north and west, and can also be found in association with the above wetland types.
Ombrotrophic	Wetlands fed only by rainfall, snowfall and mist ('cloud fed') and isolated from relatively mineral rich groundwater, resulting in acid and nutrient poor conditions *e.g.* Blanket Bog and Raised Bog.
Geotrophic or minerotrophic/rheotrophic	Wetlands fed by the earth or mineral groundwater / flowing water, which can be acidic or base-rich *e.g.* Lowland Fen, Valley Mire, Upland Spring and Flush.

TYPES OF WETLAND HABITAT

Wetland habitats can be categorized in terms of their hydrology (including the source, base-status, and nutrient status of the water), their topography, the vegetation they support, and how they have been used. Hydrology can be complex and difficult to establish simply from observation and vegetation can be similar in wetlands formed by quite different processes. In this book, wetlands are categorized according to their physical attributes and their vegetation using names that are, on the whole, commonly used and understood, although there is some variation in how they are applied. Six types of wetland are described in the following sections: three types of bog (Blanket Bog, Raised Bog and Valley Mire) as well as Lowland Fen, Reedbed and Upland Spring and Flush (which includes upland small-sedge fens). Transitional types can also be found (see *page 241*). Although marshy grasslands such as Coastal Floodplain and Grazing Marsh and Purple Moor-grass and Rush Pasture are covered within the Grassland section, they can also be considered as wetlands.

CONSERVATION INTEREST AND PROTECTION

Wetlands are greatly valued for the richness and diversity of the vegetation and wildlife they support, and for the ecological processes that functioning examples still demonstrate. They also play a key role in maintaining water quality and in flood alleviation. Intact peatlands sequester carbon – some of the carbon captured by plants is locked into peat rather than released back into the atmosphere during decomposition, and a significant amount is stored within the surface vegetation. However, this means they can also be a carbon source, and millions of tonnes of carbon dioxide are released into the atmosphere through peatland exploitation globally.

All wetland habitats, or components of them, are recognized as being of European importance (see *page 37*), with the exception of Reedbed.

'Bog bursts' occur when the surface of a bog ruptures and releases a torrent of liquid peat. Such bursts, which can be hazardous, tend to occur after intense rainfall. In the similar (if less eloquently named) case of 'peat failure', rafts of peat break away and are transported down-slope. Bog bursts are largely confined to Ireland and Northern Ireland; peat failure is also observed in Britain. Both can be triggered by anthropogenic factors, and may be affected by climate change.

HABITAT	DESCRIPTION	NOTES
Blanket Bog *page 244* *page 396*	Bog that has developed on dry land in wet climates and is rain-fed. Vegetation is relatively short and dominated by dwarf-shrubs, sedges and bog-mosses due to the low availability of minerals. Widespread and extensive in the uplands.	'Blanket mire' refers to landscapes mantled in peat that include Blanket Bog with areas of Raised Bog and transitional communities which can be hard to distinguish at first glance.
Raised Bog *page 249* *page 397*	Bog that has developed from open water and is now rain-fed. Vegetation is relatively short and dominated by dwarf-shrubs, sedges and bog-mosses due to the low availability of minerals. More common in the wetter north and west, but can form in drier areas.	Can include Quaking Bog (see *page 241*) where rafts of vegetation develop over a lens of water.
Upland Spring and Flush *page 252* *page 398*	Springs and associated flushes of water seeping over vegetation in upland settings. Acid or base-rich vegetation, usually characterized by bryophytes and small sedges.	Includes small-sedge fens.
Lowland Fen *page 256* *page 397*	Calcareous fen in floodplains, open water transitions and basins fed by base-rich ground and surface water (as well as rainwater), supporting diverse and lush vegetation including swamp vegetation and calcareous fen meadows.	Sometimes used to encompass 'poor fen' or valley Transition Mire (see *page 241*).
Valley Mire *page 260* *page 398*	Valleyhead mire that develops where water flows through a shallow valley in a heathland system, fed by groundwater and surface water (as well as rainwater).	Can technically be Transition Mire (see *page 241*) where more base-rich water enters from seepages.
Reedbed *page 265* *page 397*	Swamp vegetation dominated by Common Reed, fed by ground and standing water of variable base and nutrient status.	

NOTE: **Mire** is a term used for any ecosystem that accumulates peat; the name comes from the Scandinavian *myr*.

The oceanic climate of western Britain and Ireland allows blanket mire to develop over huge areas of the uplands, such as here in **Connemara**.

Blanket Bog and Raised Bog are locally rare peatland types for which Britain and Ireland are of particular importance. Some wetland habitats are naturally limited in their extent (*e.g.* Upland Spring and Flush), while others are very extensive (*e.g.* Blanket Bog, which covers huge areas in the uplands). In the lowlands in particular, many wetlands have been destroyed or greatly reduced in area through drainage. The remaining area of Lowland Fen and Reedbed is a tiny fragment of that in existence before drainage intensified in the 17th century. Much has also developed naturally into Wet Woodland as traditional management practices have died out over the last 100 years. In Ireland, Raised Bog has been especially devastated by peat extraction in addition to drainage for agriculture and forestry, and only around 8% now remains.

Many wetlands are currently in poor condition, although a relatively high proportion are protected through designation (*e.g.* in England about 75% are within SSSIs). Current threats to wetland habitats revolve around water availability and quality and land management practices. Many raised bogs are still threatened by commercial peat cutting, and overgrazing is an issue on many upland blanket bogs. In contrast, lack of management is impacting on raised bogs, lowland fens and reedbeds. The degree of fragmentation of lowland wetland habitats means that many are surrounded by arable land, with the consequent problems of nutrient run-off

ABOVE: Wetlands can be very small in size, such as this spring in the **Cairngorms**, or cover whole landscapes.

Cattle grazing at **Market Weston Fen, Suffolk**.

and nitrate contamination of groundwater, drainage and water extraction, and lack of grazing animals. Water availability is likely to be an ongoing issue given the increases in water consumption and the existing and predicted impacts of climate change. Peatbogs have adapted to climate change in the past, but future resilience will depend upon their condition, and specifically how active they are in terms of bog-moss growth and peat formation. Restoration projects have been carried out on many bogs of European importance, and there have been significant improvements in water quality in areas such as The Norfolk and Suffolk Broads. The Great Fen project in East Anglia is an ambitious long-term project to re-create a whole wetland landscape.

CULTURAL IMPORTANCE

It is hard to imagine the extensive wetland wildernesses that existed in the lowlands until some 400 years ago. However, although wild in aspect, many were used extensively: reed and sedge were cut for thatch, peat was cut for fuel, and they were used for grazing livestock and for wildfowling.

The cultural significance of some of these practices is still appreciated today. In contrast, wetlands still remain a key feature in upland landscapes in the form of blanket mires, and their presence is taken for granted. In Ireland, bog (both upland and lowland) still holds a unique place in the national culture, perhaps because of its prevalence. Bogs abound in Irish mythology, folklore, music and poetry, and bog is even explored as a symbol of the Irish psyche by Irish poet Seamus Heaney.

Peatlands are unique among habitats in their capacity to record the story of the landscape, and sometimes of the people who lived there. They are museums of the past, preserving in layers of peat evidence of environmental and cultural change. The Sweet Track in the Somerset Levels is one of a number of prehistoric marsh tracks that have been found within peat, and demonstrates highly developed woodworking and woodland management skills on the part of the Neolithic people who built it nearly 6,000 years ago. Artefacts and even human bodies uncovered in peatlands (such as the 2,000-year-old Lindow Man found in a Cheshire bog) suggest that some bogs were sacred places where people went to offer sacrifices to placate their gods. Paleontological records are also particularly well-preserved in wetlands. Analysis of pollen preserved in peat, and also invertebrate and wood remains, have provided invaluable insights into the development of peatlands and their responses to environmental and anthropogenic factors both spatially and through time.

Peat cutting for fuel has been practiced for millennia. Traditional, small-scale peat cutting is limited in extent and is rotational, allowing vegetation to recolonize. The cultural value of traditional peat cutting is strongly upheld where it still takes place such as here in Connemara (TOP) and Coll (ABOVE).

Reed was traditionally cut to provide thatching material, but the practice declined rapidly in the 20th century. Commercial reed-cutting has recently experienced a small resurgence (particularly in Norfolk) and is also carried out for conservation purposes.

Fens (LEFT) receive their nutrients from rocks and soils via groundwater and are relatively high in mineral nutrients, allowing lush, diverse vegetation to develop. Most bogs (RIGHT) receive their nutrients via precipitation that is acid and low in mineral nutrients and therefore support less diverse vegetation.

BOG-MOSSES

1 Red Bog-moss grows in loose carpets or soft hummocks; its red coloration is eye-catching. **2** Papillose Bog-moss is a distinctively chunky moss. **3** Feathery Bog-moss is the most aquatic bog-moss and is found in pools, runnels and ditches; it forms structure-less mats if removed from the water. **4** Golden Bog-moss is locally common in pools and hollows on the Dorset Heaths; its colour and the neat arrangement of its leaves are distinctive.

Transition Mire and Quaking Bog

Transition Mire and Quaking Bog (called after the Annex I habitat of that name) is transitional between acid bog and alkaline fen habitats. It occurs where there is lateral movement of water or groundwater influence that can ameliorate the acidic and nutrient-poor influence of the peaty substrate. This is a very wet, quaggy habitat of floating rafts of bog vegetation that tremble underfoot, of swampy open-water fringes of Bottle Sedge, or of seepages delineated with green sedges in mires. Quaking Bog of floating vegetation is also known as hover, scraw or schwingmoor, and is referred to independently in the text where it is useful to differentiate it from Transition Mire. It develops in a wide range of situations varying from the huge floodplain mire of the Insh Marshes in Speyside to the blanket mire of Rannoch Moor and quaking bogs in the valley mires of the New Forest and Dorset. It is also indicative of successional transitions (*e.g.* between Lowland Fen and Raised Bog). A characteristic feature is the presence of Bottle Sedge, a tall sedge with bottle-brush shaped heads that catch the wind, and the grey-green sward may be enriched with the white flowers of Bog Bean and the strikingly geometric, silvery leaves of Marsh Cinquefoil. Where conditions are less acidic, the sward can be more species-rich, and 'brown mosses' (a group

ABOVE: **Bottle Sedge** – a typical species of very wet mires. Its seed cases are filled with air, allowing them to float in the surrounding water. BELOW: **Insh Marshes, Speyside**, is the largest Transition Mire in Britain, occupying a five-mile stretch of the River Spey floodplain.

of yellow, brown and red coloured mosses typical of mineral-rich fens) replace bog-mosses. On the margins of lakes and pools it forms a buoyant swamp community, often with Common Sedge, Common Reed or Common Cottongrass and tall herbs including Ragged-Robin, Meadowsweet and Angelica. It is found in ladder fens and water tracks (see *page 242*) in Blanket Bog, on the marginal lagg (see *page 249*) of Raised Bog and on lochsides where water seeps down slopes. In basin mires, mobile rafts of transition vegetation can float over more base-rich water. It can also develop on the surface of cut-over mires or on partially drained bogs that have re-flooded. Transition Mire can reach into the montane zone, where small stands in hollows in calcareous montane grasslands can include Arctic-alpine species.

Transition Mire and Quaking Bog is usually a component of larger wetlands, and management therefore needs to take into account the hydrological integrity of whole sites. The tendency for rafts to consolidate and succeed to woodland contributes to habitat loss if not balanced by the development of new habitat, and sometimes artificial rejuvenation of the hydrosere may be needed.

KEY FEATURES

Hydrological features

Hydrological features add diversity to the structure and vegetation of wetlands. The terms used to describe these can be applied variably, so their usage in this book is defined here. Seepages occur where groundwater flows out from a mineral aquifer to the surface of a wetland. Runnels or rills are small lines of quite rapidly flowing water on slopes. Soakways are linear zones of flowing water and are distinguished by vegetation that differs from that of the surrounding wetland (*e.g.* Marsh St. John's-wort and Bog Pondweed may be present). Water tracks are similar but wetter, with flowing water visible on the surface running between tussocks or patches of mire vegetation. Ladder fens comprise a series of narrow pools separated by ridges aligned with the contour; this feature tends to support Transition Mire vegetation.

Hummocks and Hollows

In bogs, microtopography is a key feature, particularly in the cooler and wetter north and west. Hummocks and hollows are formed by the vertical zonation of bog-mosses in response to hydrological conditions. Hummocks of Red and Imbricate Bog-mosses often support Round-leaved Sundew. Hollows contain Papillose and Soft Bog-mosses, and deeper pools tend to support Feathery and Cow-horn Bog-mosses, with Oblong-leaved Sundew, Common Cottongrass and White Beak-sedge, or bare peat. These hummocks, hollows and pools can create distinctive patterning on the surface of bogs which differs according to topography and geographical location. It is thought that larger bog pools may persist for thousands of years.

Wetland landscapes

Wetlands are a complex group of habitats, with key features varying between different wetland types. Particular features of interest are highlighted in the relevant habitat sections (for example, surface patterning in Blanket Bog, the lagg and rand of Raised Bog, the presence of seepages and carr woodland in Valley Mire, and fen meadows in Lowland Fen). The image is annotated as an example of how to read a wetland landscape and the kind of features to look for, such as the interface between vegetation and water, different successional stages and variation in vegetation structure. In this

Minsmere, Suffolk. Key features of this Reedbed include: ❶ open water, ❷ narrow channels, ❸ fringing vegetation, ❹ early successional reedbed, ❺ drier reedbed on the landward side, ❻ scrub patches.

reedbed, channels of open water provide habitat for aquatic species (see Freshwaters, *page 270*) not found within the dense swamp vegetation. Water deeper than about one metre inhibits the growth of Common Reed, such areas contributing to the overall structural diversity of the reedbed. Narrower channels may be shallower, adding to the range of wildlife that can be supported, with fringing Common Reed providing shelter for species such as Bittern. Early successional reedbed remains wet and generally supports the greatest number of specialist wetland invertebrates, including a range of flies. Reedbeds are also important for a suite of rare moths, and other invertebrates that pupate in the litter or underground only occur where the reedbed becomes drier. Patches of scrub in drier areas are important for species such as Cetti's Warbler.

The hydrosere

Wetlands can show a variety of transitional stages represented by different vegetation types and structures. The classic development from open water through swamp and fen to carr woodland or ombrotrophic bog is referred to as a hydrosere, and reaches is full expression in the lowlands. The process of succession can take anything from 1,000 to about 4,000 years, which means that most shallow, post-glacial waterbodies have long since completed their hydrosere development. However, secondary succession can occur, as is the case in the Norfolk and Suffolk Broads, and succession is often seen in ponds and other artificial waterbodies. Succession from open water to swamp, via submerged and emergent aquatic plants, depends on the water depth being less than about one metre. Once this has occurred through siltation and the deposition of organic matter, swamp vegetation can swiftly take hold, provided there is no erosion. Fen vegetation follows and, as the sward becomes drier, the surface rises above the surrounding water-table. In some cases woody species may colonize but, where surface conditions become acidic, the growth of bog-mosses can trigger the development of Raised Bog. In some cases, paleo-ecological evidence suggests that bog-mosses have replaced woody species. Most of these stages in the hydrosere can be reversed, and are likely to be quite variable depending on local conditions. Succession plays out differently on Blanket Bog, where a wet climate creates waterlogged conditions on previously dry land, leading directly to the formation of ombrotrophic bog, although in some cases bog may have replaced woodland as the climate became wetter during the Atlantic Period 5,000–8,000 years ago.

FURTHER INFORMATION

Great Fen – a long-term project to restore an extensive area of wetland in the east of England
www.greatfen.org.uk/

Bogs: The Ecology, classification and conservation of ombrotrophic mires by Richard Lindsay (SNH, 1995).

Conserving bogs. The management handbook by Brooks and Stoneman (The Stationery Office, 1997)

Blanket Bog can be found from Dartmoor to Shetland and from Co. Cork to Co. Donegal between sea level and 1,000 m. It forms over mainly acidic soils and rock in wet, cloudy climates where rainfall outstrips evapo-transpiration and causes the formation of iron pans in the soils, creating waterlogged conditions. Bog-mosses flourish on wet, acidic ground and are resistant to decomposer microbes. Dead plant material slowly accumulates as peat, which increases waterlogging and isolates the vegetation from the groundwater and underlying soils and bedrock, further reducing nutrient availability. The resulting wet, very acidic and nutrient-poor conditions suit only a limited number of key species, particularly bog-mosses (*e.g.* Papillose, Red and Soft Bog-mosses). Cross-leaved Heath and cottongrasses grow from the bog-moss carpet, and drier areas support Heather and Deergrass.

In the cool, wet, northern and western uplands, whole landscapes are cloaked in peat. Blanket Bog is the most extensive element within these ecosystems, which are termed blanket mires. However, other habitats can also be found. Raised Bog occurs where the terrestrialization of waterbodies has taken place but the vegetation is similar to that of the surrounding Blanket Bog. Fen vegetation can be found along watercourses and flushes and ladder fens are characterized by transition communities. In the west, where rainfall is sufficient for peat formation on steeper slopes, water movement promotes vegetation more typical of Valley Mire. Peat can also form over calcareous rock if conditions are sufficiently wet.

Similar habitats

Upland Wet Heath supports many of the same species, but occurs where peat is less than half-a-metre deep and the key peat-forming species (bog-mosses and cottongrasses) are not prominent. Raised Bog can be difficult to identify within blanket mires, but lowland examples are distinctive in their form and context.

The Flow Country in Caithness and Sutherland is a huge expanse of habitat thought to be entirely natural and unparalleled in the rest of Britain and Ireland. Nearly 5% of the world's Blanket Bog occurs here. Surface patterning is particularly well developed.

Origins and development

Most blanket peat development began 5,000–6,000 years ago when the climate became warmer and wetter. In many areas the formation of Blanket Bog may have been at least partly due to forest clearance by humans. Loss of the forest canopy led to waterlogging as water-loss through transpiration decreased, resulting in conditions unsuitable for tree growth. However, in the wettest, coolest places such as the Flow Country and the Northern Isles, Blanket Bog developed naturally, forming a kind of oceanic tundra. The relative roles of both anthropogenic and natural forces on the historical and current extent of Blanket Bog is not yet fully understood.

The tradition of burning bogs to encourage palatable young growth dates back to at least the 17th century, but promotes grassy growth at the expense of peat-forming species and kills invertebrates. Drainage and sheep-grazing have also degraded extensive areas, causing peat to dry out, oxidise and erode. Thousands of hectares were lost to afforestation in the second half of the 20th century, encouraged through scandalous tax breaks. Commercial peat cutting for power production, domestic briquettes and horticulture has destroyed extensive areas.

Conservation

It is unclear how Blanket Bog will respond to climate change, and the conservation priority is therefore to restore degraded bogs to increase their resilience, which will also improve water quality, reduce flood risk farther down the catchment and sequester carbon. Models based on predicted rainfall suggest that Blanket Bog may become restricted to the north-west of Britain. However, this does not take account of biotic factors, particularly changes in the relative abundance of bog-mosses. Hummock

EXTENT IN KM^2	
Eng	2,300
Wal	532
Sco	17,590
NI	1,400
Ire	2,574

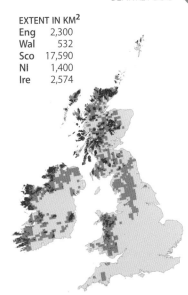

Distribution and extent

Widespread in the north and west of Britain and western Ireland. Britain and Ireland hold over 20% of the world's blanket bog. Pale shading indicates broad distribution of the Annex I Habitat blanket bogs (H7130); darker shading shows actual locations (drawn from a range of sources).

Strath Dionard, Foinaven, Sutherland – Blanket Bog occupies the flat valley floor, grading into Heather – Bilberry Upland Dry Heath then acidic Scree on the steeper sides. Greenshank breed in this bog.

mosses are likely to proliferate, but as they decompose more slowly, peat may build more rapidly and help maintain waterlogging. Blocking drainage channels is particularly important in areas where the number of rainfall days make blanket peat formation marginal, leading to drying and erosion. Allowing woodland to regenerate naturally on slopes at the margins of Blanket Bog may be beneficial where marginal erosion and instability on slopes is an issue. Efforts to curtail commercial peat cutting and the demand for horticultural peat are ongoing.

1 **Quinag, Sutherland** – blanket mires smother the landscape from high mountain slopes down to the sea in both Sutherland and Connemara; note the cut peat face. **2** **Inish Boffin, Connemara** – domestic peat cutting on a patch of Atlantic Blanket Bog just a few metres above sea level. **3** **Diamond Hill, Connemara** – erosion features such as peat hags and gullies are often found on plateaux and watershed bogs but are not fully understood; they may be natural or due to overgrazing and burning. **4** **Rannoch Moor, Highlands** – pine stumps are often exposed in peat hags in bogs that developed on forested land. Woodland has probably developed and retreated on the margins of bogs over millennia, and in other countries is still found on drier mineral ridges within and around bog systems.

1 The distinctive surface patterning found particularly in the north and west is created by the varying growth forms of different bog-mosses. Hollows and pools can be aligned in distinctive repeating patterns that change according to climate and topography. **2** From July to September look out for the dainty **Black Darter**, which breeds in bog pools and drainage ditches. In the Highlands the scarce Azure Hawker can be seen settling briefly by pools during June and July. **3** **Oblong-leaved Sundew** – a species typical of wet hollows. **4** Nutrient-poor conditions favour carnivorous plant species such as sundews, butterworts and **bladderworts**. Bladderworts take just a fraction of a second to catch prey in a highly sophisticated bladder trap where they are digested and absorbed. **5** **Cahersiveen, Iveragh** – cottongrass-dominated Blanket Bog near the summit of Bentee.

What to look for

Blanket Bog, poor in nutrients and lacking large-scale structural diversity, supports low densities of vertebrates. Look out for tundra-breeding waders such as Golden Plover, Dunlin and (in Scotland) Greenshank, joined in the far north by Arctic Skua. Golden Eagle, Hen Harrier and Short-eared Owl hunt over blanket bogs, and Otters sometimes make their way up gullies from rivers and lochs. Blanket Bog also provides seclusion for Red-throated Diver and Common Scoter breeding on lochans, and is rich in both aquatic and terrestrial invertebrates.

While the core plant species of Blanket Bog remain fairly constant throughout its range, look out for the local influence of climate and topography. Bog-myrtle, White Beak-sedge and Atlantic bryophytes such as Purple Spoonwort are typical on more oceanic western bogs, where Purple Moor-grass can dominate on steeper slopes if there is a degree of lateral flushing. Black Bog-rush is particularly common in western Ireland under the influence of wind-blown marine salts. Higher, drier eastern bogs support more Hare's-tail Cottongrass and dwarf-shrubs, with Bearberry, Mountain Crowberry, Bog Bilberry and reindeer lichens characterizing high-altitude Blanket Bog in the Cairngorms. In the north and west (particularly the Hebrides), Woolly Hair-moss co-dominates with bog-mosses. In the south Pennines and Southern Uplands swards of Hare's-foot Cottongrass cover large areas where bogs have been degraded through burning, drainage, atmospheric pollution and grazing.

How to recognize

Treeless and sodden with water, blanket bogs can be wild and desolate places. Often rainy or shrouded in cloud, their bleak beauty lies in the wide open spaces and huge skies and the strangely intimate landscape of hummocks and hollows formed of spongy, green, golden and red-coloured bog-mosses. These are often dotted with intriguing insectivorous plants and in the empty landscape, elusive waders betray their presence with distinctive, haunting calls.

On the deepest peat on level or undulating ground small lochans and pools make for treacherous walking. On slopes, small islands and cliffs of peat created through erosion (and known as peat hags) confound the unwary walker.

Many blanket bogs have been drained, burned and cut-over for peat, and this is seen in the more uniform vegetation dominated by sedges and Heather. In the best (and often most remote) sites, the water-table remains high throughout the year, and the different growth forms of bog-mosses result in striking, repeated patterns.

When to visit

Late spring–summer for breeding birds, summer–autumn for flowering plants, year-round for bog-mosses if conditions allow.

Did you know?

Peat in Blanket Bogs can reach a depth of over five metres, and accumulates at roughly half-a-millimetre per year.

Golden Plover breeds in Blanket Bog and other moorland habitats, feeding on craneflies and other invertebrates. A wary species, it is often heard rather than seen, despite its striking summer plumage.

Raised Bog

page 397

Classic lowland Raised Bog is generally found in plains and on valley floors where the topography impedes natural drainage. The dome of the bog is composed of peat particles suspended in water and contained within a living skin of bog-mosses, heathers and Hare's-tail Cottongrass, beneath which peat formation is ongoing. Bog-mosses act as a sponge, holding water gained through precipitation. This water is gradually lost through evapotranspiration, by seepage through the sides of the dome, and in some cases by streams originating within the bog. However, in some bogs a lens of water remains under the vegetative crust, creating Quaking Bog (see *page 241*). The central dome has a slightly steeper margin (the rand), which may be bordered by a lagg. The lagg forms where the bog water-table meets the water-table of the surrounding mineral soil and can support fen or Transition Mire vegetation (see *page 241*). However, most laggs have been drained and intact examples are rare throughout Europe. The wettest area is generally the relatively flat top of the domed bog, which supports similar plant communities to those of other acidic mires. Mosses include Magellanic, Papillose, Red, Feathery and Soft Bog-mosses. Cottongrasses, Deergrass, Heather and Cross-leaved Heath are common, together with Bog Asphodel and Round-leaved Sundew.

Several rare invertebrate species are found on Raised Bog, but often from just one or two sites (*e.g.* Mire Pill Beetle, Bog Bush-cricket, Bilberry Pug (a moth) and Bog Sun-jumper Spider), and it is probable that there are species still to be recorded. Remaining bogs are concentrated in the Central Belt of Scotland, the Solway region, north-west England and central Ireland.

Foulshaw Moss, Cumbria with carpets of cotton grass. This site holds breeding Osprey, Large Heath and is good for dragonflies.

EXTENT IN KM²	
Eng	174
Wal	25
Sco	208
NI	89
Ire	42

Distribution and extent

Widespread with notable local concentrations. This habitat is extremely rare globally but widely distributed in Europe, with a significant proportion in Britain and particularly Ireland. Pale green indicates shows the broad distribution of the Annex I habitats (both active and degraded raised bogs, H7110 and H7120); darker shading indicates shows locations for England, Scotland and Wales.

Similar habitats

Raised Bog supports similar species to Blanket Bog and within blanket mire complexes in wetter uplands unconfined Raised Bog can spill over onto the surrounding peatland. Erosion features typical of Blanket Bog are generally absent from Raised Bog and pools are less common (except in Ireland).

Origins and development

Raised Bog originates in shallow glacial lakes and hollows. These fill with the un-decayed remains of marginal vegetation and in-washed sediment, forming fen peat and cutting off the nutrient supply from the lake margins. The surface is colonized by bog-mosses able to flourish in the wet and nutrient-poor conditions, and bog peat begins to develop. The peat raises the vegetation above the original surface of the lake, isolating it from the groundwater, until it becomes entirely dependent on rainfall for nutrients.

Raised Bog has fared particularly badly in the last 100 years or so with only 6% of British and less than 1% of Irish bogs persisting in a relatively undisturbed condition. Many have been drained or stripped for agricultural use, or afforested. Remaining bogs are often too degraded to qualify for protection under wildlife legislation. In Ireland in particular, commercial peat stripping for fuel and horticultural use is carried out on an industrial scale. Atmospheric pollution is affecting the relative proportions of different bog-mosses.

Conservation

The conservation status of Raised Bog is poor, and ongoing effort is needed to halt its destruction and deterioration. On remaining bogs, conservation management centres on raising the water-table by blocking perimeter and internal drains, creating hydrological buffer zones at the margins and removing trees. Scrub encroachment is common on bogs, particularly those drying out as a consequence of drainage or water abstraction from underlying aquifers. However, peat-forming species can recolonize cut surfaces, and there is plenty of potential for the restoration of active peat-forming systems.

What to look for

Unsurprisingly, bogs are good for Common Toad and Common Frog, but Common Lizard and Adder may also be seen. Many specialist invertebrates are extremely rare, but Large Heath and Small Pearl-bordered Fritillary may be encountered. Characteristic plants include Cranberry, Bog-rosemary and Round-leaved Sundew, but look out also for more generalist species such as the Lesser Butterfly-orchid.

Peat cuttings in the **Carhar River basin, Iveragh** – of the original 310,000 ha of Raised Bog in Ireland, only 1% remains as active bog, although it is estimated that restoration may be possible on a further 15%.

How to recognize

Raised bogs are usually discrete entities in the landscape and, unlike blanket bogs, are often individually named. They are formed of a dome of peat that can rise up several metres above the surrounding agricultural land, although this can be hard to appreciate on the ground. Wet terrain makes Raised Bogs tricky to explore and it is often difficult to get a feel for a whole site unless there is a view from a nearby hill.

On pristine bogs, colourful carpets of bog-mosses patterned with hollows and hummocks are interspersed with sedges and heathers. Many sites are now degraded, having been drained or cut over for peat. These are more heathery and sometimes support an open canopy of birch, pine and Rhododendron woodland. Most Raised Bog is found in the lowlands, but upland examples in blanket mire occur.

When to visit

June–August for drier conditions, flora and invertebrates (including midges and mosquitoes!). A hard frost can make walking easier in winter, which is a good time to look out for raptors hunting over the bog.

1 **Flanders Moss, Stirlingshire** – one of the biggest (and best) raised bogs in the UK. Drier areas are often invaded by trees such as Downy Birch, which are removed where possible to prevent them from drying out the bog further. However, marginal scrub is important for invertebrates. **2** **Hare's-tail Cottongrass** can be particularly abundant on degraded bog. **3** **Bog-mosses** intertwined with **4** **Cranberry** at Carsegowan Moss, Galloway, a remnant of the once extensive Solway peatlands that formed over estuarine clays.

Wherever the water-table is high and water cannot percolate into the substrate, water is forced to the surface, either bubbling out from an obvious springhead or seeping through the vegetation. If the substrate remains impermeable down-slope or is saturated with water, the water flows over the surface in rills or more diffusely in flushes. The vegetation is strongly influenced by the mineral content of the rock through which the water flows, and also the temperature of the water.

Spring water from calcareous rocks is rich in dissolved calcium carbonate, which precipitates out on contact with the air and leaves a crunchy yellowish deposit of calcium (tufa) behind that can help build up low mounds of mosses such as the soft orange-brown Curled Hook-moss. Base-rich flushes and small-sedge fens retain a well-developed bryophyte layer, usually of brown mosses (see *page 241*). These are joined by small sedges such as Flea Sedge and Carnation Sedge, and Common Butterwort, Bird's-eye Primrose and Grass-of-Parnassus may be present. Taller swards can include Angelica, Meadowsweet, Marsh-marigold, Globeflower and Ragged-Robin.

The bright green Fountain Apple-moss often marks out springs on acid rocks, sometimes with the golden-green Marsh Forklet-moss and the dark green or purple liverwort Water Earwort. In acid flushes, a green layer of bog-mosses is sometimes joined by Upland Wet Heath species, and sedges can include Bottle Sedge and Star Sedge.

In the montane zone, Spring and Flush vegetation is enriched with Arctic-alpines. It is also found associated with ice-cold springs and channels of meltwater in late-lying snow-beds (see High Montane Heath and Snow-bed, *page 208*). In the warmer oceanic regions of south-west England and Wales, small, well-defined stands of Round-leaved Crowfoot and Blinks emerge from running water in rills and small streams.

Springs and Flushes form permanent wetland features in the landscape and so are important for insects, spiders and other invertebrates with an annual life-cycle. Cranefly larvae feed among mosses and emerge in

A flush on **Carn Ban Mor, Cairngorm.**

great numbers in the summer, providing food for upland wader and grouse chicks, Ring Ouzels, Wheatears and other upland birds.

Similar habitats

Upland Springs and Flushes can be quite sharply delineated or more diffuse, gradually merging into the surrounding heathland or grassland. On lower hillsides, flushed gullies support Sharp-flowered and Soft Rushes in Upland Acid Grassland and Upland Rush Pasture.

Origins and development

Spring and Flush vegetation in the montane zone is natural, maintained by the harsh climate, but at lower altitudes within moorland and upland grassland it is generally grazed. Grazing can help maintain species-richness by removing tall rushes and grasses and keeping the surface open for small flowers and sedges; however, these small features are vulnerable to trampling damage, particularly where there are tufa formations. Bryophytes are particularly susceptible to air-borne pollutants but the 'critical load' beyond which habitat deterioration will occur is not known. Changes in the extent and duration of snow cover will affect high-altitude Springs and Flushes.

Conservation

Upland springs and flushes are typically very small, and are therefore usually subject to management decisions made about wider areas. Greater awareness of their presence and sensitivities would help ensure that management is not harmful. At high altitudes, this is probably a climax vegetation type, although the presence of willows in related Scandinavian vegetation and also Mountain Ledge hints at the potential presence of montane willows under lighter grazing regimes. Climate change may result in the loss of montane species.

EXTENT UNKNOWN

Distribution and extent

Widely distributed throughout the uplands. Extent unknown as some features can be very small. Pale shading indicates the broad distribution of 4 relevant Annex I habitats (H7220, H7240, H7210, H7140) [note that these Annex I types do not necessarily always correspond well to Upland Spring and Flush]; darker shading shows actual locations where recorded (no data for Ireland).

LEFT: **Balnakiel, Sutherland** – a calcareous flush with brown mosses and Carnation Sedge almost at sea level on Durness limestone. RIGHT: **Alpine Silverwort** growing with Lindberg's Bog-moss.

What to look for
Curled Hook-moss growing with Hooked Scorpion-moss and
Yellow Starry Feather-moss is a good indicator of species-rich
flushes. At medium and high altitudes, look out for Yellow
Saxifrage and Russet Sedge.

How to recognize
Small and richly coloured patches
of vegetation that catch the eye
amongst duller upland swards indicate
the presence of springs and flushes.
Springs are often surrounded by
plush cushions and mats of mosses
and liverworts that are saturated with
water, and the sound of flowing water
is never far away. Where the water
seeps diffusely over the surface in
flushes, the ground can be open and
stony, or support thick vegetation
comprising small sedges, rushes and
herbs. These upland jewels are always
worth investigating and can support
beautiful plants, many of which are
uncommon or rare.

When to visit
Year-round for bryophytes (conditions
permitting); summer for flowering
plants.

1 Starry Saxifrage can be found in wet flushes up to 1,000 m. **2** Common Butterwort is a characteristic species
of base-rich flushes and obtains nutrients from small flies caught in its sticky leaf rosette. **3** Coire an Lochain,
Cairngorms – an acidic flush rich in bog-mosses and other bryophytes. **4** Whernside, Yorkshire Dales – this acid
spring below the summit feeds a nearby tarn.

Creag Meagaidh, Central Highlands – Springs and Flushes are most common in the uplands where the water-table is constantly topped up by rain, mist and snow.

Lowland Fen   page 397

Lowland Fen is found where the ground remains waterlogged for most of the year or is periodically inundated in floodplains. It occurs in shallow valleys and adjoining open water and is fed by surface and groundwater, as well as rainwater. Conditions are variable, and can be acid to base-rich and nutrient-poor to fertile. This is reflected in the vegetation, which also varies according to past management. Grazing, mowing, draining and peat-digging all interact with hydrological factors to shape the flora and the structure of vegetation. The small-sedge fens of Anglesey and Ireland are found in alkaline conditions with low nutrient levels. The classic tall-herb and sedge fens of The Norfolk and Suffolk Broads are found on peat of nearly neutral pH in more fertile conditions.

Lowland Fen can be a particularly species-rich habitat, although many of these species are not wetland specialists, and their presence is a reflection of the diversity of conditions found. The fenland fauna includes particularly large numbers of species of flies, beetles and moths. The diversity of invertebrates is reliant upon structural variety: bare areas, tussocks, deep litter, shaded areas, pools and transitions to swamp, carr woodland and Fen Meadow are all important.

Similar habitats

Reedbed is similar to Lowland Fen but can be both wetter and taller, and is almost exclusively dominated by Common Reed. Grazed areas of Lowland Fen supporting Fen Meadow vegetation in northern England can be transitional to Northern Hay-meadows, with Globeflower and Marsh Hawk's-beard. Transitions to Wet Woodland are common.

Origins and development

Lowland Fen develops where landscape features prevent drainage and create waterlogged conditions (*e.g.* the floodplain fens of The Norfolk and Suffolk Broads and basin fens of central Ireland) or where there is a constant flow of water (*e.g.* the spring-fed fens of Anglesey). Lowland Fen is a transitional habitat that would, over time, succeed to Wet Woodland or, where the development of peat isolates the vegetation from the

Thelnetham Fen, Suffolk – a spring-fed valley fen comprising Fen Meadow, Saw-sedge fen and small-sedge fen.

groundwater, to Raised Bog. Various land-use practices including mowing, grazing and peat digging have arrested this successional process, helping to retain wet conditions by removing plant litter, exposing springs and preventing the establishment of woody species. The decline of such practices since the mid-20th century has seen a deterioration in the quality of many fens, although some are still cut for thatch or marsh hay or for conservation purposes. Fens are also very vulnerable to river engineering that modifies flooding regimes. Vast areas that once supported Lowland Fen have been drained and used for agriculture, and most Lowland Fen is now confined to protected sites.

EXTENT IN KM²

Eng	119
Wal	49
Sco	17
NI	1
Ire	195

Conservation

The area of Lowland Fen has declined significantly over the last century across Europe, and Britain and Ireland hold a large proportion of that which remains. However, in Ireland, Lowland Fen is often threatened by polluted groundwater and in Britain by nearby water extraction or lack of flooding due to river engineering. Paradoxically, it can also be threatened if it remains part of intact floodplain systems due to the effects of river-borne nutrients. Attempts to maintain high water levels have included the installation of impermeable liners (*e.g.* at Wicken Fen) and irrigation (*e.g.* at Redgrave and Lopham Fen). Landscape-scale conservation is particularly important for wetland sites, and initiatives such as the Great Fen project in East Anglia are looking to link and buffer existing sites with re-created wetlands. Such initiatives can help to ameliorate some of the effects of climate change, particularly those relating to water levels and nutrient enrichment. Greater management effort may be needed to counter a likely increase in more generalist invasive species.

What to look for

On Anglesey, in the shallow East Anglian valleys and on the Carboniferous limestone of Ireland look out for small-sedge

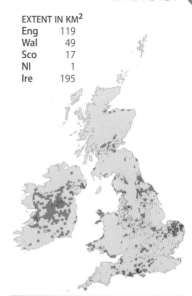

Distribution and extent

Scattered across lowland Britain and Ireland; extensive areas are now confined to East Anglia, Anglesey and Lough Erne. Generally rare in Europe. Pale shading indicates the broad distribution of the Annex I habitats representing calcareous fens (H7210) and alkaline fens (H7230); darker shading shows Lowland Fen locations drawn from a range of sources. Extent figures are for the two Annex I habitats combined.

LEFT: **Redgrave and Lopham Fen, Suffolk** – swamp vegetation is found on the margins of fens and lining dykes where is colonizes open water, sometimes forming floating rafts of vegetation (called hover) over water, liquid peat or older rafts. RIGHT: **Upton Fen, Norfolk** – Marsh Fern is a characteristic component of Common Reed and Saw-sedge fen.

ABOVE: **Swallowtail** – the iconic Swallowtail is now limited to The Norfolk and Suffolk Broads, where it can be seen on various reserves. It lays its eggs on tall plants of Milk-parsley, on which the caterpillar (RIGHT) feeds. Look for the butterfly (LEFT) on a windless day in the early morning between late May and mid-July. In some years there is a second brood in mid-August–September. BELOW: **How Hill, Norfolk** – much of what is traditionally considered as fen in The Norfolk and Suffolk Broads is dominated by Common Reed and has been created through centuries of reed cutting.

fens. They occur near seepages and springs where the summer water-table is close to the surface and are characterized by Black Bog-rush and Blunt-flowered Rush. Look for small sedges and herbs in damp runnels between tussocks and more acid-loving species such as Tormentil and Bog Asphodel on tussock tops. Uncommon and rare species include Pugsley's Marsh-orchid, Grass-of-Parnassus and Slender Tufted-sedge.

In the classic tall-herb fens of The Norfolk and Suffolk Broads and Wicken Fen look out for Milk-parsley and Marsh Pea in swards of Common Reed or Reed Sweet-grass, together with bulky herbs such as Yellow Loosestrife, Purple-loosestrife, Meadowsweet, Yellow Iris, Common Valerian, Hemp-agrimony and Wild Angelica. Particularly species-rich swards can be found where cutting followed by grazing creates Fen Meadow communities (see Purple Moor-grass and Rush Pasture, *page 174*).

In East Anglia, keep an eye out for the strangely tusked Chinese Water Deer, an introduced species that favours swampy vegetation (Britain now holds one tenth of its world population). Other fenland mammals include Harvest Mouse, Water Shrew and Water Vole, although they are typically hard to see. Listen out

for Grasshopper Warbler, Sedge Warbler and Reed Warbler (favoured by Cuckoo as a host) and, in Britain, Barn Owl is a frequent sight quartering marshes.

How to recognize

Lowland Fen supports tall, dense swards of reeds, large sedges and rushes or a shorter, tussocky sward of rushes and small sedges. It is often rich in other flowering plants, including many conspicuous and attractive species.

Many sites are small and isolated, set within drained farmland, but more extensive areas are still found where wetland landscapes have escaped conversion to agriculture.

The water-table is rarely far below the surface making Lowland Fen hard to explore, particularly where it is dissected by deep dykes or dotted with pools and swampy hollows. At many sites, particularly in East Anglia, the limited access routes are clearly defined by mown trails, raised paths or boardwalks. These can add structural diversity, and are good places to watch for flying insects such as the iconic Broadland species, Swallowtail and Norfolk Hawker. However, some fens are only accessible by boat.

When to visit

Summer for insects and plants.

Did you know?

The Fen Raft Spider is a prodigious hunter, able to take dragonflies and sticklebacks. First discovered in 1956 at Redgrave and Lopham Fen, it is known from only a small handful of sites, and young spiders reared in captivity have been released to try and safeguard the species from extinction in Britain.

1 **Saw-sedge** forms distinctive stands that were traditionally cut in the summer to provide tough thatch for roof ridges. Species-rich examples of Saw-sedge fen (which are of European importance) can include plants such as Fen Orchid, Marsh Helleborine, Lesser Tussock-sedge and Slender Sedge. **2** **Yellow Iris** – a common component of tall-herb fens. **3** **Southern Marsh-orchid** – A diversity of orchids can be found in fens, including this species, Early Marsh-orchid, Common Spotted-orchid, Marsh Helleborine, and the rare Pugsley's Marsh-orchid and Fen Orchid. **4** **Grass-of-Parnassus** is a delicate plant that flowers from July to September. It can be found in small-sedge fens and fen meadows or along rides cut in tall-herb fens; it is also typical of upland flushes.

Valley Mire is best known from lowland heathland landscapes, but also occurs in the uplands. Variation in Valley Mire vegetation is generally due to hydrological factors. The water percolating through the underlying sands and gravels is mostly acid and nutrient-poor. However, in any one valley it may come from a variety of sources, and seepages and springs often introduce more base-rich water, increasing the complexity and diversity of the vegetation. The lateral movement of water contributes to the zonation seen in many larger mires where nutrients tend to accumulate along the central axis. As the ground gets wetter, vegetation dominated by heathers gives way to an open community of bog-mosses with a scattering of vascular plants such as Bog Asphodel and Round-leaved Sundew. Towards the centre of the mire this can be replaced with Black Bog-rush along soakways, the wettest of which may support Marsh St. John's-wort and Bog Pondweed. Birch or willow-dominated woodland can sometimes develop in the centre of mires. Dense patches of Purple Moor-grass may be associated with areas where the water is well-oxygenated, or in valley bottoms where nutrients accumulate. Valley Mire generally shows some surface patterning, with hollows, hummocks and bog pools. In some places, such as Hartland Moor in Dorset, buoyant rafts of vegetation can form over liquid peat (see Transition Mire and Quaking Bog, *page 241*).

Similar habitats

Lowland fens within valleys tend to be larger, usually within agricultural landscapes, and support tall herbs and large sedges characteristic of more alkaline conditions. Lowland Wet Heath shares many species with Valley Mire, but bog-mosses are confined to the small and neat Compact and Soft Bog-mosses, often only

Hartland Moor, Dorset – White Beak-sedge flowers in July and August and is more widespread than the scarce Brown Beak-sedge, which flowers in June–July. Brown Beak-sedge (INSET) can be identified by its broader, yellower leaves and chestnut spikelets with a projecting bract. In autumn, the fruits of White Beak-sedge also turn brown, and the two species can be confused at first glance.

present as discrete cushions. Where it occurs within blanket mire in the uplands, Valley Mire can support more Purple Moor-grass, Bog Asphodel, Bog-myrtle and Oblong-leaved Sundew than the surrounding vegetation.

Origins and development

In the warm and dry southern lowlands mires can only form in hollows or shallow valleys where water is held back by topographical features or vegetation. Valley Mire peat is rarely very deep, usually no more than 1·5 m, sometimes only 20 cm or so, but there is evidence at some sites to suggest that mire vegetation has been constantly present over thousands of years. Mires have been affected by peat cutting in the past, and some floating rafts of vegetation are found over what may be re-flooded turbaries (peat diggings). Although usually dependent on natural topographic features, Valley Mire is also found in ball-clay mines on the Dorset Heaths and tin workings on Dartmoor.

Drainage has affected many mires, either directly or through water extraction/drainage on nearby sites lowering the water-table. Drier mires are also more vulnerable to burning. Recreational disturbance has possibly had a role in the declines of breeding waders (*e.g.* in the New Forest).

Conservation

Valley Mire conservation centres around maintaining (or recreating) suitable hydrological conditions. For example, in the New Forest attempts have been made to slow the loss of water from mires by modifying drainage systems. On the Dorset Heaths, extensive grazing has been reintroduced to prevent coarse vegetation from gradually building up and creating drier conditions, and to maintain an open sward suitable for bog-mosses and small perennials such as sundews.

EXTENT UNKNOWN

Distribution and extent

Can be found in the uplands in areas supporting blanket mire. Scarce in the lowlands. Many sites are very small and the map shows selected key locations in England and Scotland simply as dots. In Wales actual sites are shown. No data for Ireland.

LEFT: **Stoborough Heath, Dorset** – in summer the mossy-green wetland species in the shallow valley stand out against the heathery background of Lowland Dry Heath. RIGHT: **Hartland Moor, Dorset** – in winter the pale litter of Purple Moor-grass and tussocks of Black Bog-rush highlight the curving mire in the shallow valley bottom, with willows in the centre.

1 **Raft Spiders** can be seen from May to August resting on the surface of bog pools and use their legs to sense vibrations in the surface of the water that might indicate the approach of potential prey. **2** **Bog Asphodel** – a classic bog species that flowers from July to September. **3** **Morden Bog, Dorset** – Common Cottongrass stands out when in flower in June.

1 **Stoborough Heath, Dorset** – Black Bog-rush growing along a central water track, with Bog Asphodel, White Beak-sedge and Cross-leaved Heath growing among Bog-myrtle to the side. **2** **Godlingston Heath, Dorset** – a Valley Mire sward dominated by Bog Asphodel. **3** **Bog Orchid** is threatened throughout its European range; it favours areas with some water movement, and is found growing both on bog-moss lawns on the edge of runnels and deeper within rushy swards towards the centre of mires. **4** Bog pools and wet hollows are a key component of Valley Mire, and can support floating mats or spongy carpets of bog-mosses, including **Golden Bog-moss** (hummocks) and **Feathery Bog-moss** (hollows) seen here. Vascular plants include **White Beak-sedge** and Common Cottongrass, with Bog-bean, Lesser Bladderwort and Bog Pondweed in deeper water. **5** **Pale Butterwort** is a perennial species that flowers from June to October and forms large, long-lived seed banks from which it regenerates readily following disturbance. Insectivorous plants such as butterworts and sundews are widespread in Valley Mire, reflecting the limited availability of nutrients.

What to look for

Many species of dragonfly and damselfly are associated with bog pools and runnels, including Small Red Damselfly, Keeled Skimmer and Black Darter. The conical nests of the endangered Black Bog Ant can be found at the transition between Valley Mire and Wet Heath, and the velvety, striped Raft Spider can be seen on the surface of pools. Characteristic breeding birds to look out for include Snipe and Curlew, and Hen Harrier can roost in some mires in winter.

A distinctive habitat of European significance to look out for in Valley Mire is peaty depressions dominated by White Beak-sedge. Found next to bog pools, on flushed areas on the sides of Valley Mire and disturbed areas such as tracks, it can support scarce species such as Brown Beak-sedge, Marsh Clubmoss and Bog Orchid. Only about 400 ha of this habitat remains in and associated with Valley Mire, but it is also found on Blanket Bog and Raised Bog in western Britain and the west and midlands of Ireland.

In soakways, water tracks and shallow pools look for a distinctive community with Marsh St. John's-wort, Bog Pondweed and Cow-horn Bog-moss. It is found in clear, still or only gently moving waters where the water-table fluctuates, so that it is above water during the summer months. It can occasionally include an unusual creeping fern, Pillwort, which also grows at the margins of heathland ponds where there is some clay in the soil and where there has been a long tradition of heavy grazing.

How to recognize

In the lowlands, Valley Mire stands out as a distinctive element in the landscape. Soft, jewel-bright patches of bog-mosses line small channels where the water trickles almost imperceptibly. Dark bog pools are spiked with Common Cottongrass and White Beak-sedge, and in summer the brown, peaty water is warm to the touch. The mires are busy with insects, although even damselflies can be caught by the sticky, insectivorous sundews that speckle the bog-mosses.

Some mires squelch underfoot, others quake treacherously over an unknown depth of liquid peat. In places, tall tussocks of Purple Moor-grass and spicy-scented Bog-myrtle make walking all but impossible.

In the uplands, Valley Mire can be easily spotted where it has developed in, for example, hanging valleys, but it can be harder to pick out where it forms part of the overall landscape of blanket peat.

When to visit

Valley Mire is slow to come alive in the spring (but listen out for Snipe drumming); it looks best in late summer when most characteristic species are still in flower.

Did you know?

The New Forest contains 75% of the lowland Valley Mire of north-west Europe

Keeled Skimmer – the larvae inhabit debris at the bottom of runnels and pools for two years before emerging. Males often perch nearby and can be locally abundant from June to September.

Reedbed

page 397

Reedbed is essentially swamp dominated by Common Reed. It is found in a wide range of conditions in the lowlands on permanently waterlogged or seasonally dry situations of differing nutrient status, although it is typical of more nutrient-enriched waters. Common Reed has a vigorous rhizomatous growth form and is adapted to waterlogged conditions (the previous year's stems remain standing for several seasons, helping to aerate the rhizomes), allowing to it maintain its dominance in extensive stands.

Reedbed is a transitional habitat found between water and land. Where it fringes open water, it can give way to floating or submerged aquatics where the water becomes deeper. On the landward margin it can be replaced by Saw-sedge (in nutrient-poor, base-rich waters) or Greater Tussock-sedge and other swamp species (where there are more nutrients). Where conditions are drier, it may grade directly into tall-herb fen, although intact sequences are quite rare due to drainage. The diversity of habitat structure provided by different successional stages, including open wet areas, pools, reed fringes and stands of different ages, is important for wildlife.

In north-west England and Scotland, Reedbed tends to be less extensive and is restricted to more nutrient-rich areas in lakes (*e.g.* the deltas of inflowing streams where Common Reed often forms a patchwork with Bottle Sedge or Bladder-sedge).

Similar habitats

Reedbed forms transitions with tall-herb and sedge Lowland Fen, often in a complex patchwork resulting from varied management. It can be differentiated from tall-herb fen and other swamp communities by the overwhelming dominance of Common Reed.

Radipole, Dorset – this Reedbed in the centre of Weymouth supports Bearded Tit and Bittern.

EXTENT IN KM²

Eng	70
Wal	5
Sco	11
NI	32
Ire	n/k

Distribution and extent

Widespread throughout the lowlands. The map shows actual Reedbed sites, drawn from a range of sources. Many sites are small and may not be mapped. Key areas with extensive habitat include the north side of the Tay Estuary, the Suffolk Coast, the Broads, the Somerset Levels, the Humber Estuary and Morecambe Bay.

Origins and development

Common Reed is an active colonizer of open water, and can persist for a long time in areas that are regularly flooded (including tidal areas) – some clones have been aged at over 1,000 years. Elsewhere, the formation of peat and build up of litter leads to the development of Lowland Fen and then Wet Woodland (carr). In the past this process was often set back indefinitely by winter-only cropping of the upright, bare stems (mainly for thatch), which helped to perpetuate dense, single-species stands.

Reedbeds were once extensive, particularly in the fens of eastern England, but were lost to agriculture once large-scale drainage schemes started in the 17th century. A decline in reed-cutting throughout the 20th century, together with nutrient enrichment from fertilizer run-off, caused a decline in the quality of the remaining sites, often with the loss of key species.

Conservation

Of the 900 or so reedbeds in the UK, only about 50 are greater than 20 ha (the minimum size required for breeding Bittern). Conservation effort has focussed on expanding and re-creating reedbeds on inland sites to compensate for expected losses through coastal flooding. In the face of reduced precipitation, increases in temperature and greater demand for water abstraction, the maintenance of water levels will be a priority (Common Reed requires surface water throughout the year). Recent projects have addressed issues around setting back succession and creating variation in structure in ways that support the reed-cutting industry and use of cut reed for biofuel and composting. Livestock grazing, used more widely in continental Europe, is also being explored, and may have a role in creating habitat mosaics on larger sites.

TOP: **Deben Estuary, Suffolk** – Common Reed can tolerate moderately saline water, and is common in brackish estuaries and dykes. BOTTOM: Reed cutting results in an immediate reduction in breeding birds. Ideally cutting should be carried out on a rotational basis. The interface between mosaics of differently aged patches of reed are favoured by several species.

1 **Bearded Tit** is a reedbed specialist that lives off reed aphids in the summer and reed seeds in the winter. 2 **Bittern** – the British population dipped to just 11 booming males at seven sites in 1997 but has since recovered (mainly as a result of habitat creation projects) and almost 200 booming males were recorded in 2019. 3 **Westwood Marshes, Walberswick, Suffolk** – this 18th century mill was used to drain the surrounding land for agricultural use before the area was re-flooded as part of Second World War defence works.

1 **Cley Marshes, Norfolk** – many coastal reedbeds, such as those at Cley, are threatened by sea-level rise. In north Norfolk new wetlands are being created on farmland farther inland to compensate for the habitat that is likely to be lost. **2** **Ant Broads and Marshes, Norfolk**. The margins of reedbeds provide habitat for nesting wildfowl and for invertebrates and fishes. Bitterns hunt for fish, amphibians, birds and mammals along the reed/water interface where the water depth is about 15–30 cm; sites with a high ratio of reedbed edge to area support the highest densities of Bittern.
3 **Hickling, Norfolk** contains one of the largest reedbeds in England. Bittern was first photographed by ornithologist Emma Turner here after its return to Britain as a breeding species in the early 20th century. Its subsequent decline prompted a programme of Reedbed restoration projects.

What to look for

Reedbed is highly valued for the characteristic suite of birds it can support, some of which only breed in this habitat. Listen out for the distinctive booming of Bittern at dawn and dusk between March and June. Other species to look out for include Bearded Tit, Marsh Harrier, Reed Warbler, Water Rail and Reed Bunting. In coastal areas of southern England and Wales, the robust, explosive song of Cetti's Warbler is an increasingly familiar sound around scrubby Reedbed margins. Reedbed also provides late-summer roost sites for large flocks of migrant Swallow and Sand Martin, and in the winter is used by roosting raptors and Starling. Huge flocks of Starling create an astonishing spectacle, swirling overhead in constantly changing formations. There are also a number of very rare birds associated with Reedbed, such as Little Bittern and Savi's Warbler.

In Britain, Grass Snake may be seen swimming in open water or basking in dry areas. Keep an eye open for Water Vole – Reedbed provides this species with an important refuge from Mink. Fishes, such as Rudd and Eel, are also an important component of ecosystems in which Reedbed is found. At least 25 species of invertebrates are dependent on Reedbed, and up to 700 species have been recorded. A complete transition from open water to fen provides the greatest number of niches, with older, drier parts having the highest invertebrate density. Rare species of conservation importance include the White-mantled Wainscot moth.

Reedbed is intrinsically poor in plants species. Look for Water Mint and Marsh Bedstraw where the reed cover is quite open in shallow water and in denser swards Cowbane, Greater Spearwort and Water Dock. The more nutrient-poor reedbeds of lakes in the north and west can support Bogbean, Marsh Cinquefoil, Bottle Sedge and Water Horsetail.

How to recognize

Common Reed can be found fringing still or slow-moving open water, or forming impenetrable expanses in floodplains.

In summer the thick blue-green stands are quite monotonous, although in drier areas they can be laced with sprawling Bittersweet or Hedge Bindweed, and tall-herbs such as Yellow Iris and Great Willowherb add the occasional patch of colour. In winter the reed drops its leaves, and the rustling stands of bleached, brittle stems are quietly atmospheric.

Often growing in standing water, or through thick litter of indeterminate firmness, reedbeds are hard to explore, and are most easily appreciated from their margins or where board-walks have been constructed. Hides are usually the best places to go to catch a glimpse of Bittern skulking through poolside reeds, but Bearded Tits are easier to see as they flit over reed heads.

When to visit

Winter for raptors and Starling roosts; spring for breeding birds.

Did you know?

Common Reed can grow in water that is over a metre deep and can produce over 200 shoots per square metre.

ABOVE: After suffering heavily from habitat loss and illegal persecution, **Marsh Harrier** numbers increased in the late 20th century and it is once again a regular sight flying over Reedbed in some parts of the country. RIGHT: **Reed Leopard** is a local and scarce moth, occurring in East Anglia and Dorset. The larvae feed inside Common Reed stems.

FRESHWATERS

ORIGINS

Freshwaters encompass a wide range of habitats from high mountain tarns to large sluggish rivers in the lowlands. Nowhere in Britain or Ireland is very far from the sea so very large rivers are absent, but the generally high level of precipitation means that rivers and streams form a key component of most landscapes. River water is derived from precipitation via surface run-off, springs or snow-melt, and usually collects in a drainage basin from which it flows downhill in a channel eroded by the river. In the uplands, fast-flowing rivers can erode 'V'-shaped valleys. As the water flow slows in the middle reaches, the valley becomes shallower and broader and the river starts to meander over the valley bottom floodplain. Upland rivers can also follow 'U'-shaped valleys gouged out by glaciers. Most natural lakes owe their origins to glacial deposits creating dams, or to glaciers over-deepening valleys. England was less heavily glaciated than the rest of Britain and Ireland and, in the lowlands, natural lakes with glacial origins (such as the Shropshire and Cheshire meres) are rare and limited in distribution. There are some natural lakes around the coast where coastal sediment has trapped freshwater (such as Slapton Ley in Devon). However, most lowland lakes are artificial, created through mineral extraction, as drinking water reservoirs, ornamental lakes, moats or canal feeder reservoirs. Ponds and pools across the lowlands are often legacies of small-scale mineral workings or were dug to stock fish or to provide water for livestock; the Norfolk and Suffolk Broads are flooded medieval peat diggings. On a geological time-scale, lakes are temporary features in the landscape, as they gradually trap sediment brought in by rivers and the process of hydrosere succession starts (see Wetlands *page 234*).

Many of the rare species of the **New Forest** live at the grazed margins of shallow, vegetation-filled waterbodies. The rare Southern Damselfly breeds on this slow-flowing stream.

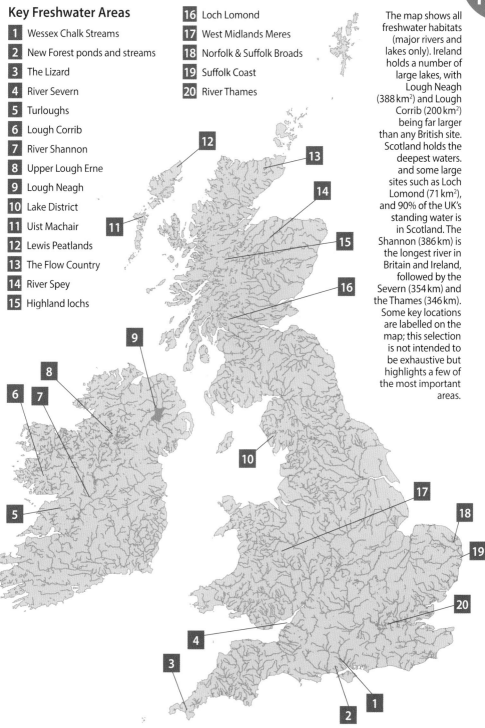

Key Freshwater Areas

1. Wessex Chalk Streams
2. New Forest ponds and streams
3. The Lizard
4. River Severn
5. Turloughs
6. Lough Corrib
7. River Shannon
8. Upper Lough Erne
9. Lough Neagh
10. Lake District
11. Uist Machair
12. Lewis Peatlands
13. The Flow Country
14. River Spey
15. Highland lochs
16. Loch Lomond
17. West Midlands Meres
18. Norfolk & Suffolk Broads
19. Suffolk Coast
20. River Thames

The map shows all freshwater habitats (major rivers and lakes only). Ireland holds a number of large lakes, with Lough Neagh (388 km²) and Lough Corrib (200 km²) being far larger than any British site. Scotland holds the deepest waters. and some large sites such as Loch Lomond (71 km²), and 90% of the UK's standing water is in Scotland. The Shannon (386 km) is the longest river in Britain and Ireland, followed by the Severn (354 km) and the Thames (346 km). Some key locations are labelled on the map; this selection is not intended to be exhaustive but highlights a few of the most important areas.

TYPES OF FRESHWATER HABITAT

The character of all freshwaters is shaped by the landscape in which they are found. The underlying geology of the catchment influences the water chemistry and physical characteristics such as size, depth or flow. Upland lakes, rivers and streams tend to be low in dissolved nutrients ('oligotrophic'), while in the lowlands glacial deposits create naturally productive, nutrient-rich waters ('eutrophic'). These are simple extremes and a wide variety of intermediate types exist. Humans have had a substantial impact by raising nutrient levels and acidifying waters.

Standing Waters

Standing waters include open waters that lack a unidirectional flow, and can be permanent or seasonal. They have traditionally been classified as oligotrophic or eutrophic according to their nutrient status. Alkalinity (the amount of dissolved calcium carbonate) and pH (the ratio of hydrogen to hydroxyl ions) also influence the overall character of waterbodies. In general, oligotrophic lakes tend to be acidic and eutrophic lakes more alkaline. Oligotrophic waters are most common in the uplands where acidic rocks dominate and the deepest lakes are found. Alkaline waters occur mainly in the lowlands of England and Ireland where rivers and streams drain limestone, and are often eutrophic. Mesotrophic waters are intermediate in their productivity and alkalinity and are generally found in the north and west. Changes in plant and animal communities according to water nutrient status are shown in the chart on *page 277*.

Freshwater habitats in two contrasting parts of Britain (both maps are at the same scale). The **Frome and Piddle river valleys** in Dorset (LEFT IMAGE AND MAP) contain Floodplain Grazing Marsh and Ditch systems. There are small areas of standing water in this un-glaciated landscape and the porous chalk geology means that there are relatively few tributaries. In contrast, in upland landscapes (RIGHT IMAGE AND MAP), the hard bedrock means that there is a much higher density of streams and rivers and there are large areas of standing water of glacial origin (such as **Loch Maree** in Wester Ross, shown here).

HABITAT	DESCRIPTION
STANDING WATER	
Nutrient-rich (Eutrophic) Lake *page 282 | page 388*	Nutrient rich and often alkaline, found in the lowlands. Some naturally mesotrophic lakes are now eutrophic due to pollution.
Upland Lake, Loch and Tarn *page 285 | page 390*	Nutrient poor, acidic waterbodies found in the uplands.
Peat-stained (Dystrophic) Waters *page 288 | page 389*	Very acidic and nutrient-poor pools found within peatlands.
Turlough and Fluctuating Mere *page 291 | page 389*	Aquifer-fed waterbodies that fluctuate with the water-table and may dry out completely.
Other Lake Types *pages 294–297 | page 388*	Mesotrophic Lake, Marl Lake, Lowland Nutrient-poor Lake and Brackish Lake.
Pond *page 298 | page 389*	Small (< 2 ha), widespread and usually isolated waterbodies.
Ditch *page 301 | page 389*	Shallow and linear artificial boundary or drainage features.
Canal *page 304 | page 389*	Shallow, linear waterbodies that join river catchments and were constructed for transport purposes.
FLOWING WATER	
Fast-flowing River and Stream *page 307 | page 390*	Actively eroding natural watercourses, usually in the uplands, with fast-flowing and clear water.
Sluggish River and Stream *page 310 | page 390*	River systems with slow-flowing and cloudy water that deposit fine sediment on the river bed, usually in the lowlands. Most have been modified.
Chalk River and Stream *page 313 | page 390*	Lowland fast-flowing rivers and streams with clear water derived from chalk aquifers, typically supporting water-crowfoot vegetation communities.

This mid-channel bar in the **River Avon on the Dorset /Hampshire border** is composed of fine shingle. It is re-shaped when the river floods, but in the summer supports sparse ruderal vegetation.

Besides the three main trophic levels, there are other types of standing water where the water chemistry is particularly distinctive: dystrophic waters are peat-stained, highly acidic and poor in nutrients; marl lakes are very alkaline; and brackish waters are partially saline and fluctuate with the tide. Alkalinity, depth, colour, area, altitude, substrate and shape of water bodies all contribute to differences in the plant and animal communities present. Of the 24 aquatic vegetation communities described in the British National Vegetation Classification (NVC), 21 can be found in standing waters. In practice, individual sites are not always easy to categorise and detailed analysis has resulted in various approaches that identify up to 11 types of lake. Seven types of standing water are described in detail in this book, and a summary is provided of four more unusual types.

Flowing Waters

Flowing waters are often shallower than standing waters and are linear. Their character is influenced by flow rate (which is linked to topography), in addition to both land-use and geology within the catchment (which affect water chemistry). Flow characteristics have a strong influence on the plant and animal communities present, as fast-flowing water presents a fundamental challenge for many aquatic life forms, and here we separate streams and rivers according to flow rate (*i.e.* fast-flowing, eroding watercourses and sluggish streams and rivers that deposit sediment). The dividing line is an arbitrary one, reflecting an essentially upland/lowland split. A single watercourse can include both types and water chemistry may vary along its length, but there is often a change in species and character when it crosses from the uplands into the arable zone. Chalk streams and rivers are described separately, as they are both distinctive and rare. The difference between rivers and streams is again arbitrary. Ordnance Survey maps at a scale of 1:25,000 indicate watercourses that are wider than 8·25 metres with two blue lines (as opposed to one) and this width is often taken as the threshold beyond which a watercourse is considered as a river.

River plant communities are harder to classify than those of standing waters due to the variations in water chemistry within single watercourses. Aquatic plants (macrophytes) occur in both lakes and rivers but in flowing water phytoplankton are not a key part of the flora as they are washed away. Fourteen NVC communities occur in flowing water. As with standing waters, detailed analysis has revealed the complexity of flowing waters, and 10 types have been identified.

THREATS AND ISSUES

Most freshwater habitats are intricately linked to the landscape around them. For rivers and streams and the lakes they feed, those links extend to the entire catchment upstream and consequently human impacts are not limited to those directly affecting the waterbody, but extend into the catchment. Afforestation affects water flow and results in acidification; soil management and overgrazing influence the amount of sediment; artificial fertilizers and pesticides affect water quality; and water abstraction reduces water levels. These factors, combined with run-off from roads and urban areas and sewage effluents, means that few waters are unpolluted. Changes in phosphorous levels started nearly two centuries ago – sediment cores from some lakes in the Lake District indicate changes in the diatom assemblage dating back to the mid-1800s, corresponding to increases in the local human population and tourist use. Nutrient enrichment is now thought to be affecting 80% of UK lakes, and studies of streams have suggested that once agriculture exceeds 30–50% of the catchment area, their condition deteriorates. The impacts of nutrient enrichment are different for each kind of waterbody, but typically result in a loss of key species. Solutions to all these issues are limited and complex, particularly for large waterbodies.

Modification and drainage also affect many watercourses. Channels that have been straightened, embanked or canalized within hard walls are a common sight, and few rivers now have natural braids or are unconstrained within their floodplains; only 11% of the total length of all rivers and streams in England and Wales is thought to be unmodified and near-natural.

A further factor impacting on the ecology of waterbodies is the scale of colonization by invasive non-native species. The connectivity of waterbodies means that plants and animals can spread quickly. For example, Canadian Pondweed is thought to have been introduced to Ireland from Canada in around 1836. By 1880 it had spread to England and Scotland and was hindering navigation in many watercourses. Now it is widespread but seldom abundant. Himalayan Balsam is the most common non-native bankside plant, particularly along larger rivers. It forms dense stands that out-compete other plants and substantially reduces the abundance of invertebrates associated with the vegetation. Countless introductions of non-native fish (often for angling) have also impacted on other wildlife (*e.g.* Zander suppress other fish populations, carp increase turbidity and remove aquatic macrophytes, and farmed fish reduce genetic diversity within natural fish stocks). American Mink and Signal Crayfish have been associated with the decline of some native species such as Water Vole and White-clawed Crayfish.

Rivers and streams are particularly sensitive to climate change as water temperature tends to track air temperature closely. Most river organisms are cold-blooded and therefore sensitive to temperature changes. Temperature also affects water chemistry, including oxygen concentration. Water temperature in streams and rivers has already increased by around 1–3°C over the last three decades. Changes in rainfall due to climate change will also affect river flow, which will impact on the distribution and abundance of many river animals. Any reductions in water flow are likely to be exacerbated by high levels of water abstraction in many areas. On the other hand, increases in the intensity of flooding are likely to exacerbate siltation and nutrient enrichment in watercourses, adversely effecting species dependent on coarse sediment and clean, well-oxygenated water (*e.g.* Atlantic Salmon, Freshwater Pearl Mussel and stoneflies). Depending on how increased flooding is managed, the increase in the frequency and extent of flooding may, however, facilitate the recovery of rivers currently constrained by flood defences.

Himalayan Balsam is a garden escape that has rapidly colonized river banks. Like Japanese Knotweed, another invasive non-native, it smothers other vegetation and leaves banks bare and vulnerable to erosion in the winter.

Hatchet Pond, New Forest, Hampshire. Conservation issues here include nutrient enrichment, invasive plants (New Zealand Pigmyweed) and carp, introduced by anglers. Nutrient enrichment is likely to be result of atmospheric deposition, run-off from the car-park, the use of ground-bait by anglers, food given to waterfowl and as a legacy of the use of the area during the Second World War.

CULTURAL IMPORTANCE

Freshwaters have played a key part in determining where people live. Access to freshwater, the importance of water for transport, the presence of crossing points and flood risk have all influenced the location of settlements. Rivers lie at the heart of many cities such as London (the Thames) and Dublin (the Liffey) and have often been used as boundaries (such as the Wye, on the border between England and Wales). Freshwaters provide drinking water (for people and their livestock) and power (now generally hydroelectricity, but water-powered mills were essential to rural life in the past). Rivers and canals have been important transport routes, and freshwaters have provided important food sources (fish and wildfowl). Today in the UK, every person uses around 150 litres of water per day and demand is increasing. Around two-thirds of the UK's water comes from surface sources rather than groundwater.

People are often drawn to water, and many waterbodies are used extensively for recreational pursuits including the use of various watercraft and for angling and bankside walks. Many myths, legends and stories also include water as a key element, often with some kind of mystery attached (such as the Loch Ness monster, or the Waters of Avalon in the legends of King Arthur). Freshwaters are portrayed in many artforms, including books such as Kenneth Grahame's childrens' story *Wind in the Willows*.

CONSERVATION IMPORTANCE AND PROTECTION

Freshwater and wetland habitats together occupy just 3% of the UK's land surface but support around 10% of its species, including around 4,000 invertebrate taxa. Freshwater habitats are protected through a range of legislation. For example, in England there are 28,693 ha of open water within the SSSI network, of which 20,458 ha are standing waters and 7,881 ha are rivers and streams. There are 44 English rivers that, at least in part, are designated as SSSI. Nine freshwater Annex I habitat types are present in Britain and Ireland, two of which are Priority Habitats and one (rivers with floating vegetation often dominated by water-crowfoots) for which the UK has a special responsibility (see *page 37*). The European Water Framework Directive required the development of catchment-scale management plans detailing actions needed to maintain and improve the ecological status (among other requirements) of waterbodies up to 2027.

TOP: Fish ponds were widespread in the Middle Ages and were an important food source. Fishing is a popular modern pastime and many freshwaters are artificially stocked. MIDDLR: Many gravel pits and reservoirs now fulfil a range of roles, including recreation, education and nature conservation. BOTTOM: Otters disappeared from most of England in the latter part of the 20th century due to pollution and habitat destruction, but can once again be found across Britain and Ireland thanks to conservation efforts. Otters use all parts of the catchment, including ditches and small streams – they can even occasionally be seen in Blanket Bog.

	Dystrophic	Oligotrophic	Mesotrophic	Eutrophic	Hypereutrophic
Phytoplankton					
Submerged aquatic plants					
Benthic animals					
Cyprinid fish (Chubb, Dace, Roach, Rudd *etc.*)					
Whitefish (Vendace, Powan, Pollan)					

The abundance of different groups of plants and animals varies with the nutrient status of the water. This table shows the notional abundance of different groups within different standing water habitats.

Solving water-quality issues: Lessons learned from the Norfolk Broads

The Norfolk Broads were dominated by diverse submerged plant communities until around the middle of the 20th century when most were lost as a consequence of increases in nutrient levels that resulted in dense phytoplankton growth. In the early 1980s, Cockshoot Broad was dammed off from the adjacent River Bure in order to isolate it from the source of further nutrient enrichment, and phosphorus-rich sediment was removed to a depth of almost one metre in an attempt to restore the plant communities. Although submerged plants began to recolonize soon after phosphorous levels dropped, the main area of the Broad was slow to be colonized and, by the mid-1980s, plants began to decline and phytoplankton levels started rising again. It appeared that the fish population had increased and the fish were eating the zooplankton (which control the level of phytoplankton). In 1989 virtually all the fish (nearly 100,000) were removed from the Broad, allowing zooplankton to increase again, and aquatic plants began to recolonize the main part of the Broad. However, the process has been slow, and this has been attributed to waterfowl damage to plants and the arrival of a predatory shrimp (that preys on zooplankton). Levels of aquatic macrophytes have fluctuated markedly since the original fish removal, but on the whole the approach seems to have been successful. This example highlights the complexities and difficulties involved in resolving water quality issues in large waterbodies.

TYPES OF AQUATIC PLANTS

Aquatic plant species have a range of growth forms. **Emergent aquatics** have their roots underwater but their leaves and flowers above (*e.g.* Arrowhead, Flowering-rush and Greater Spearwort). Some have leaves floating on the surface (*e.g.* Yellow and White Water-lilies). **Submerged aquatics,** such as most pondweeds, have all their leaves submerged in the water. Water-crowfoots have both submerged leaves and floating leaves. There are also some species that are entirely **free-floating**, such as Water-soldier, Frogbit and duckweeds.

Emergent plants

Yellow Water-lily

Greater Spearwort

Submerged aquatic plants

Spiked Water-milfoil

Three-lobed Water-crowfoot

Free-floating

Frogbit

Common Duckweed

F

F

DRAGONFLIES AND DAMSELFLIES

A range of dragonflies is associated with flowing water. **1** **White-legged Damselfly** prefer slow-flows and muddy sediment; **2** **Beautiful Demoiselle** and **3** **Golden-ringed Dragonfly** are associated with gravelly streams.

FRESHWATER INVERTEBRATES

Insects that can be found on the surface or under the water include: **4** **pond skaters**; **5** **Great Diving Beetle**; **6** Dragonfly nymphs such as this **Common Blue Damselfly**.

279

KEY FEATURES

Margins

Sites with a complete hydrosere (see *page 243*) from open water to Wet Woodland have the potential to support the widest range of species. A key part of this is the marginal zone of bank and shallow water, which can be especially diverse, particularly where there is a gently sloping transition rather than an abrupt change. It provides habitat for plants and animals that require both aquatic and terrestrial conditions, and can be particularly rich in invertebrates. Look for a range of shallow water and marginal plant species and invertebrates such as dragonflies, mayflies and craneflies.

Exposed Riverine Sediments

Exposed riverine sediments are shoals of bare sand and shingle that can form spits, bars and islands. They are dynamic, temporary features that are reshaped by every flood and are widespread and common – around 47% of the total length of rivers in England and Wales contains un-vegetated bars. Often a mix of substrates will be present as successive floods deposit different sizes of sediment. They lack continuous vegetative cover, but a suite of specialist invertebrates, including ground beetles, rove beetles, flies and spiders, occupy a range of microhabitats provided by the transition from stonier sediments on the upstream end to the finer sediments at the tail-end. Where vegetation is present, it can be varied and may include heathland species and sometimes montane species washed down from the uplands. Both Common Sandpiper and Little Ringed Plover breed on exposed riverine sediments.

Eroding Banks and River Cliffs

Where rivers are able to move naturally across floodplains, faster-flowing water on the outside of meanders erodes the banks and can create cliffs and exposed areas that gradually shift over time. The un-vegetated, loose material can be important for a range of specialist invertebrates, and the cliffs provide nesting sites for Kingfisher and Sand Martin.

River Wye, Gloucestershire. This meander shows some key features of flowing waters such as: ❶ backwater, ❷ cliff exposed through erosion, ❸ exposed riverine shingle, ❹ woody debris, here including willows that are still growing following the collapse of the bank.

FURTHER INFORMATION
Freshwater Habitats Trust: www.freshwaterhabitats.org.uk/
Freshwater Biological Association: www.fba.org.uk/
Rivers by Holmes & Raven (Bloomsbury Publishing, 2018)

Woody Debris and Log Jams

Although often removed from rivers to allow water to flow easily, whole trees, limbs or branches that fall into waterbodies create an important range of microhabitats. Large pieces of debris add complexity and can modify flows, create pools and catch sediment. They provide shelter, shade and spawning sites for fish, and a variety of conditions for invertebrates and algae, while the smaller organic debris that collects around it provides nutrients. Protruding debris helps the terrestrial adult stage of river flies (mayflies, stoneflies, caddisflies) and dragonflies to emerge from the water, and can provide resting places for mammals and birds. Woody debris is most commonly found in steep-sided, woodland headwater streams, where its role in flood alleviation is increasingly recognized, as it slows the water flow. It also reduces bank erosion and stabilizes the stream bed. Its scarcity elsewhere is due the lack of riverine woodland as well as river management practices. However, 're-snagging', the introduction of woody debris, is now a recognized river rehabilitation technique. At a number of sites, Beaver have been released (generally within confined areas) to help slow water flow, create pools and increase the amount of water debris in water courses.

Chalk Stream in the Frome Valley, Dorset.
Key features include: ❶ submerged macrophytes, ❷ emergent plants, ❸ riparian vegetation on river bank, ❹ fast-flowing section with gravelly bottom.

Pond, Dowrog Common, Pembrokeshire.
Key features include: ❶ shallow, poached margin, ❷ emergent plants, ❸ overhanging willow scrub, ❹ succession from swamp vegetation to scrub.

Nutrient-rich (Eutrophic) Lake page 388

Naturally nutrient-rich (eutrophic) lakes typically occur in areas with sedimentary rocks or drift deposits from which the nutrients are derived. They are often located within the hard water areas of the un-glaciated southern and eastern lowlands of Britain, and in Ireland they are mainly found in the midlands and the north-east. The bottom sediment is derived from decayed organic matter and, where aerobic conditions develop as a result of bacterial activity, only a specialist fauna (*e.g.* nematode worms) will occur. The relatively high levels of dissolved nutrients in the water support abundant planktonic algae, and these in turn provide the foundation of a complex food web of zooplankton (*e.g.* cyclops and water fleas), larger invertebrates (including snails, dragonflies and water beetles) and fishes (predominantly Cyprinids such as Roach, Rudd and Tench, as well as Perch and Pike). The fish in turn support breeding bird species such as Great Crested Grebe. Amphibians, including Great Crested Newt, are often present. Where algae is dense, it may limit submerged aquatic plants to the shallow water where light can still penetrate, but a rich flora including pondweeds, water-milfoils and Yellow Water-lily is found at the best sites. In many waterbodies the nutrient levels are artificially high as a consequence of agricultural run-off or sewage effluent and the flora and fauna are impoverished.

Similar habitats

Pond and Canal can hold eutrophic water, as can Turlough and Fluctuating Mere, which differs in its hydrology and is also largely restricted to Breckland and western Ireland. Other types of waterbody generally have clearer water and often a rocky shoreline.

Hoveton Great Broad, Norfolk, has lost much of its aquatic flora due to over-enrichment. **Water fleas** (INSET) and other zooplankton form a rich 'soup' visible to the naked eye that in turn supports a range of larger invertebrates.

Origins and development

Most nutrient-rich lakes are artificial, having been created deliberately for a variety of functions. Many are the remnants of extraction, such as gravel pits, or the special case of the Norfolk and Suffolk Broads, which were created when medieval peat diggings were subsequently flooded. Others were created as reservoirs. A scattering (*e.g.* the Shropshire and Cheshire Meres) have natural origins, having been created by glacial action. Historically, many sites have been lost through drainage – much of Fenland would once have been covered by shallow, eutrophic lakes – and the remainder have been degraded by pollution. Elevated levels of nutrients (in particular phosphorus) lead to the dominance of algae, turning the water dark green and excluding macrophytes and impoverishing fish communities.

Conservation

The restoration of nutrient-rich lakes is complex and expensive, but is worth attempting provided the input of pollutants can be stopped. Successful projects have involved phosphate stripping at sewage works discharging into upstream rivers and the removal of nutrient-enriched mud from lake beds. Other threats to nutrient-rich lakes include recreational use (boats increase the turbidity of the water) and invasion by non-native species. Management of the immediate surroundings is integral to the management of the waterbody as many aquatic species (*e.g.* amphibians and invertebrates) spend part of their life-cycles in the adjacent terrestrial habitats.

EXTENT IN KM²

Eng	204
Wal	9
Sco	7
NI	151
Ire	144

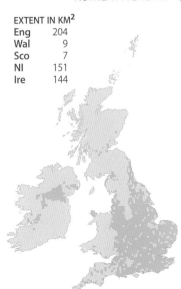

Distribution and extent

Widely scattered. Uncommon in Europe due to pollution. Map shows broad extent of Annex I habitat (H3150) and the extent figures are from the reporting for freshwaters that fall into this category.

BOTTOM LEFT: **How Hill, Norfolk** – open water with Yellow Water-lily is backed by swamp vegetation of Common Reed and Bulrush with Hemp-agrimony.

What to look for

The presence of various pondweeds and stoneworts is a good indication of unpolluted water. Large numbers of waterfowl may be seen in winter.

How to recognize

Nutrient-rich Lake includes any waterbody between a small pool and a large lake that has a high level of nutrients. Found in the lowlands, some are natural waters (*e.g.* Slapton Ley in Devon, Upper Loch Erne in Fermanagh and Loch Leven in Kinross); others are artificial waterbodies such as flooded gravel pits, ornamental lakes and moats.

The high nutrient level can often be deduced from the greenish water and abundant vegetation. The water clarity varies, but by summer is often quite murky with a distinctive swampy smell. The bottom, which is not often visible, is muddy, deep in rich organic sediment. In the lowlands, robust fringing vegetation and muddy margins can make it hard to reach the shore, and it is often difficult to see the whole extent of a lake. On some sites, a succession from open water through submerged and emergent communities to Reedbed, Lowland Fen and Wet Woodland can be observed, especially from out on the water looking towards the shore.

When to visit

Mid-winter is the peak time to see wildfowl, ideally at dawn or dusk. Visit in the summer to see many of the invertebrates and plants.

1 Nutrient-rich waters can support high densities of a range of fishes such as **Rudd** (shown), Roach, Tench and Pike. **2** Once believed extinct in Britain, **Medicinal Leech** inhabits warm, shallow water with plenty of vegetation. Amphibians, birds and fish are its main prey. **3** Spiked Water-milfoil can tolerate nutrient-rich waters and is widespread. **4** **Small Red-eyed Damselfly** – a recent colonist that can be seen on marginal vegetation and floating vegetation in July and August. Densities of **5** **Great Crested Grebe** are highest on the most nutrient-rich sites.

F

Upland Lake, Loch and Tarn

page 390

Upland waterbodies have low levels of nutrients (they are 'oligotrophic') and are not productive. The water is usually very clear because the low nutrient levels limit the growth of phytoplankton, although the leaching of humic substances from the catchment may cause some brown coloration. A variable community of unrelated but distinctive plants called 'isoetids' is associated with oligotrophic lakes. These plants, which absorb carbon dioxide through their roots, have shuttlecock-like rosettes of narrow leaves and include Shoreweed, Quillwort, Water Lobelia, Awlwort and, mainly in western Ireland and the Hebrides, Pipewort. The clear water allows good light penetration and some plants will grow down to a depth of eight metres, although most grow in shallow water. In shallow waters, Bog Pondweed, water-starworts and Floating Bur-reed may be present, while Bottle Sedge and Common Club-rush fringe sheltered bays. With relatively little plant life, there are correspondingly small numbers of plant-eating invertebrates; however, caddisflies, water beetles and water-boatmen are typically present, and River Limpet and freshwater shrimps may be seen around the shoreline. Some deep-water invertebrates and zooplankton only found in oligotrophic lakes may be glacial relics. Brown Trout, Arctic Charr and whitefish are found in lochs up to about 500 m. At higher altitudes, newts may be the top predator in the food chain. Black-throated Diver, Common Scoter, Goldeneye and Red-breasted Merganser breed on upland lochs, which can be some of the least disturbed aquatic habitats in Britain and Ireland.

Coire an Lochain, Cairngorms – one of the highest waterbodies in Britain and Ireland, this corrie lake freezes over for most of the winter and holds a very limited fauna.

EXTENT IN KM^2	
Eng	89
Wal	20
Sco	201
NI	24
Ire	78

Distribution and extent

Widespread in the uplands. Map shows broad extent of Annex I habitat (H3130) and the extent figures are from the reporting for freshwaters that fall into this category.

Similar habitats

The water of Mesotrophic Lake is also clear, but contains lush fringing and aquatic vegetation (some of the Lake District waters are mesotrophic), while the organic shoreline of Nutrient-rich Lake is often fringed with swamp and fen vegetation. Peat-stained (Dystrophic) Waters are typically dark brown.

Origins and development

Upland lake, loch and tarn basins were formed as a result of glacial scour in hard rock landscapes. Tarns (or lochans) are often found in corries, among glacial moraine and in kettle-holes, while larger, deeper lochs and lakes are in 'U'-shaped valleys. Although some smaller examples have been lost through drainage, the number of larger oligotrophic waterbodies has remained stable. However, many have been degraded by inputs of nutrients from agricultural run-off and small domestic point sources. Non-native species are a problem at some sites, in particular fish (*e.g.* Ruffe, which feed on Powan eggs and fry) and plants (*e.g.* New Zealand Pigmyweed).

Conservation

Conservation measures involve ensuring stable nutrient levels and good water quality, and appropriate land management within the catchment is vital. Diffuse pollution from agriculture is an ongoing problem, and drainage of surrounding peatlands can also be an issue. Atmospheric pollution remains a threat for high altitude lochs, while those near the coast may be affected by salinity due to changes in sea level. Climate change is also likely to worsen eutrophication and sedimentation problems and may threaten species on the southern limit of their range such as Arctic Char.

1 Clear waters of **Loch Gamhna, Rothiemurchus, Inverness-shire**. **2** **Coire an Lochain, Cairngorms** – seen from above (see also *page 285*). **3** **Pipewort** (top left and centre of image) is found on peaty substrates, and is seen growing here with Least Bur-reed (bottom right). **4** **Marsh Clubmoss** belongs to one of the most ancient groups of land plants and requires a symbiotic fungi in order to develop. It is found in bare places where there is little competition.

What to look for

In the summer, look out for Floating Water-plantain and the elusive Slender Naiad, also exposed populations of Shoreweed or Bog Hairgrass and Marsh Clubmoss on dry shores. Breeding Black-throated Diver, Common Scoter and Goldeneye may also be present in the summer, and Otter can be seen year-round.

How to recognize

Upland Lake, Loch and Tarn includes the biggest and deepest waterbodies in Britain and Ireland, such as great lochs of Loch Ness and Loch Maree, and many of the lakes of the Lake District and Snowdonia. Their stony, wave-washed shores and deep, cold water can look forbidding on a bleak day, but in the sunshine the glittering water and often stunning scenery have a more accessible beauty, and they are some of the best-loved features in our landscape.

This habitat type also includes smaller, shallower tarns and lochans, many of which are unnamed. Found high up in mountain corries or on the fells, they are beautiful, solitary places, with just a thin scattering of plants. They often freeze over completely in the winter.

When to visit

Summer for breeding birds and aquatic plants.

Did you know?

Loch Morar, the deepest in the UK, reaches a depth of 310 m, while Loch Ness holds more water than all the lakes in England and Wales put together.

TOP: **Loch Maree, Wester Ross**, is a large, relatively pristine loch where Otter and **Black-throated Diver** (BOTTOM) feed on Atlantic Salmon and Brown Trout. Submersion within its waters was once considered a cure for lunacy.

Peat-stained (Dystrophic) Waters page 389

Dystrophic waters are highly acidic and poor in nutrients. They contain dissolved humic acid derived from peat, which also stains the water a dark brown. The coloration makes for poor light penetration, and this, together with the low nutrient content, means that relatively few plant species are able to thrive. Common Cottongrass, Lesser Bladderwort, Bogbean and Bog Pondweed are characteristic, and bog-mosses sometimes dominate, for example in many of the dubh (black) lochans of north-west Scotland. The fringing vegetation is not generally distinctive but tends to reflect that of the surrounding land. Invertebrates include water beetles, caddisfly larvae, water-boatmen and some scarce dragonflies. In small pools, the invertebrate population includes a high proportion of carnivorous species which prey mostly on terrestrial invertebrates that drop into the water. The lack of suitable food means that mayflies and stoneflies (which are largely herbivorous) are mostly absent and many pools are too acidic to support fish. Although individual pools are species-poor, the degree of variation between them means that, at a landscape level, the habitat has greater diversity. Lowland dystrophic pools can be more species-rich than those in the uplands as a result of additional nutrient input from the adjacent land.

Similar habitats

Dystrophic waters occur within mire systems and are linked to Blanket Bog, Raised Bog and Valley Mire. Some oligotrophic waters can also be brown-coloured and the two can be difficult to separate.

A dubh lochan on **Rannoch Moor** with **Bog Bean** flowering in the foreground. The pools of Rannoch Moor include an unusual diversity of size, depth and shoreline types.

Origins and development

Most dystrophic waters are found within blanket mire in the uplands (particularly north-west Scotland and western Ireland). Examples are also found farther south, such as in the mosses of the West Midlands where kettle-holes have developed into basin mires. In southern Britain a few are found over Tertiary sands between Surrey and Dorset, but in most of the mire systems in this area there is little open water; Woolmer Pond in Hampshire is thought to be an ancient peat cutting. Dystrophic waters have been lost from areas such as the Irish Midlands through drainage, peat extraction and forestry.

Conservation

Given their often remote nature, many peaty pools are relatively unaffected by the nutrient enrichment that impacts on other standing waterbodies, and there is little need for conservation intervention beyond that needed for the surrounding habitat. Blanket Bog restoration projects involve restoring the natural hydrology of sites and allowing new pools to form.

What to look for

Look in dystrophic pools for insectivorous plants such as bladderworts. In Scotland, look for Azure Hawker, White-faced Darter and Black Darter, which is also found on southern sites with Emerald Damselfly and, in England and Wales, Small Red Damselfly. In the Shetlands, Orkney and Hebrides, listen out for the strange repetitive call of breeding Red-throated Diver.

EXTENT IN KM^2

Eng	13
Wal	1
Sco	9
NI	1
Ire	27

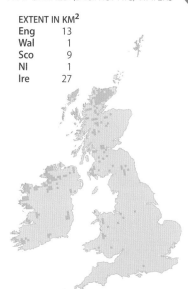

Distribution and extent

Mostly confined to the north and west of Britain and the Atlantic fringe of Ireland. Peat-stained Waters are rare in the lowlands. Map shows broad extent of Annex I habitat (H3160) and the extent figures are from the reporting for freshwaters that fall into this category.

Lake District – many small, unnamed peaty pools are found in the uplands.

How to recognize

These are the dark, peaty pools and lakes found scattered across our remotest uplands. They are also found in Raised Bog and Valley Mire in the lowlands, but most are an intrinsic part of Blanket Bog where, even on the dullest day, they catch the light and add a sparkle to the otherwise sombre landscape. They are generally small and can occur in isolation or dispersed among knolls and hollows where their prevalence makes it hard to pick a straight route through the bog.

In north-west Scotland, they form ordered linear or concentric patterns. Sometimes they are capped with a quaking mat of mosses and vascular plants (which cannot necessarily take a person's weight).

Larger dystrophic lakes with sandy or gravelly shores are also (rarely) found. Lowland pools tend to be deeper than their upland counterparts.

When to visit

June for Bogbean and Common Cottongrass in flower and various dragonfly species.

Did you know?

The low levels of nutrients in Peat-stained Waters is a challenge for many plants, but the resulting lack of competition is ideal for bladderworts, which use a suction trap to capture and digest tiny invertebrates.

1 Flow Country, Sutherland – patterning of dubh lochans.
2 Bog-bean. **4** Abernethy, Speyside – a dystrophic pool created by damming a stream; pools such as this provide habitat for the rare **3** Northern Damselfly, which is restricted to only about 30 sites in central Scotland.

Turlough and Fluctuating Mere

page 389

Turloughs and Fluctuating Meres occur in depressions in Carboniferous limestone and chalk respectively. Springs, swallow holes and openings into underground drainage systems allow limestone basins to fill with groundwater and empty again, while the porous nature of chalk means that water can percolate through it. The variation in water level may be up to six metres, and often follows a seasonal pattern. Turloughs tend to fill around mid-autumn, and empty the following spring. In contrast, fluctuating meres may become fuller in the summer in a delayed response to high winter groundwater levels. They can also dry out altogether for prolonged periods; the process by which they fluctuate is not fully understood.

Plant communities are determined by the period of inundation and the water level. The lowest parts of the basin can be marshy and support Common Sedge, or muddy in which case species such as Knotgrass, Amphibious Bistort and Water-purslane readily grow. Silverweed is particularly characteristic, and can be found across the damper centre and some way up the sides of the basin, usually giving way to a springy turf of Carnation Sedge and wet-meadow species in turloughs, or a band of Reed Canary-grass in fluctuating meres. The aquatic flora is better developed in fluctuating meres than turloughs, and can include pondweeds and stoneworts. Both habitats support a range of

EXTENT IN KM²
Eng <1
Wal <1
NI <1
Ire 57

Water levels in the turloughs of **the Burren, Co. Clare**, seen here in August, respond particularly rapidly to changes in groundwater level usually linked to rainfall, although Cahergassaun Lough near the coast empties and refills twice daily with the tide in summer. Greater awareness of turloughs is needed to ensure their protection. Many have been lost through drainage, and more recently, suspected turloughs have been lost to development including a bypass and a car salesroom (subsequently abandoned when it flooded!).

Distribution and extent

Turloughs are largely restricted to the central western lowlands of Ireland; fluctuating meres are only found in the East Anglian Breckland. These habitats are unique to Britain and Ireland. Dots on the map indicate sites, with those in Ireland drawn from the EPA turlough database. Extents for Ireland, Wales and Northern Ireland drawn from the Annex I reporting (H3180).

291

invertebrates, usually species adapted to temporary waterbodies. Some are highly mobile (*e.g.* dragonflies), whilst others have forms that can withstand periods of dessiccation (*e.g.* water fleas and Fairy Shrimp, which can flourish in the warm, fish-free water during wet periods). Each site tends to have a different invertebrate fauna according to factors such as water depth and grazing. The waterbodies also provide spawning sites for amphibians, and Great Crested Newt is found in some fluctuating meres. During the winter, turloughs provide important winter feeding grounds for waterfowl, and water-filled fluctuating meres can support breeding wildfowl.

Similar habitats

Turloughs and fluctuating meres are similar to lakes when the water levels are high, but unlike lakes can support fen or grassland communities when the water levels drop. Temporary ponds are smaller.

Origins and development

Turloughs form where glacial drift is thin or absent over depressions in grey calcarenite, a type of limestone through which water is able to flow particularly easily. The origins of Breckland's fluctuating meres are unknown, but they also depend on geomorphological features. The absence of a water inlet means that Turloughs and Fluctuating Meres are not prone to silting up, and may be ancient, although many turloughs contain a layer of marl in the soil profile, suggesting that they were once permanently flooded. Shallow ridges indicate where turloughs were used for cultivation when the human population density was higher, and fluctuating meres have also very occasionally been cropped during dry spells. Grazing systems are integral to the management and diversity of turloughs and larger turloughs are usually commons.

Conservation

While 79 of the 300 turloughs in Ireland are designated as SACs, there is comparatively little in place to ensure their protection, and smaller turloughs may not even be mapped. Lack of awareness and incomplete understanding of their hydrology inhibit long-term conservation planning. Loss of traditional grazing

Shrubby Cinquefoil can be found flowering in June and July at the high water mark of turloughs.

systems linked to the ephemeral nature of turloughs threatens their wildlife interest, as does increased nutrient input through agricultural intensification. Fluctuating meres are more reliably protected, but water abstraction may be prolonging dry periods.

What to look for

Look out for Fen Violet, Water Germander, Shrubby Cinquefoil, Whooper Swan and Scarce Emerald Damselfly in turloughs. Two distinctive mosses, the blackish Smaller Lattice-moss and the large, branched Greater Water-moss, can be seen on the rocks of swallow holes and the bottom of fluctuating meres. When fluctuating meres are water-filled, look for breeding Little Grebe, Tufted Duck, Gadwall and Pochard.

How to recognize

Turloughs and Fluctuating Meres are strange, otherworldly places. Their shallow basins have no apparent outlet or inlet, but fill with groundwater according to complex hydrologies that are not fully understood, emptying again to reveal a pattern of concentrically zoned vegetation that looks alien in the surrounding rocky or heathy landscape.

Turloughs tend to fill in winter, and dry out in summer, although shallow pools of water may remain and can enlarge rapidly following rainfall. Fluctuating meres are less predictable and, although they may fluctuate seasonally, they can also remain dry for several years.

When empty, the shallow basins may be grazed by livestock, and some turloughs are divided into fields by radiating stone walls that are submerged in winter. When full, they can support large numbers of wildfowl.

When to visit

Turloughs are likely to hold water in winter, so this is a good time to visit for wildfowl, while late spring and summer are optimal for plants and dragonflies. Fluctuating meres are of interest at any time of year, but keep an open mind about what wildlife might be present.

Did you know?

Not all of Breckland's meres fluctuate as some are permanent waterbodies on clay. Langmere and Ringmere at East Wretham Heath are the best known fluctuating meres.

TOP: **Scarce Emerald Damselfly**, sometimes called the Turlough Spreadwing in Ireland, is particularly associated with turloughs. BOTTOM: **Langmere, East Wretham, Norfolk** – During dry phases the muddy bottom supports ruderal species including Common Nettle. Breckland holds six fluctuating meres and another six smaller fluctuating pools.

Other types of Lake page 388

Mesotrophic Lake

These are neutral to base-rich lakes usually found on the fringes of the uplands, often where calcareous and acidic bedrocks meet. They tend to have hard, rocky bottoms and clear water that allows light to penetrate. With a moderate nutrient status ('mesotrophic'), these lakes can be particularly rich in aquatic plants, unlike the more barren oligotrophic lakes, although most have an upland 'feel'. A range of different aquatic plant communities can occur, depending on the substrate, water depth and exposure. Sheltered areas with a stable water column may hold Alternate Water-milfoil and a variety of pondweeds, while areas with fine sediments (*e.g.* outflows) may support stoneworts. Look out for scarce plants such as Six-stamened Waterwort and Pillwort. Classic sites include Bassenthwaite and Windermere in the Lake District, Loch of the Lowes in Perthshire, and Llyn Eiddwen and Llyn Fannod in Ceredigion.

TOP: **Broad-leaved Pondweed** is a typical Mesotrophic Lake species, and can sometimes be found with **Pillwort**, a tiny fern that flourishes in bare livestock-poached margins; BOTTOM: **Loch Insh, Speyside** – the River Spey flows through this loch and there is an exceptionally fast through-flow of water.

Marl Lake

Marl Lakes occur in limestone areas and have very clear water with a characteristic blue tint. Marl is calcium carbonate that has precipitated out of the water primarily as a result of the removal of carbon dioxide by aquatic plants. This precipitation removes dissolved nutrients from the water and, as a consequence, phytoplankton levels are low. However, macrophytes can obtain nutrients from the marl that forms the bottom sediment and, because of the clarity of the water, can grow at great depths (exceptionally down to 12 m). The flora can be very rich, and stoneworts (large algae that superficially resemble vascular plants and are coated with deposits of calcium carbonate) are a notable feature. The invertebrate fauna is variable, with some lakes supporting a rich diversity of species similar to those found in eutrophic waters, while isolated and upland marl lakes support relatively few invertebrates. Classic sites include the Durness lochs of Sutherland, Malham Tarn (North Yorkshire), Lough Bunny (Co. Clare), Lough Owel (Co. Westmeath) and Lough Carra (Co. Mayo). The Cotswold Water Park is a network of artificial waterbodies including marl lakes that were created through gravel extraction.

TOP: **Malham Tarn, North Yorkshire,** a classic and much-studied site, is the highest Marl Lake in the UK; BOTTOM: **Loch Caladail, near Durness, Sutherland** – one of a cluster of three marl lakes known for their very clear water.

Other types of Lake   page 388

Lowland Nutrient-poor Lake

There are some lowland sites where lakes lie on sandy, acidic substrates and are low in nutrients. Such lakes are similar in their chemistry, and much of their flora to upland oligotrophic lakes, They can support 'isoetid' species such as Water Lobelia, Shoreweed and Quillwort, which may be zoned in single-species lawns. In the UK, these lakes are scarce and occur only at a few heathland and Machair locations; classic sites include Hatchet Pond (New Forest, Hampshire), Little Sea (Studland, Dorset) and Oak Mere (Cheshire) and the South Uist Machair lochs. Ireland is a stronghold for Lowland Nutrient-poor Lakes, with 32 SACs designated for this habitat type, including Lough Corrib, an unusual site with features characteristic of both Marl Lake and Lowland Nutrient-poor Lake in basins in limestone and acidic rocks respectively.

TOP: **Water Lobelia** is one of the more distinctive 'isoetids' when in flower during July and August; BOTTOM: **Little Sea, Studland, Dorset** is a shallow lake that formed when sea water became landlocked by accreting sand dunes. The water is now fresh and is replenished by acidic, oligotrophic water draining off the adjacent heathland. Much of the aquatic vegetation has disappeared in recent years, probably due to the introduction of Carp.

Brackish Lake

Brackish lakes, which can be eutrophic or oligotrophic, are slightly saline, and their water levels show some fluctuation with the tide. In The Broads of East Anglia, Hickling, Horsey and Martham fall into this category. In Scotland there are lochs where sea water can enter at high tide through a narrow inlet. Such sites are rocky and have a gradient from fresh to more saline water along their length; they include Harray and Stenness on Orkney (eutrophic) and Loch an Duin on South Uist (oligotrophic).

TOP: Tasselweeds are sumberged grass-like herbs found in shallow, brackish waters. They have long-stalked fruits and a single midrib. **Beaked Tasselweed** and the rarer Spiral Tasselweed are best differentiated by examination of the ripe fruits in summer; BOTTOM: **Hickling Broad, Norfolk**, is connected to the sea by the rivers Thurne and Bure.

Pond

page 389

Ponds are very diverse and this habitat type supports a correspondingly diverse flora and fauna. Some individual ponds support over 40 aquatic plant species and over 50 large invertebrates. Overall, ponds support a similar number of plant species to lakes, and more large invertebrates than rivers; some two-thirds of freshwater species have been recorded in ponds. Most ponds gradually silt up over time and examination of old maps suggests that many field ponds only last a century or so. However, deeper ponds may be more permanent and some ground ice depressions (sometimes called pingos) have held water for 14,000 years. Many gardens contain ponds, and these can also be rich in wildlife, particularly where they have shallow edges, marginal vegetation and nearby plant cover. Temporary pools that dry out annually are distinctive and, as they tend not to silt up (the dry spells allow organic matter to oxidise), may be a more permanent feature in the landscape than deeper pools. They also lack predatory fish, and so may support different invertebrate communities from those ponds or pools that remain water-filled year-round.

Similar habitats

Ponds are distinctive in being small in size and lacking connectivity. Lakes have a true open-water zone in which algae and submerged plants are dominant. Temporary ponds in heavily grazed grassland are associated with mosaics of acid and neutral grassland and are best seen in the New Forest.

Large pond at **Aylesbeare Common, Devon**.

Origins and development

Natural ponds are found in solution hollows, seasonally flooded depressions and pingos dating from the end of the last glaciation. Artificial ponds include those deliberately created as waterbodies such as dew ponds (for watering livestock), decoys (to draw wildfowl for hunting) and pools used for leather and hemp processing. Others were created as a result of the extraction of minerals such as stone (including flint), sand, gravel, clay, brickearth and marl (chalky soil used as a fertilizer). There are also about 5,000 moats that probably date from the 13th century onwards. Many ponds will silt up unless periodically cleared out. Changes in rural practices have often made ponds redundant and so they have been allowed to dry out. Others have been drained or lost to development; 50% of the estimated one million ponds that existed in Britain 100 years ago have vanished.

Conservation

Ponds are vulnerable to pollution (mainly nutrient enrichment from agricultural run-off) and neglect. Temporary ponds are particularly threatened as the small water volume means that they are more vulnerable to drainage and pollution. Some old ponds may benefit from careful restoration, and there are ambitious targets to re-create ponds – the Freshwater Habitats Trust aims to ensure that by 2050 there are once again one million ponds in the UK. New ponds are an effective way of creating new freshwater habitat that is relatively easy to protect from nutrient-enrichment.

NUMBER OF PONDS
Eng 234,000
Wal 47,000
Sco 198,000
NI n/k
Ire n/k

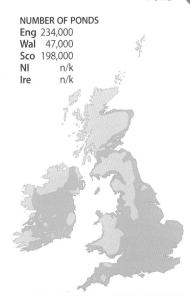

Distribution and extent

Ponds are widely distributed, predominantly in the lowlands. Figures are 2007 UK Countryside Survey estimates.

A temporary pool on a **New Forest** lawn. Ponds only need to hold water for a few months each year to support a suite of aquatic species. This pond supports Tadpole Shrimp and Fairy Shrimp.

What to look for

Search the drying edges of temporary pools for Pennyroyal (in the New Forest), Pigmy Rush (on the Lizard) and Yellow Centaury (south-west England and Ireland). Keep an eye open for Fairy Shrimp when pools refill. Look for Great Crested Newt in permanent ponds with a water depth of over 50 cm and abundant aquatic plants, the much less widespread Natterjack Toad in temporary pools in Sand Dune and lowland heathland. Pond-dipping can reveal a great diversity of invertebrates, including water beetles, diving beetles, water fleas, pond snails, caddisfly larvae and dragonfly nymphs.

How to recognize

Ponds are small waterbodies (up to 2 ha) that hold water for all or part of the year and are not fed by a stream or river, but depend on rain and groundwater. They are characterized by shallow-water and swamp vegetation, with little deep, open water and can be found in gardens, on village greens, in corners of farmland, deep within woods, and on pastures and heathlands. Ponds are sometimes hidden, lost in overgrown, forgotten tangled thickets.

Unpolluted and not overly shaded ponds can be teeming with wildlife, supporting a wide array of invertebrates and diverse plant species, and providing habitat for amphibians and birds. In some areas they are a characteristic feature of the landscape, such as the 'pingos' of East Anglia, the Cheshire marl pits and the forest and moorland pools of Speyside.

When to visit

Spring for tadpoles; summer for 'bug-hunting' and aquatic and marginal plants; winter for Fairy Shrimp.

Did you know?

The Anglo-saxons had seven words for different kinds of ponds. The word pond is derived from pund, meaning enclosure, and reflects the artificial origins of many ponds.

TOP: Village pond, **Redgrave, Suffolk**. Ponds often form a focal point in villages and historically would have fulfilled a range of roles, including water for animals and fish for food. BOTTOM: **Pennyroyal** flowers during August and September and is associated with temporary pools on heavily grazed village greens. It experienced a drastic decline in the 20th century as habitat was destroyed, or changed as grazing decreased.

Ditch

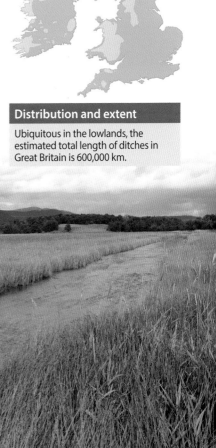

page 389

EXTENT UNKNOWN

In areas that were once extensive wetlands, ditches are the remnant of wetland habitats that have long since disappeared, and provide a continuous link with those habitats. These ditches can be centuries old, and are particularly rich in aquatic plants and invertebrates. Since most ditches are nutrient-rich, differences in vegetation composition are determined by salinity, water depth and flow, substrate type and management. The diversity of the fauna depends on the structural variety within a ditch, and is greatest where there is a mixture of marginal vegetation of different heights, open water, shallow trampled edges and different bank profiles – steep sides are favourable for Water Vole but gentle, shallow edges are preferred by many invertebrate species. Ditches in coastal grazing marshes often contain brackish water, and this adds another suite of specialist species (although influxes of strongly saline water into freshwater ditches can result in low species diversity). Shaded ditches and those colonized by invasive non-native plant species (see Canal, *page 304*) are less diverse. Ditches where some form of management takes place are generally richer in plant and invertebrate species and have a greater abundance of amphibians and visiting birds.

Similar habitats

Ditches can be confused with heavily engineered small streams and may be similar to canals, although the latter are generally wider.

Insh Marshes, Speyside – this site has a very complex hydrology. The wide ditch was constructed in the 19th Century for drainage purposes.

Distribution and extent

Ubiquitous in the lowlands, the estimated total length of ditches in Great Britain is 600,000 km.

301

Origins and development

Most ditches were dug to drain land and make it suitable for cultivation or grazing animals, although some were created to transport materials (such as peat or reeds) or to form livestock barriers (known as wet fences). In some grazing marshes, ditches were used to help maintain high water levels in the summer to encourage grass growth, and in places where wetland habitats are being restored, ditches are once again used to bring water onto the site rather than to drain it. Threats include major fluctuations in water level, pollution, invasive non-native species and inappropriate management (either over-management or a lack of management, resulting in the loss of open water).

1 **Frome Valley, Dorset** – a recently cleared ditch. Ditches in this valley support a range of uncommon plants such as Red Pondweed and Lesser Water-plantain. **2** **Loch Gruinart, Islay** – an extensive ditch network in coastal grazing marsh. **3** **Arne Moors, Dorset** – a relatively nutrient-poor ditch in acid peat. **4** Ditch within Coastal and Floodplain Grazing Marsh at **Southwold, Suffolk**.

Conservation

Regular cutting of aquatic and bankside vegetation and the occasional removal of silt is usually necessary to keep ditches open, and is best staggered over time, with stretches left uncut to ensure a wide range of conditions and provide a refuge for species likely to be lost during ditch clearance. Maintaining good water quality is a challenge in areas with intensive farming where nutrient run-off frequently pollutes ditches. Current large-scale wetland restoration projects should benefit ditches.

What to look for

Key plant species include Frogbit, Tubular Water-dropwort, Sharp-leaved Pondweed and Water-soldier, and some ditch systems support stoneworts (look in recently cleared areas). Look for Sea Club-rush, Brackish Water-crowfoot, Spiral Tasselweed and Beaked Tasselweed in brackish ditches. Rare invertebrates include Great Silver Water Beetle and Norfolk Hawker, but more widespread species such as Ruddy Darter and Hairy Dragonfly are easier to see.

Ditches are generally a feature of flat land close to sea level and are typically found in Coastal and Floodplain Grazing Marsh, Lowland Fen or farmland, although they extend into the uplands too. They are artificial features that are usually straight and often follow field boundaries. Generally constructed for the purpose of draining the adjacent land, ditches range in size from a spade's width to wide agricultural drains.

The best ditches provide a refuge for wetland species that were once more widespread in the landscape. Rare plants can be found among the marginal and aquatic vegetation, which can support a diverse array of invertebrates including numerous rare water beetles and other scarce and threatened species. Ditches in arable land only rarely support such rich assemblages.

When to visit

Mid-summer (July) is a good time for flowering plants. June is the best time to see dragonflies such as Norfolk Hawker.

1 **How Hill, Norfolk** – a species-rich ditch supporting a range of aquatic plants including **Frogbit** and **Water-soldier** (**2**). **3** **Norfolk Hawker** – distinguished by its brown body, clear wings and green eyes, is an iconic species of the Norfolk Broads, where its return from near-extinction signifies the success of conservation projects.

Canals lack strongly flowing water, and the resulting absence of currents and bank erosion means that they have more ecological similarity with standing water and ponds than rivers. Canals vary markedly in their character, generally depending on water characteristics, the amount of boat traffic and how banksides are managed. For example, the canals of southern England and the English Midlands are eutrophic; those in north-west England receive their water from the Pennines and are mesotrophic, while the Caledonian Canal, which runs through the Great Glen, is oligotrophic.

Aquatic macrophytes can include Rigid Hornwort, Spiked Water-milfoil, pondweeds, duckweeds and Yellow Water-lily, while rare species include Grass-wrack Pondweed and Floating Water-plantain. Invertebrates can include a diversity of dragonflies, beetles, bugs and molluscs, and submerged infrastructure can support freshwater sponges. Where boat traffic is limited, fishes such as Perch, Tench, Rudd and Pike may inhabit the canal. The wildlife interest is not limited to the water; the Greywell Tunnel on the Basingstoke Canal is one of the largest winter bat roosts in the UK.

Canals are often accompanied by linear strips and pockets of other habitat (*e.g.* woodland, scrub, and grassland) which, together with the marginal and aquatic communities of the canal itself, provide corridors of semi-natural habitat linking otherwise isolated sites within agricultural or urban landscapes. Canals can also link autonomous river catchments.

Similar habitats

Canals can be separated from Ditches by their width and function. Rivers 'canalized' for transport purposes or in urban settings can look similar, but have a visible flow of water.

Canal boats moored on the **Kennet and Avon Canal** at Devizes, Wiltshire.

Origins and development

The Romans were the first to build canals in Britain, but they did not become widespread until the Industrial Revolution. Most were constructed between 1750 and 1870 to extend water transport for the large-scale movement of materials and goods for which trains of packhorses on poorly surfaced roads were inadequate. Canals made a dramatic impact on the landscape, to which there was often opposition. They started to fall into decline with the advent of rail transport and later, road haulage, and many were closed. However, from the 1960s recreational interest in canals was sufficient to stop further closures, and canals that were already closed began to be restored by groups of enthusiasts. There are plans to build new canals to enhance existing networks for recreational purposes.

Conservation

The wildlife interest of canals is threatened by poor water quality and excessive siltation leading to the loss of open water in derelict canals, and by bank erosion and high water turbidity caused by recreational boat traffic in navigable canals. Canals often run through densely populated areas where urban pressures are high. Non-native invasive species (*e.g.* Mink, Signal Crayfish, New Zealand Pigmyweed and Parrot's-feather) can disperse readily along canal networks. Today, management has to balance heritage, recreation and nature conservation interests, and obtaining the often considerable funding necessary to maintain canals can be challenging.

EXTENT IN KM

Eng	3,300
Wal	200
Sco	200
NI	110
Ire	300

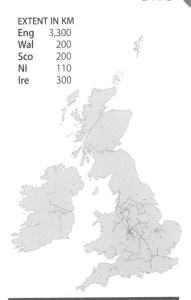

Distribution and extent

Widespread, particularly in lowland England.

Wey and Arun Canal, West Sussex – abandoned in 1871, this 37 km stretch of canal linked two rivers. It shows how, without maintenance and regular boat traffic, open water is gradually colonized by swamp vegetation.

What to look for

Look out for Water Vole and also Kingfisher, which can be seen even in urban environments. Canals are often good places to see a wide range of dragonflies associated with standing water.

1 Kingfisher is a widespread species that is often encountered on canals where water quality has been improved. **2** The Basingstoke Canal, Hampshire, is nationally important for its large range of aquatic plants and invertebrates. Heavily shaded sections tend to be less species-rich. **3** Floating Water-plantain can carpet stretches of little-used canals in England and Wales, which provide a substitute for its former habitat of slow-moving, mesotrophic rivers; the UK holds a significant proportion of the world population of this plant (which is also found pools and lakes).

How to recognize

Canals are artificial inland waterways that were constructed to create an interconnected water transport system. They are easily recognized as they tend to be relatively straight with a parallel towpath, and are quite uniform, usually 10–20 m wide and 1–2 m deep. The water level is controlled, there is little or no flow, and there is associated infrastructure such as locks, cuttings, embankments, bridges and tunnels.

Now used predominantly for recreational purposes, they can be pleasant, tranquil places, and many support diverse wildlife, particularly where boat traffic is not too heavy and marginal vegetation is present.

When to visit

Spring and summer for invertebrates and aquatic flora.

Did you know?

In England and Wales 18 canals are designated as SSSIs, and three (the Cannock Extension Canal, Rochdale Canal and the Montgomery Canal) are SACs, designated for their populations of Floating Water-plantain.

Fast-flowing River and Stream

page 390

EXTENT UNKNOWN

Fast-flowing, turbulent waters are a challenging environment for plants and animals. They occur in areas with high rainfall, steep slopes and impervious substrates, and most show marked variations in water flow. When rivers are in spate, the erosive power of the water increases dramatically. The strength of the current is fundamental in determining the species likely to be present. Water chemistry is less important – most Fast-flowing Rivers and Streams are nutrient-poor. Where the bottom is composed of shifting and unstable stones, the only vegetation present is algae coating some stones, though mosses and liverworts can be found where the sediment is more stable. When streams converge to form rivers the current still causes erosion but the water loses speed and finer sands and gravels may accumulate. However, the substrates are often still too mobile for plants to take hold. Marginal aquatic vegetation is scarce but may include Alternate Water-milfoil and Bulbous Rush.

Turbulent water is rich in oxygen, and suits animals that have a high oxygen demand and strategies that enable them to cope with fast flows. Atlantic Salmon and Brown Trout (salmonids) are strong swimmers and lay their eggs in carefully constructed redds (depressions on the river bed) to prevent them from being washed away, although when the eggs hatch the young head downstream where more food is available. Freshwater Pearl Mussel lives buried or partly buried in coarse sand and fine gravel and has a larval phase that attaches to the gills of juvenile salmonids; it is a good indicator of pollution-free water but is declining severely.

Distribution and extent

Widespread in the uplands.

River Grudie, Wester Ross. The large boulders reveal the strength and variation in the water flow. Cobbles trap detritus and organic matter, which are exploited by detritivore invertebrates.

Other invertebrates, such as stoneflies, mayflies and caddisflies, use gaps between coarse sediment particles to shelter from the current, and some caddisfly larvae attach themselves to rocks within silk cocoons.

Similar habitats

Some watercourses, such as those on the seaward sides of mountains in Ireland and western Scotland, are fast-flowing for their whole length, while others may be fast-flowing in their headwaters and then gradually slow down. Slow-flowing watercourses can be differentiated by their silty substrate and meandering form (unless modified) and they generally hold more in-stream and marginal vegetation.

Origins and development

Fast-flowing River and Stream is a habitat of upland environments where multitudinous small flushes, rills and runnels gradually merge, firstly into small streams, then into larger tributary streams, before finally forming rivers. Such rivers and streams are essentially eroding systems that carry fine particles, pebbles and boulders with them as they flow downstream.

Increases in both nutrients and sediment, together with artificial changes in water flow (*e.g.* through abstraction or damming for reservoirs), have led to increased plant growth and a shift in invertebrate and fish communities in some upland rivers and streams. Acidification through atmospheric pollution and catchment afforestation is widespread.

Conservation

Recent improvements seen in lowland rivers, particularly in urban areas, have not been reflected in the uplands. Conservation measures need to address catchment management, including issues surrounding afforestation, heather-burning, overgrazing and, at lower altitudes, agricultural pollution. Impacts on Fast-flowing River and Stream have cumulative implications for water quality and flow farther downstream, potentially affecting a range of other habitats including Sluggish River and Stream.

What to look for

Particularly characteristic birds of fast-flowing streams include Dipper and Grey Wagtail, which are joined by Red-breasted Merganser and Common Sandpiper in broader reaches. Brown Trout, Grayling and Bullhead can be present, and during the 'salmon run', look out for Atlantic Salmon leaping waterfalls. Near waterfalls, it is worth searching shaded, constantly damp streamside boulders for tiny filmy-ferns.

The River Feshie, Speyside is one of Britain's most dynamic river systems. Its 'flashy' flow regime, soft banks and the abundance of loose sediment result in a continually evolving braided channel.

How to recognize

Fast-flowing River and Stream is characteristic of the uplands, where turbulent water tumbles down steep hillsides in a series of riffles, waterfalls and pools. In their upper reaches, watercourses are often incised into the underlying bedrock. Lower down, where streams flatten out and widen into rivers, boulders, pebbles and gravel start to accumulate but the flow remains relatively fast, and species diversity is low compared to that of slow-flowing lowland rivers.

Loud and exhilarating after rain, fast-flowing rivers and streams can dry rapidly in droughty conditions, exposing spongy cushions of aquatic mosses on boulders and stranding Brown Trout in shrinking pools. Dippers bob on waterside boulders regardless of the water flow, occasionally diving for mayfly nymphs and caddisfly larvae, while in the spring Red-breasted Merganser might be seen around islets and promontories.

When to visit

Year-round for Dipper and bryophytes, autumn after rain for the salmon run. Access can be difficult after heavy rain.

TOP: **Creag Meagaidh, Central Highlands** – upland streams are often relatively straight due to the fast-flowing water. This stream is fed by snow-melt that collects in a tarn in the corrie (just out of view). BOTTOM: **Dippers** are characteristic of fast-flowing and well-oxygenated streams and rivers, usually in the uplands.

F

Sluggish River and Stream page 390

As rivers broaden out and the water flow slows down, the temperature and the amount of sediment on the river bed increase, resulting in a different suite of species from those in the faster-flowing headwaters. Phytoplankton, which is washed away in fast-flowing watercourses, can develop sizeable populations, particularly in backwaters and, together with suspended sediment, makes the water cloudy. In-stream vegetation of pondweeds, water-starworts, water-milfoils and the submerged cabbage-like leaves of Yellow Water-lily can be sufficiently abundant to slow the water flow further, promoting the deposition of sediments and detritus and providing shelter for aquatic fauna. Invertebrates (which include filter-feeders, detritivores, grazers and predators) also shelter in snagged debris and in the bottom sediment, or can be found on the surface film. Insects are the most abundant group, although molluscs are also present. Fishes include Bream, Roach, Dace, Perch, Eel and Pike (a powerful predator), and Brown Trout and Atlantic Salmon may pass through. Marginal vegetation is abundant where the bottom sediment facilitates rooting, and includes robust plants such as Common Reed, Reed Sweet-grass, Bulrush, Hemp-agrimony and water-parsnips, with smaller herbs such as Water Mint, bur-marigolds and Brooklime on shallow edges. In their lower reaches, rivers are influenced by salt water and tides and, where they merge into estuaries, marine species such as mullet, Sea Bass and Flounder may be present.

Similar habitats

Transitional zones intermediate between Fast-flowing and Sluggish River and Stream are found, and there is also overlap between the vegetation of Sluggish River and Stream and Nutrient-rich (Eutrophic) Lake.

A backwater of the **River Nene, Earls Barton, Northamptonshire.**

Origins and development

EXTENT UNKNOWN

Naturally dynamic, slow-flowing rivers and streams shape the surrounding landscape. They gradually migrate across the floodplain as sediment is eroded from the outside of a bend and deposited on the inside. Additional meanders can form on existing loops, and ox-bow lakes develop where meanders are cut off from the main channel. Slow-flowing backwaters are found where the river divides into more than one channel. All these features add to the diversity of species present.

A desire to use flat, fertile floodplains for agriculture and development has meant that extensive stretches of lowland rivers have been engineered and contained. Our rivers are no longer wild; they are often confined to a single channel, prevented from flooding and, in urban areas, diverted into tunnels. As a result they are commonly perceived as a linear entity within a valley, rather than an integral part of a wider wetland system. The character and conservation interest of many rivers has also been severely affected by pollution and water abstraction. However, over the last few decades efforts to clean up pollution and 're-naturalise' rivers have resulted in a return of macrophytes, fish and invertebrates.

Conservation

Distribution and extent

Widespread in the lowlands.

River restoration projects seek to find the balance between protecting human use of riparian environments and allowing rivers to function naturally. Flood risk can be reduced by setting back embankments and reinstating flood meadows, washlands and grazing marshes. Diffuse pollution from agriculture remains an issue, and can usually only be addressed through catchment-scale changes in land management practices. At a more local scale, the management of river banks to provide a diverse range of vegetation structures is important. Increasing the extent of riverine woodland to create a patchwork of shady conditions will help combat temperature increases resulting from climate change at the same time as providing woody debris.

LEFT: **The River Wampool, near Angerton, Cumbria** meanders through agriculturally improved pasture as it approaches the Solway, where the pasture grades into Saltmarsh. RIGHT: **Mill Lawn Brook, New Forest** – New Forest streams originating in semi-natural habitat are unpolluted, varied in character and support a range of invertebrates.

How to recognize

Sluggish rivers and streams meander slowly through the lowland countryside, depositing fine sediments and organic detritus as they flow seawards. In their natural state, they curve sinuously through their floodplain and include looped meanders, shallow and deep pools, backwaters and mid-channel bars. However, the rivers of Britain and Ireland have largely been tamed and confined, and these dynamic elements are often no longer formed.

Unpolluted waters can still be rich in wildlife. Thick marginal vegetation of 'reedy' species and robust herbs gives way to usually rather cloudy open water with both submerged and emergent aquatic plants. and there can be a host of invertebrate species. Large, pollarded willows often line the river banks, and in some places the floodplains still support Floodplain Grazing Marsh or Lowland Meadow and Pasture, habitats that, together with wetlands and floodplain woodlands, would once have formed an integral part of lowland river systems.

When to visit

Early–mid-summer for flowering plants and invertebrates.

Did you know?
The economic cost of flood damage in England over the winter of 2013/14 was estimated to be over £1 billion.

1 **River Waveney, Suffolk/Norfolk** border. Several surviving fens and marshes hint at the extensive wetland habitat that would once have lined the river valley, including Redgrave and Lopham, the largest remaining river valley fen in England. **2** **Banded Demioselle** – one of the most attractive damselflies and a species that is typical of sluggish rivers and streams. **3** **The River Shannon** is the longest river in Britain and Ireland and flows through 11 counties with an average flow rate of over 200 m³ per second.

Chalk River and Stream

page 390

Chalk rivers and streams always originate in chalk springs but they do not necessarily flow over chalk for their entire length. Water is steadily released from the aquifer, although upper reaches show gentle seasonal fluctuations and some headwater sections include winterbournes that run dry in late summer (and support their own distinctive species including Pond Water-crowfoot and rare river flies). Having percolated through the chalk the water is very pure and rich in minerals, and its temperature remains fairly constant throughout the year. These factors combine to allow Chalk River and Stream to support characteristic aquatic plant communities that can be very species-rich – 50 species per kilometre have been recorded from two classic chalk rivers in Hampshire, the Test and the Itchen. Water-cress and Lesser Water-parsnip are common along shallow edges, while the channel holds Stream Water-crowfoot and water-starworts, with River Water-crowfoot more common in downstream reaches. These in-stream plants slow the water flow in the summer and trap sediment, as well as provide food and shelter for invertebrates and fishes. Where there are clean gravels, fishes such as Bullhead, Brook Lamprey and Atlantic Salmon breed; some rivers are also stocked with Brown Trout and Rainbow Trout. The highest diversity and abundance of invertebrates is found on stretches of river bordered by wetland habitats with a range of vegetation structures present.

EXTENT IN KM
Eng 3,900

River Itchen, near **Ovington, Hampshire** – The Itchen is famous for trout fishing and its designation as an SAC reflects the presence of other species such as Bullhead, Atlantic Salmon and Brook Lamprey.

Distribution and extent

There are around 200 chalk rivers in the world, of which around 85% are in England.

Similar habitats
Chalk River and Stream is distinguished from other lowland waters by the clarity of the water.

Origins and development
Natural channel geomorphology can no longer be seen on chalk rivers – they have been modified by people over millennia for a variety of activities including transport, milling, fishing, irrigation, drainage and Water-cress beds. Some also have strong links with nearby cities, for example, the Avon (Salisbury), the Itchen (Winchester) and the Wensum (Norwich), and where they occur in densely populated parts of the country impacts relating to recreational pressure and water extraction are correspondingly high. Chalk catchments also include a particularly high proportion of arable land.

Conservation
Some rivers are virtually dry in the summer and over-abstraction of water is a major threat that needs to be addressed. Other issues are the physical modification of banks and channels, pollution from agricultural fertilizers and pesticides, increased amounts of sediment from eroded soil, and intensive fisheries management (such as regular weed cutting, stabilization of banks and stocking with farm-reared fish). However, there are a number of chalk river conservation projects that aim to maintain a mosaic of habitats in the catchment to restore aquifers and to protect the water from nutrient enrichment, and also to raise the profile of the habitat. The spread of non-native species (*e.g.* Japanese Knotweed and Himalayan Balsam) along banksides is an increasing challenge.

1 A tributary of the **River Piddle, Dorset** – chalk streams probably once arose in willow and Alder carr (although this is rarely the case today) and the water-crowfoot beds that are considered to be a characteristic feature of this habitat type would have been limited to stretches where there were gaps in the tree canopy. **2** The bed of chalk rivers and streams is usually composed of gravel from flint deposits within the chalk, and fine sediment is limited to slow-flowing outer bends in the river. **3** **The River Avon** on the Hampshire/Dorset border as winter flood waters retreat. The Avon is the longest chalk river in Europe.

What to look for

Aquatic vegetation is often eye-catching and can include five species of water-crowfoot. Fishes include Brown Trout, Brook Lamprey and Grayling, and Bullhead can sometime be seen under stones. Birds to look out for include Kingfisher and Reed Bunting, and adjacent grazing marsh may support breeding waders.

1 **Mayflies** spend most of their life underwater as a nymph, then emerge synchronously over a few days in late May when they mate and lay their eggs before dying, all in a matter of a few hours.
2 **Tributary of the River Itchen** with water-crowfoot beds clearly visible mid-channel. White-clawed Crayfish, once very common in hard waters but declining rapidly, is still found in the Itchen.
3 **Stream Water-crowfoot** – often the dominant plant in Chalk River and Stream.

How to recognize

Chalk Rivers and Streams are some of our most iconic freshwater sites. They can be particularly serene and equable watercourses, where mats of white-flowered water-crowfoots float in the shallow, crystal-clear water that flows swiftly over a gravelly bed. Low banks are fringed with Water-cress and Water Forget-me-not, backed by lush reed-grasses and colourful tall-herbs.

In May, thousands of mayflies emerge together and dance over the water's surface. Swallows swoop down to catch the flying adults and an occasional splash and circle of ripples shows where a Brown Trout has risen to the surface.

Old mills are a common sight, and some rivers have historic structures relating to old irrigation systems. Famous for fly-fishing, some chalk rivers have river keepers and are managed very carefully for angling, while commercial Water-cress beds are associated with some headwaters.

When to visit

Late spring–early summer for water-crowfoots in flower. The last week in May and first week in June is the peak time for mayfly emergence and is known in the trout-fishing world as 'duffer's fortnight' as even incompetent anglers can apparently make a catch!

COASTAL HABITATS

At around 31,000 km, the UK has one of the longest national coastlines in Europe, whilst that of Ireland extends to 6,000 km. Found along these coasts are some of our most important and unique habitats. The coastline is hugely variable and encompasses towering sea stacks; cliffs of black basalt, white chalk and red sandstone; shifting sand dunes; shingle ridges; saltmarshes and mudflats. Some of our oldest shores are composed of rocks that are three billion years old, while shingle and dune systems are dynamic habitats that can be seen to have changed with each visit. Natural features such as Fingal's Cave, the Giant's Causeway, the Cliffs of Moher, the Old Man of Hoy and Durdle Door draw visitors from far and wide, while the islands of Bardsey, Lindisfarne and Iona have both spiritual and cultural importance.

ORIGINS

Many factors have played a part in creating the coastline that we see today: geology, glaciation, sea-level change, sediment supply, wind, wave, tide and human activities all play a role. Britain and Ireland are unusual in having a large tidal range and stormy conditions, and as a consequence the coast is particularly dynamic. Tidal range is highest in the Severn Estuary and varies around the coast; wave energy is greatest on western coasts exposed to the north Atlantic, while the Irish Sea and North Sea are relatively sheltered.

Geology, and in particular rock strength, plays a fundamental role in dictating the shape of the coastline. Rocks that are easily eroded allow bays to develop while more resistant rocks form headlands. Soft rocks generally form sloping cliffs, whereas erosion-resistant rocks are more likely to form vertical cliffs. Geology also determines the character of beaches that develop where eroded sediment from cliffs or from offshore sandbanks is washed ashore by the waves and current. Sand is composed of silica derived from quartz, which is highly resistant to weathering, and can be mixed with shell fragments that raise the pH. Shingle is composed of flints and glacial deposits. Soft shorelines can also form on less exposed coasts where silty

Kynance, Cornwall, at low tide. At high tide the sand is under water. The middle shore (thick brown lower band), upper shore (black stripe) and splash zone are discernable. Cliff slope grassland at the top of the cliffs is still within reach of the spray in strong winds and storms.

HABITAT	DESCRIPTION
Mudflat and Sandflat *page 326 | page 386*	Bare expanses of open sand or mud in the intertidal zone.
Saltmarsh *page 329 | page 387*	Low vegetation growing on the landward edge of mudflats in sheltered bays and estuaries.
Sand Dune *page 332 | page 387*	Mobile and stable ridges and hollows created when sand from the intertidal zone is blown inland. Supports a succession of vegetation communities.
Machair *page 338 | page 386*	A cultural landscape comprizing a mosaic of dune grassland, wetlands and cultivated land (only found on the northern Atlantic fringe).
Coastal Vegetated Shingle *page 342 | page 386*	Shingle ridges shaped by currents, tides and storm surges that have become stable enough to supporting a range of vegetation.
Saline Lagoon *page 348 | page 387*	Coastal lagoons holding salt water but often with no direct connection to the sea.
Rocky Shore *page 352 | page 386*	Boulders and jumbled rocks extending into the intertidal zone, rich in seaweeds.
Soft Cliff *page 355 | page 388*	Unstable, sloping cliffs of soft rock often supporting a range of vegetation types.
Hard Cliff and Cliff Slope *page 358 | page 386*	Sheer rocky cliffs and associated cliff slope vegetation.

The rare **Sea Stock** is found on young dunes, which are particularly vulnerable to trampling (Port Eynon, Gower).

material washed down in rivers is deposited and builds up over time to form mudflats and saltmarshes. Soft shorelines are therefore closely linked to areas where the sediment originates, and are influenced by any changes that occur in these places.

Changes in sea levels over time have had dramatic impacts on the coastline. Sea levels rose rapidly when the ice retreated some 11,500 years ago. Added to this, as northern areas lost the weight of ice, the crust sprang upwards, and a see-saw effect ('isostatic rebound') is still causing parts of southern Britain to sink. The landbridge linking eastern England to the continent disappeared around 7,500 years ago. Seabed surveys show that this area was once a rolling plain with over a thousand kilometres of rivers, 24 lakes and extensive marshes and forests. Peat and pieces of tree trunk visible along the beaches of north Norfolk are a legacy of this lost landscape. Evidence of rising sea waters can be seen elsewhere along the coast. On the beach at Borth in North Wales, the roots of the forest that once filled Cardigan Bay can be seen at low tide, and human footprints from 8,000 years ago have been found in silt deposits exposed in the Severn Estuary. Some shingle beaches, such as Blakeney Point in Norfolk and Chesil in Dorset, have their origins in offshore gravel, pushed to shore by sea levels that rose as ice melted around 7,000 years ago. Individual storms and surges can also have long-lasting affects. Layers of sand overlying clay soils on raised beaches on the east coast of Scotland are thought to have their origins in tsunamis some 7,000 years ago.

TYPES OF COASTAL HABITAT

Coastal habitats are all found at the interface between land and sea, but vary in the degree to which they extend into the intertidal zone (which is regularly inundated but exposed at low tides), or above the limit of extreme high tides. Beyond the high tide mark is a zone that is still strongly affected by the sea through wind-blown salt spray and sand. The maritime influence extends even farther inland due to the effects of high winds, small temperature ranges and high atmospheric humidity.

Coastal habitats can be conveniently divided into eroding and accreting systems, which are linked through the transfer of sediment from one to the other. In many areas the sea erodes the land to form cliffs, which may be formed of hard or soft rock. Hard cliffs are sheer and support only crevice vegetation; many have caves near their base. They are battered by waves particularly during storms, and salt spray influences the cliff slope vegetation. Rocky shores are made up of rocks, boulders and pools within, and just above, the intertidal zone and are found at the base of hard cliffs and shorelines. Soft cliffs are composed of less resistant rock and are often slumped. Their more gentle slopes and terraces can support a range of other habitats. Sediment that is eroded from cliffs enters the water and, depending on tides and currents, is later re-deposited on the shore.

Accreting coastal habitats are formed where eroded sediment carried by currents, tides and waves is deposited on or near the shore in shallow water. Mudflat and Sandflat are almost level areas of fine sediment that are exposed at low tide and are devoid of vascular plants, although they can be rich in invertebrates. Where mud accumulates in sheltered bays and estuaries, it can be colonized by a distinctive suite of vascular plants and the process of succession leads to the formation of Saltmarsh. Not all Saltmarsh plants are restricted to the coastal zone as in rare circumstances some can occur inland – there is a natural salt spring

Blakeney Point, Norfolk is a four-mile-long shingle spit. Barrier beaches and spits occur in areas with a low tidal range such as East Anglia. Wave action is focused on a narrower band and can have a particularly strong influence.

Raised beaches on **Mull** (looking east from Tostary towards Tràigh na Cille and Ben More) are a dramatic testament to changes in sea level over the past 500,000 years.

Mudflat with eelgrass beds

Sandflat

Mudflat

embryo
Sand Dune
(now eroded)

mobile Sand Dune

pioneer Saltmarsh

fixed Sand Dune
grassland

Saltmarsh

Rocky Shore

Variation in the strength of wave action within and outside of the **Exe Estuary in Devon** has resulted in the development of a range of soft-shore coastal habitats for which the site is of international importance.

C

Caraun Point, Co. Mayo. Shifting sand can reveal middens and other archaeological features either in vertical sand faces or in the bottom of blow-outs. Middens, the rubbish dumps of our ancestors, can date back 7,000 years and contain abundant winkle and oyster shells.

with inland Saltmarsh vegetation in Staffordshire. Beaches are found where coarse sediments accumulate along the shoreline, including within bays between headlands on hard coasts. The intertidal area can be quite dynamic, but on the landward side of the beach, Coastal Vegetated Shingle or Sand Dune can develop and stabilize the sediment, again leading to a succession of plant communities. Soft shorelines can erode if the supply of sediment is disrupted or through storm damage.

On the north-west coast of Ireland and north-west Scotland (especially the Outer Hebrides), the extreme winds give rise to a unique sandy plain known as Machair. Lagoons of salt water trapped by a rocky sill are also found in the Hebrides, while in East Anglia, such lagoons are often associated with shingle areas.

THREATS AND ISSUES

Sea defences restrict the natural dynamism of coastal habitats by interfering with both erosion and accretion and preventing the coastline from shifting in response to changing conditions. In the last 10,000 years, the sea has risen by around 30 m and is currently rising at an estimated 2 mm per year. Coastal habitats are increasingly squeezed as they are eroded at the seaward edge but are unable to roll inland because of the presence of sea defences. Sea-level rise affects all coastal habitats but is a particular issue for soft shorelines. Many soft shores are eroding rather than accreting due to insufficient sediment supplies, often linked to the presence of hard sea defences. Accretion can only keep pace with sea-level rise where there is sufficient sediment. Climate change will also quicken coastal erosion through increased storms, accelerating habitat loss. Many coastal areas, particularly within bays and along estuaries, support high human populations. Ports, docks, industry and all of our nuclear power stations are found on the coast. Added to this, nowhere in Britain is farther than 110 km from the sea (the distance is even less in Ireland), making the shore easily accessible by a high proportion of the population. The pressure on coastal habitats is often substantial. Excessive trampling, and in some cases wear from vehicles, can damage Sand Dune (particularly foredunes), Saltmarsh, Coastal Vegetated Shingle and Rocky Shore. Disturbance is an issue for breeding and wintering birds, and seals on both hard and soft shores. The impacts of recreation are exacerbated where habitats are constrained and limited in extent.

CULTURAL IMPORTANCE

The coast has always been of great cultural importance in Britain and Ireland. It has provided access to a range of resources including food, transport opportunities and often flat and fertile terrain for agriculture, but nowadays many people choose to live by the coast for aesthetic reasons and for the recreational opportunities our coastlines offer. However, the coast can be a hostile place to live. In 1953, 326 people died along the east coast of England and Scotland when a combination of high tides, strong winds and low pressure pushed water levels over five metres above mean sea level in some places. In 2014, several storms wreaked havoc along the coasts of Britain and Ireland, with substantial damage to properties and transport infrastructure, in addition to changes to much-loved landmarks, some of which vanished under the waves. Coastal communities have always been vulnerable. Skara Brae in Orkney is the best-preserved prehistoric village in northern Europe. It was engulfed in sand by a storm around 4,500 years ago and remained buried until another storm revealed it in the 1800s. Along the Suffolk coast the coastline has moved 1·5 km inland since Roman times. In the 12th and 13th centuries, the prosperous city of Dunwich was one of the biggest ports in Suffolk. The harbour is now silted up and a tiny village is all that remains. Along the same coast, Orford was an important commercial and naval port, located just by the mouth of the River Alde in the 16th century. Now the mouth of the estuary is some 9 km downriver. As we reassess the wisdom of defending undeveloped land along our shores, change may become a more accepted element of the coastal landscape.

Near **Ballyconneely, Connemara**. Heavily sheep-grazed Machair with four-wheel drive tracks. Not all coastal sites are protected nature reserves.

Calshot, Hampshire. Beach huts and wooden sea defences, including groynes installed to trap the shingle. Trampling is limiting the vegetation growth on the stabilized shingle.

Snettisham, Norfolk. This section of beach supported a healthy population of Ringed Plover before hard sea defences were constructed at the end of the 20th century.

Kite surfing and other forms of recreation are popular in **Poole Harbour, Dorset.** In Britain and Ireland, many important sites for nature conservation are also a focus for recreation, whereas in many other parts of the world the two are often separated; it is in coastal habitats that the issues associated with recreation and nature conservation are perhaps most apparent.

Managed realignment at **Paull Holme Strays, on the Humber** – image taken in 2013, ten years after the defences were breached.

CONSERVATION IMPORTANCE AND PROTECTION

Twenty-two Annex I habitats (see *page 37*) are associated with the coastal habitats covered in this book, and of these the UK and/or Ireland has special responsibility for estuaries, coastal shingle vegetation, vegetated sea cliffs, several dune grassland types, humid dune slacks and machair. England has over half of Europe's chalk coasts and Britain holds some of the most important shingle and coastal lagoon sites in Europe. Machair is unique to Britain and Ireland. Our coastal habitats are important in a global context for a range of species including breeding seabirds, waders, and Grey Seal.

The most complex and difficult decisions regarding coastal habitats often revolve around sea defences. Over 45% of England's coastline is fortified, although the figure is much less in Ireland at about 8%. These structures can be costly and difficult to maintain, yet the economic, political and social implications of letting them go are substantial. There are conservation implications too, as important freshwater habitats may occur just inland of sea defences. Coastal habitats such as Saltmarsh can act as natural flood defences, as they dissipate wave energy, but this function is compromised by coastal squeeze. In 'managed realignment' the sea defences are deliberately breached to allow new areas of habitat, particularly Saltmarsh, to form farther inland; *for example at Freiston* in Lincolnshire and Tollesbury in Essex. Local erosion may also reinvigorate accretion elsewhere. Cost benefit analyses indicate that 'managed realignment' is economically viable in the long-term, with the value of lost farmland or other habitats offset by the costs saved in maintaining flood defences. For nature conservation, it means that some areas of coastal habitats are able to function dynamically once more, although space must be found farther inland for displaced semi-natural habitats previously found just inside the sea wall.

Most coastal habitats need little land management to maintain their conservation interest, as the influence of the sea is the overriding factor shaping the plant and animal communities present. Grazing can be important in maintaining species-diversity on heathland and grassland found on cliff slopes and in sand dune systems, and also on Saltmarsh sites with a long history of grazing. However, grazing regimes can be difficult to maintain where the habitat may be unproductive and challenging for livestock and where recreational access levels are high. Machair is unique among coastal habitats in being dependent on traditional crofting.

Balancing recreation and nature conservation is a challenge, particularly in popular tourist destinations or areas with high local populations. Measures relating to resolving access impacts, such as wardening, education, interpretation, boardwalks, seasonal no-access zones and dog restrictions are in place at many sites.

Where the natural dynamism of habitats has been restricted, options to ensure the full range of communities is present are often limited. Bulldozers have been used to shift dunes in South Wales in a last-ditch attempt to save Fen Orchid and dune slack vegetation communities. Terns and breeding waders such as Ringed Plover are – around most of England's coastline – now restricted to small fenced exclosures that keep people, dogs and predators such as foxes out. Colonies expand inside the fences but the relatively high concentration of birds can draw predators such as Kestrel, owls and Hedgehog (which are difficult to exclude), and they are more vulnerable to chance events.

Durl Head, Devon – these cliff slopes are famed amongst botanists for a suite of rare and scarce plants including **Small Restharrow** (BELOW).

THE DYNAMIC COASTLINE

Coastal habitats are naturally dynamic, constantly changing as tides, currents and storms erode or build shorelines. The balance between land and sea in the coastal zone is one that humans have long sought to control. Sea defences were built from Roman times onwards, both as part of land claim and to protect farmland, settlements and industrial sites from flooding. Modern day sea defences include embankments and hard sea walls, and groynes and other beach structures designed to trap sediment and slow its movement. However, on some coasts, too much sediment is a problem and it is removed. Material dredged from shipping channels is often deposited offshore or used to build up eroding beaches.

Creation of Coastal Habitats

The **Wallasea Island Wild Coast** project in **Essex** is the UK's largest coastal wetland habitat creation project. Innovative work led by the RSPB has created nearly 700 ha of coastal habitats on what was previously low-lying arable land as part of a coastal realignment scheme. Around 3 million tonnes of inert material extracted from underneath London as part of the works on Crossrail were used as the basis of new Mudflat, Saltmarsh and Coastal and Floodplain Grassland, complete with ditches, lagoons and a network of creeks. Carefully designed with a gently sloping topography, the ground now rises up to a metre above the current level of the highest astronomical tides. The area, which is now a nature reserve, has, in part, been designed to attract breeding birds – both those that already breed in Essex and also those that could occur in the future given the warming climate (such as Spoonbill and Black-winged Stilt). Pools with predator-free islands have been dug to optimize conditions for nesting, and early successes

have included a range of breeding waders, gulls and terns. Over 13,000 wintering waterbirds were counted in 2018.

The image was taken in 2019 and key parts of site (and when they were created) are:

1 **Allfleets Marsh: Saltmarsh** – first managed realignment (2006);

2 **Jubilee Marsh:** Mudflat, Saltmarsh, Saline Lagoons, islands and non-tidal grassland – created using material from London's Crossrail works (2015);

3 **Pool Marsh:** Saline Lagoons – created with a regulated tidal exchange system that allows the water levels and salinity to be carefully manipulated (2018);

4 **Permanent Saline Lagoons** – the last element of habitat creation to be completed (2018);

5 **Pool with islands** – designed to attract breeding birds and located within Jubilee Marsh (2015);

6 **Very gently sloping grassland above the level of current highest astronomical tides** – areas such as this will persist even with rising sea levels and provide space for coastal habitats to develop in the future.

KEY FEATURES

Zonation

The influence of the sea is all-important, and a sequence of zones with decreasing proximity and exposure to waves and spray is found in all coastal habitats. Different zones are worth searching for, as each can support distinctive species within the habitat. These zones can be vertical or horizontal (see Ardnamurchan images *opposite*). Structure is also important, with, for example, ledges on Hard Cliff support breeding seabirds (see Fair Isle image *below*), while caves or boulders add to the range of nesting opportunities for species such as Chough and Storm Petrel respectively.

Transience

Transient features are important components of many coastal habitats. Slumps and landslips on Soft Cliff create a variety of microhabitats for plants and are particularly important for invertebrates; sand bars and new areas of dune habitat are used by nesting birds; and temporary pools in dune slacks are sometimes home to Natterjack Toad. Freshwater inputs from streams result in areas with decreased salinity and are often used by birds such as feeding waders, loafing gulls and wildfowl.

Exposure

Headlands are the most maritime element of coasts, particularly where they face the prevailing wind. Look here for plant communities maintained by natural exposure, and in autumn and spring for migrant birds.

Fair Isle, Shetland. Key features include: ❶ sea cave, ❷ boulder beach, ❸ cliff slope with maritime vegetation maintained through exposure, ❹ exposed ledges (here supporting a Gannet colony).

FURTHER INFORMATION
British Trust for Ornithology (publications and data relating to birds and coastal sites, especially estuaries) www.bto.org/

Common Seaweeds, Lichens of Rocky Shores and Rock Shore Communities (Field Studies Council laminated guides)

Saltmarsh by Clive Chatters (Bloomsbury Publishing, 2017)

Rocky Shores by John Archer-Thompson & Julian Cremona (Bloomsbury Publishing, 2019)

Sanna, Ardnamurchan, Argyll. Key features include: ❶ freshwater input, ❷ strandline, ❸ embryo dune, ❹ mobile (yellow) dune, ❺ fixed dune, ❻ sand hills, ❼ blowout, ❽ dune scrub.

Sheltered Rocky Shore, Ardnamurchan, Argyll. Key features include: ❶ splash zone, ❷ upper shore, ❸ middle shore, ❹ lower shore.

Mudflat and Sandflat page 386

This habitat incorporates all intertidal areas of sand and mud. The main factor influencing the structure and composition of Mudflat and Sandflat communities is exposure to wave action, although salinity and length of tidal immersion also play a role. In sheltered areas where silt is deposited, the substrate has a high organic content and is highly productive. Mudflat can be teeming with polychaete worms, bivalves and mud snails. The number of species is low, but the density of individuals can be very high. Sandy substrates have a low organic content and can dry out when exposed. They are inhabited by far fewer invertebrates but can support amphipod crustaceans such as sandhoppers, polychaetes, bivalves such as cockles, and burrowing echinoderms. Muddy sands with intermediate characteristics can be found on the landward side of barrier islands and in estuary mouths and can support Mussel beds where there is some stone or shell to which the mussels can attach. The surface of intertidal flats usually appears bare, although mats of microalgae can be present on mud, binding the surface together. Beds of Dwarf Eelgrass may occur in sheltered locations.

The abundant invertebrates in Mudflat provide an important food source for a wide range of waders and wildfowl including Knot, Dunlin, Oystercatcher and Shelduck, while Brent Goose and Wigeon feed on eelgrasses. Over one and a half million waterfowl spend the winter in Britain and Ireland, drawn by the abundant food and relatively mild winters.

Similar habitats

Tidal Saline Lagoon includes Mudflat, which can also grade into Saltmarsh. Sandflat is a prerequisite for the formation of Sand Dune and Machair.

Medway, Kent – the meandering central channel gives an indication of the depth of the mud and the tidal reach in this creek.

Origins and development

Mudflat and Sandflat is an entirely natural habitat that forms as a result of waterborne particles settling on the sea or estuary bed. The underlying geology and topography of a coastline determines its basic shape and its potential to accumulate and hold sediment. Sandflat is found on open coasts, beaches and bays where vigorous wave action prevents the deposition of silt, Mudflat occurs in sheltered areas such as estuaries where much finer particles (<0·125 mm) of clay and silt derived from rivers accrete in less energetic waters. In many places the habitat has been reduced by land claim.

Conservation

Pollution from agricultural, industrial and domestic effluents is an issue in some areas. Many harbours and estuaries require dredging to maintain shipping access, and this can reduce the quantity of sediment available within the wider area, affect sediment quality, and release heavy metals or other toxins from below the surface. Fishing, bait digging, commercial shellfish harvesting and recreation bring further pressures and can cause significant disturbance to birds. Mudflat and Sandflat plays a vital

EXTENT IN KM^2

Eng	5,584
Wal	2,526
Sco	5,794
NI	701
Ire	6,075

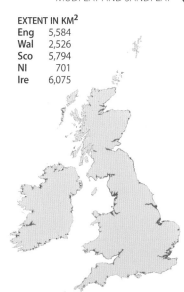

Distribution and extent

The habitat as a whole is widespread on soft shorelines, particularly the North Sea coast. Map based on satellite data (CORINE). Dots indicate sites (SPAs) designated for their assemblage of wintering water birds; these are the large estuary sites that support internationally important numbers of birds in winter. Extent figures are drawn from the relevant Annex I reporting (covering codes H1130, H1140 and H1160).

LEFT: Bait-diggers are a common sight on many intertidal flats, searching for **Lugworm** (cast shown ABOVE) and Ragworm, which they use for angling.

role in coastal protection, dissipating wave energy and reducing the likelihood of coastal erosion, damage to sea defences or flooding. However, where fixed sea defences are present, intertidal flats may be lost through coastal squeeze (*i.e.* when the rate of relative sea-level rise is greater than the rate of accretion).

What to look for

A wide range of waders and wildfowl can occur on Mudflat, and Common and Grey Seal can be seen basking on Sandflat. Common Shore Crab is often seen on both.

1 **Knot** at Snettisham on The Wash. Over 80% of all the Knot that breed in high-arctic Canada and Greenland spend the winter on just 15 British estuaries. The Wash holds the largest number of wintering waterbirds of any site in Britain and Ireland, with counts in some years of over 400,000 birds. **2** **Holme, Norfolk** – extensive Sandflat extends for hundreds of metres at low tide. Near the shore, it has accumulated on top of a layer of peat that was formed before melting glacial ice filled the North Sea basin. **3** Mats of **Sea Lettuce** in Poole Harbour, Dorset. Algal mats such as this tend to be most visible in the summer and indicate high nutrient inputs.

How to recognize

Intertidal flats are wide, open spaces where land, sea and sky seem to merge. They are governed by the tide and currents in a shifting and changing realm that seems to lie beyond everyday human influence. Sandflat is found in exposed locations where silt cannot settle, and appears bare and pale from a distance. Mudflat is typical of estuaries and sheltered bays, and retains a watery sheen even at low tide. In some places it is relatively firm underfoot and can be crossed; in others it is soft and treacherous. Sandflat is generally firmer to walk on than Mudflat.

On both Sandflat and Mudflat the incoming tide can outstrip a running person, and local knowledge and a tide table are needed before venturing out. One of the most characteristic features of intertidal flats is best seen from slightly higher land on the shore – the spectacular numbers of waders and wildfowl that can be present in the autumn and winter.

When to visit

September–March for waders and wildfowl.

Did you know?

One cubic metre of Mudflat may contain well over 1,000 worms.

Saltmarsh

page 387

Saltmarsh supports a series of communities of salt-tolerant plants that can be seen in a successional sequence (known as the halosere) from open Mudflat to mature marsh. This sequence is determined by the frequency and period of inundation and can be seen running parallel to the shore, reflecting the development of the saltmarsh. It can also be found in disturbed areas of the upper marsh and within depressions known as pans.

Areas of open mud that are still regularly inundated by the tide support a sparse cover of pioneer plant species. These slow the water, allowing more sediment to accumulate. As the surface of the mud becomes raised up, other species are able to become established, until at the landward side of the marsh species that can only tolerate occasional immersion are found. Erosion also takes place, mainly on meanders in estuaries and along the creeks that form as depressions are scoured out by water draining away on the ebb tide.

There is substantial variation in Saltmarsh across Britain and Ireland. This variation is due to differences in climate, past and present management (including land claim and grazing), and the relative rates of erosion and accretion. At many sites in the south, pioneer marsh is being eroded as sea levels rise.

Nearly 300 species of invertebrate are associated with Saltmarsh, of which around 150 are exclusive to the habitat. In the winter, Saltmarsh provides important feeding and roosting opportunities for birds, notably for seedeaters such as Twite and for wildfowl and waders. Saltmarsh also holds around half of the UK's population of breeding Redshank, and creeks can be important nursery sites for several species of fish.

Saltmarshes on the west coast of Wales, northern England and Galloway are often grazed and the resulting grassy sward and can support grazing ducks and geese. The **Solway Firth** marshes (shown here) support large numbers of Pink-footed and Barnacle Geese in the winter.

EXTENT IN KM²	
Eng	224
Wal	78
Sco	56
NI	2
Ire	38

Distribution and extent

Found in large, sheltered estuaries around Britain and Ireland. Also occurs on Atlantic coasts in western Europe. Pale blue shading indicates broad distribution of Annex I habitats (H1310, H1330 and H1420, plus H1410 in Ireland); darker shading actual Saltmarsh derived from satellite imagery (CORINE) and other data. Extent figures drawn from the reporting for the Annex I habitats.

Similar habitats

Mudflat and Saltmarsh are similar and the transition between them can be continuous. However, Mudflat is typically unvegetated, lower and more homogenous in profile. Saltmarsh can also occur in transitions with Coastal and Floodplain Grazing Marsh, Sand Dune and Vegetated Shingle.

Origins and development

Saltmarsh develops on Mudflat on sheltered coasts where the accumulating mud becomes sufficiently raised above the water level for Saltmarsh plants to become established. The plants stabilize the substrate and help capture more particles suspended in the sea water – and the marsh keeps building so long as it is subject to tidal inundation. Saltmarsh can also form on different habitats if coastal geomorphological processes change. For example, some Saltmarsh in the Hebrides was formerly Machair, and there is a unique type of Saltmarsh on the west coast of Ireland that formed on Blanket Bog following sea-level rise 2,000–4,000 years ago. Some Saltmarsh is of much more recent origin. Common Cord-grass was planted to help stabilize Mudflat and has spread rapidly around the coast, although in some places it is now dying back naturally. Over millennia, large areas of Saltmarsh have been claimed for farmland and, as a consequence, upper Saltmarsh communities are under-represented in much of southern and eastern England. Recent losses are thought to have been caused by increased storm activity, increases in tidal range and water velocities caused by land claim and seawalls, and a reduction in sediment supply caused by the prevention of erosion of Soft Cliff.

Conservation

Saltmarsh is particularly vulnerable to climate change. The overall area is likely to continue to decrease as sea defences prevent it from moving inland in response to sea-level rise (a process called 'coastal squeeze'). However, the important role that this habitat plays in the accumulation of sediment and in diffusing wave action is now recognized, and area of Saltmarsh may be expanded in places where sea defences are 'realigned'. This may result in a shift in vegetation as Saltmarsh created through re-alignment ends to be dominated by Sea Purslane and lacks other characteristic species such as Common Sea-lavender.

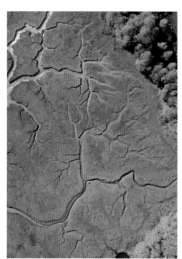 

LEFT: **Poole Harbour, Dorset** – an aerial view of Saltmarsh showing a network of creeks that drains into the harbour towards the left of the image. Creeks are not permanent features, and can change course over time, collapse or become treacherously overgrown by the surrounding vegetation. RIGHT: Chenier banks are occasionally found on Saltmarsh where wave action is sufficient to throw shells up onto the marsh where they form distinctive banks, sometimes supporting strandline species (*e.g.* Grass-leaved Orache).

What to look for

Look out for rare and scarce sea-lavenders, although these are absent from Scotland. In western Scotland, Saltmarsh Flat-sedge and Slender Spike-rush can be found, while Marsh-mallow inhabits brackish patches in the south of England and Wales. Grazed Saltmarsh can support large flocks of wildfowl.

How to recognize

Saltmarsh forms a soft fringe of low vegetation on sheltered coasts where the land gradually merges into the sea. It is found within bays, natural harbours, the heads of sheltered lochs, estuaries, lagoons and behind shingle bars, and can stretch for miles along the coast in a flat, wide band or can form smaller patches or narrow strips.

Saltmarsh is only completely submerged by spring high tides, but with every tide water creeps rapidly and silently up a branching network of sinuous creeks to flood the lower marsh. As the tide ebbs again, it reveals thick, soft mud in creeks and pans; the unwary walker will soon sink boot or even thigh deep into black, smelly mud below the glossy surface.

In the winter saltmarshes can seem bleak places, bereft of colour and inhabited only by wildfowl and roosting waders. However, in the early summer they are brightened by flowering Thrift and the call of breeding Redshank, and later in the summer marshes in the south can turn purple with sea-lavenders.

When to visit

Winter for geese and autumn to spring for high-tide wader roosts; May for Thrift in flower, July/August for Common Sea-lavender in flower.

Did you know?
Cord-grasses can trap and stabilize up 10 cm of sediment a year on Saltmarsh.

1 Higher up the marsh, species typically include Sea Purslane, **Common Sea-lavender** (**2**), Sea Aster and Common Saltmarsh-grass. **3** **Glassworts** are plants of pioneer Saltmarsh, where they help slow the flow of water and encourage ongoing silt deposition. Known collectively as samphire, glassworts are harvested as a delicacy in some areas. **4** **Long-spiked** (*left*) and **Yellow Glassworts** (*right*).

Sand Dune

page 387

Sand dunes develop in places that are inhospitable to the vast majority of plants, as they are dry, salty, unstable, lack nutrients and are liable to inundation. Yet specialist species are able to colonize the bare sand, and in doing so alter the structure, stability, nutrient content, microclimate and hydrology of the incipient sand dune system, allowing other plants to colonize. The classic succession from strandline vegetation through pioneer and mobile dunes to fixed dune grassland, wet dune slacks and scrub is usually more haphazard than the text books suggest; a consequence of storm damage, erosion by people or quirks in the development of individual sites. In reality, on many sites sea-level rise and recreational pressure mean that strandline and embryonic dunes are often absent, while mobile dunes may have been immobilized by sea defences, or the supply of sand cut off altogether by dredging or by the prevention of erosion elsewhere.

The variation in conditions favours a great variety of plant species. Rarities include dune specialists (*e.g.* Sea Stock and Dune Gentian) as well as those also found in other habitats (*e.g.* Round-leaved Wintergreen, Scottish Primrose and Fen Orchid). Warm, open conditions mean that sand dune systems are rich in invertebrates, including butterflies, moths and burrowing bees and wasps – in the UK over 100 invertebrate species are restricted to dunes, and hundreds more are associated with them.

Similar habitats

The early-successional stages of sand dunes support unique vegetation communities, but the vegetation of fixed dunes and slacks is similar to that of Lowland Dry and Wet Heath, Lowland Fen and acid and calcareous grasslands. Machair is a distinctive coastal habitat related to dunes that is restricted to Scotland and Ireland.

Whiteford Burrows, Gower – primary dune slacks form when a new dune cuts off an area of beach and changes its hydrology. Secondary slacks occur where the wind scours away the sand (a blow out) until the water-table (which is domed in sand dune systems) is reached. Slacks are seasonally flooded and remain wet or damp in the summer, apparent here from the greener colour of the vegetation at the base of the slack.

Origins and development

Sand dunes form by a combination of natural geomorphological and biological processes. Sand brought to the beach by tides and currents is blown inland when the intertidal zone is exposed and dries out. The sand that is deposited starts to accumulate behind any obstacle that slows the wind (*e.g.* vegetation or debris). Hindshore dunes form in bays or where strong winds and a plentiful supply of sand allow dunes to be pushed some way inland and often include dune slacks (*e.g.* the Sefton Coast in Merseyside). Climbing sand dunes can form where strong winds push sand up over rising ground (*e.g.* Stackpole, Pembrokeshire). Frontshore systems project out into the sea across inlets (*e.g.* the Inch Strand, Co. Kerry), at the mouth of an estuary (*e.g.* the Sands of Forvie, Aberdeenshire), where longshore drift acting in opposing directions comes together or where sediment is particularly abundant (*e.g.* Romney Warren, Kent).

Conservation

Sand dunes are dynamic systems that need space and freedom to move. This is a challenge when they are hemmed in by hard sea defences, agricultural land, golf courses, urban development and coniferous plantations (planted to stabilize the dunes); many dunes systems in the UK are in effect over-stabilized and lack bare sand and early-successional habitats. Although climate change may lead to erosion (through increased storm intensity and sea-level rise) it could also lead to the over-stabilization of mobile dunes through a reduction in the amount of blown sand and increased grass growth, while summer drought will lead to the loss of characteristic vegetation in dune slacks. A strategic approach is needed to tackle issues related to shoreline management, particularly where sea defences prevent dune systems from rolling inland in response to sea-level rise.

EXTENT IN KM^2
Eng	73
Wal	37
Sco	132
NI	11
Ire	93

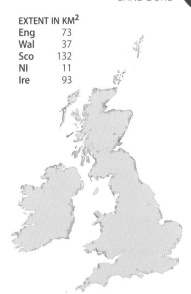

Distribution and extent

Occurs widely around the coastline of Britain and Ireland. Pale blue shading indicates broad distribution of Annex I habitats; darker shading actual Sand Dune derived from satellite imagery (CORINE) and other data. Extent figures drawn from the reporting for multiple Annex I habitats (H210, H2120, H2130, H2140, H2150, H2160, H2170, H2190 and H2250).

LEFT: **Holkham, Norfolk** – in drought-prone systems where the accreting sand is acidic, or where leaching is sufficiently strong to remove the calcareous influence of shell sand, lichens (RIGHT) give the sward a characteristic grey tinge.

Recreational pressure is often high, and damage to embryonic dunes, which are particularly vulnerable, affects the functioning of entire systems. Strandline and mobile dune communities are natural, but livestock and/or Rabbit grazing are important in retaining the character of fixed dune grassland and some slacks.

ABOVE: **1** **Dawlish Warren** – Dune scrub develops on stabilized dunes, although historically this was often prevented by grazing livestock. If the substrate becomes particularly leached, or is acid to begin with, dune heath can develop (see Lowland Dry Heath, *page 130*). Here the presence of a golf course interrupts the natural transition to Saltmarsh at the back of the spit. **2** Dune slacks can be flower-rich. This slack at **Braunton Burrows, Devon** supports Creeping Willow, Bird's-foot-trefoil and Lesser Centaury. **3** **Holme Dunes, Norfolk**. Accreting dunes require considerable volumes of fresh sand.

FACING PAGE: **4** **Strandline** (Saltfleetby – Theddlethorpe, Lincolnshire). Plants such as oraches are able to colonize the beach along the drift line and, together with any debris, start the process of sand accumulation. It is a transitional habitat, either being washed away or developing into dunes. **5** **Foredune** (Braunton Burrows, Devon). Once sand accretion has started, Sand Couch or Lyme-grass can colonize by seed or rhizome fragments and stabilize the pioneer dune – mainly through horizontal growth. **6** **Mobile (yellow) dune** (Studland Beach, Dorset). Once the dune is beyond the limit of tidal inundation, Marram takes hold. The rapid vertical growth of its shoots (about one metre per year) means that dunes can build quickly. The sand at the surface remains loose, and can be blown from the windward face of the dune and deposited in its lee, causing the dune gradually to roll inland. **7** **Fixed dune** (Kilinallen, Islay). As new dunes develop in front of the mobile dune, the supply of sand lessens and Marram becomes less vigorous. Mosses, and then lichens, fine grasses and herbs help stabilize the dune and increase the organic matter in the soil.

What to look for

Along the strandline look for annual species including Prickly Saltwort, Sea Rocket, Sea Sandwort and oraches, the seeds of which can wash up and germinate at the upper limit of the tidal reach. The strandline community, which is usually discontinuous or scattered, is a good indicator of the functional health of a sand dune system, as it requires a constant supply of sand. It can provide habitat for a number of invertebrates, including the Beachcomber Beetle, which feeds on sandhoppers under large pieces of debris. Oystercatcher and Ringed Plover may sometimes be found nesting near the strandline.

Brighter green swards of Sand Couch or silvery Lyme-grass indicate pioneer dunes, but these species soon give way to Marram as sand accretion increases. Mobile dunes are a challenging environment for most plants, but look for Sea Spurge, Sea Bindweed and Sea-holly among the Marram. Mobile dunes warm up quickly and provide shelter, and can be attractive to invertebrates, although more stable sand is preferred by burrowing bees and digger wasps – look out for miniature spoil heaps. Lizard trails can also be seen in the bare sand of mobile dunes. Sand-hill Screw-moss can play an important role in stabilizing the sand surface; its tightly twisted leaves unscrewing remarkably rapidly when it becomes wet. Associated species include the annuals Common Whitlowgrass, Early Hair-grass, Sea Fern-grass and Dune Fescue.

On fixed dunes where conditions become too stable for Marram, look for dune grassland with Red Fescue, Lady's Bedstraw and Cat's-ear. Differences in the substrate type, hydrology, climate and grazing pressure mean that dune grassland is very variable. Calcareous dune grassland is the most species-rich, and typically supports Common Centaury, Kidney Vetch, various clovers, Yellow-wort, Pyramidal Orchid and Carline Thistle. Fixed dunes on the east coast of England can support native stands of Sea-buckthorn, and Common Juniper thickets occur on dunes in the north of Scotland. Mixed Scrub is often widespread where it is not prevented from developing by Rabbit or livestock grazing. It can provide valuable shelter for migratory birds, particularly on foreshore systems.

Dune slacks tend to be found on larger sites, and particularly (but not exclusively) in the wetter north and west. Slack vegetation is also very variable, but often supports ankle to knee-deep Creeping Willow. Calcareous slacks can be species-rich, supporting plant communities similar to those of small-sedge Lowland Fen, while acid slacks can support Lowland Wet Heath vegetation.

LEFT: **Sea Holly** is a distinctive plant of sand dunes. A waxy covering on the leaves helps to prevent dessication in this arid habitat. RIGHT: The diminutive **Fen Orchid** is threatened in every country within its range. It is now very rare in Britain and is found in young dune slacks in South Wales, where conservation measures include digging up areas of dune grassland to create suitable early-successional slacks. A taller form is known from a handful of fenland sites in the Norfolk Broads.

How to recognize

Sand Dune is a familiar habitat, found wherever sandy beaches are wide enough for sand to dry out and blow inland. In some places, a thin strip of parallel dunes at the top of the beach soon gives way to managed countryside. Elsewhere, a confusing maze of sand hills and hollows extends inland, and requires repeated visits to explore.

Many areas are heavily impacted by humans. Sea defences often form a hard interface with the beach, while networks of sandy paths and huge wind-hollowed 'blow outs' show where the vegetation has been eroded away by thousands of feet. But sand dunes are also some of our wildest places, where natural processes are still paramount despite our best efforts, and where a single winter storm can re-shape the seaward face of a dune system, shifting untold tonnes of sand overnight. On windy days, young dunes can be harsh, challenging places; the sand slips constantly underfoot and stings the eyes, and Marram whips the legs. However, within the lee of dunes the flower-rich grassland is more sheltered, and is particularly pleasant on warm summer evenings on sites where Natterjack Toads croak from dune slack pools.

When to visit

The summer months are most rewarding for wildlife; winter visits can be exhilarating and offer the experience of geomorphological processes in action.

Did you know?

Some dunes date back at least 5,000–6,000 years (nearer 9,000 years in the Outer Hebrides), while others are just a few hundred years old.

1 **Rhossili, Gower** – a distinctive type of dune grassland dominated by Bloody Crane's-bill, also found in Northumberland. **2** The scarce **Dune Tiger Beetle** can be seen in the intertidal and around drift lines, where it hunts for insects. **3** **Natterjack Toad** is endangered in Britain and Ireland, although it has been reintroduced to a number of sites. It spawns in shallow pools in dunes (and heaths) where seasonal desiccation reduces the numbers of invertebrate predators.

Machair

page 386

Machair is essentially calcareous fixed dune grassland found as part of a distinctive cultural landscape on the Atlantic fringe. Strong onshore winds provide a constant top-dressing of calcareous shell sand and fragments of calcareous seaweed, and this prevents the soil becoming leached of nutrients despite the wet climate. The grassland is rich in plant species (up to 45 species per square metre) and can be quite variable as a result of historical and current management, in addition to environmental factors such as the proximity of the water-table to the surface.

The word 'machair' is also sometimes used to refer to the wider mosaic of wet grassland, tussocky marshland and small arable plots within which Machair is found. This patchwork of habitats means that several wader species can be found breeding in close proximity. Lapwing is the most common, with Dunlin, Redshank and Snipe in wetter areas, while Oystercatcher and Ringed Plover nest on dry cultivated ground. Corncrake also nests in Machair hay meadows but is much harder to see. Other birds associated with Machair are Twite, Chough and Corn Bunting. The small-scale variation in habitats favours a wide range of invertebrates, including rare beetles and weevils, and the flower-rich grassland is an abundant source of nectar; both the very rare Great Yellow Bumblebee and the scarce Moss Carder Bumblebee are particularly associated with Machair.

Similar habitats

The unique character and limited distribution of Machair make it easy to differentiate from Sand Dune and grassland habitats.

Stadhlaigearraidh, South Uist – Machair grassland is characterized by its rich abundance of flowering plants, although none are unique to the habitat.

Origins and development

The beaches and dunes of Machair systems were built up thousands of years ago as broken seashells and glacial sediment (washed into the sea at the end of the last glaciation) were brought ashore by wave action. Powerful winds created dunes at the top of the beach, which were periodically eroded, blowing sand far inland. Humans have played a role in the development of Machair since the Mesolithic period, when the light birch and Hazel scrub that had developed on the thin sandy soils was cleared. By the Bronze Age, Machair plains were being used for agriculture, and a system of light cattle-grazing, hay cutting and low-intensity rotational cropping evolved that shaped the vegetation into a landscape similar to that seen today. However, Machair systems are very vulnerable to the changes in traditional crofting practices that have occurred over the past century.

Conservation

A switch to sheep and year-round grazing, earlier harvesting or conversion to silage, drainage, the increased use of artificial fertilizers and the homogenization of management within Machair systems are all problematic, and ongoing support is needed to help maintain the traditional management on which Machair depends. Climate change may lead to increased inundation by seawater and freshwater flooding, which could further jeopardise traditional management, already barely economically viable. Inappropriate recreational use is a particular issue on some Irish sites.

EXTENT IN KM²

Sco	117
Ire	31

Distribution and extent

Unique to Britain and Ireland, Machair is restricted to the north and west coasts of Scotland (particularly the Outer Hebrides) and Ireland. Pale shading on map indicates the broad extent of the Annex I habitat (H21A0); dark shading shows actual locations. Extent figures from Annex I reporting.

LEFT: **Machair Bay, Connemara** – tightly grazed Machair with the Twelve Bens mountain range behind.
RIGHT: Rotational cultivation is a characteristic of Machair systems.

1 The **Corncrake** was once widespread in Britain and Ireland but suffered heavy losses in the 20th century due to changes in meadow mowing practices. Agri-environment schemes and reintroductions have resulted in a partial recovery but the Machair of the Hebrides remains a stronghold. **2** The **Belted Beauty** moth is rare in Britain and Ireland outside of the Machair of Galway, Mayo and the west coast of Scotland. Females are flightless – one suggestion is that they reached offshore islands by floating on driftwood. **3** **Corn Bunting** – In the past Hebridean Machair held the highest densities of this species in Britain. Rapid recent declines are linked to a lack of winter grain. **4** **Great Yellow Bumblebee** – Hebridean Machair is the key habitat for the remaining populations of this species, which was once found across the UK. **5** **Chough** – Machair is a favourite foraging habitat for Chough along the west coast of Ireland and on Islay and Colonsay. **6** Declines in the breeding populations of waders such as **Dunlin** were linked to the introduction of Hedgehog to South Uist in 1974. However, declines in areas without Hedgehog indicate that there are wider issues affecting the birds that relate to changes in agricultural practices and other pressures.

1

What to look for

Orchids, including particular varieties of Common Spotted-orchid and Early Marsh-orchid, and the rare Irish Lady's-tresses and Lesser Butterfly-orchid. Listen out for Corncrake.

How to recognize

Machair is a particularly attractive type of exceptionally flower-rich dune grassland. It is found in a unique landscape shaped by the oceanic climate and the traditional crofting practices of the west coasts of Scotland and Ireland.

The flat or gently undulating grassland that extends inland from Atlantic beaches typically includes Red Fescue, Lady's Bedstraw, Common Bird's-foot-trefoil, Daisy, Yarrow, Eyebright and Red Clover. Its colour changes subtly throughout the season as different species become dominant in the sward. In some places it is interspersed with cultivated patches, which can hold eye-catching arable weeds such as Corn Marigold, Sun Spurge, and Wild Pansy. Inland, it is usually backed by lochs surrounded by marshy grassland.

Machair is famous for its breeding waders, and in early summer their distinctive calls can be heard all around, while the rasping "*crek crek*" of the secretive Corncrake may be heard from deep within iris beds.

When to visit

June–August for Machair flora, April–June for breeding waders and Corncrake.

Did you know?

Winds are exceptional on Machair sites. On the Outer Hebrides gale force winds are recorded on 50 or more days a year and winds of 6 or more on the Beaufort Scale are recorded for over 20% of the year.

Coastal Vegetated Shingle

page 386

Shingle beaches form on exposed coasts where the wave action is sufficiently forceful to bring ashore sediment between 2 mm and 200 mm in diameter. Only a proportion of the 3,500 km or so of coastal shingle around Britain and Ireland can support vegetation, as shingle features often remain mobile and shift with storms and changing currents. Vegetation is usually best developed on stable spits, barriers, barrier islands and cuspate forelands (rounded protrusions of shingle that develop where longshore drift acting in opposition converges).

On larger shingle sites, an intact succession from strandline vegetation to scrub or stunted woodland of oaks or Holly can be seen. Intermediate stages include communities of perennial shingle specialists, grassland, Shingle Heath with lichens and Heather (or Crowberry and Common Juniper in the north) and, in wet hollows, Lowland Fen or Wet Woodland. In Scotland, complete succession to Caledonian Forest is found in Spey Bay. Some of the vegetation communities present are unique to shingle, while others are rare shingle versions of more terrestrial communities.

Similar habitats

Communities transitional to Sand Dune or Saltmarsh develop where shingle is overlain with blown sand, or behind spits where mud collects. Some shingle sites include Saline Lagoon.

Shingle Street, Suffolk. When shingle becomes stable, a sparse cover of large, deep-rooted perennials (*e.g.* Curled Dock, Yellow Horned-poppy and Sea-kale) develops, interspersed with mats of Sea Campion, Sea Mayweed and Sea Pea.

Origins and development

Most shingle systems in Britain and Ireland were formed by about 4,000 years ago and have been naturally dynamic ever since. However, shingle communities are inherently fragile and easily damaged, and human pressures have substantially degraded and reduced the area of vegetated shingle. At many sites the vegetation and associated fauna have been destroyed, and the shingle structures themselves immobilized by development (*e.g.* power plants, defence structures and housing estates). Many beaches also suffer from the removal or redistribution of shingle for coastal management purposes, the removal of shingle for construction aggregate, water extraction and/or recreational pressure.

Conservation

Although most Coastal Vegetated Shingle is protected by conservation designations, its prospects are poor and increased storm events and changes in sediment budgets will bring new challenges. Emphasis needs to be put on restoring the mobility of shingle systems and allowing the full range of successional stages

EXTENT IN KM²

Eng	42
Wal	1
Sco	12
NI	1
Ire	2

Distribution and extent

The largest shingle structures are in north-east Scotland, East Anglia and the south coast of England. The UK (together with New Zealand and Japan) is of global importance for shingle. Pale shading on map indicates the broad extent of the relevant Annex I habitats (H1210 and H1220); darker shading show actual locations. Extent figures from Annex I reporting.

Near Lepe, Hampshire. Strandline vegetation (such as the orache community seen here) is able to take hold in relatively mobile shingle wherever sufficient rotting seaweed is washed up. Sea Beet is also common, replaced by Sea Mayweed, Cleavers and Chickweed on moist, sheltered sites farther north.

to develop. This involves reviewing the reliance on shingle structures for flood defence and the use of groynes and sea walls to prevent shingle features from moving, so that shingle features can migrate in response to changes in sea levels. Recreational pressure also needs to be managed to avoid damage to vegetation and associated fauna, and to minimize disturbance to birds.

TOP: **Bawdsey, Suffolk**. As an increasing amount of organic matter aids water retention and grassland or lichen heath develops, with species such as Red Fescue, Cat's-ear, stonecrops, *Cladonia* lichens and Cypress-leaved Plait-moss. BOTTOM: **Yellow Horned-poppy** is a highly toxic plant that is adapted to coastal environments. Its leaves are crumpled and have a waxy coating to help reduce moisture-loss, while silver hairs reflect light.

LEFT: **Orford Lighthouse, Suffolk** – with shingle ridges in the foreground. RIGHT: **Dungeness, Kent**. Stabilized shingle supporting Gorse and Blackthorn scrub with open, lichen-rich areas.

ORFORD VILLAGE

Coastal grazing marsh

Saltmarsh

Stable vegetated shingle

Splash zone

Saline lagoon
(HAVERGATE ISLAND)

Stable vegetated shingle

Orfordness, Suffolk, looking north. This spit is 16 km long and is formed by longshore drift. Until about 900 years ago the village of Orford faced the open sea.

What to look for

Look out for ridges, which indicate areas that have been relatively undamaged by trampling. They are formed when wave-sorting of shingle results in large pebbles lying in the hollows between ridges of smaller pebbles. Shingle with smaller pebbles retains water and organic matter, making it easier for seeds to germinate and causing characteristic stripes of vegetation. On stable shingle look for patches of Shingle Heath, scrub and even stunted woodland. Different sites or stretches of coast are also noted for particular plants, for example Cottonweed (Wexford), Sea Pea (common in East Anglia), Nottingham Catchfly (Dungeness and the Solent), Little-Robin (the Solent) and Oysterplant (Scottish sites). Where Saltmarsh has developed behind a shingle ridge (*e.g.* at sites like Blakeney Point or Chesil) look for a drift-line community dominated by Shrubby Sea-blite.

A range of bees and other nectar feeders can be found on vegetated shingle, including important populations of Shrill and Brown-banded Carder Bees. There is also a range of specialist invertebrates including those that occur below the surface in the shingle matrix, and some exceptionally rare invertebrates, such as the Sussex Emerald moth and the Gilkicker Weevil, are limited to single sites.

Breeding waders are characteristic of undisturbed areas (*e.g.* Ringed Plover and Oystercatcher) while tern and gull colonies are a feature at many sites (such as Cemlyn Bay, Scolt Head, Blakeney Point, Orfordness and Dungeness). Predators such as Stoat, Hedgehog and Fox are often drawn to the breeding bird colonies, and Brown Hare can be seen at some sites such as Orfordness, Dungeness and Snettisham.

TOP: **Common Terns** nest in colonies in a range of habitats that include shingle spits and lagoon islands, from which they fly up to 15 km to feed in shallow, inshore waters.. BOTTOM: **Ringed Plover** nests between April and August, and is most likely be found on relatively open shingle near to mudflats. Look in areas with low levels of disturbance and listen out for alarm calls that will indicate birds with eggs or chicks.

How to recognize

Shingle beaches are dynamic places, constantly shifting and changing shape as a result of storms and longer-term wave action. Each of the relatively few key shingle sites has its own unique character, a combination of the formative coastal processes and past and present uses.

Shingle sites often have a curiously ambivalent feel; many have been used for nuclear or military installations, and have hard sea defences imposed on them, evidenced in a scattering of concrete structures and fences and nearby edifices. Yet away from these intrusions they are wild places where the power of the elements is overwhelmingly present. The wildlife is unique and distinctive, typified by elusive Ringed Plovers, large perennial plants such as Sea-kale and Yellow Horned-poppy, and intriguing invertebrates including the Whelk-shell Jumping Spider (which lives in washed up whelk shells) and the Scaly Cricket.

When to visit

April–May for breeding waders and terns, May–August for flowering plants, winter for Snow Bunting and other passerines.

Did you know?
Ness (derived from Old Norse for headland) refers to a rounded promontory, and is often found in place names of shingle sites.

1 Scaly Cricket – a Mediterranean species found at a few localities along the south coast of England and Wales. It scavenges at night around the upper drift line and during the day can be found by turning over seaweed and pieces of rubbish. **2** Sea Pea is a splash zone specialist with a circumpolar range. Its seeds are dispersed by the sea, and remain viable in salt water for up to five years. **3** Sea-kale – another splash zone specialist with buoyant seeds; genetic studies show that there has been a mixing of genes between populations of this plant in France and England, presumably due to dispersal by currents.

Saline Lagoon page 387

Saline Lagoons are very variable in the plants and animals they support, due largely to differences in geomorphology. Isolated lagoons are separated from the sea by a barrier of shingle or sand through which sea water percolates, and can become in-filled over time. Percolation lagoons are ponded water found within depressions in soft sediments, and may rise and fall with the tide. They are often transient, shifting with the substrate. Silled lagoons (found in Scotland) are basins with a rock barrier that retains the water at low tide. Lagoons can also be inlets into which the sea enters with each tide, in some cases through sluices or culverts. The key factor is the salinity of the water, which varies according to the freshwater input, the frequency with which the lagoon is replenished with salt water, and evaporation, and lagoons can be anything from brackish to hypersaline. Only a limited range of plants is found and includes marine species (*e.g.* eelgrasses, wracks and Sugar Kelp), brackish (*e.g.* tassleweeds) and freshwater species (*e.g.* pondweeds). Invertebrates that are particularly associated with Saline Lagoon include Starlet Sea Anemone, Lagoon Sandworm and Lagoon Sand-shrimp. The muddy and sparsely vegetated margins support a diverse range of beetles and flies, some of which are rare or scarce.

Similar habitats

The fauna and flora of Saline Lagoons are similar to those of estuaries, brackish ditches and some artificial harbours.

Walberswick, Suffolk – these lagoons support breeding Avocet and Starlet Sea Anemone. They sit behind an artificially created shingle bank.

Origins and development

Saline lagoons can be created through natural geomorphological processes, but some have formed as a consequence of the construction of sea defences and can be found on their landward as well as seaward side, for example within Coastal Grazing Marsh and former creeks in Saltmarsh. Saline lagoons around the Solent were used in medieval times for commercial salt production, and some of those in Chichester Harbour were mill ponds.

Conservation

Lagoons are often naturally transient features and habitat continuity can be a problem for some of the resident species if new lagoons are not formed. Threats include sea-level rise, coastal development, and pollution and nutrient enrichment from agricultural run-off and sewage outlets. Unusual tidal incursions or marked changes in the inflow of freshwater can also be damaging as plant and animal communities within individual lagoons are adapted to the specific conditions found there. Lagoons have been successfully created at some sites such as Minsmere in Suffolk.

EXTENT IN KM^2

Eng	14
Wal	1
Sco	35
NI	2
Ire	24

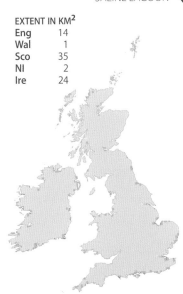

Distribution and extent

Uncommon, with concentrations on the east coast of Britain and the Outer Hebrides. Scarce in Europe. Pale shading on map indicates the broad extent of the Annex I habitat (H1150); darker shading shows actual locations. Extent figures from the Annex I reporting for Coastal Lagoons.

Cemlyn Lagoon, Anglesey supports a diverse range of lagoon species. It is separated from the sea by a shingle ridge. Sea water enters through an inlet with a sluice and by percolation through the shingle.

Chesil Fleet at Ferrybridge (TOP) and **from Portland, Dorset** (BOTTOM) – this 13 km-long tidal lagoon, up to 5 m deep, was formed around 5,000 years ago and runs behind Chesil Beach, which creates a barrier from the sea. There is an inlet at its eastern end. Some 150 species of seaweed, 25 species of fish and 60 species of mollusc have been recorded.

What to look for

Breeding birds including terns, Ringed Plover and Avocet; wintering wildfowl; specialist invertebrates such as Starlet Sea Anemone; Beaked Tasselweed.

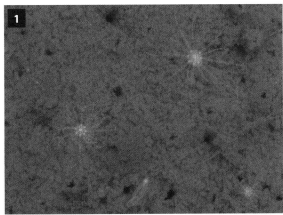

How to recognize

Saline Lagoons are pools of saline water that are at least partially cut off from the sea by a barrier (often of shingle) that retains water at low tide. They are often shallow and their water level fluctuates little (if at all) with the tide. Those on soft shores can be small and transient, and are a special feature of dynamic sites where natural change is a defining element. Longer-lived lagoons also occur, sometimes in bedrock.

Although lagoons are not species-rich compared to marine habitats, they support specialist invertebrates and plants adapted to the variable conditions, and are always worth investigating. Larger lagoons can support breeding and wintering waders, wildfowl and gulls and terns.

When to visit

Spring–autumn for invertebrates, year-round for bird interest.

Did you know?

Saline lagoons can be smaller than one hectare, but the largest (Loch of Stenness, Orkney) is 800 ha.

1 **Starlet Sea Anemone** occurs in muddy lagoon margins from Dorset round to the Humber. **2** **Avocet** nests primarily in Saline Lagoon; it recolonized the UK after an absence of about 100 years once sea defences were allowed to breach during the Second World War. **3** An isolated lagoon at **Shingle Street, Suffolk** – lagoons here change frequently as storm events shift huge amounts of shingle, filling in some lagoons and creating new ones.

C

Rocky Shore page 386

Life on the rocky shore is influenced predominantly by the reach of the waves and a series of zones is usually visible on the rocks. The width and character of each zone is variable and is influenced by tidal range, degree of exposure to wave action, slope and aspect. Conditions higher up the shore are more demanding for marine species, and species diversity (and competition between species) generally increases along a gradient down the shore. Plants such as Rock Sea-lavender and Thrift occur on the upper edge of the 'splash zone', the zone above the high tide mark that is not submerged, but is splashed by breaking waves and is dominated by black and orange crustose lichens. Below the splash zone, the 'upper shore zone' is submerged by high tides, but for relatively short periods and not on every tide. Here, green seaweeds can dominate, especially where freshwater runs across the shore. The 'middle shore zone' is submerged for longer and tends to be dominated by tough brown seaweeds (such as Bladder Wrack and Spiral Wrack) that can out-compete seaweeds characteristic of the upper zone. The 'lower shore zone' is submerged most of the time and red seaweeds are common, with large kelps on the extreme lower shore. Exposed shores tend to be less diverse than sheltered shores, as high-energy waves damage seaweeds, but they are still inhabited by sedentary animals that can attach firmly to rocks, including limpets, barnacles and mussels.

Similar habitats

Rocky Shore is often found below Hard Cliff and Cliff Slope, and there is overlap between the splash zone of Rocky Shore and cliff bottoms.

Conservation

In general, conservation management revolves around protection from damaging activities and over-harvesting (commercial harvesting of shellfish and seaweed occurs in some locations). Threats include pollution, both marine (*e.g.* oil spills) and from the land (*e.g.* sewage effluent). There is also some evidence

Cemlyn, Anglesey – This rocky shore has a good assemblage of seaweeds, including coralline and red encrusting algae in the more exposed rock pools.

that trampling and harvesting can reduce species diversity. Rocky shores are wonderful places in which to observe a great diversity of species at close quarters and are often visited by school and university field trips. They play an important role in inspiring an interest in ecology and public awareness of the marine environment.

What to look for

Rocky Shore life-forms are very diverse. Look out for Sea Slater (a littoral woodlouse) in the splash zone, sandhoppers (tiny shrimp-like crustaceans) under piles of seaweed on the upper shore, Common Hermit Crab inhabiting old Dog Whelk or Common Periwinkle shells, and pipefish camouflaged among weeds. On the lower shore, look out for Sea Lemon (a sea slug), Star Sea Squirt (which grow in jelly-like colonies) and Bread-crumb Sponge and, from the upper shore down, a variety of seaweeds.

EXTENT UNKNOWN

Distribution and extent

Widely distributed around the coasts of Britain and Ireland. Map indicates general areas with rocky shores and shading also includes the broad distribution of the Annex I habitat for submerged or partly submerged sea caves (H8330).

LEFT: **Handa, Sutherland** – various zones are visible on this exposed rocky shore: The **SPLASH ZONE** is just visible in the top of the image; **Twisted Wrack** is a species of the **UPPER SHORE ZONE**, while **Dulse** (dark red) and **Oar Weed** (in pool) are **LOWER SHORE ZONE** species. ABOVE: **Limpets** – found in the middle shore zone, each limpet has a 'home' where its shell forms a tight fit to the rock. The limpets graze on algae and move when submerged (and at night), returning to their home spot as the tide retreats.

SPLASH ZONE

UPPER SHORE ZONE

Twisted Wrack

LOWER SHORE ZONE

Dulse

Oar Weed

How to recognize

Rocky Shore is a jumble of boulders and ledges of various shapes and sizes, most of which are periodically submerged by sea water. When the tide falls, hollows and channels retain sea water and hold a microcosm of the marine environment, with a great diversity of life-forms including seaweeds, sea sponges, sea anemones, sea urchins, crustaceans, shellfish and small fish. Rock slippery with thick seaweed and speckled with barnacles and limpets is exposed briefly before the tide starts to rise again.

Rocky Shore is a common coastal habitat, found on a range of coasts from exposed Atlantic headlands to the sheltered shores of sea lochs, and is the main coastal habitat of the north and west.

When to visit

Year-round. Check a tide table and try to visit at low tide when the greatest area of shore is exposed – spring tides are best.

Did you know?

Over 500 species of seaweed have been identified in Irish waters. Seaweeds have long been harvested for food and also as a fertilizer. Seaweed was particularly important in areas with poor soil, allowing human settlement and cultivation in areas that would otherwise have been uninhabitable.

1 **Clifden, Connemara** – on sheltered rocky shores, zones are less obvious and seaweed dominates.
2 **Achmelvich, Assynt** – Rock pools can change markedly in temperature, salinity and oxygen content over a relatively short time period. Species that live in them have to be able to tolerate these challenging conditions. Look out for crabs and prawns and fishes such as Butterfish and gobies in larger rock pools. **3** **Kimmeridge, Dorset** – a large area of this gently shelving beach is revealed at low tide, exposing intertidal boulders, rock pools, wave-cut platforms and channels. It supports a range of unusual seaweeds including Bushy Rainbow Wrack.
4 **Beadlet anemones** (red and green forms together) – crevices provide shelter from desiccation.

Soft Cliff page 388

Soft Cliff is characterized by slumps and landslips caused by the erosion of the cliff base by the sea and by rain and percolating groundwater. These features create a complex environment on a small scale, which is ideal for invertebrates. Twenty-nine species of invertebrate (of which 22 are rare) are, in the UK, limited to Soft Cliff, while another 75 are closely associated with this habitat. The presence of terraced or shallow slopes of different gradients, bare ground, early-successional communities and scrub create a diverse range of vegetation types and structures that influence temperature and soil moisture content and provide suitable conditions for a range of species. For example, dry, friable soils are suitable for burrowing insects while flower-rich vegetation provides nectaring opportunities. Wet areas are used by water beetles, soldier flies and craneflies, and are a source of wet mud used by some solitary bees and wasps for nest building. The warm microclimate of bare areas prolongs the active period of warmth-loving species. This diversity also allows invertebrates to meet the varying requirements of different stages in their life-cycles.

Bare areas of Soft Cliff are colonized by pioneer plants such as Colt's-foot while more stable areas support grassland with Creeping Bent and flowering herbs such as Common Bird's-foot-trefoil and Wild Carrot. Seepages can be rich in orchids. If undisturbed, these communities progress to scrub and eventually woodland.

EXTENT UNKNOWN

Distribution and extent

Unprotected Soft Cliff is concentrated in England and Wales. Difficult to map as habitat often vertical or near vertical. Britain and Ireland hold a significant proportion of the Soft Cliff habitat in north-west Europe.

Eype, Dorset – exposed upper cliff with scrub developing on slumps part-way down the cliff face.

Similar habitats

Soft Cliff contains small patches of many other habitat types including grassland, wetland, heathland and scrub. The continuity of varied early-successional communities that is characteristic of Soft Cliff is also found on some Brownfield sites, but is otherwise now scarce throughout the countryside.

Origins and development

Soft Cliff is typically formed of soft mudstones, friable sands, shales, glacial deposits, soft chalk or silty limestones that offer little resistance to coastal erosion and weathering. In many places intensive management or development nearby (*e.g.* car parks, caravan parks, agriculture, nearby water abstraction and sea defences) has disrupted the natural processes of erosion and degraded the habitat. Sea-level rise and increasing storminess may lead to increased erosion.

Conservation

Soft cliffs are one of the few habitats in Britain and Ireland where a lack of intervention is crucial. Allowing natural processes to continue is fundamental in ensuring a continuity of varied early-successional habitats. The creation of cliff top buffer strips would allow space for coastal erosion and people. Although recognized for its geomorphological importance, the ecological importance of Soft Cliff has perhaps been rather overlooked in the past.

TOP: **Dunwich, Suffolk** – Soft Cliff of Norwich Crag is situated between Coastal Vegetated Shingle and Lowland Dry Heath, creating a continuum of semi-natural habitat. BOTTOM: **Burning Cliff, Dorset** – the vegetated slumped cliff shown here was the site of a fire in 1826 that continued for several years. The fire is believed to have been started by heat generated by the decomposition of pyrite within the shale.

What to look for

Look in different microhabitats for a range of invertebrates such as mining bees, solitary wasps, rove beetles and butterflies including blues, skippers and the rare Glanville Fritillary. Scrub can hold migrant birds in the spring and autumn and some soft cliffs support Sand Martin colonies. Look out for fossils after cliff falls.

How to recognize

The unstable, soft substrate of Soft Cliff readily slumps and it is rarely sheer like Hard Cliff. The crumbly ground makes access difficult and sometimes dangerous, but the jumbled, untamed wildness of Soft Cliff invites exploration. Heavy rain can cause sections of the cliff to collapse and it can change dramatically and suddenly.

The profile of taller Soft Cliff is often stepped where sections of cliff have slipped, creating flat areas that hold a mix of scrub, grassland, pools, and reedy patches surrounded by open or bare areas. The complex mosaic of a range of microhabitats in a small area make it particularly rich in invertebrates.

When to visit

Summer for invertebrates and safer access.

Did you know?

Fossils revealed in Soft Cliff (e.g. at Lyme Regis, Dorset) have helped shape our understanding of evolution and extinction with the discovery of marine reptiles such as ichthyosaurs.

1 **Chapman's Pool, Dorset** – the cliffs in the foreground are composed of Kimmeridge Clay, in the distance Houns-tout is capped with Portland Stone. **2** **Cliff Tiger Beetle** occurs around wet flushes on Soft Cliff along the south coast of England and can be spotted running over bare ground. **3** **Colt's-foot** is a distinctive pioneer species of landslips, Its flowers appearing before the leaves in March.

The vegetation of Hard Cliff and Slope varies according to the degree of exposure to wind and salt-spray, the soil type and stability, climate and factors such as grazing. On very exposed or sheer cliffs only lichens grow, although salt-tolerant higher plants such as Rock Samphire or, farther north, Scots Lovage, can be found on ledges and in crevices. The influence of salt-spray can extend inland for 500 m, but drops off rapidly, and grazing and the nature of the soil then become more important. A distinctive maritime form of Red Fescue occupies much of the lower cliff slope, with Thrift and Sea Campion or, on more calcareous soils, Yorkshire-fog and Sea Carrot. Grazing increases the relative abundance of rosette-forming plants such as plantains that are resistant to grazing. Around seabird colonies the soil is nutrient-enriched and supports oraches and Sea Beet in a community that is also found along strandlines. In more sheltered sites, Bluebell can be prominent in the vegetation, often under a canopy of Bracken. Cliff top vegetation can grade into Maritime Heath (*page 137*) or Lowland Calcareous Grassland depending on the substrate. In very exposed positions, 'perched' sand dunes can occur on cliff tops.

Hard Cliff provides disturbance-free nesting locations for raptors such as Peregrine and, in Scotland, White-tailed Eagle, but the most abundant cliff-breeding birds are seabirds. Cliffs are

EXTENT IN KM²
Eng	137
Wal	32
Sco	120
NI	3
Ire	55

Distribution and extent

Widely distributed, particularly on western and northern coast and on parts of the east coast of Scotland. England holds a significant proportion of Europe's chalk cliffs. Hard Cliff and Cliff Slopes are difficult to map as habitat often vertical or near vertical. Pale shading indicates the broad extent of the Annex I habitat (H1230); darker shading shows actual sites, where data exists. Dots are the locations with large seabird colonies (>10,000 colonial nesting seabirds). Extents are from the Annex I reporting.

Gannet colony, Noss Shetland – Gannets were first seen prospecting the east-facing cliffs in 1911 and the first breeding was noted in 1914; by 1939 there were 1,830 pairs and numbers have continud to rise, with almost 10,000 apparently occupied nests (AON) in 2008 and over 13,000 AON in 2019.

Cliff top grassland

Black Tar Lichen

Orange Sea Lichen

Nesting auks

Thrift

Nesting Fulmars

Handa Island, Sutherland has the largest seabird colonies in Britain and Ireland.

relatively predator-free and easily accessible from the sea, and millions of seabirds breed on them. Seabirds are good indicators of the health of the marine environment, and worrying declines have been linked to a reduction in the quality and quantity of prey species (*e.g.* sandeels) associated with changes in fishing practices and climate change; weather conditions and the impacts of predators have also played a role.

Similar habitats

Hard Cliff and Slope is closely linked to Rocky Shore, Maritime Heath and grassland habitats. Hard Cliff can sometimes be found interspersed with Soft Cliff, which is crumbly and usually has a slumped profile.

Origins and development

Hard Cliff is a natural habitat created by past or present erosion by wind and water of hard rocks. Some cliff slope swards are maintained as grassland through exposure and the thin soils, or by intense physical disturbance from seabirds. Others are maintained through livestock and Rabbit grazing. In other cases, livestock and Rabbit grazing prevents the development of coarser vegetation and scrub. Natural gradations are truncated where cultivated land approaches the cliff top, but in other places cliff slope vegetation grades into inland heathland, grassland or scrub.

Conservation

Disturbance to nesting seabirds from recreational use of the coast can be an issue at more accessible sites – breeding success can be reduced if birds are stressed, and when birds leave their nests, eggs and chicks are susceptible to predation. Rat eradication programmes on some islands (*e.g.* Lundy) have been successful in re-establishing seabird colonies. Invasive, non-native plants such as Hottentot Fig can become dominant in some areas (*e.g.* on the Lizard and at some Irish sites) and the management of these species is difficult in challenging terrain.

Exposed, west-facing cliffs on **Lundy Island**, topped with cliff grassland and some Maritime Heath. The island is an important site for breeding seabirds and the more sheltered cliffs hold an endemic plant, Lundy Cabbage (which in turn supports two endemic invertebrates).

1 **Portland, Dorset** – stepped undercliffs such as this can support scrub and stunted woodland, which, in inaccessible areas, may be some of the most natural habitat in lowland Britain and Ireland. **2** **The Lizard, Cornwall** – Cliff Slope grassland with **Dyer's Greenweed** in the foreground. **3** **Wild Cabbage** flowers between May and August and is found in a localized community on calcareous cliff tops, including at **Ballard Down, Dorset**. Hard chalk cliffs such as these are relatively uncommon and occur predominantly in southern England. **4** **Skomer, Pembrokeshire** – this short, Thrift-dominated sward is maintained by exposure and Rabbit grazing.

What to look for

The cliffs of Britain and Ireland hold internationally important colonies of seabirds – 68% of the world's Gannets and 90% of the world's Manx Shearwaters breed here, and in total some eight million seabirds nest around our coastline. From a distance look out for splashes of white guano, that indicate ledges supporting colonies of Guillemot, Razorbill and/or Kittiwake. Search the cliffs for the more scattered nests of Shag, Fulmar, Great Black-backed Gull and Herring Gull. Cormorants also breed at some sites, and build conspicuously large and untidy nests. Where there are no rats (which eat eggs and chicks), Puffin, Manx Shearwater and Leach's Petrel nest on the cliff slopes (the last two species are nocturnal). Manx Shearwaters abandon their chicks at about 10 weeks, and the youngsters are left to find their own way from their burrow out to sea, where they immediately head south to their wintering quarters off South America. Guillemots do not desert their chicks and can be seen below the cliffs on calm evenings in early July, calling to entice their offspring to plunge off the ledges to join them. Gannets mostly breed on remote outcrops and islands – there are 21 gannetries around Britain and Ireland. Black Guillemot (a northern species) nests in rock crevices and under boulders away from seabird colonies, while Chough nests in sea caves on some west coasts sites. Swift and House Martin also breed on coastal cliffs.

The hard cliffs of the west and south support some specialist invertebrates, including moths such as Thrift Clearwing and Fiery Clearwing (the latter restricted to the chalk cliffs of Kent and Sussex). There is even a water beetle that is restricted to seepages on sandstone cliffs. Relatively few plant species are found on Hard Cliff, but look out for Sea Aster, Rock Samphire, Rock Sea-spurrey, Golden Samphire and, in the north, Scots Lovage and Roseroot. On drought-prone cliff-edge swards look for spring-flowering annuals, together with Spring Squill and, in Scotland, Purple Milk-vetch. A group of rarities particularly associated with The Lizard includes rare clovers, Chives, Hairy Greenweed, Fringed Rupturewort and Autumn Squill).

1 **Roseroot** growing in a cliff crevice on Handa Island, Sutherland. The wet climate ameliorates the influence of salt-spray, and allows some species associated with Mountain Ledge to flourish on sheltered maritime cliffs. **2** **Orange Sea Lichen** and **Sea Ivory** are distinctive lichens often found on Hard Cliff. **3** **Skomer, Pembrokeshire** – Cliff top grassland in spring with Sea Campion, Bluebell and Red Campion.

How to recognize

Hard Cliff and Slope is found in exhilarating and sometimes intimidating locations where more or less sheer faces of granite, sandstone, limestone or basalt are eroded by the sea. Headlands and sites facing the prevailing south-westerly winds tend to be the most maritime in character, pounded by waves and scorched by salt-laden winds.

Cliffs, usually topped with a sparsely to densely vegetated slope, can drop directly into the sea or down to a rocky intertidal zone of fallen boulders.

The sheer rock can be coloured with splashes of lichens and dotted with crevice plants, while cliff slopes often support eye-catching Sea Campion, Thrift, Kidney Vetch or other plants. Some cliffs support seabird colonies, particularly in more remote locations, – these are unforgettable places with thousands of birds flying around the cliffs and bobbing on the water below.

When to visit

Spring–summer for seabirds and cliff flora.

Did you know?

In the past, both eggs and birds were collected from seabird colonies and, although this practice has almost entirely ceased, Gannet chicks are still harvested from Sula Sgeir each year by the men of Ness (Isle of Lewis).

1 Thrift Clearwing flies in June and July around rocky coastlines. The larvae feed in the roots and stems of Thrift, especially on plants growing in rock crevices near the splash zone. **2 Golden-hair Lichen** is very sensitive to air pollution; once widespread in the UK, it is now mainly limited to windy cliff-tops. **3 Puffins** typically nest in burrows on the cliff slope, and birds, once their eggs have hatched, can be seen flying in with beaks full of silvery sandeels. **4 Razorbills** nest in crevices and among boulders, often near **5 Guillemots**, which line up along narrow ledges.

363

OTHER HABITATS

ORIGINS AND TYPES

This section includes a handful of habitats that do not fit neatly into any one of the other habitat categories: **Arable, Brownfield, Traditional Orchard** and **Garden**.

The common denominator is that they are all more heavily influenced by humans than other habitats, and are farther along the spectrum between semi-natural and artificial. However, this does not mean that they are devoid of wildlife. The best examples can be wonderfully rich in species – for example, Brownfield can contain as many invertebrates as ancient woodland and Arable supports a unique suite of species, many of which are becoming increasingly rare. These habitats do, however, have some major ecological differences. Arable is regularly and frequently disturbed, and supports plant species that are able to regenerate rapidly from the seed bank and complete their life-cycle within a short space of time. Traditional Orchard, on the other hand, supports species such as epiphytic lichens that require long periods of stability. Nevertheless, continuity can be important for both of these habitat types (*e.g.* some arable weeds only occur on sites where they have had a long history). Brownfield is similar to Arable in that it provides bare substrate, but as it remains undisturbed, primary succession is able to take place. Both Arable and Brownfield support large numbers of introduced species, which is unsurprising given how closely linked they are with people, and the opportunities provided for colonization. For example, around 3,000 non-native species (of which well over half are flowering plants) occur in England (this figure excludes garden plants), and around 11% are species that occur in Brownfield.

Some other habitats that are not semi-natural but can include excellent wildlife habitat are gardens, allotments and churchyards. Gardens occupy over 400,000 ha in the UK and contain around three million ponds and nearly 30 million trees. It is thought that over 12 million UK households actively provide food for birds. Allotments are similar to Arable in that they are regularly disturbed and can support arable weeds. They often include untended patches, scrubby corners, ponds, ditches and hedges that all add to the potential for wildlife. Churchyards can also be rich in wildlife, including species-rich unimproved grassland, hedgerows and veteran trees, and old gravestones may support many species of lichen. Yew trees in particular have an association with old churches – 75% of the ancient Yews in Britain are thought to be within churchyards, many of which are older than the church itself.

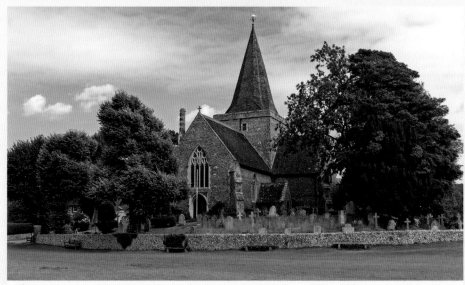

Alfriston Churchyard, East Sussex. In summer the churchyard is left uncut for wild flowers.

HABITAT	DESCRIPTION
Arable *page 368 | page 394*	Land cultivated for annual crops. Uncultivated margins and unsprayed headlands are of particular interest for wildlife.
Brownfield *page 372 | page 394*	Developed land that has been abandoned and re-colonized by widlife, typically industrial sites, railway sidings and quarries. Technically known as 'Open Mosaic Habitat'.
Traditional Orchard *page 375 | page 395*	An enclosed area planted with widely spaced fruit trees, usually in permanent grassland that is left unmown during the summer.
Garden *page 378 | page 395*	An area of land used for growing ornamental and/or food and medicinal plants and for recreation, often enclosed and usually adjacent to property.

Intensive farming leaves little room for wildlife.

CONSERVATION

The species-richness of Arable and Traditional Orchard is highly dependent upon sympathetic management and is particularly susceptible to economic pressures that may either result in intensification (in the case of Arable) or abandonment (in the case of Traditional Orchard). Arable weeds are the most endangered group of plants in Britain, and farmland birds have been identified as the most endangered avian group across Europe; 60% of farmland species are in decline and reversing this trend is proving challenging. A wider uptake of measures such as leaving field margins fallow, reducing pesticide use, and setting aside areas for wildlife would benefit both groups, but require key changes to the European Common Agricultural Policy. The threats to Brownfield are different, and revolve around planning procedures. Current policy is a presumption in favour of developing brownfield sites provided they are not of high environmental value; the challenge is to ensure their value is identified and recognized through designation as SSSI.

FURTHER INFORMATION

Common Ground – a charity that explores the relationship between nature and culture and works to promote community orchards – www.commonground.org.uk

The Orchard Network – www.ptes.org/campaigns/traditional-orchard-project/orchard-network/

Arable Plants: A Field Guide by Phil Wilson & Miles King (WILD*Guides*, 2004)

Arable Bryophytes by Ron Porley (WILD*Guides*, 2008)

Caring for God's Acre – www.caringforgodsacre.org.uk/

Buglife Brownfield Hub – www.buglife.org.uk/brownfield-hub

Key events relating to Arable, Brownfield and Traditional Orchard

4500 BCE	Neolithic arable cultivation starts.
2000 BCE	Arable cultivation is well established and Arable forms a key part of the landscape.
0	The Romans arrive into a landscape already deforested and supporting rotational cropping. Large estates come to dominate the farming system; a demand-led economy develops.
7th century	After the Roman period, towns become depopulated, subsistence agriculture returns and scrub and woodland regenerate.
11th century	The feudal landscape is well established, with common grazing land and open field systems.
14th century	After three centuries of agricultural growth, the Black Death results in the abandonment of much land and sparks changes in the feudal system.
17th–18th century	The Enclosures (of common land) result in a reduction in small-scale, mixed farming.
18th–19th century	The Agricultural Revolution allows sustained population growth; landowners become capitalist farmers. The Highland Clearances, the arrival of cheap food imports and the Irish potato famine saw the amount of land under arable cultivation drop.
19th century	The Industrial Revolution creates the first Brownfield sites and paves the way for future industry. Britain becomes the world's first urban nation.
20th century	Emphasis turns to increasing self-sufficiency and productivity after the Second World War. New technology, cropping systems, pesticides and artificial fertilizers significantly change agriculture. Many orchards are neglected or destroyed. Brownfield becomes a key haven for wildlife in an increasingly intensively used landscape. From 1985, agri-environment schemes provided some financial support for wildlife-friendly farming.
Early 21st century	Focus on public services offered by farming (including benefits to wildlife) increases, yet key opportunities to reform CAP are missed and populations of many species continue to decline.

Quarrying creates abundant bare ground that, if managed sensitively, can provide habitat for species such as Sand Martin and a suite of bare ground invertebrates. **Pennyroyal** (INSET) is one species that has unexpectedly benefited from quarry tracks in Dorset.

Allotments can be a haven for wildlife. This site in Dorset holds good numbers of Slow-worm and Adder is occasionally seen, while Weasel's-snout is a common 'arable weed'.

Wild corners often provide opportunities for wildlife, such as this Corn Marigold.

Marsh Helleborine on a damp roadside ditch in Dorset.

Urban parks can provide habitat for wildilfe. Here in Poole, Dorset, **Brent Geese** feed on nutrient-rich amenity grassland once food becomes depeleted in Poole Habour as the winter progresses.

Arable

page 394

Arable land, cultivated to grow a variety of short-term crops such as cereals, oil-seed rape, sugar beet, beans and potatoes, covers about 25% of Britain and 15% of Ireland. As it is regularly disturbed, it can only support species able to exploit the periodically open conditions created by ploughing and harvesting. A suite of ephemeral plants ('arable weeds') was once widespread across arable land, but has suffered badly from the use of agrochemicals and intensive farming techniques. Arable weeds are mostly annual, and some can produce seeds in as little as six weeks following germination and which can then survive for many years in the soil. Some species, such as Corncockle, have short-lived seed, and are reliant upon the seed being harvested with the crop and re-sown for the next season – an unlikely scenario in modern agriculture. Other species, such as Darnel, are now extinct in the UK but have survived in areas such as the Aran Islands where less intensive farming practices persist.

Weedy strips are important foraging habitat for seed-eating invertebrates and, where flowers occur, a range of nectar-feeding invertebrates may be present. Some invertebrates are associated with disturbed ground, such as the Necklace Ground Beetle and the Set-aside Downy-back Beetle (whose name is a reminder of the set-aside areas intended to decrease arable surpluses in the late 20th century – set-aside strips are now created to benefit wildlife). The bird community of arable land includes a declining suite of species such as Lapwing, Yellow Wagtail, Corn Bunting and Yellowhammer which, together with rare species such as Montagu's Harrier, Stone-curlew, Quail and Cirl Bunting, have suffered from changes in management that have reduced breeding productivity and (for residents) winter survival.

A colourful field margin near Swaffham, Norfolk. Most arable land has now lost its arable flora, including species that were once abundant.

Origins and development

The origins of arable production extend right back to the Neolithic, when an agriculturally based culture gradually expanded across Europe from the Middle East. Many arable weeds are now regarded as ancient introductions that arrived with crop seed, although some were already present in disturbed areas. Together with a range of invertebrates, birds and mammals, they are now closely associated with human agricultural activities. However, modern agriculture, with its efficient seed-cleaning, widespread adoption of pesticides, new crop types, increased fertilizer use, changes in crop rotation, better drainage and switch to winter-sown cereals, has led to severe declines in species.

Conservation

The conservation challenge is to reverse the declines in species associated with arable farming across land that is owned by many different individuals and managed commercially. Government funding through agri-environment schemes has provided for a suite of measures such as beetle banks, skylark plots, uncultivated field margins and unsprayed conservation headlands. However, although there is evidence that such measures can be beneficial, the declines are continuing; for example, the farmland bird index (which uses amalgamated trend data for 19 species) continues to decrease. A number of nature reserves, such as Fivehead Arable Fields in Somerset, have been created solely to support populations of rare arable weeds. Climate change may result in changes in land-use practices – this will present both challenges and opportunities for species currently relying on arable land.

EXTENT IN KM^2	
Eng	47,749
Wal	1,003
Sco	6,799
NI	954
Ire	11,608

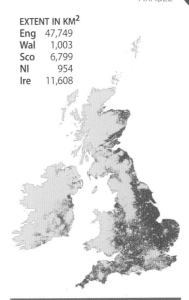

Distribution and extent

Widespread across Britain and Ireland, particularly abundant in the south and east of England. Arable weed hotspots are concentrated on the chalk of south-east England and the Atlantic fringes where less intensive farming has persisted. Map derived from satellite imagery (CORINE).

Common Poppy is still widespread on Arable land, but other poppy species such as Prickly Poppy are much scarcer. Some arable weeds have long-lived seed banks, and can reappear in cultivated, uncropped field margins. A great many of the declining arable weeds (see *page 370*) such as **Corn Marigold** were once so common and widespread that they were considered to be pests.

What to look for

Check winter stubble for farmland birds and look out for Brown Hare in the spring (Britain only). Look for uncommon arable plants such as Round-leaved Fluellen, Sharp-leaved Fluellen, Small Toadflax and Dwarf Spurge, which may indicate the presence of other rarer plants.

'Arable weeds' have declined drastically due to seed cleaning, a switch to autumn-sown crops, the development of highly competitive crop varieties, the use of herbicides and the loss of arable margins. Many are archaeophytes, plants that arrived with crop seed from the Neolithic period onwards. **1** **Corn Marigold** was viewed as a serious weed in Victorian times but is now considered vulnerable. **2** **Cornflower** is often included in wildflower seed mixes and only a small number of 'natural' populations are known. **3** **Prickly Poppy** can be distinguished from other poppies by the seed heads, which are long, thin and covered with prickles. **4** **Dwarf Spurge** is found on chalky soils, along arable margins and on drought-prone grassland. **5** **Large Venus's-looking-glass** has striking bright purple flowers and is naturalized in arable fields in Hampshire; it can also occur as a garden escape. **6** **Round-leaved Fluellen** is found on light soils over chalk and calcareous boulder-clay. **7** **Small Toadflax** is a spring-germinating annual of arable fields but can also be found on tracks, walls and even railways. **8** **Fine-leaved Fumitory** is typically found in spring-sown crops on chalky soils and is largely confined to southern and eastern England. **9** **Shepherd's-needle** was once controlled as a pernicious weed, but is now considered to be critically endangered in Britain.

How to recognize

Arable is, by its very nature, primarily managed for food production, and over the last 70 years or so this has usually resulted in large, featureless fields that are treated with pesticides and inorganic fertilizers and hold little natural cover. However, some small areas of arable land are managed less intensively, sometimes with wildlife as well as food production in mind. The best sites are easily spotted in the summer by a splash of colour along field margins where arable weeds are still flourishing, and by the presence of thick hedgerows and unmanaged corners that still hold farmland birds such as Turtle Dove, Yellowhammer and Grey Partridge.

When to visit

July–August for arable weeds; winter for farmland bird flocks.

Did you know?

The word archaeophyte refers to species that were introduced as a consequence of human activity in ancient times. Many arable weeds are archaeophytes.

1 With its blunt nose and furry ears, **Harvest Mouse** is distinctive but hard to see. Woven nests above the ground in dense vegetation, such as cereal crops, are the best indication of its presence. **2 Skylark** is the commonest bird to nest in fields but has declined markedly since the 1970s. This decline has been linked to the loss of mixed farming and a switch from spring-sown to autumn-sown cereal crops. **3 Brown Hare** was introduced to Britain in the Iron Age. It tends to occur in very open habitats, such as arable, and does not burrow underground. To avoid predators they rely on speed, reaching up to 70km/h.

Brownfield page 394

Brownfield (technically known as 'open mosaic habitat') has become a refuge for early-successional species that are scarce or absent in the wider urban landscape. The legacy of past industrial use can sometimes be found in piles of fuel ash and other waste products and the thin soils vary markedly in their chemical content and pH, even within a single site. These skeletal soils are crucial in maintaining the habitat in an early-successional stage, an element that is rare in the lowlands. The habitat can be dominated by lichens and mosses, or by tall ruderal herbs such as Rosebay Willowherb, and often includes pools and inundated areas, short open turf, flower-rich grassland and scrub.

The unusual habitat structure and chemical composition of the soil can lead to some unexpected species, and there is also an element of chance in terms of the species that arrive. A range of flowering plants (including non-native species) provides abundant nectar sources for invertebrates, while open bare ground, rubble and exposed concrete provide warm areas for basking, good foraging areas for visual predators and potential sites for burrowing invertebrates. Scrub provides shelter and further structural diversity. Built structures can be colonized too – for example, numbers of Black Redstart peaked in London after the Second World War, when it bred in bomb sites and derelict buildings.

Similar habitats

Brownfield sites can encompass vegetation associated with Lowland Dry Heath, a range of grassland types, scrub and secondary woodland, but are uniquely urban. Calaminarian Grassland (specifically associated with substrates with toxic levels of heavy metals) is also found in post-industrial landscapes.

Isle of Grain Power Station, Kent – The Isle of Grain holds a number of Brownfield sites that support rare and endangered invertebrates, and has seen a number of battles between conservation organizations and developers with conflicting interests.

Origins and development

The origins of Brownfield sites are very varied, but all Brownfield sites have been developed and subsequently abandoned. However, they are often threatened, as planners seek to contain development within urban areas rather than extending onto greenfield sites. The importance of Brownfield sites for wildlife is not widely recognized, although open mosaic habitat is a Priority Habitat in the UK.

Conservation

The conservation of Brownfield sites involves raising awareness of the importance of the habitat, undertaking comprehensive survey work of potential sites and ensuring long-term continuity of the habitat. It may be possible for redevelopment proposals to incorporate the wildlife interest by providing new habitat and retaining key features.

What to look for

Brownfield sites can be especially rich in invertebrates, including bees (*e.g.* Brown-banded and Shrill Carder Bees), solitary wasps (including weaver wasps), jumping spiders and a range of beetles. They often provide ideal habitat for reptiles (Slow-worm, Common Lizard, Grass Snake and Adder), and pools can support amphibians (*e.g.* newts and Common Frog). Birds particularly associated with Brownfield include Black Redstart and Little Ringed Plover. Look out for orchids, including Bee Orchid and Chalk Fragrant-orchid.

EXTENT UNKNOWN

Distribution and extent

Brownfield sites can occur anywhere there has been development. The map is derived from satellite imagery (CORINE) and shows land classified as construction sites, continuous urban fabric, industrial or commercial units, port areas, road and rail networks and associated land.

LEFT: **West Thurrock Marshes, Essex** was the subject of a long-running legal battle to protect an important Brownfield site from development, which was ultimately unsuccessful. The bare ground in the foreground is pulverized fuel ash (waste from a coal power station); this can provide an important substrate for a range of lichens. RIGHT: **Canvey Wick, Essex** was transformed from coastal grazing marsh in the 1970s to create an oil refinery that was decommissioned in 1973 without ever opening. This was Britain's first Brownfield SSSI and 1,400 invertebrate species have been recorded from this site.

1 Brownfield sites are now key habitats for **Shrill Carder Bee** that requires flower-rich areas and long, tussocky grass in which to nest. **2** **Grayling** is a relatively scarce butterfly that is often found on Brownfield sites. **3** **Slow Worm** is a legless lizard that rarely basks in the open; on Brownfield sites it can often be found under rocks, bricks and other debris. **4** **Brandon, Suffolk** – this 0·1 ha nature reserve in an industrial estate supports a suite of rare species, including Field Wormwood and the Wormwood Moonshiner beetle. Regular soil disturbance is required to maintain the wildlife interest.

How to recognize

Brownfield is developed land that has become derelict. Generally encountered in urban or industrial settings, it can include corners of industrial estates, abandoned factories, railway sidings, disused power stations, airfields, and even old quarries and brick-pits. Once disused, these sites rapidly take on a wild feel as plants and animals quickly colonize.

Industrial waste, spoil heaps and exposed substrate make for infertile soils and droughty conditions, and as a consequence weeds and species typical of early-successional habitats often dominate, interspersed with scrub, built structures, patches of grassland and bare ground in a higgledy-piggledy mosaic. Part of the attraction of Brownfield is the degree of uncertainty about just what might be found. It is also often the nearest area of habitat for many wildlife lovers.

When to visit

Spring and summer for flowers and invertebrates.

Did you know?
Up to 15% of all the rare and scarce invertebrates in the UK have been recorded on Brownfield sites, and at least 40 invertebrate species are wholly confined to this habitat.

Traditional Orchard

page 395

The ecological interest of Traditional Orchard (*i.e.* orchard managed in a low-intensity way) is found in the old-growth fruit and nut trees which, together with associated hedgerows, boundary trees, grassland, streams and ponds, can support a large number of plants and animals including rare and scarce species – 1,800 species have been recorded from orchards. Old fruit trees may be retained in Traditional Orchards, and their hollow trunks, rot holes and split bark are good for fungi, lichens, invertebrates and birds such as Lesser Spotted Woodpecker. Fruit trees have a limited life-span (an apple tree has an approximate life of 80–120 years; a plum 50–70 years), and for specialist beetles and lichens to be present, trees must be allowed to age and replacements planted to ensure continuity of old trees.

Trees in Traditional Orchards are often planted at low densities and grown as standards, meaning that their crowns are high enough to allow hay-cutting or grazing. Where orchard grassland has been traditionally managed without artificial fertilizers or pesticides it can hold an interesting flora including species such Green-winged Orchid and Cowslip. Waxcap fungi can sometimes be found if the field layer is kept short.

Orchards can play an important role in contributing to a network of habitats such as Wood Pasture, ancient woodland and Hedgerow, which offer continuity for species requiring stability over time.

EXTENT IN KM^2	
Eng	170
Wal	10
Sco	n/k
NI	n/k
Ire	n/k

Middlebere Farm, Dorset – A small farmhouse orchard that has been replanted with a variety of traditional apple varieties.

Distribution and extent

Widespread, particularly in the English lowlands, with concentrations in Herefordshire, Worcestershire, Gloucestershire, Somerset and Kent. Orchards are hard to map as they are often small and associated with gardens and other private land. Map shows inventory undertaken by the People's Trust for Endangered Species for Natural England and Natural Resources Wales and also includes orchards mapped from satellite data (CORINE, minimum size 25 ha). Inventory data are not available for Scotland, Northern Ireland or Ireland.

Origins and development

Over 2,400 apple varieties are thought to occur in British and Irish orchards, and DNA evidence indicates that they are descendents of the wild apple of Asia rather than the native Crab Apple. The Romans probably first introduced cultivated apples to Britain, and their fruit-growing skills were perhaps perpetuated in monasteries through the medieval period. By 1700, orchards were a well-established feature of the countryside in key areas, and most farms had their own orchards to provide fruit, and also cider, which was a component of farm workers' wages. From the 1950s, changes in farming practices resulted in the inevitable loss of orchards, cheap supermarket imports reduced the economic viability of commercial orchards, and remaining sites were often neglected. However, there is a resurgence of interest in locally grown varieties, and the social role of orchards is being seen once again in the recent rise of community orchards.

Similar habitats

Traditional Orchards are structurally similar to Wood Pasture, although the tree species are cultivated and managed for fruit production. The grassland can be similar to Lowland Meadow and Pasture.

Conservation

Sympathetic management involves the appropriate pruning of old trees, regenerating orchards through planting new trees, avoiding the use of pesticides and artificial fertilizers and suitable grassland management. Traditional Orchards are usually very small and variable in the species they support, so measures to ensure connectivity between orchards and nearby similar habitat is important in order to support some of the rarer wildlife. The rich heritage of local fruit varieties is maintained by the National Fruit Collection at Brogdale in Kent.

What to look for

Lesser Spotted Woodpecker, Bullfinch and Redstart; a wide range of invertebrates including Noble Chafer and Mistletoe Marble Moth; epiphytic lichens and fungi; Mistletoe.

TOP: Within the UK there are over 2,400 different varieties of apple, 500 varieties of pear and 300 types of plum. BOTTOM: Veteran tree features such as rot holes are important for invertebrates and can be used by nesting birds and roosting bats.

How to recognize

With their gnarled old fruit trees and long grass rich in flowers, Traditional Orchards seem quintessentially English. Once a ubiquitous feature of the lowland countryside, they can still be found tucked away on the edges of villages and behind farmhouses. They are usually small and may contain a variety of different fruit and nut trees including apple, cherry, pear, plum, damson, quince, walnut and cobnut (a type of hazelnut), many of which may be local varieties.

The trees are widely spaced and scattered over permanent grassland that is often left to grow long in the summer, unlike in modern commercial orchards where dwarf or bush trees grow closely together over mown grass.

When to visit

April/May for blossom; summer for invertebrates and flowering plants; autumn for species drawn to fallen fruit including Fieldfare and Badger.

Did you know?

Over 50% of traditional orchards in England were lost in the second half of the 20th century, but more recently there has been a resurgence of interest in small traditional orchards.

1 The blossom of fruit trees is a source of nectar for many invertebrates. **2** **Redstart** is a hole-nesting species that can be found in orchards with old trees. **3** **Mistletoe**, which is semi-parasitic, is commonly found in orchards – six species of invertebrate are associated with this plant: a moth, a weevil and four bugs.

Garden

Gardens, allotments and parks are the greenspaces on our doorsteps. Some are ornamental, some grow food and others are managed for amenity or tended for wildlife – many fulfil all of these roles. These places are often predominantly planted up with non-native or cultivated species. However, many native plants, some of which may be the predecessors of cultivated varieties, can also be present, either having been deliberately planted as part of the design or having simply arrived of their own accord.

There are a huge number of gardens in Britain and Ireland. Estimates vary but, for example, around 22 million homes (around 87%) in the UK have a garden. It is also estimated that around 28% of households put out food for birds, that around 16% of gardens have at least one nest box, and that 10% contain a pond. The range of wildlife species that inhabit a garden partly depends on environmental factors (such as soil type, aspect, climate, size and geographic location) but the diversity of microhabitats and structure of the garden, its previous use and its current management are also important. With the general demise of nature in the wider countryside and urban areas, gardens can have a role in providing refuges for wildlife and potential stepping stones between patches of wilder habitat.

Origins and development

In Britain, the history of gardens can be traced back to Roman times (*i.e.* around 100 CE), when formal, geometric gardens were laid out around large villas, while in Ireland there are written accounts of vegetable gardens from roughly this period. Medieval gardens, such as monastic or cottage gardens, provided herbs, vegetables and enclosed spaces for domestic livestock; it was only later that gardens were designed to be aesthetically pleasing. Through the ages, garden design has reflected changing fashions. The formal patterns of the enclosed Renaissance gardens of the 15th and 16th centuries gave way to the more naturalistic landscape gardens made famous by Capability Brown in the 18th century. In the Victorian era, public

In this garden, raised beds allow high-density planting, leaving space for wildlife corners.

gardens planted up with ornamental flowers became popular, as did informal 'cottage gardens' with jumbles of flowers, herbs and vegetables growing together. Gardening history generally dwells on the activities of affluent landowners, but most people probably used small gardens and backyards to provide food regardless of changing fashions in garden design.

As the extent of semi-natural habitats in the countryside became reduced and fragmented during the second half of the 20th century, and the species dependent upon them declined, gardening specifically to encourage wildlife emerged as a new horticultural trend. Today, eco-gardening (including practices to avoid wider environmental damage, to create niches for wildlife and to provide locally grown food) has become widespread. How to recognize

EXTENT IN KM^2
UK 4,329
Ire n/k

Similar habitats

Brownfield habitat is found where urban or industrial spaces have been left derelict and lack active management. Traditional Orchard can be part of gardens. The landscaped gardens of some country houses may be associated with Wood Pasture.

Conservation

Gardens with scruffy corners can offer much for wildlife and there are many ways to enhance them further. Features such as shady log piles, bird feeders, ponds, bug hotels, bird boxes and wildflower patches, together with wildlife-friendly horticultural practices, all make gardens better places for wildlife. Unfortunately, pressure for development often means that new

Distribution and extent

Gardens occur wherever people live. Map based on satellite data (CORINE) and shows areas classified as urban fabric, green urban areas or sport and leisure facilities.

Cowslip flourishing in a garden wildflower patch.

housing is built at high densities and as a consequence many new homes have limited garden space, while so-called 'garden grabbing' has resulted in new developments replacing existing gardens. Front gardens have increasingly disappeared under tarmac or gravel to create off-road parking, and decking and paving have edged out back lawns and borders. Slug pellets and other garden pesticides not only kill invertebrates and plants but can also accumulate in the food chain. Fences and walls act as barriers, preventing species such as Hedgehogs moving between gardens.

Although the proportion of homes with gardens is decreasing, interest in wildlife gardening is burgeoning, and a number of national initiatives such as RSPB's Big Garden Birdwatch, Plantlife's Every Flower Counts, Butterfly Conservation's Big Butterfly Count and a joint campaign involving the Royal Horticultural Society (RHS) and The Wildlife Trusts called Wild About Gardens, are further raising awareness of garden wildlife.

What to look for

Check feeders for a variety of birds, including tits, finches, Nuthatch and Great Spotted Woodpecker. Mammals such as Hedgehog, Fox and Badger can also be drawn to feeding stations in gardens. Gardens with a variety of plants flowering throughout the year can be great places for bees, hoverflies, butterflies and other nectar feeders and pollinators. Garden ponds may hold amphibians such as Common Frog and Common Toad and attract dragonflies. Rotting wood in gardens in the south-east of England may hold Stag Beetle. Unmown lawns can contain surprises such as Bee Orchid.

LEFT: This garden at the **Bug Farm in Pembrokeshire** has been deliberately designed with wildlife in mind.
RIGHT: Creating a bug hotel can be a fun way to provide opportunities for observing a range of invertebrates at close quarters.

FACING PAGE: **1** As well as the expected finches and tits, feeders can attract other species including Nuthatch and **Great Spotted Woodpecker**. **2** The once-ubiquitous **House Sparrow** was considered a pest but has now gone from many urban areas. It can still be found in many gardens. **3** **Fox** densities are highest in urban areas, where they are actively fed in some gardens. **4** Common Frog breeds in many garden ponds, where its jelly-like globules of spawn are seen in early spring.

How to recognize

Gardens are enclosed, cultivated spaces generally immediately adjacent to properties, which makes them excellent places to observe wildlife – many children have their very first wildlife encounters in a garden. Gardens range in size and scale from tiny patios or courtyards with planters to designed landscapes associated with large country houses. Those with, for example, monoculture lawns, impenetrable fences, expanses of paving or gravel on an impermeable membrane, and just the occasional ornamental shrub or patch of bulbs, present plenty of opportunities to make improvements that would encourage wildlife. However, at their best, gardens can be excellent for wildlife, particularly those that are hugely varied, with unkempt corners, native trees, berry-bearing hedges, climbing plants, ponds, dead wood, uncut seed heads and stems and a variety of plants flowering continuously throughout the season. Parks (public open spaces managed for recreation) may contain specimen trees, small wooded areas, larger waterbodies and designated wildlife areas, but are often heavily managed with pesticides and mowers. Allotments are communal plots of land typically used for growing fruit, vegetables, herbs and flowers: often scruffier than gardens, they can also be excellent for wildlife.

When to visit

Winter for birds around feeding stations, early spring for breeding amphibians in garden ponds, late spring and summer for insects.

Did you know?

Jennifer Owen, a zoologist who studied the wildlife in her modest suburban garden in Leicester over a 30-year period, recorded over 2,600 species of animals and plants (including 20 insect species new to Britain).

Habitat Correspondence Tables

These tables show how the habitat types described in this book are aligned with commonly used classification systems (see page 35), including Annex I habitats, UK BAP priority habitats, UK Habitat Classification, British Plant Communities (National Vegetation Classification), the UK Phase 1 Habitat Classification, the Fossitt Habitats of Ireland and the Irish Vegetation Classification. The various systems all use codes as abbreviations of the habitat/vegetation types, and these are also listed in the tables for convenience.

These systems were designed for different purposes, and so do not always correspond neatly. For example, Lowland Mixed Oak and Ash Wood was not identified as being of most need of conservation at a European level, and so is not an Annex I habitat. However, one component of Lowland Mixed Oak and Ash Wood (woodland found in south-east England characterized by oaks and Hornbeam) is an Annex I type (namely '9160 Sub-Atlantic and medio-European oak or oak-hornbeam forests of the *Carpinion betuli*'). Lowland Mixed Oak and Ash Wood is itself only one component of the UK Priority Habitat 'Lowland Mixed Deciduous Woodland', which also includes Lowland Dry Oak and Birch Wood, Wet Woodland and Beech Wood. The Phase 1 category 'A111 Broadleaved woodland - semi-natural' is similarly broad. One Irish habitat falls within Lowland Mixed Oak and Ash Wood ('WN2 Oak – Ash – Hazel woodland') and there is overlap with a second ('WN4 Wet Pedunculate Oak – Ash woodland') although a component of this falls with Wet Woodland. Similarly, vegetation described in two NVC communities (W8 *Fraxinus excelsior – Acer campestre – Mercurialis perennis* woodland and W10 *Quercus robur – Pteridium aquilinum – Rubus fruticosus* woodland) is found in Lowland Mixed Oak and Ash Wood, but some elements of these communities describe vegetation found within Lowland Dry Oak and Birch Wood, Wood Pasture, Upland Oak Wood and Upland Mixed Ash Wood. The various relationships can be quite complex, and the following table shows how habitats and communities within each classification either equate to, overlap with or fall within the habitat types described in this book. The National Biodiversity Network (NBN) Habitat Directory available on the NBN gateway website is an interactive resource through which most of the relationships between the other classifications can be more fully explored. The Irish Vegetation Classification (available online) provides information on the relationship of communities with various habitat classifications and the British National Vegetation Classification. Note that a number of rare, transitional or ubiquitous communities have not been included.

Key

Ann. I: Annex I – habitats considered to be most in need of conservation within Europe for which Special Areas of Conservation (SACs) are designated (habitat descriptions can be found on the Joint Nature Conservation Committee (JNCC) website jncc.defra.gov.uk/).

UKPH: UK priority habitats – habitats considered to be under threat in the UK because of their rarity or rate of decline (habitat descriptions can be found via the JNCC website).

UKHab: The UK Habitat Classification is a hierarchical approach that has been designed to incorporate the other UK habitat schemes. Further information can be found at ecountability.co.uk/ukhabworkinggroup-ukhab.

NVC: British Plant Communities – plant communities described within the National Vegetation Classification (published by Cambridge University Press in a five-volume series entitled *British Plant Communities* edited by John Rodwell).

P1: Phase 1 – A standardized system for recording semi-natural vegetation and other wildlife habitats

in the UK (described in *Handbook for Phase 1 habitat survey - a technique for environmental audit*, JNCC, 2010).

GHI: Guide to the Habitats of Ireland – a standard scheme for describing habitats in Ireland (described in *A Guide to Habitats in Ireland* by Julie Fossitt, An Chomhairle Oidhreachta /The Heritage Council, 2000).

IVC: Irish Vegetation Classification – a hierarchical vegetation classification. Community descriptions can be found online on the National Biodiversity Data Centre website biodiversityireland.ie/projects/national-vegetation-database/irish-vegetation-classification/explore/. Develpment of the IVC is ongoing – communities published online up to July 2020 are included.

▉ : contained within classification

▉ : overlaps with classification

☐ : roughly equivalent to classification

▉ : no equivalent classification

Phase 1 habitats are shaded in the tables according to the colour coding used for Phase 1 surveys.

The following list provides the commonly used English names for species that are included in the plant community summary descriptions in the National Vegetation Classification.

NVC name [Stace 4 name] .... Common name

Acer campestre .... Field Maple
Agrimonia eupatorium .... Agrimony
Agrostis .... bent grasses
Agrostis capillaris .... Common Bent
Agrostis curtisii .... Bristle Bent
Agrostis stolonifera .... Creeping Bent
Alchemilla alpina .... Alpine Lady's-mantle
Alchemilla glabra .... A Lady's-mantle
Alnus glutinosa .... Alder
Alopecurus geniculatus .... Marsh Foxtail
Alopecurus myosuroides .... Black-grass
Alopecurus pratensis .... Meadow Foxtail
Ammophila arenaria .... Marram Grass
Angelica sylvestris .... Wild Angelica
Anthelia julacea .... Alpine Silverwort
Anthoxanthum odoratum .... Sweet Vernal-grass
Arctostaphylos alpinus .... Arctic Bearberry
Arctostaphylos uva-ursi .... Bearberry
Armeria maritima .... Thrift
Arrhenatherum elatius .... False Oat-grass
Artemisia maritima
  [=Seriphidium maritimum] .... Sea Wormwood
Arthrocnemum perenne
  [=Sarcocornia perennis] .... Perennial Glasswort
Asplenium ruta-muraria .... Wall-rue
Asplenium trichomanes .... Maidenhair Spleenwort
Asplenium viride .... Green Spleenwort
Aster tripolium .... Sea Aster
Athyrium distentifolium .... Alpine Lady-fern
Atriplex prostrata .... Spear-leaved Orache
Avenula pratensis
  [=Helictochloa pratensis] .... Meadow Oat-grass
Avenula pubescens
  [=Helictotrichon pubescens] .... Downy Oat-grass

Beta vulgaris ssp. maritima .... Sea Beet
Betula pendula .... Silver Birch
Betula pubescens .... Downy Birch
Betula spp. .... birches
Blysmus rufus .... Saltmarsh Flat-sedge
Brachypodium pinnatum .... Tor-grass
Brassica oleracea .... Wild Cabbage
Bromus erectus [=Bromopsis erecta] .... Upright Brome
Bryum pseudotriquetrum .... Marsh Bryum

Cakile maritima .... Sea Rocket
Calliergon cuspidatum
  [=Calliergonella cuspidata] .... Pointed Spear-moss
Calliergon giganteum .... Giant Spear-moss
Callitriche stagnalis .... Common Water-starwort
Calluna vulgaris .... Heather
Caltha palustris .... Marsh-marigold
Campylium stellatum .... Yellow Starry Feather-moss
Capsella bursa-pastoris .... Shepherd's-purse

Carex arenaria .... Sand Sedge
Carex bigelowii .... Stiff Sedge
Carex curta .... White Sedge
Carex dioica .... Dioecious Sedge
Carex flacca .... Glaucous Sedge
Carex nigra .... Common Sedge
Carex panicea .... Carnation Sedge
Carex paniculata .... Greater Tussock-sedge
Carex riparia .... Greater Pond-sedge
Carex rostrata .... Bottle Sedge
Carex saxatilis .... Russet Sedge
Carex vesicaria .... Bladder-sedge
Carex viridula ssp. oedocarpa .... Common Yellow Sedge
Carlina vulgaris .... Carline Thistle
Centaurea nigra .... Common Knapweed
Cerastium diffusum ssp. diffusum
  [=Cerastium glomeratum] .... Sticky Mouse-ear
Ceratophyllum demersum .... Rigid Hornwort
Ceratophyllum submersum .... Soft Hornwort
Chara spp. .... stoneworts
Chrysanthemum segetum .... Corn Marigold
Cirsium dissectum .... Meadow Thistle
Cirsium palustre .... Marsh Thistle
Cladium mariscus .... Saw Sedge
Cladonia arbuscula .... a lichen
Cornicularia aculeata [=Cetraria aculeata] .... a lichen
Corylus avellana .... Hazel
Corynephorus canescens .... Grey Hair-grass
Crataegus monogyna .... Hawthorn
Cratoneuron commutatum
  [=Palustriella commutata] .... Curled Hook-moss
Crepis paludosa .... Marsh Hawk's-beard
Crithmum maritimum .... Rock Samphire
Cryptogramma crispa .... Parsley Fern
Cynosurus cristatus .... Crested Dog's-tail
Cystopteris fragilis .... Brittle Bladder-fern

Daucus carota ssp. gummifer .... Sea Carrot
Deschampsia cespitosa .... Tufted Hair-grass
Deschampsia flexuosa [=Avenella flexuosa] .. Wavy Hair-grass
Dicranum majus .... Greater Fork-moss
Dryas octopetala .... Mountain Avens

Eleocharis palustris .... Common Spike-rush
Eleocharis uniglumis .... Slender Spike-rush
Elodea canadensis .... Canadian Waterweed
Elymus farctus ssp. borealis-atlanticus
  [=Elymus junceiformis] .... Sand Couch
Elymus pycnanthus [=Elytrigia athericus] .... Sea Couch
Elymus repens .... Common Couch
Empetrum nigrum .... Crowberry
Erica ciliaris .... Dorset Heath
Erica cinerea .... Bell Heather
Erica tetralix .... Cross-leaved Heath
Erica vagans .... Cornish Heath
Eriophorum angustifolium .... Common Cottongrass
Eriophorum vaginatum .... Hare's-tail Cottongrass
Eupatorium cannabinum .... Hemp-agrimony

Fagus sylvatica .... Beech
Festuca ovina .... Sheep's-fescue

Festuca rubra	Red Fescue
Filipendula ulmaria	Meadowsweet
Frankenia laevis	Sea-heath
Fraxinus excelsior	Ash
Galium aparine	Cleavers
Galium palustre	Marsh Bedstraw
Galium saxatile	Heath Bedstraw
Galium sterneri	Limestone Bedstraw
Galium verum	Lady's Bedstraw
Geranium sanguineum	Bloody Crane's-bill
Geranium sylvaticum	Wood Crane's-bill
Geum rivale	Water Avens
Glaucium flavum	Yellow Horned-poppy
Glyceria maxima	Reed Sweet-grass
Gymnocarpium robertianum	Limestone Fern
Halimione [=Atriplex] portulacoides	Sea-purslane
Hedera helix	Ivy
Hieracium pilosella	
[=*Pilosella officinarum*]	Mouse-ear-hawkweed
Hippophae rhamnoides	Sea-buckthorn
Holcus lanatus	Yorkshire-fog
Honckenya peploides	Sea Sandwort
Hyacinthoides non-scripta	Bluebell
Hydrocharis morsus-ranae	Frogbit
Hylocomium splendens	Glittering Wood-moss
Hypericum elodes	Marsh St. John's-wort
Ilex aquifolium	Holly
Inula crithmoides	
[=*Limbarda crithmoides*]	Golden-samphire
Iris pseudacorus	Yellow Iris
Isoetes lacustris	Quillwort
Isoetes setacea [= *Isoetes echinospora*]	Spring Quillwort
Juncus acutiflorus	Sharp-flowered Rush
Juncus bulbosus	Bulbous Rush
Juncus effusus	Soft Rush
Juncus maritimus	Sea Rush
Juncus subnodulosus	Blunt-flowered Rush
Juncus trifidus	Three-leaved Rush
Juniperus communis ssp. *communis*	Common Juniper
Juniperus communis ssp. *nana*	Dwarf Juniper
Kiaeria starkei	Starke's Forkmoss
Koenigia islandica	Iceland-purslane
Lemna gibba	Fat Duckweed
Lemna minor	Common Duckweed
Leymus arenarius	Lyme-grass
Ligusticum scoticum	Scots Lovage
Limonium binervosum	Rock Sea-lavender
Littorella uniflora	Shoreweed
Lobelia dortmanna	Water Lobelia
Lolium perenne	Perennial Rye-grass
Luzula sylvatica	Great Wood-rush
Lysimachia nemorum	Yellow Pimpernel
Matricaria maritima	
[=*Tripleurospermum maritimum*]	Sea Mayweed

Matricaria perforata	
[=*Tripleurospermum inodorum*]	Scentless Mayweed
Mercurialis perennis	Dog's Mercury
Minuartia verna	Spring Sandwort
Molinia caerulea	Purple Moor-grass
Montia fontana	Blinks
Myriophyllum alterniflorum	Alternate Water-milfoil
Myriophyllum spicatum	Spiked Water-milfoil
Nardus stricta	Mat-grass
Narthecium ossifragum	Bog Asphodel
Nuphar lutea	Yellow Water-lily
Nymphaea alba	White Water-lily
Origanum vulgare	Wild Marjoram
Oxalis acetosella	Wood-sorrel
Papaver rhoeas	Common Poppy
Peucedanum palustre	Milk-parsley
Phalaris arundinacea	Reed Canary-grass
Philonotis fontana	Fountain Apple-moss
Phragmites australis	Common Reed
Pinguicula lusitanica	Pale Butterwort
Pinus sylvestris	Scots Pine
Plantago spp.	plantains
Poa annua	Annual Meadow-grass
Pohlia wahlenbergii var. *glacialis*	Mountain Thread-moss
Polygonum amphibium	
[=*Persicaria amphibia*]	Amphibious Bistort
Polytrichum alpinum	
[=*Polytrichastrum alpinum*]	Alpine Haircap
Polytrichum sexangulare	Northern Haircap
Potamogeton natans	Broad-leaved Pondweed
Potamogeton pectinatus	
[=*Stuckenia pectinata*]	Fennel Pondweed
Potamogeton perfoliatus	Perfoliate Pondweed
Potamogeton polygonifolius	Bog Pondweed
Potentilla anserina	Silverweed
Potentilla erecta	Tormentil
Prunus spinosa	Blackthorn
Pteridium aquilinum	Bracken
Puccinellia distans	Reflexed Saltmarsh-grass
Puccinellia maritima	Common Saltmarsh-grass
Quercus spp.	oaks
Quercus petraea	Sessile Oak
Quercus robur	Pedunculate Oak
Racomitrium heterostichum	Bristly Fringe-moss
Racomitrium lanuginosum	Woolly Fringe-moss
Ranunculus aquatilis	Common Water-crowfoot
Ranunculus fluitans	River Water-crowfoot
Ranunculus omiophyllus	Round-leaved Crowfoot
Ranunculus peltatus	Pond Water-crowfoot
Ranunculus penicillatus	
ssp. *pseudofluitans*	Stream Water-crowfoot
Rhodiola rosea	Roseroot
Rubus chamaemorus	Cloudberry
Rubus fruticosus	Bramble
Rumex acetosa	Common Sorrel
Rumex acetosella	Sheep's Sorrel

Rumex crispus .... Curled Dock

Sagina maritima .... Sea Pearlwort
Sagina nodosa .... Knotted Pearlwort
Salicornia .... glassworts
Salix cinerea .... Grey Willow
Salix herbacea .... Dwarf Willow
Salix lapponum .... Downy Willow
Salix pentandra .... Bay Willow
Salix repens .... Creeping Willow
Salix repens ssp. argentea [=Salix repens] .... Creeping Willow
Sanguisorba officinalis .... Great Burnet
Saxifraga aizoides .... Yellow Saxifrage
Saxifraga stellaris .... Starry Saxifrage
Scabiosa columbaria .... Small Scabious
Schoenus nigricans .... Black Bog-rush
Scilla verna .... Spring Squill
Scirpus cespitosus [=Trichophorum cespitosum] .... Deergrass
Scirpus lacustris ssp. lacustris
     [=Schoenoplectus lacustris] .... Common Club-rush
Scirpus lacustris ssp. tabernaemontani
     [=Schoenoplectus tabernaemontani] .... Grey Club-rush
Scirpus maritimus
     [=Bolboschoenus maritimus] .... Sea Club-rush
Senecio vulgaris .... Groundsel
Sesleria albicans [=Sesleria caerulea] .... Blue Moor-grass
Sibbaldia procumbens .... Sibbaldia
Silene acaulis .... Moss Campion
Sorbus aucuparia .... Rowan
Sparganium erectum .... Branched Bur-reed
Spartina .... cord-grasses
Spartina alterniflora .... Smooth Cord-grass
Spartina anglica .... Common Cord-grass
Spartina maritima .... Small Cord-grass
Spergula arvensis .... Corn Spurrey
Spergularia marina .... Lesser Sea-spurrey

Spergularia rupicola .... Rock Sea-spurrey
Sphagnum auriculatum
     [=Sphagnum denticulatum] .... Cow-horn Bog-moss
Sphagnum capillifolium .... Red Bog-moss
Sphagnum compactum .... Compact Bog-moss
Sphagnum cuspidatum .... Feathery Bog-moss
Sphagnum denticulatum .... Cow-horn Bog-moss
Sphagnum fallax .... Flat-topped Bog-moss
Sphagnum papillosum .... Papillose Bog-moss
Sphagnum russowii .... Russow's Bog-moss
Sphagnum warnstorfii .... Warnstorf's Bog-moss
Spirodela polyrhiza .... Greater Duckweed
Stachys arvensis .... Field Woundwort
Stellaria media .... Common Chickweed
Stratiotes aloides .... Water-soldier
Suaeda maritima .... Annual Sea-blite
Suaeda vera .... Shrubby Sea-blite

Taxus baccata .... Yew
Thymus praecox [=Thymus drucei] .... Wild Thyme
Thymus pulegioides .... Large Thyme
Triglochin maritima
     [=Triglochin maritimum] .... Sea Arrowgrass
Typha angustifolia .... Lesser Bulrush
Typha latifolia .... Bulrush

Ulex europaeus .... Gorse
Ulex gallii .... Western Gorse
Ulex minor .... Dwarf Gorse
Urtica dioica .... Common Nettle

Vaccinium myrtillus .... Bilberry
Veronica persica .... Common Field-speedwell
Veronica polita .... Grey Field-speedwell
Viola arvensis .... Field Pansy
Viola riviniana .... Common Dog-violet

COASTAL HABITATS 1/2

Coastal Vegetated Shingle — page 342

UKHab	s3b Coastal vegetated shingle
P1	H3 Shingle above high tide mark
Ann. I	H1210 Annual vegetation of drift lines
	H1220 Perennial vegetation of stony banks
UKPH	Coastal vegetated shingle
NVC	SD1 *Rumex crispus – Glaucium flavum* shingle community
	SD2 *Honckenya peploides – Cakile maritima* strandline community
	SD3 *Matricaria maritima – Galium aparine* strandline community
	MC6 *Atriplex prostrata – Beta vulgaris* ssp. *maritima* sea-bird cliff community
GHI	CB1 Shingle and gravel banks
	LS1 Shingle and gravel shores
IVC	ST1 Spear-leaved Orache – Sea Sandwort strandline group

Hard Cliff and Cliff Slope — page 358

UKHab	s2a5 Vegetated sea cliffs
P1	**H81 Maritime cliff and slope – hard cliff**
	H83 Maritime cliff and slope – crevice/ledge vegetation
	H84 Maritime cliff and slope – coastal grassland
	H85 Maritime cliff and slope – coastal heathland
Ann. I	H1230 Vegetated sea cliffs of the Atlantic and Baltic coasts
UKPH	Maritime cliff and slope
NVC	MC1 *Crithmum maritimum – Spergularia rupicola* maritime rock-crevice community
	MC2 *Armeria maritima – Ligusticum scoticum* maritime rock-crevice community
	MC3 *Rhodiola rosea – Armeria maritima* maritime cliff-ledge community
	MC4 *Brassica oleracea* maritime cliff-ledge community
	MC5 *Armeria maritima – Cerastium diffusum* ssp. *diffusum* maritime therophyte community
	MC6 *Atriplex prostrata – Beta vulgaris* ssp. *maritima* sea-bird cliff community
	MC7 *Stellaria media – Rumex acetosa* sea-bird cliff community
	MC8 *Festuca rubra – Armeria maritima* maritime grassland
	MC9 *Festuca rubra – Holcus lanatus* maritime grassland
	MC10 *Festuca rubra – Plantago* spp. *maritime* grassland
	MC11 *Festuca rubra – Daucus carota* ssp. *gummifer* maritime grassland
	MC12 *Festuca rubra – Hyacinthoides non-scripta* maritime bluebell community

Hard Cliff and Slope (contd.) — page 358

NVC (contd.)	H7 *Calluna vulgaris – Scilla verna* heath
	H8 *Calluna vulgaris – Ulex gallii* heath
	+ overlap with scrub (W21–25) communities
GHI	CS1 Rocky sea cliffs
	CS2 Sea stacks and islets
IVC	RH4A Sea Spleenwort crevice community
	GL3F Red Fescue–Bird's-foot-trefoil grassland

Machair — page 338

UKHab	s3a7 (26) Dune grassland (machair)
P1	H6 Sand dune
Ann. I	H21A0 Machairs
UKPH	Machair
NVC	SD8 *Festuca rubra – Galium verum* fixed dune grassland
GHI	CD6 Machair
IVC	DU2C Red Fescue – Ribwort Plantain – Sand Sedge duneland
	DU2D Red Fescue – Wild Thyme duneland
	DU3C Creeping Bent – Red Fescue – Sand Sedge duneland
	DU3D Red Fescue – Daisy duneland

Mudflat and Sandflat — page 326

UKHab	t2 Intertidal mudflats and sandflats
P1	H11 Intertidal – mud/sand
Ann. I	H1130 Estuaries
	H1140 Mudflats and sandflats not covered by seawater at low tide
	H1160 Large shallow inlets and bays
UKPH	Intertidal mudflats
NVC	—
GHI	LS2 Sand shores
	LS3 Muddy sand shores
	LS4 Mud shores
	MW2 Sea inlets and bays
	CW2 Tidal rivers
IVC	—

UKHab	t1 Littoral rock
P1	H13 Intertidal – boulders/rocks
Ann. I	H8330 Submerged or partially submerged sea caves
H1170 Reefs
UKPH	Intertidal underboulder communities
Intertidal chalk
NVC	—
GHI	LR1 Exposed rocky shores
LR2 Moderately exposed rocky shores
LR3 Sheltered rocky shores
LR5 Sea caves
IVC	—

Saline Lagoon	page 348
UKHab	t2g Saline lagoons
P1	G16 Standing water – brackish
Ann. I	H1150 Coastal lagoons
UKPH	Saline lagoons
NVC	SM19 Blysmus rufus salt-marsh community
SM20 Eleocharis uniglumis salt-marsh community
GHI	CW1 Lagoons and saline lakes
IVC	SW1A Beaked/Spiral Tasselweed lagoon community

Saltmarsh	page 329
UKHab	t2a Coastal saltmarsh
P1	H2 Saltmarsh
Ann. I	H1310 Salicornia and other annuals colonizing mud and sand
H1320 Spartina swards (Spartinion maritimae)
H1330 Atlantic salt meadows (Glauco-Puccinellietalia maritimae)
H1420 Mediterranean and thermo-Atlantic halophilous scrubs (Sarcocornetea fruticosi)
UKPH	Coastal saltmarsh
NVC	SM4 Spartina maritima salt-marsh community
SM5 Spartina alterniflora salt-marsh community
SM6 Spartina anglica salt-marsh community
SM7 Arthrocnemum perenne stands
SM8 Annual Salicornia salt-marsh community
SM9 Suaeda maritima salt-marsh community
SM10 Transitional low marsh vegetation with Puccinellia maritima, annual Salicornia species and Suaeda maritima
SM11 Aster tripolium var. discoideus salt-marsh community
SM12 Rayed Aster tripolium stands
SM13 Puccinellia maritima salt-marsh community
SM14 Halimione portulacoides salt-marsh community
SM15 Juncus maritimus – Triglochin maritima salt-marsh community

Saltmarsh (contd.)	page 329
NVC (contd.)	SM16 Festuca rubra salt-marsh community
SM17 Artemisia maritima salt-marsh community
SM18 Juncus maritimus salt-marsh community
SM19 Blysmus rufus salt-marsh community
SM20 Eleocharis uniglumis salt-marsh community
SM21 Suaeda vera – Limonium binervosum salt-marsh community
SM22 Halimione portulacoides – Frankenia laevis salt-marsh community
SM23 Spergularia marina – Puccinellia distans salt-marsh community
SM24 Elymus pycnanthus salt-marsh community
SM25 Suaeda vera drift-line community
SM26 Inula crithmoides on salt-marshes
SM27 Ephemeral salt-marsh vegetation with Sagina maritima
SM28 Elymus repens salt-marsh community
GHI	CM1 Lower salt marsh
CM2 Upper salt marsh
IVC	SM1 Glasswort – Cord-grass group
SM2 Common Saltmarsh-grass – Greater Sea-spurrey group
SM3 Sea Plantain – Thrift saltmarsh group
SM4 Red Fescue – Sea Wormwood group
SM5 Sea Rush – Parsley Water-dropwort group
SM6 Creeping Bent - Saltmarsh Rush

Sand Dune	page 332
UKHab	s3a (+ 28) Coastal sand dunes (+ Dunes with creeping willow)
P1	H6 Sand dune
Ann. I	H2110 Embryonic shifting dunes
H2120 Shifting dunes along the shoreline with Ammophila arenaria (`white dunes`)
H2130 Fixed dunes with herbaceous vegetation (`grey dunes`)
H2140 Decalcified fixed dunes with Empetrum nigrum
H2150 Atlantic decalcified fixed dunes (Calluno-Ulicetea)
H2160 Dunes with Hippophae rhamnoides
H2170 Dunes with Salix repens ssp. argentea (Salicion arenariae)
H2190 Humid dune slacks
H2250 Coastal dunes with Juniperus spp.
UKPH	Coastal sand dunes

387

COASTAL HABITATS 2/2 *page 316*

Sand Dune (contd.)		*page 332*
NVC	SD2 *Honckenya peploides – Cakile maritima* strandline community	
	SD4 *Elymus farctus* ssp. *boreali-atlanticus* foredune community	
	SD5 *Leymus arenarius* mobile dune community	
	SD6 *Ammophila arenaria* mobile dune community	
	SD7 *Ammophila arenaria – Festuca rubra* semi-fixed dune community	
	SD8 *Festuca rubra – Galium verum* fixed dune grassland	
	SD9 *Ammophila arenaria – Arrhenatherum elatius* dune grassland	
	SD11 *Carex arenaria – Cornicularia aculeata* dune community	
	SD12 *Carex arenaria – Festuca ovina – Agrostis capillaris* dune grassland	
	SD13 *Sagina nodosa – Bryum pseudotriquetrum* dune-slack community	
	SD14 *Salix repens – Campylium stellatum* dune-slack community	
	SD15 *Salix repens – Calliergon cuspidatum* dune-slack community	
	SD16 *Salix repens – Holcus lanatus* dune-slack community	
	SD17 *Potentilla anserina – Carex nigra* dune-slack community	
GHI	CD1 Embryonic dunes	
	CD2 Marram dunes	
	CD3 Fixed dunes	
	CD5 Dune slacks	
IVC	**DU1 Sand Couch – Marram group**	
	DU2 Red Fescue – Lady's Bedstraw group	
	DU3 Creeping Bent – Sand Sedge group dunelands	
	FE3A Common Sedge – Lesser Spearwort fen	
	FE3B Common Sedge – Silverweed fen	
	FE3C Common Spike-rush –Creeping Bent marsh/ fen	
	FE3D Common Sedge – Pointed Spear-moss fen	

Soft Cliff		*page 355*
UKHab	**s2a6 Soft rock sea cliffs**	
P1	**H82 Maritime cliff and slope – soft cliff**	
Ann. I	H1230 Vegetated sea cliffs of the Atlantic and Baltic coasts	
UKPH	Maritime cliff and slope	
NVC	*Much of the vegetation does not fit within the NVC, although a range of grassland, scrub and wetland communities may be present*	
GHI	CS3 Sedimentary sea cliffs	
IVC	Much of the vegetation does not fit within the IVC, although a range of grassland, scrub and wetland communities may be present	

FRESHWATERS 1/2

STANDING WATER

Nutrient-rich (Eutrophic) Lake		*page 282*
UKHab	**r1a Eutrophic standing water**	
	f2d Aquatic marginal vegetation	
P1	**F2 Marginal and inundation**	
	G11 Standing water – eutrophic	
Ann. I	H3150 Natural eutrophic lakes with *Magnopotamion* or *Hydrocharition*-type vegetation	
UKPH	Eutrophic standing waters	
NVC	A1 *Lemna gibba* community	
	A2 *Lemna minor* community	
	A3 *Spirodela polyrhiza – Hydrocharis morsus-ranae* community	
	A5 *Ceratophyllum demersum* community	
	A6 *Ceratophyllum submersum* community	
	A8 *Nuphar lutea* community	
	A11 *Potamogeton pectinatus – Myriophyllum spicatum* community	
	A12 *Potamogeton pectinatus* community	
	A15 *Elodea canadensis* community	
	A19 *Ranunculus aquatilis* community	
	A20 *Ranunculus peltatus* community	
	S3 *Carex paniculata* swamp	
	S4 *Phragmites australis* swamp and reed-beds	
	S5 *Glyceria maxima* swamp	
	S6 *Carex riparia* swamp	
	S8 *Scirpus lacustris* ssp. *lacustris* swamp	
	S12 *Typha latifolia* swamp	
	S13 *Typha angustifolia* swamp	
	S14 *Sparganium erectum* swamp	
	S20 *Scirpus lacustris* ssp. *tabernaemontani* swamp	
	S21 *Scirpus maritimus* swamp	
	S28 *Phalaris arundinacea* tall-herb fen	
GHI	FL5 Eutrophic lakes	
IVC	**FW2F Fennel Pondweed – Spiked Water-milfoil aquatic community**	
	FW3I Grey Club-rush swamp	

Other types of Lake		*page 294*
UKHab	**r1b5 (142) Calcium-rich nutrient-poor lakes lochs and pools**	
	r1 (+ 138) Mesotrophic lakes (+ saline influence)	
	f2d Aquatic marginal vegetation	
	r1c6 Nutrient-poor shallow waters with aquatic vegetation on sand	
P1	**F2 Marginal and inundation**	
	G12 Standing water – mesotrophic	
	G15 Standing water – marl	
	G16 Standing water – brackish	
Ann. I	H3110 Oligotrophic waters containing very few minerals of sandy plains (*Littorelletalia uniflorae*)	
	H3140 Hard oligo-mesotrophic waters with benthic vegetation of *Chara* spp.	
UKPH	Mesotrophic lakes	

Other types of Lake (contd.)
page 294

NVC	A2 *Lemna minor* community A3 *Spirodela polyrhiza – Hydrocharis morsus-ranae* community A4 *Hydrocharis morsus-ranae – Stratiotes aloides* community A8 *Nuphar lutea* community A9 *Potamogeton natans* community A10 *Polygonum amphibium* community A11 *Potamogeton pectinatus – Myriophyllum spicatum* community A13 *Potamogeton perfoliatus – Myriophyllum alterniflorum* community A19 *Ranunculus aquatilis* community A20 *Ranunculus peltatus* community A22 *Littorella uniflora – Lobelia dortmanna* community A23 *Isoetes lacustris/setacea* community
GHI	FL3 Limestone/marl lakes FL4 Mesotrophic lakes
IVC	FFW1A Shoreweed – Lesser Spearwort aquatic community FW1B Pipewort – Water Lobelia aquatic community FW1C Bulbous Rush aquatic community FW2A Greater Water-moss – Alternate Water-milfoil aquatic community FW3A White Water-lily – Common Reed aquatic community FW3D Common Club-rush swamp FW3J Broad-leaved Pondweed – Water Horsetail aquatic community FE2A Water Horsetail – Bogbean mire

Peat-stained (Dystrophic) Waters
page 288

UKHab	r1c6 Oligotrophic and dystrophic lakes
P1	G14 Standing water – dystrophic
Ann. I	3160 Natural dystrophic lakes and ponds
UKPH	Oligotrophic and Dystrophic Lakes
NVC	A24 *Juncus bulbosus* community, often in association with various mire communities (M1–3, M15–21)
GHI	FL1 Dystrophic lakes
IVC	FW1C Bulbous Rush aquatic community FE2B Bog-sedge – Bogbean mire

Pond, Ditch, Canal
pages 298–304

UKHab	r1e Canals r1 (361) Standing open water or canals (natural lake or pond) f2d Aquatic marginal vegetation
P1	G11 Standing water – eutrophic G12 Standing water – mesotrophic G13 Standing water – oligotrophic G14 Standing water – dystrophic F2 Marginal and inundation

Pond, Ditch, Canal (contd.)
pages 298–304

Ann. I	H3170 Mediterranean temporary ponds H3130 Oligotrophic to mesotrophic standing waters with vegetation of the *Littorelletea uniflorae* and/or of the *Isoeto-Nanojuncetea* H3140 Hard oligo-mesotrophic waters with benthic vegetation of *Chara* spp. H3150 Natural eutrophic lakes with *Magnopotamion* or *Hydrocharition*-type vegetation H3160 Natural dystrophic lakes and ponds
UKPH	Ponds
NVC	A wide variety of aquatic (A1–12, A15, A16, A20, A21), swamp and fen communities plus vegetation of open habitats (OV28–OV35)
GHI	FL8 Other artificial lakes and ponds FW3 Canals FW4 Drainage ditches
IVC	—

Turlough and Fluctuating Mere
page 291

UKHab	FW2A Greater Water-moss – Alternate Water-milfoil aquatic community FW3C Bottle Sedge swamp/fen
P1	F2 Marginal and inundation G11 Standing water – eutrophic G12 Standing water – mesotrophic
Ann. I	H3180 Turloughs
UKPH	Aquifer fed naturally fluctuating water bodies
NVC	S11 *Carex vesicaria* swamp S19 *Eleocharis palustris* swamp W3 *Salix pentandra – Carex rostrata* woodland
GHI	FL6 Turloughs
IVC	FW2A Greater Water-moss – Alternate Water-milfoil aquatic community FW3C Bottle Sedge swamp/fen FW3J Broad-leaved Pondweed – Water Horsetail aquatic community FE3A Common Sedge – Lesser Spearwort fen FE3B Common Sedge – Silverweed fen FE3C Common Spike-rush – Creeping Bent marsh/fen FW3J Broad-leaved Pondweed –Water Horsetail aquatic community

FRESHWATERS 2/2 *page 270*

Upland Lake, Loch and Tarn	*page 285*
UKHab	r1c5 Clear-water lakes or lochs with aquatic vegetation
P1	F2 Marginal and inundation
	G13 Standing water – oligotrophic
Ann. I	H3130 Oligotrophic to mesotrophic standing waters with vegetation of the Littorelletea uniflorae and/or of the Isoëto-Nanojuncetea
UKPH	Oligotrophic and Dystrophic Lakes
NVC	A22 *Littorella uniflora* – *Lobelia dortmanna* community
	A23 *Isoetes lacustris/setacea* community
GHI	FL2 Acid oligotrophic lakes
IVC	FW1A Shoreweed – Lesser Spearwort aquatic community
	FW1B Pipewort – Water Lobelia aquatic community
	FW1C Bulbous Rush aquatic community

RUNNING WATER

Chalk River and Stream	*page 313*
UKHab	r2a5 (144) Rivers with floating vegetation (chalk rivers)
	f2d Aquatic marginal vegetation
P1	F2 Marginal and inundatation]
	G22 Running Water – mesotrophic
Ann. I	H3260 Water courses of plain to montane levels with the *Ranunculion fluitantis* and *Callitricho-Batrachion* vegetation
UKPH	Rivers
NVC	A16 *Callitriche stagnalis* community
	A17 *Ranunculus penicillatus* ssp. *pseudofluitans* community
	A19 *Ranunculus aquatilis* community
	A20 *Ranunculus peltatus* community
GHI	—
IVC	—

Fast-flowing River and Stream	*page 307*
UKHab	r2a5 Rivers with floating vegetation
	f2d Aquatic marginal vegetation
P1	F2 Marginal and inundation
	G23 Running water – oligotrophic
Ann. I	H3260 Water courses of plain to montane levels with the *Ranunculion fluitantis* and *Callitricho-Batrachion* vegetation
UKPH	Rivers

Fast-flowing River and Stream (contd.)	*page 307*
NVC	A9 *Potamogeton natans* community
	A14 *Myriophyllum alterniflorum* community
	A17 *Ranunculus penicillatus* ssp. *pseudofluitans* community
	A18 *Ranunculus fluitans* community
GHI	FW1 Eroding/upland rivers
IVC	FW2A Greater Water-moss – Alternate Water-milfoil aquatic community
	FW2B Long-beaked Water Feather-moss – St Winifred's Moss aquatic community
	FW2C Stream Water-crowfoot – Greater Water-moss aquatic community
	FW2D Fool's-watercress – Stream Water-crowfoot aquatic community
	FW2E Fool's-water-cress – Watercress aquatic community

Sluggish River and Stream	*page 310*
UKHab	r2a6 Other priority habitat rivers
P1	F2 Marginal and inundation
	G21 Running water – eutrophic
Ann. I	H3270 Rivers with muddy banks with *Chenopodion rubri* and *Bidention* vegetation (Ireland)
UKPH	Rivers
NVC	A5 *Ceratophyllum dermersum* community
	A7 *Nymphaea alba* community
	A8 *Nuphar lutea* community
	A9 *Potamogeton natans* community
	A10 *Polygonum amphibium* community
	A11 *Potamogeton pectinatus* – *Myriophyllum spicatum* community
	A12 *Potamogeton pectinatus* community
	A15 *Elodea canadensis* community
	A16 *Callitriche stagnalis* community
	+ many swamp (S4–9, S11–14, S16–19, S22) and open (OV28–32) communities
GHI	FW2 Depositing/lowland rivers
IVC	FW2C Stream Water-crowfoot – Greater Water-moss aquatic community
	FW2D Fool's-watercress – Stream Water-crowfoot aquatic community
	FW2F Fennel Pondweed – Spiked Water-milfoil aquatic community
	FW2G Common Club-rush – Branched Bur-reed swamp

Calaminarian Grassland	page 195
UKHab	s1c Calaminarian grasslands
P1	**I12 Scree**
	I22 Spoil
Ann. I	H6130 Calaminarian grasslands of the *Violetalia calaminariae*
UKPH	Calaminarian grassland
NVC	OV37 *Festuca ovina – Minuartia verna* community
GHI	GS1 Dry calcareous and neutral grassland
IVC	RH3A Greater Copperwort – Heath Threadwort mine-spoil community
	RH3B Sea Campion – Eyebrights mine-spoil community

Coastal and Floodplain Grazing Marsh	page 177
UKHab	g3c (25) Other neutral grassland (coastal and floodplain grazing marsh)
P1	**B5 Marsh/marshy grassland**
Ann. I	—
UKPH	Coastal and floodplain grazing marsh
NVC	MG6 *Lolium perenne – Cynosurus cristatus* grassland
	MG10 *Holcus lanatus – Juncus effusus* rush-pasture
	MG11 *Festuca rubra–Agrostis stolonifera – Potentilla anserina* grassland
	MG13 *Agrostis stolonifera – Alopecurus geniculatus* grassland
	+ overlaps with various other grassland (MG4, 7–9, 12) and swamp (S5–7) and fen (M22–25) communities
GHI	GS4 Wet grassland
	GA1 Improved agricultural grassland
IVC	GL2A Creeping Bent – Creeping Buttercup marsh-grassland
	GL2B Soft Rush – Yorkshire-fog grassland
	GL2C Yorkshire-fog – Perennial Rye-grass grassland

Lowland Calcareous Grassland	page 162
UKHab	g2a Lowland calcareous grassland
P1	**B3 Calcareous grassland**
Ann. I	H6210 Semi-natural dry grasslands and scrubland facies: on calcareous substrates (*Festuco-Brometalia*)
UKPH	Lowland calcareous grassland
NVC	CG1 *Festuca ovina – Carlina vulgaris* grassland
	CG2 *Festuca ovina – Avenula pratensis* grassland
	CG3 *Bromus erectus* grassland
	CG4 *Brachypodium pinnatum* grassland
	CG5 *Bromus erectus – Brachypodium pinnatum* grassland
	CG6 *Avenula pubescens* grassland
	CG7 *Festuca ovina – Hieracium pilosella – Thymus praecox/pulegioides* grassland
	CG8 *Sesleria albicans – Scabiosa columbaria* grassland
	CG9 *Sesleria albicans – Galium sterneri* grassland

Lowland Calcareous Grassland (contd.)	page 162
GHI	GS1 Dry calcareous and neutral grassland
IVC	GL3A Quaking-grass – Wild Thyme grassland
	GL3C Red Fescue – Ribwort Plantain grassland

Lowland Dry Acid Grassland	page 168
UKHab	g1a Lowland dry acid grassland
P1	**B1 Acid grassland**
Ann. I	H2330 Inland dunes with open *Corynephorus* and *Agrostis* grasslands
UKPH	Lowland dry acid grassland
NVC	U1 *Festuca ovina – Agrostis capillaris – Rumex acetosella* grassland
	U2 *Deschampsia flexuosa* grassland
	U3 *Agrostis curtisii* grassland
	U4 *Festuca ovina – Agrostis capillaris – Galium saxatile* grassland
	SD10 *Carex arenaria* dune community
	SD11 *Carex arenaria – Cornicularia aculeata* dune community
GHI	GS3 Dry-humid acid grassland
IVC	GL4A Common Bent – White Clover grassland

Lowland Meadow and Pasture	page 171
UKHab	g3a Lowland meadow
P1	**B2 Neutral grassland**
Ann. I	H6510 Lowland hay meadows (*Alopecurus pratensis, Sanguisorba officinalis*)
UKPH	Lowland Meadows
NVC	MG4 *Alopecurus pratensis – Sanguisorba officinalis* grassland
	MG5 *Cynosurus cristatus – Centaurea nigra* grassland
	MG8 *Cynosurus cristatus – Caltha palustris* grassland
GHI	GS2 Dry meadows and grassy verges
IVC	GL3C Red Fescue – Ribwort Plantain grassland
	GL3D Crested Dog's-tail – Red Clover grassland
	GL3E Red Fescue – Yellow Rattle grassland

Northern Hay Meadow	page 186
UKHab	g3b5 Mountain hay meadows
P1	**B2 Neutral grassland**
Ann. I	H6520 Mountain hay meadows
UKPH	Upland hay meadow
NVC	MG3 *Anthoxanthum odoratum – Geranium sylvaticum* grassland
GHI	—
IVC	—

Purple Moor-grass and Rush Pasture	*page 174*
UKHab	f2b Purple moor grass and rush pastures
P1	**B5 Marsh/marshy grassland**
Ann. I	H6410 Purple Moor-grass meadows
UKPH	Purple Moor-grass and rush pasture
NVC	M22 *Juncus subnodulosus – Cirsium palustre* fen-meadow M23 *Juncus effusus/acutiflorus – Galium palustre* rush-pasture M24 *Molinia caerulea – Cirsium dissectum* fen-meadow M25 *Molinia caerulea – Potentilla erecta* mire M26 *Molinia caerulea – Crepis paludosa* mire
GHI	GS4 Wet grassland
IVC	**GL1A Sharp-flowered Rush – Yorkshire-fog grassland** **GL1B Creeping Bent – Meadowsweet marsh-grassland** **GL1C Purple Moor-grass – Devil's-bit Scabious grassland** **GL1D Purple Moor-grass – Tormentil – Creeping Bent grassland** **GL1E Sharp-flowered Rush – Springy Turf-moss grassland** **GL4D Velvet/Brown Bent – Springy Turf-moss grassland**

Upland Acid Grassland	*page 192*
UKHab	g1b Upland acid grassland
P1	**B1 Acid grassland**
Ann. I	—
UKPH	—
NVC	U2 *Deschampsia flexuosa* grassland U3 *Agrostis curtisii* grassland U4 *Festuca ovina – Agrostis capillaris – Galium saxatile* grassland U5 *Nardus stricta – Galium saxatile* grassland M25 *Molina caerulea – Potentilla erecta* mire
GHI	GS3 Dry-humid acid grassland
IVC	**GL4A Common Bent – White Clover grassland** **GL4B Mat-grass – Tormentil grassland** **GL4C Common Bent – Tormentil grassland**

Upland Calcareous Grassland	*page 183*
UKHab	g2b Upland calcareous grassland
P1	**B3 Calcareous grassland**
Ann. I	H6210 Semi-natural dry grasslands and scrubland facies: on calcareous substrates (*Festuco-Brometalia*) H6230 Species-rich *Nardus* grassland, on siliceous substrates in mountain areas (and submontane areas in continental Europe)
UKPH	Upland calcareous grassland
NVC	CG9 *Sesleria albicans – Galium sterneri* grassland CG10 *Festuca ovina – Agrostis capillaris – Thymus praecox* grassland CG11 *Festuca ovina – Agrostis capillaris – Alchemilla alpina* grassland CG13 *Dryas octopetala – Carex flacca* heath U4 *Festuca ovina – Agrostis capillaris – Galium saxatile* grassland U5c *Nardus stricta – Galium saxatile* grassland
GHI	GS1 Dry calcareous and neutral grassland GS3 Dry-humid acid grassland
IVC	**GL3A Quaking-grass – Wild Thyme grassland**

Upland Rush Pasture	*page 189*
UKHab	g3c8 (14) Holcus-Juncus neutral grassland (scattered rushes)
P1	**B5 Marsh/marshy grassland**
Ann. I	—
UKPH	—
NVC	MG10 *Holcus lanatus – Juncus effusus* grassland M23 *Juncus effusus/acutiflorus – Galium palustre* rush-pasture
GHI	GS4 Wet grassland
IVC	**GL4D Velvet/Brown Bent – Springy Turf-moss grassland**

HEATHLANDS

Lowland Dry Heath		page 130
UKHab	h1a5 Dry heaths; lowland h1a6 Dry coastal heaths with Cornish heath	
P1	D1 Dry dwarf shrub heath	
	D3 Lichen/bryophyte heath	
	H66 Sand-dune – dune heath	
	H85 Maritime cliff and slope – coastal heathland	
Ann. I	H4030 European dry heaths	
UKPH	Lowland heathland	
NVC	H1 *Calluna vulgaris – Festuca ovina* heath H2 *Calluna vulgaris – Ulex minor* heath	
	H3 *Ulex minor – Agrostis curtisii* heath H4 *Ulex gallii – Agrostis curtisii* heath	
	H7 *Calluna vulgaris – Scilla verna* heath H8 *Calluna vulgaris – Ulex gallii* heath	
	H11 *Calluna vulgaris – Carex arenaria* heath	
GHI	HH1 Dry siliceous heath	
IVC	HE2A Western Gorse – Bell Heather heath HE2C Heather – Common Bent heath	

Upland Dry Heath		page 143
UKHab	h1b5 Dry heaths; upland	
P1	D1 Dry dwarf shrub heath	
	D5 Dry heath/acid grassland	
Ann. I	H4030 European dry heaths	
UKPH	Upland heathland	
NVC	H4 *Ulex gallii – Agrostis curtisii* heath H8 *Calluna vulgaris – Ulex gallii* heath	
	H9 *Calluna vulgaris – Deschampsia flexuosa* heath H10 *Calluna vulgaris – Erica cinerea* heath H12 *Calluna vulgaris – Vaccinium myrtillus* heath H16 *Calluna vulgaris – Arctostaphylos uva-ursi* heath H18 *Vaccinium myrtillus – Deschampsia flexuosa* heath H21 *Calluna vulgaris – Vaccinium myrtillus – Sphagnum capillifolium* heath	
GHI	HH1 Dry siliceous heath	
IVC	HE2B Heather – Heath Plait-moss heath HE2C Heather – Common Bent heath	
	HE3A Heather – Glittering Wood-moss heath HE3B Heather – Western Earwort heath	

Lowland Wet Heath		page 140
UKHab	h1a7 Wet heathland with cross-leaved heath; lowland h1a8 Wet heathland with Dorset heath and cross-leaved heath	
P1	D2 Wet dwarf shrub heath	
Ann. I	H4010 Northern Atlantic wet heaths with *Erica tetralix* H4020 Temperate Atlantic wet heaths with *Erica ciliaris* and *Erica tetralix*	
UKPH	Lowland Heathland	
NVC	H3 *Ulex minor – Agrostis curtisii* heath H4 *Ulex gallii – Agrostis curtisii* heath	
	H5 *Erica vagans – Schoenus nigricans* heath	
	M16 *Erica tetralix – Sphagnum compactum* wet heath	
GHI	HH3 Wet heath	
IVC	HE2A Western Gorse – Bell Heather heath HE2C Heather – Common Bent heath HE4D Purple Moor-grass – Tormentil – Cross-leaved Heath heath	
	HE4E Purple Moor-grass – Heather – Cross-leaved Heath heath	

Upland Wet Heath		page 149
UKHab	h1b6 Wet heathland with cross-leaved heath; upland	
P1	D2 Wet dwarf shrub heath	
	D6 Wet heath/acid grassland	
Ann. I	H4010 Northern Atlantic wet heaths with *Erica tetralix*	
UKPH	Upland heathland	
NVC	M15 *Scirpus cespitosus – Erica tetralix* wet heath	
	M16 *Erica tetralix – Sphagnum compactum* wet heath	
GHI	HH3 Wet heath	
IVC	HE2C Heather – Common Bent heath HE2D Heather – Purple Moor-grass – Bell Heather heath	
	HE2E Heather – Deergrass heath	
	HE4A Purple Moor-grass – Deergrass bog/heath HE4B Purple Moor-grass – Mat-grass heath HE4C Purple Moor-grass – Black Bog-rush bog/heath	
	BG2F Deergrass – Common Cottongrass bog/heath	

MOUNTAINS
page 198

High Montane Heath and Snow-bed
page 208

UKHab	g1b5 Montane acid grasslands
	g2b5 Alpine and subalpine calcareous grasslands
P1	D3 Lichen/bryophyte heath
	D4 Montane heath/dwarf herb
	B3 Calcareous grassland
Ann. I	H6150 Siliceous alpine and boreal grasslands
	H6170 Alpine and subalpine calcareous grasslands
UKPH	—
NVC	U7 *Nardus stricta – Carex bigelowii* grass-heath
	U8 *Carex bigelowii – Polytrichum alpinum* sedge-heath
	U9 *Juncus trifidus – Racomitrium lanuginosum* rush-heath
	U10 *Carex bigelowii – Racomitrium lanuginosum* moss-heath
	U11 *Polytrichum sexangulare – Kiaeria starkei* snow-bed
	U12 *Salix herbacea – Racomitrium heterostichum* snow-bed
	U13 *Deschampsia cespitosa – Galium saxatile* grassland
	U14 *Alchemilla alpina – Sibbaldia procumbens* dwarf-herb community
	CG12 *Festuca ovina – Alchemilla alpina – Silene acaulis* dwarf-herb community
GHI	—
IVC	GL3A Quaking-grass – Wild Thyme grassland

Montane Dwarf-shrub Heath
page 204

UKHab	h1c5 Alpine and subalpine heaths
P1	D4 Montane heath/dwarf herb
Ann. I	H4060 Alpine and boreal heaths
UKPH	Upland heathland
NVC	H13 *Calluna vulgaris – Cladonia arbuscula* heath
	H14 *Calluna vulgaris – Racomitrium lanuginosum* heath
	H15 *C. vulgaris – Juniperus communis* ssp. *nana* heath
	H17 *C. vulgaris – Arctostaphylos alpinus* heath
	H19 *Vaccinium myrtillus – Cladonia arbuscula* heath
	H20 *V. myrtillus – Racomitrium lanuginosum* heath
	H22 *V. myrtillus – Rubus chamaemorus* heath
GHI	HH4 Montane heath
IVC	HE3C - Heather – Mat-grass heath

Montane Scrub
page 215

UKHab	h1c6 Mountain willow scrub (H4080)
P1	A2 Scrub
Ann. I	H4080 Sub-Arctic *Salix* spp. scrub
UKPH	Inland rock outcrop and scree habitats
NVC	W20 *Salix lapponum – Luzula sylvatica* scrub
GHI	—
IVC	—

Mountain Ledge
page 212

UKHab	s1a9 Tall herb communities
P1	C2 Upland species-rich ledges
Ann. I	H6430 Hydrophilous tall herb fringe communities of plains and of the montane to alpine levels
UKPH	Inland rock outcrop and scree habitats
NVC	U15 *Saxifraga aizoides – Alchemilla glabra* banks
	U16 *Luzula sylvatica – Vaccinium myrtillus* tall-herb community
	U17 *Luzula sylvatica – Geum rivale* tall-herb community
	CG14 *Dryas octopetala – Silene acaulis* ledge community
GHI	—
IVC	RH2D Wild Angelica – Golden-head Moss ledge community

OTHER HABITATS
page 364

Arable
page 368

UKHab	c1a Arable field margins
	c1c Cereal crops
	c1d Non-cereal crops
P1	J11 Cultivated/disturbed land – arable
Ann. I	—
UKPH	Cereal field margins
NVC	OV3 *Papaver rhoeas – Viola arvensis* community
	OV4 *Chrysanthemum segetum – Spergula arvensis* community
	OV7 *Veronica persica – Veronica polita* community
	OV8 *Veronica persica – Alopecurus myosuroides* community
	OV9 *Matricaria perforata – Stellaria media* community
	OV10 *Poa annua – Senecio vulgaris* community
	OV11 *Poa annua – Stachys arvensis* community
	OV13 *Stellaria media – Capsella bursa-pastoris* community
GHI	BC1 Arable crops
IVC	WE1 Annual Meadow-grass - Chickweed group

Brownfield
page 372

UKHab	u1a Open mosaic habitats on previously developed land
P1	J13 Cultivated/disturbed land – ephemeral/short perennial
Ann. I	—
UKPH	Open mosaic habitats on previously developed land
NVC	Characteristic open communities show a poor fit to NVC communities. There is overlap with grasslands (MG1–2, MG9–11, MG13, CG10, U1–2), scrub (W6, W23) and a variety of aquatic and swamp communities
GHI	ED3 Recolonizing bare ground
IVC	—

Garden	page 378
UKHab	200, 231, 900, 910 Secondary codes for Parks and gardens, Vegetated garden, Small-scale food growing, Allotments may apply
P1	J Various miscellaneous codes may apply
Ann. I	—
UKPH	—
NVC	—
GHI	Various codes may apply
IVC	Various codes may apply

Traditional Orchard	page 375
UKHab	920 Orchard
P1	A12 Plantation
Ann. I	—
UKPH	Traditional orchards
NVC	MG5 Cynosurus cristatus – Centaurea nigra grassland MG6 Lolium perenne – Cynosurus cristatus grassland W24 Rubus fruticosus – Holcus lanatus underscrub
GHI	WD5 Scattered trees and parkland
IVC	—

ROCKY HABITATS
page 218

Limestone pavement	page 230
UKHab	s1b4 Limestone pavement
P1	I12 Scree
Ann. I	H8240 Limestone pavements
UKPH	Inland rock outcrop and scree habitats
NVC	OV38 Gymnocarpium robertianum – Arrhenatherum elatius community OV39 Asplenium trichomanes – Asplenium ruta-murariae community OV40 Asplenium viride – Cystopteris fragilis community + overlaps with woodland (W9), grassland (CG9, CG10, CG13, M5) and mire (M10, M26, M27) communities
GHI	ER2 Exposed calcareous rock
IVC	RH1B Wood Sage – Wall Lettuce pavement community RH1A Maidenhair Spleenwort – Comb-moss crevice community

Rocky Slopes	page 224
UKHab	s1a7 Plants in crevices in base-rich rocks (H8210) s1a8 Plants in crevices in acid rocks (H8220)
P1	I11 Inland cliff
Ann. I	H8220 Siliceous rocky slopes with chasmophytic vegetation H8210 Calcareous rocky slopes with chasmophytic vegetation
UKPH	Inland rock outcrop and scree habitats
NVC	U18 Cryptogramma crispa – Athyrium distentifolium snow-bed U21 Cryptogramma crispa – Deschampsia flexuosa community OV39 Asplenium trichomanes – Asplenium ruta-murariae community OV40 Asplenium viride – Cystopteris fragilis community
GHI	ER1 Exposed siliceous rock ER2 Exposed calcareous rock
IVC	RRH1A Maidenhair Spleenwort – Comb-moss crevice community RH2A Wilson's Filmy -Fern – Mouse-tail Moss crevice community

Scree	page 227
UKHab	s1a5 Acidic scree (H8110) s1a6 Base-rich scree (H8120)
P1	I12 Scree
Ann. I	H8110 Siliceous scree of the montane to snow levels H8120 Calcareous and calcschist screes of the montane to alpine levels
UKPH	Inland rock outcrop and scree habitats
NVC	U18 Cryptogramma crispa – Athyrium distentifolium snow-bed U21 Cryptogramma crispa – Deschampsia flexuosa community OV38 Gymnocarpium robertianum – Arrhenatherum elatius community
GHI	ER3 Siliceous scree and loose rock ER4 Calcareous scree and loose rock
IVC	RH1A Maidenhair Spleenwort – Comb-moss crevice community RH2A Wilson's Filmy-fern – Mouse-tail Moss crevice community RH2B Green Mountain Fringe-moss – Viviparous Fescue scree community RH2C Woolly Fringe-moss – Heath Plait-moss scree community

SCRUB
page 100

Bracken	*page 117*
UKHab	g1c Bracken
P1	C1 Bracken
Ann. I	—
UKPH	—
NVC	W25 *Pteridium aquilinum – Rubus fruticosus* underscrub
GHI	HD1 Dense bracken
IVC	SC1C Bracken – Bramble scrub

Hedgerow	*page 111*
UKHab	h2a Hedgerow (priority habitat)
P1	J2 Hedges
Ann. I	—
UKPH	Hedgerows
NVC	W21 *Crataegus monogyna – Hedera helix* scrub W22 *Prunus spinosa – Rubus fruticosus* scrub W23 *Ulex europaeus – Rubus fruticosus* scrub
GHI	WL1 Hedgerows
IVC	SC1 Bramble – Cleavers group

Mixed Scrub	*page 108*
UKHab	h3h Mixed scrub
P1	A111 Broadleaved woodland – semi-natural
Ann. I	—
UKPH	—
NVC	W21 *Crataegus monogyna – Hedera helix* scrub W22 *Prunus spinosa – Rubus fruticosus* scrub + provisional NVC *Agrimonia eupatoria – Origanum vulgare* community, *Corylus avellana – Geranium sanguineum* community
GHI	WS1 Scrub
IVC	SC1A Blackthorn – Hawthorn scrub SC1B Hawthorn – Bramble scrub

WETLANDS 1/2

Blanket Bog	*page 244*
UKHab	f1a Blanket bog
P1	E161 Blanket sphagnum bog E17 Wet modified bog E18 Dry modified bog
Ann. I	H7130 Blanket bogs 7150 Depressions on peat substrates of the Rhynchosporion 7140 Transition mires and quaking bogs
UKPH	Blanket Bog
NVC	M1 *Sphagnum denticulatum* bog pool community M2 *Sphagnum cuspidatum/fallax* bog pool community M3 *Eriophorum angustifolium* bog pool community M15 *Scirpus cespitosus – Erica tetralix* wet heath M17 *Scirpus cespitosus – Eriophorum vaginatum* blanket mire M18 *Erica tetralix – Sphagnum papillosum* raised and blanket mire M19 *Calluna vulgaris – Eriophorum vaginatum* blanket mire M20 *Eriophorum vaginatum* blanket and raised mire M25 *Molinia caerulea – Potentilla erecta* mire
GHI	PB2 Upland blanket bog PB3 Lowland blanket bog PB5 Eroding blanket bog PB4 Cutover bog PF3 Transition mire and quaking bog
IVC	HE4A Purple Moor-grass – Deergrass bog/heath HE4B Purple Moor-grass – Mat-grass heath HE4C Purple Moor-grass – Black Bog-rush bog/heath HE4D Purple Moor-grass – Tormentil – Cross-leaved Heath heath BG1A Feathery Bog-moss – Cow-horn Bog-moss bog BG1B White Beak-sedge – Bog Asphodel bog BG1C Black Bog-rush – Common Cottongrass bog BG1D Common Cottongrass – Heath Star-moss bog BG2C Cross-leaved Heath – Purple Moor-grass – Reindeer Lichen bog/heath BG2D Cross-leaved Heath – Black Bog-rush bog BG2E Heather – Cottongrass bog BG2F Deergrass – Common Cottongrass bog/heath

Lowland Fen	page 256
UKHab	f2a Lowland fen
P1	E2 Flush and spring
	E3 Fen
	F1 Swamp
Ann. I	H7210 Calcareous fens with *Cladium mariscus* and species of the *Caricion davallianae*
	H7230 Alkaline fens
UKPH	Lowland fens
NVC	S2 *Cladium mariscus* swamp and sedge beds
	S24 *Phragmites australis – Peucedanum palustre* tall-herb fen
	S25 *Phragmites australis – Eupatorium cannabinum* tall-herb fen
	M9 *Carex rostrata – Calliergon cuspidatum/giganteum* mire
	M13 *Schoenus nigricans – Juncus subnodulosus* mire
	M22 *Juncus subnodulosus – Cirsium palustre* fen-meadow
	M24 *Molinia caerulea – Cirsium dissectum* fen-meadow
	M25 *Molinia caerulea – Potentilla erecta* mire
	M27 *Filipendula ulmaria – Angelica sylvestris* mire
	M28 *Iris pseudacorus – Filipendula ulmaria* mire
	+ overlap with other swamp (S1–28) communities
GHI	PF1 Rich fen and flush
	FS1 Reed and large sedge swamps
	FS2 Tall-herb swamps
	GM1 Marsh
IVC	FW3F Meadowsweet – Common Reed tall-herb swamp
	FW3H Great Fen-sedge – Common Reed swamp
	FE1A Black Bog-rush – Yellow Starry Feather-moss fen
	FE1B Black Bog-rush –Devil's-bit Scabious fen
	FE1C Carnation Sedge –Yellow Sedge fen
	FE2F Bogbean –PointedSpear-moss mire
	FE3A Common Sedge –Lesser Spearwort fen

Raised Bog	page 249
UKHab	f1b Lowland raised bog
P1	E162 Raised sphagnum bog
	E17 Wet modified bog
	E18 Dry modified bog
Ann. I	H7110 Active raised bogs
	H7120 Degraded raised bogs still capable of natural regeneration
	H7150 Depressions on peat substrates of the Rhynchosporion
	H7140 Transition mires and quaking bogs
UKPH	Raised Bog

Raised Bog (contd.)	page 249
NVC	M1 *Sphagnum denticulatum* bog pool community
	M2 *Sphagnum cuspidatum/fallax* bog pool community
	M3 *Eriophorum angustifolium* bog pool community
	M15 *Scirpus cespitosus – Erica tetralix* wet heath
	M18 *Erica tetralix – Sphagnum papillosum* raised and blanket mire
	M19 *Calluna vulgaris – Eriophorum vaginatum* blanket mire
	M20 *Eriophorum vaginatum* blanket and raised mire
	W4 *Betula pubescens – Molinia caerulea* woodland
GHI	PB1 Raised bog
	PB4 Cutover bog
	PF3 Transition mire and quaking bog
IVC	BG1A Feathery Bog-moss – Cow-horn Bog-moss bog
	BG1D Common Cottongrass – Heath Star-moss bog
	BG2A Hare's-tail Cottongrass – Cranberry bog
	BG2B Cross-leaved Heath – Bog-rosemary bog

Reedbed	page 265
UKHab	f2e Reedbeds
P1	F1 Swamp
Ann. I	—
UKPH	Reedbed
NVC	S4 *Phragmites australis* swamp and reed-beds
	S25 *Phragmites australis – Eupatorium cannabinum* tall-herb fen
	S26 *Phragmites australis – Urtica dioica* tall-herb fen
GHI	FS1 Reed and large sedge swamps
IVC	FW3B Common Reed – Bulrush swamp
	FW3E Common Reed – Water Horsetail swamp
	FW3G Water Horsetail – Common Spike-rush swamp

WETLANDS 2/2 page 234

Upland Spring and Flush		page 252
UKHab	f2c Upland flushes, fens and swamps	
P1	E2 Flush and spring	
	E3 Fen	
Ann. I	H7220 Petrifying springs with tufa formation (*Cratoneurion*) H7240 Alpine pioneer formations of the *Caricion bicoloris-atrofuscae*	
	7210 Calcareous fens with *Cladium mariscus* and species of the *Caricion davallianae* 7140 Transition mires and quaking bogs	
UKPH	Upland flushes, fens and swamps	
NVC	M7 *Carex curta – Sphagnum russowii* mire M8 *Carex rostrata – Sphagnum warnstorfii* mire M9 *Carex rostrata – Calliergon cuspidatum/giganteum* mire M10 *Carex dioica – Pinguicula lusitanica* mire	
	M11 *Carex viridula* ssp. *oedocarpa – Saxifraga aizoides* mire	
	M12 *Carex saxatilis* mire M31 *Anthelia julacea – Sphagnum auriculatum* spring M32 *Philonotis fontana – Saxifraga stellaris* spring M33 *Pohlia wahlenbergii* var. *glacialis* spring M34 *Carex demissa – Koenigia islandica* flush	
	M35 *Ranunculus omiophyllus – Montia fontana* rill	
	M37 *Palustriella commutata – Festuca rubra* spring M38 *Cratoneuron commutatum – Carex nigra* spring	
	+ overlaps with other mire (M4–7, M27–29) and swamp (S9–11, S19, S27) communities	
GHI	FP1 Calcareous springs FP2 Non-calcareous springs	
IVC	FE1C Carnation Sedge –Yellow Sedge fen	

Valley Mire		page 260
UKHab	f2a8 Transition mires and quaking bogs; lowland	
P1	E31 Fen – valley mire	
Ann. I	H7140 Transition mires and quaking bogs H7150 Depressions on peat substrates of the Rhynchosporion	
UKPH	Lowland fens	
NVC	M1 *Sphagnum denticulatum* bog pool community M14 *Schoenus nigricans – Narthecium ossifragum* mire M21 *Narthecium ossifragum – Sphagnum papillosum* valley mire M29 *Hypericum elodes – Potamogeton polygonifolius* soakway	
GHI	PF3 Transition mire and quaking bog	
IVC	FW3C Bottle Sedge swamp/fen	

WOODLANDS 1/2 page

Atlantic Hazel Wood		page 91
UKHab	h3b5 Atlantic hazel	
P1	A111 Broadleaved woodland – semi-natural	
Ann. I	—	
UKPH	Upland Mixed Ashwoods	
NVC	W9 *Fraxinus excelsior – Sorbus aucuparia – Mercurialis perennis* woodland W11 *Quercus petraea – Betula pubescens – Oxalis acetosella* woodland W17 *Quercus petraea – Betula pubescens – Dicranum majus* woodland	
GHI	WN2 Oak – Ash – Hazel woodland	
IVC	WL2E Hazel – Barren Strawberry woodland WL1Cii Sessile Oak – Hazel woodland, Ash sub-community	

Beech Wood		page 60
UKHab	w1c5 Beech forests on acid soils w1c6 Beech forests on neutral to rich soils	
P1	A111 Broadleaved woodland – semi-natural	
Ann. I	H9120 Atlantic acidophilous Beech forests with *Ilex* and sometimes also *Taxus* in the shrublayer H9130 *Asperulo-Fagetum* Beech forests	
UKPH	Lowland Beech and Yew Woodland	
NVC	W12 *Fagus sylvatica – Mercurialis perennis* woodland W14 *Fagus sylvatica – Rubus fruticosus* woodland W15 *Fagus sylvatica – Deschampsia flexuosa* woodland	
GHI	—	
IVC	—	

Caledonian Forest		page 86
UKHab	w2a5 Caledonian forest	
P1	A131 Mixed woodland – semi-natural	
Ann. I	H91C0 Caledonian Forest	
UKPH	Native pine woods	
NVC	W18 *Pinus sylvestris – Hylocomium splendens* woodland	
	W11 *Quercus petraea – Betula pubescens – Oxalis acetosella* woodland W17 *Quercus petraea – Betula pubescens – Dicranum majus* woodland W19 *Juniperus communis* ssp. *communis – Oxalis acetosella* woodland	
GHI	—	
IVC	—	

Coniferous Plantation

page 97

UKHab	w2b Other Scot's Pine woodland w2c Other coniferous woodland
P1	A122 Coniferous woodland – plantation
Ann. I	—
UKPH	—
NVC	—
GHI	WD4 Conifer plantation
IVC	—

Lowland Dry Oak and Birch Wood

page 57

UKHab	w1f5 Dry oak-dominated woodland
P1	A111 Broadleaved woodland – semi-natural
Ann. I	H9190 Old acidophilous oak woods with *Quercus robur* on sandy plains
UKPH	Lowland Mixed Deciduous Woodland
NVC	W10 *Quercus robur* – *Pteridium aquilinum* – *Rubus fruticosus* woodland W16 *Quercus* spp. – *Betula* spp. – *Deschampsia flexuosa* woodland
GHI	—
IVC	—

Lowland Mixed Oak and Ash Wood

page 52

UKHab	w1f6 Oak-hornbeam forests w1f7 Other Lowland mixed deciduous woodland
P1	A111 Broadleaved woodland – semi-natural
Ann. I	H9160 Sub-Atlantic and medio-European oak or oak – Hornbeam forests of the *Carpinion betuli*
UKPH	Lowland Mixed Deciduous Woodland
NVC	W8 *Fraxinus excelsior* – *Acer campestre* – *Mercurialis perennis* woodland W10 *Quercus robur* – *Pteridium aquilinum* – *Rubus fruticosus* woodland
GHI	WN2 Oak – Ash – Hazel woodland
	WN4 Wet Pedunculate Oak – Ash woodland
IVC	WL1A Pedunculate Oak – Great Wood-rush woodland WL2A Pedunculate Oak – Enchanter's-nightshade woodland WL2B Ash – Wood Avens woodland WL2C Ash – Sycamore woodland WL2D - Beech – Ivy woodland

Upland Birch Wood

page 94

UKHab	w1e Upland birchwoods
P1	A111 Broadleaved woodland – semi-natural
Ann. I	—
UKPH	Upland Birchwoods
NVC	W4 *Betula pubescens* – *Molinia caerulea* woodland W11 *Quercus petraea* – *Betula pubescens* – *Oxalis acetosella* woodland W17 *Quercus petraea* – *Betula pubescens* – *Dicranum majus* woodland
GHI	WN1 Oak – birch – Holly woodland
IVC	WL4A Downy Birch – Bilberry woodland WL4B Downy Birch – Common Bent woodland WL4D Downy Birch – Bramble woodland WL4F Downy Birch – Bracken woodland

Upland Mixed Ash Wood

page 83

UKHab	w1f6 Oak-hornbeam forests w1b5 Lime-maple woodlands of rocky slopes (H9180) w1b6 Other upland mixed ashwoods s1b Limestone pavements
P1	A111 Broadleaved woodland – semi-natural
Ann. I	H9180 *Tilio-Acerion* forests of slopes, screes and ravines
	H8240 Limestone Pavements
UKPH	Upland Mixed Ashwoods
NVC	W8 *Fraxinus excelsior* – *Acer campestre* – *Mercurialis perennis* woodland W9 *Fraxinus excelsior* – *Sorbus aucuparia* – *Mercurialis perennis* woodland
GHI	—
IVC	WL1Cii Sessile Oak Hazel woodland, Ash sub-community WN2 Oak – Ash – Hazel woodland

WOODLANDS 2/2

Upland Oak Wood	page 78
UKHab	w1a5 Western acidic oak woodland
P1	A111 Broadleaved woodland – semi-natural
Ann. I	H91A0 Old oak woods with *Ilex* and *Blechnum* in the British Isles
UKPH	Upland Oak Woods
NVC	W10 *Quercus robur – Pteridium aquilinum – Rubus fruticosus* woodland W11 *Quercus petraea – Betula pubescens – Oxalis acetosella* woodland W16 *Quercus* spp. – *Betula* spp. – *Deschampsia flexuosa* woodland W17 *Quercus petraea – Betula pubescens – Dicranum majus* woodland
GHI	WN1 Oak – birch – Holly woodland
IVC	WL1B Sessile Oak – Great Wood-rush woodland WL1C Sessile Oak – Hazel woodland WL1D Sessile Oak – Bilberry woodland

Wet Woodland	page 66
UKHab	w1d Wet woodland
P1	A111 Broadleaved woodland – semi-natural
Ann. I	H91E0 Alluvial forests with *Alnus glutinosa* and *Fraxinus excelsior* H91D0 Bog woodlands
UKPH	Wet Woodland
NVC	W1 *Salix cinerea – Galium palustre* woodland W2 *Salix cinerea – Betula pendula – Phragmites australis* woodland W3 *Salix pentandra – Carex rostrata* woodland W5 *Alnus glutinosa – Carex paniculata* woodland W6 *Alnus glutinosa – Urtica dioica* woodland W7 *Alnus glutinosa – Fraxinus excelsior – Lysimachia nemorum* woodland W18 *Pinus sylvestris – Hylocomium splendens* woodland W4 *Betula pubescens – Molinia caerulea* woodland
GHI	WN5 Riparian woodland WN6 Wet willow-alder-ash woodland WN7 Bog woodland WN4 Wet Pedunculate Oak – Ash woodland
IVC	WL3 Alder – Meadowsweet group WL4C Downy Birch – Blunt-leaved Bog-moss woodland WL4E Downy Birch – Grey Willow woodland

Wood Pasture	page 72
UKHab	Various + 20 wood-pasture and parkland
P1	A31 Parkland and scattered trees – broadleaved
Ann. I	—
UKPH	Wood pasture and parkland
NVC	W10 *Quercus robur – Pteridium aquilinum – Rubus fruticosus* woodland W11 *Quercus petraea – Betula pubescens – Oxalis acetosella* woodland W14 *Fagus sylvatica – Rubus fruticosus* woodland W15 *Fagus sylvatica – Deschampsia flexuosa* woodland W16 *Quercus* spp. – *Betula* spp. – *Deschampsia flexuosa* woodland W17 *Quercus petraea – Betula pubescens – Dicranum majus* woodland + various open habitat types
GHI	WD5 Scattered trees and parkland
IVC	Overlaps with various woodland and open communities

Yew Wood	page 63
UKHab	w1c7 Yew-dominated woodland
P1	A131 Mixed woodland – semi-natural A121 Coniferous woodland – semi-natural
Ann. I	H91J0 *Taxus baccata* woods of the British Isles
UKPH	Lowland Beech and Yew Woodland
NVC	W13 *Taxus baccata* woodland
GHI	WN3 Yew woodland
IVC	WL2F Yew – Holly woodland

Species referred to in the text

English names have been used wherever possible throughout this book when referring to species, in an attempt to ensure that the text is as accessible as possible for readers who are not familiar with scientific names. English names are in any case most commonly used for groups such as birds, butterflies, mammals and higher plants. For other groups, such as lower plants and some invertebrates, many naturalists are only familiar with the scientific names and although English names have been derived for most, these have only recently started to be used. However, for consistency, and because scientific names may be off-putting, these English names have also been used for the species within these groups. The scientific names for all the species mentioned in the text are listed in this section for the benefit of readers who are only familiar with scientific names or who wish to know what its scientific name is. Details of the sources for the nomenclature used are given on *page 39*.

The following abbreviations are used:

agg. (aggregate) – a group of microspecies that are commonly referred to as a single species.

sens. lat. (*sensu lato*) – the species name is used in the broadest sense.

spp. (species) – use where more than one species of a particular genus is referred to.

ssp. (subspecies) – a taxonomic rank below that of species.

var. (variety) – a taxonomic rank below that of species used for some plants, algae and fungi.

* Not the common name used by the relevant authority but nonetheless more widely used.

Flowering Plants

Adder's-tongue	*Ophioglossum vulgatum*
Alder	*Alnus glutinosa*
Allseed	*Linum radiola*
Alpine Bartsia	*Bartsia alpina*
Alpine Bistort	*Bistorta vivipara*
Alpine Blue-sow-thistle	*Cicerbita alpina*
Alpine Catchfly	*Lychnis alpina*
Alpine Cinquefoil	*Potentilla crantzii*
Alpine Clubmoss	*Diphasiastrum alpinum*
Alpine Forget-me-not	*Myosotis alpestris*
Alpine Gentian	*Gentiana nivalis*
Alpine Hair-grass	*Deschampsia cespitosa* var. *pulchra*
Alpine Lady's-mantle	*Alchemilla alpina*
Alpine Lady-fern	*Athyrium distentifolium*
Alpine Meadow-rue	*Thalictrum alpinum*
Alpine Mouse-ear	*Cerastium alpinum*
Alpine Pearlwort	*Sagina saginoides*
Alpine Pennycress	*Thlaspi caerulescens*
Alpine Saw-wort	*Saussurea alpina*
Alpine Saxifrage	*Saxifraga nivalis*
Alpine Speedwell	*Veronica alpina*
Alpine Woodsia	*Woodsia alpina*
Alternate Water-milfoil	*Myriophyllum alterniflorum*
Amphibious Bistort	*Persicaria amphibia*
Angular Solomon's-seal	*Polygonatum odoratum*
Annual Knawel	*Scleranthus annuus*
Apple	*Malus domestica*
Arctic Mouse-ear	*Cerastium arcticum*
Arctic Sandwort	*Arenaria norvegica* ssp. *norvegica*
Ash	*Fraxinus excelsior*
Aspen	*Populus tremula*
Autumn Lady's-tresses	*Spiranthes spiralis*
Autumn Squill	*Scilla autumnalis*
Awlwort	*Subularia aquatica*
Baneberry	*Actaea spicata*
Barberry	*Berberis vulgaris*
Bastard Balm	*Melittis melissophyllum*
Bastard-toadflax	*Thesium humifusum*
Bay Willow	*Salix pentandra*
Beaked Tasselweed	*Ruppia maritima*
Bearberry	*Arctostaphylos uva-ursi*
Bee Orchid	*Ophrys apifera*
Beech	*Fagus sylvatica*
Beech Fern	*Phegopteris connectilis*
Bell Heather	*Erica cinerea*
Bilberry	*Vaccinium myrtillus*
Bird's-foot Sedge	*Carex ornithopoda*
Bird's-nest Orchid	*Neottia nidus-avis*
Bird's-eye Primrose	*Primula farinosa*
Biting Stonecrop	*Sedum acre*
Bittersweet	*Solanum dulcamara*
Bitter-vetch	*Lathyrus linifolius*
Black Bog-rush	*Schoenus nigricans*
Black Bryony	*Tamus communis*
Black Medick	*Medicago lupulina*
Black-poplar	*Populus nigra* ssp. *betulifolia*
Blackthorn	*Prunus spinosa*
Bladder Campion	*Silene vulgaris*
Bladder-sedge	*Carex vesicaria*
bladderworts	*Utricularia* spp.
Blinks	*Montia fontana*
Bloody Crane's-bill	*Geranium sanguineum*
Blue Heath	*Phyllodoce caerulea*
Blue Moor-grass	*Sesleria caerulea*
Bluebell	*Hyacinthoides non-scripta*
Blunt-flowered Rush	*Juncus subnodulosus*
Bog Asphodel	*Narthecium ossifragum*
Bog Bilberry	*Vaccinium uliginosum*
Bog Orchid	*Hammarbya paludosa*

Bog Pondweed	*Potamogeton polygonifolius*
Bogbean	*Menyanthes trifoliata*
Bog-myrtle	*Myrica gale*
Bog-rosemary	*Andromeda polifolia*
Bottle Sedge	*Carex rostrata*
Box	*Buxus sempervirens*
Bracken	*Pteridium aquilinum*
Brackish Water-crowfoot	*Ranunculus baudotii*
Bramble	*Rubus fruticosus* agg.
Bristle Bent	*Agrostic setacea*
Brittle Bladder-fern	*Cystopteris fragilis*
Broad Buckler-fern	*Dryopteris dilatata*
Broad-leaved Helleborine	*Epipactis helleborine*
Broad-leaved Pondweed	*Potamogeton natans*
Brooklime	*Veronica beccabunga*
Broom	*Cytisus scoparius*
Brown Beak-sedge	*Rhynchospora fusca*
Buck's-horn Plantain	*Plantago coronopus*
Buckthorn	*Rhamnus cathartica*
Bugle	*Ajuga reptans*
Bulbous Rush	*Juncus bulbosus*
Bulrush	*Typha latifolia*
Bur Medick	*Medicago minima*
Burnet Rose	*Rosa pimpinellifolia*
Burnt-tip Orchid	*Orchis ustulata*
Butcher's-broom	*Ruscus aculeatus*
buttercups	*Ranunculus* spp.
butterworts	*Pinguicula* spp.
Carline Thistle	*Carlina vulgaris*
Carnation Sedge	*Carex panicea*
Cat's-ear	*Hypochaeris radicata*
Cedar-of-Lebanon	*Cedrus libani*
Chaffweed	*Lysimachia minima*
Chalk Eyebright	*Euphrasia pseudokerneri*
Chalk Fragrant-orchid	*Gymnadenia conopsea*
Chalk Milkwort	*Polygala calcarea*
Chickweed-wintergreen	*Lysimachia europaea*
Chives	*Allium schoenoprasum*
Cleavers	*Galium aparine*
Cloudberry	*Rubus chamaemorus*
clovers	*Trifolium* spp.
Clustered Clover	*Trifolium glomeratum*
Cock's-foot	*Dactylis glomerata*
Coltsfoot	*Tussilago farfara*
Common Bent	*Agrostis capillaris*
Common Bird's-foot-trefoil	*Lotus corniculatus*
Common Butterwort	*Pinguicula vulgaris*
Common Centaury	*Centaurium erythraea*
Common Club-rush	*Schoenoplectus lacustris*
Common Cord-grass	*Spartina anglica*
Common Cottongrass	*Eriophorum angustifolium*
Common Cow-wheat	*Melampyrum pratense*
Common Dog-violet	*Viola riviniana*
Common Gorse	*Ulex europaeus*
Common Knapweed	*Centaurea nigra*
Common Milkwort	*Polygala vulgaris*
Common Nettle	*Urtica dioica*
Common Poppy	*Papaver rhoeas*
Common Reed	*Phragmites australis*
Common Rock-rose	*Helianthemum nummularium*
Common Saltmarsh-grass	*Puccinellia maritima*
Common Sea-lavender	*Limonium vulgare*
Common Sedge	*Carex nigra*
Common Sorrel	*Rumex acetosa*
Common Spotted-orchid	*Dactylorhiza fuchsii*
Common Stork's-bill	*Erodium cicutarium* agg.
Common Twayblade	*Listera ovata*
Common Valerian	*Valeriana officinalis*
Common Water-crowfoot	*Ranunculus aquatilis*
Common Whitlowgrass	*Erophila verna*
Compact Rush	*Juncus conglomeratus*
Coral Necklace	*Illecebrum verticillatum*
Coralroot Orchid	*Corallorhiza trifida*
cord-grasses	*Spartina* spp.
Corn Marigold	*Chrysanthemum segetum*
Corncockle	*Agrostemma githago*
Cornflower	*Centaurea cyanus*
Cornish Heath	*Erica vagans*
Cottonweed	*Otanthus maritimus*
Cow Parsley	*Anthriscus sylvestris*
Cowbane	*Cicuta virosa*
Cowberry	*Vaccinium vitis-idaea*
Cowslip	*Primula veris*
Crab Apple	*Malus sylvestris*
Cranberry	*Vaccinium oxycoccos*
Creeping Bent	*Agrostis stolonifera*
Creeping Buttercup	*Ranunculus repens*
Creeping Lady's-tresses	*Goodyera repens*
Creeping Soft-grass	*Holcus mollis*
Creeping Willow	*Salix repends*
Crested Dog's-tail	*Cynosurus cristatus*
Cross-leaved Heath	*Erica tetralix*
Crowberry	*Empetrum nigrum*
Cuckooflower	*Cardamine pratensis*
Curled Dock	*Rumex crispus*
Curved Wood-rush	*Luzula arcuata*
Cyphel	*Cherleria sedoides*
Daisy	*Bellis perennis*
Dandelions	*Taraxacum* agg.
Dark-leaved Willow	*Salix myrsinifolia*
Dark-red Helleborine	*Epipactis atrorubens*
Darnel	*Lolium temulentum*
Deergrass	*Trichophorum cespitosum*
Dense-flowered Orchid	*Neotinea maculata*
Devil's-bit Scabious	*Succisa pratensis*
Devon Whitebeam	*Sorbus devoniensis*
Diapensia	*Diapensia lapponica*
Divided Sedge	*Carex divisa*
Dogwood	*Cornus sanguinea*
Downy Birch	*Betula pubescens*
Downy Currant	*Ribes spicatum*
Downy Willow	*Salix lapponum*
Drooping Saxifrage	*Saxifraga cernua*
Dropwort	*Filipendula vulgaris*
duckweeds	*Lemnaceae*
Dune Fescue	*Vulpia fasciculata*

Lady's Bedstraw .... *Galium verum*
Lady's-mantle .... *Alchemilla* spp.
Large Venus's-looking-glass .... *Legousia speculum-veneris*
Large-leaved Lime .... *Tilia platyphyllos*
Lemon-scented Fern .... *Oreopteris limbosperma*
Lesser Bladderwort .... *Utricularia minor*
Lesser Butterfly-orchid .... *Platanthera bifolia*
Lesser Celandine .... *Ranunculus ficaria*
Lesser Pond-sedge .... *Carex acutiformis*
Lesser Skullcap .... *Scutellaria minor*
Lesser Twayblade .... *Listera cordata*
Lesser Water-parsnip .... *Berula erecta*
Lesser Water-plantain .... *Baldellia ranunculoides*
Lily-of-the-valley .... *Convallaria majalis*
Limestone Bedstraw .... *Galium sterneri*
Limestone Fern .... *Gymnocarpium robertianum*
Little Mouse-ear .... *Cerastium semidecandrum*
Little-Robin .... *Geranium purpureum*
Lizard Orchid .... *Himantoglossum hircinum*
Long-spiked Glasswort .... *Salicornia dolichostachya*
Lousewort .... *Pedicularis sylvatica*
Lundy Cabbage .... *Coincya wrightii*
Lyme-grass .... *Leymus arenarius*
Mackay's Heath .... *Erica mackaiana*
Maiden Pink .... *Dianthus deltoides*
Maidenhair Fern .... *Adiantum capillus-veneris*
Maidenhair Spleenwort .... *Asplenium trichomanes*
Male-fern .... *Dryopteris filix-mas*
Man Orchid .... *Aceras anthropophorum*
Many-stalked Spike-rush .... *Eleocharis multicaulis*
Marram .... *Ammophila arenaria*
Marsh Arrowgrass .... *Triglochin palustre*
Marsh Bedstraw .... *Galium palustre*
Marsh Cinquefoil .... *Potentilla palustris*
Marsh Clubmoss .... *Lycopodiella inundata*
Marsh Fern .... *Thelypteris palustris*
Marsh Foxtail .... *Alopecurus geniculatus*
Marsh Gentian .... *Gentiana pneumonanthe*
Marsh Hawk's-beard .... *Crepis paludosa*
Marsh Helleborine .... *Epipactis palustris*
Marsh-mallow .... *Althaea officinalis*
Marsh Pea .... *Lathyrus palustris*
Marsh St. John's-wort .... *Hypericum elodes*
Marsh-marigold .... *Caltha palustris*
Mat-grass .... *Nardus stricta*
Meadow Buttercup .... *Ranunculus acris*
Meadow Crane's-bill .... *Geranium pratense*
Meadow Oat-grass .... *Helictochloa pratensis*
Meadow Saffron .... *Colchicum autumnale*
Meadow Thistle .... *Cirsium dissectum*
Meadowsweet .... *Filipendula ulmaria*
Melancholy Thistle .... *Cirsium heterophyllum*
Military Orchid .... *Orchis militaris*
Milk-parsley .... *Peucedanum palustre*
Mistletoe .... *Viscum album*
Monkey Orchid .... *Orchis simia*
Moonwort .... *Botrychium lunaria*
Moschatel .... *Adoxa moschatellina*

Moss Campion .... *Silene acaulis*
Mossy Stonecrop .... *Crassula tillaea*
Mountain Avens .... *Dryas octopetala*
Mountain Crowberry* [Crowberry]
.... *Empetrum nigrum* ssp. *hermaphroditum*
Mountain Everlasting .... *Antennaria dioica*
Mountain Male-fern .... *Dryopteris oreades*
Mountain Pansy .... *Viola lutea*
Mountain Sorrel .... *Oxyria digyna*
Mountain Willow .... *Salix arbuscula*
Mouse-ear-hawkweed .... *Pilosella officinarum*
Mousetail .... *Myosurus minimus*
Mudwort .... *Limosella aquatica*
Musk Orchid .... *Herminium monorchis*
Myrtle-leaved Willow .... *Salix myrtilloides*
Narrow-leaved Helleborine .... *Cephalanthera longifolia*
Narrow-leaved Water-dropwort .... *Oenanthe silaifolia*
Narrow-lipped Helleborine .... *Epipactis leptochila* agg.
Net-leaved Willow .... *Salix reticulata*
Nettle-leaved Bellflower .... *Campanula trachelium*
New Zealand Pigmyweed .... *Crassula helmsii*
Northern Rock-cress .... *Arabis petraea*
Norwegian Mugwort .... *Artemisia norvegica*
Nottingham Catchfly .... *Silene nutans*
Oak Fern .... *Gymnocarpium dryopteris*
Oblong Woodsia .... *Woodsia ilvensis*
Oblong-leaved Sundew .... *Drosera intermedia*
One-flowered Wintergreen .... *Moneses uniflora*
Opposite-leaved Golden-saxifrage
.... *Chrysosplenium oppositifolium*
oraches .... *Atriplex* spp.
Orpine .... *Hylotelephium telephium*
Oxeye Daisy .... *Leucanthemum vulgare*
Oxlip .... *Primula elatior*
Oysterplant .... *Mertensia maritima*
Pale Butterwort .... *Pinguicula lusitanica*
Parrot's-feather .... *Myriophyllum aquaticum*
Parsley Fern .... *Cryptogramma crispa*
Parsley-piert .... *Aphanes arvensis* agg.
Pasqueflower .... *Pulsatilla vulgaris*
Pedunculate Oak .... *Quercus robur*
Pennyroyal .... *Mentha pulegium*
Pepper-saxifrage .... *Silaum silaus*
Perennial Knawel .... *Scleranthus perennis*
Perennial Rye-grass .... *Lolium perenne*
Petty Whin .... *Genista anglica*
Pigmy Rush .... *Juncus pygmaeus*
Pignut .... *Conopodium majus*
Pill Sedge .... *Carex pilulifera*
Pillwort .... *Pilularia globulifera*
Pipewort .... *Eriocaulon aquaticum*
plantains .... *Plantago* spp.
Plymouth Pear .... *Pyrus cordata*
Pond Water-crowfoot .... *Ranunculus peltatus*
pondweeds .... *Potamogeton* spp.
Portland Spurge .... *Euphorbia portlandica*
Prickly Poppy .... *Papaver argemone*
Prickly Saltwort .... *Salsola kali*

Primrose .... *Primula vulgaris*
Pugsley's Marsh-orchid .... *Dactylorhiza traunsteinerioides*
Purple Gromwell .... *Aegonychon purpureocaeruleum*
Purple Milk-vetch .... *Astragalus danicus*
Purple Moor-grass .... *Molinia caerulea*
Purple Ramping-fumitory .... *Fumaria purpurea*
Purple Saxifrage .... *Saxifraga oppositifolia*
Purple-loosestrife .... *Lythrum salicaria*
Purple-stem Cat's-tail .... *Phleum phleoides*
Pyramidal Orchid .... *Anacamptis pyramidalis*
Pyrenean Scurvygrass .... *Cochlearia pyrenaica*
Quaking-grass .... *Briza media*
Quillwort .... *Isoetes lacustris*
Ragged-Robin .... *Lychnis flos-cuculi*
Ramsons .... *Allium ursinum*
Red Campion .... *Silene dioica*
Red Clover .... *Trifolium pratense*
Red Currant .... *Ribes rubrum*
Red Fescue .... *Festuca rubra* agg.
Red Helleborine .... *Cephalanthera rubra*
Red Pondweed .... *Potamogeton alpinus*
Reed Sweet-grass .... *Glyceria maxima*
Ribwort Plantain .... *Plantago lanceolata*
Rigid Bucker-fern .... *Dryopteris submontana*
Rigid Hornwort .... *Ceratophyllum demersum*
Rock Samphire .... *Crithmum maritimum*
Rock Sea-lavender .... *Limonium binervosum* agg.
Rock Sea-spurrey .... *Spergularia rupicola*
Rhododendron .... *Rhododendron ponticum*
Rosebay Willowherb .... *Chamaenerion angustifolium*
Roseroot .... *Rhodiola rosea*
Rough Hawkbit .... *Leontodon hispidus*
Round-headed Rampion .... *Phyteuma orbiculare*
Round-leaved Crowfoot .... *Ranunculus omiophyllus*
Round-leaved Fluellen .... *Kickxia spuria*
Round-leaved Sundew .... *Drosera rotundifolia*
Round-leaved Wintergreen .... *Pyrola rotundifolia*
Rowan .... *Sorbus aucuparia*
Royal Fern .... *Osmunda regalis*
Rustyback .... *Ceterach officinarum*
Salad Burnet .... *Sanguisorba minor* ssp. *minor*
Saltmarsh Flat-sedge .... *Blysmus rufus*
Saltmarsh Rush .... *Juncus gerardii*
Sand Catchfly .... *Silene conica*
Sand Couch .... *Elymus junceiformis*
Sand Sedge .... *Carex arenaria*
Sanicle .... *Sanicula europaea*
Saw Sedge .... *Cladium mariscus*
Scaly Male-fern .... *Dryopteris affinis*
Scots Lovage .... *Ligusticum scoticum*
Scots Pine .... *Pinus sylvestris*
Scottish Asphodel .... *Tofieldia pusilla*
Scottish Primrose .... *Primula scotica*
Sea Aster .... *Tripolium pannonicum*
Sea Beet .... *Beta vulgaris* ssp. *maritima*
Sea Bindweed .... *Calystegia soldanella*
Sea Campion .... *Silene uniflora*
Sea Carrot .... *Daucus carota* ssp. *gummifer*

Sea Clover .... *Trifolium squamosum*
Sea Club-rush .... *Bolboschoenus maritimus*
Sea Fern-grass .... *Catapodium marinum*
Sea Lettuce .... *Ulva latuca*
Sea Mayweed .... *Tripleurospermum maritimum*
Sea Pea .... *Lathyrus japonicus*
Sea Plantain .... *Plantago maritima*
Sea Purslane .... *Atriplex portulacoides*
Sea Rocket .... *Cakile maritima*
Sea Sandwort .... *Honckenya peploides*
Sea Spurge .... *Euphorbia paralias*
Sea Stock .... *Matthiola sinuata*
Sea-buckthorn .... *Hippophae rhamnoides*
Sea-holly .... *Eryngium maritimum*
Sea-kale .... *Crambe maritima*
sea-lavenders .... *Limonium* spp.
Selfheal .... *Prunella vulgaris*
Sessile Oak .... *Quercus petraea*
Shallon .... *Gaultheria shallon*
Sharp-flowered Rush .... *Juncus acutiflorus*
Sharp-Leaved Fluellen .... *Kickxia elatine*
Sharp-leaved Pondweed .... *Potamogeton acutifolius*
Sheep's-fescue .... *Festuca ovina*
Sheep's Sorrel .... *Rumex acetosella* ssp. *acetosella*
shield-ferns .... *Polystichum* spp.
Shepherd's-needle .... *Scandix pecten-veneris*
Shepherd's Cress .... *Teesdalia nudicaulis*
Shetland Mouse-ear .... *Cerastium nigrescens*
Shoreweed .... *Littorella uniflora*
Shrubby Cinquefoil .... *Dasiphora fruticosa*
Shrubby Sea-blite .... *Suaeda vera*
Sibbaldia .... *Sibbaldia procumbens*
Silver Birch .... *Betula pendula*
Silverweed .... *Potentilla anserina*
Six-stamened Waterwort .... *Elatine hexandra*
Slender Hare's-ear .... *Bupleurum tenuissimum*
Slender Naiad .... *Najas flexilis*
Slender Sedge .... *Carex lasiocarpa*
Slender Spike-rush .... *Eleocharis uniglumis*
Slender Tufted-sedge .... *Carex acuta*
Small Cow-wheat .... *Melampyrum sylvaticum*
Small Restharrow .... *Ononis reclinata*
Small Scabious .... *Scabiosa columbaria*
Small Toadflax .... *Chaenorhinum minus*
Small-leaved Lime .... *Tilia cordata*
Small-white Orchid .... *Pseudorchis albida*
Smooth Cat's-ear .... *Hypochaeris glabra*
Smooth Hawk's-beard .... *Crepis capillaris*
Snow Pearlwort .... *Sagina nivalis*
Snowdon Lily .... *Lloydia serotina*
Soft Rush .... *Juncus effusus*
Solomon's-seal .... *Polygonatum multiflorum*
Southern Marsh-orchid .... *Dactylorhiza praetermissa*
Spanish Catchfly .... *Silene otites*
Spiked Speedwell .... *Veronica spicata*
Spiked Water-milfoil .... *Myriophyllum spicatum*
Spindle .... *Euonymus europaeus*
Spiral Tasselweed .... *Ruppia spiralis*

Spring Gentian .... *Gentiana verna*
Spring Sandwort .... *Sabulina verna*
Spring Speedwell .... *Veronica verna*
Spring Squill .... *Scilla verna*
Squinancywort .... *Asperula cynanchica*
St. Dabeoc's Heath .... *Daboecia cantabrica*
Star Sedge .... *Carex echinata*
Starry Saxifrage .... *Saxifraga stellaris*
Stemless Thistle .... *Cirsium acaule*
Stiff Sedge .... *Carex bigelowii*
stonecrops .... *Sedum* spp.
Strawberry-tree .... *Arbutus unedo*
Stream Water-crowfoot .... *Ranunculus penicillatus*
Subterranean Clover .... *Trifolium subterraneum*
Suffocated Clover .... *Trifolium suffocatum*
Sun Spurge .... *Euphorbia helioscopia*
sundews .... *Drosera* spp.
Sweet Chestnut .... *Castanea sativa*
Sweet Vernal-grass .... *Anthoxanthum odoratum*
Sycamore .... *Acer pseudoplatanus*
Tea-leaved Willow .... *Salix phylicifolia*
Teesdale Sandwort .... *Sabulina stricta*
Teesdale Violet .... *Viola rupestris*
Three-leaved Rush .... *Juncus trifidus*
Three-lobed Crowfoot .... *Ranunculus tripartitus*
Thrift .... *Armeria maritima*
Thyme-leaved Sandwort .... *Arenaria serpyllifolia*
Tor-grass .... *Brachypodium pinnatum*
Tormentil .... *Potentilla erecta*
Trailing Azalea .... *Loiseleuria procumbens*
Traveller's-joy .... *Clematis vitalba*
Tubular Water-dropwort .... *Oenanthe fistulosa*
Tufted Hair-grass .... *Deschampsia cespitosa*
Tunbridge Filmy-fern .... *Hymenophyllum tunbrigense*
Turkey Oak .... *Quercus cerris*
Twinflower .... *Linnaea borealis*
Twin-headed Clover .... *Trifolium bocconei*
Violet Helleborine .... *Epipactis purpurata*
Viviparous Fescue .... *Festuca vivipara*
Wall-rue .... *Asplenium ruta-muraria*
Water Avens .... *Geum rivale*
Water Dock .... *Rumex hydrolapathum*
Water Forget-me-not .... *Myosotis scorpioides*
Water Germander .... *Teucrium scordium*
Water Horsetail .... *Equisetum fluviatile*
Water Lobelia .... *Lobelia dortmanna*
Water Mint .... *Mentha aquatica*
Water-cress .... *Rorippa nasturtium-aquaticum*
water-milfoils .... *Myriophyllum* spp.
water-parsnips .... *Berula* spp.
Water-purslane .... *Lythrum portula*
Water-soldier .... *Stratiotes aloides*
water-starworts .... *Callitriche* spp.
Wavy Hair-grass .... *Avenella flexuosa*
Wavy St. John's-wort .... *Hypericum undulatum*
Wayfaring-tree .... *Viburnum lantana*
Weasel's-snout .... *Misopates orontium*
Western Gorse .... *Ulex gallii*

Western Marsh-orchid .... *Dactylorhiza majalis*
White Beak-sedge .... *Rhynchospora alba*
White Clover .... *Trifolium repens*
White Helleborine .... *Cephalanthera damasonium*
whitebeams .... *Sorbus* spp.
Whorled Caraway .... *Carum verticillatum*
Wild Angelica .... *Angelica sylvestris*
Wild Cabbage .... *Brassica oleracea* var. *oleracea*
Wild Carrot .... *Daucus carota*
Wild Cherry .... *Prunus avium*
Wild Gladiolus .... *Gladiolus illyricus*
Wild Pansy .... *Viola tricolor*
Wild Privet .... *Ligustrum vulgare*
Wild Service-tree .... *Sorbus torminalis*
Wild Strawberry .... *Fragaria vesca*
Wild Thyme .... *Thymus drucei*
Wilson's Filmy-fern .... *Hymenophyllum wilsonii*
Wood Anemone .... *Anemone nemorosa*
Wood Crane's-bill .... *Geranium sylvaticum*
Wood Sage .... *Teucrium scorodonia*
Wood Stitchwort .... *Stellaria nemorum*
Wood-sorrel .... *Oxalis acetosella*
Woolly Willow .... *Salix lanata*
Wych Elm .... *Ulmus glabra*
Yarrow .... *Achillea millefolium*
Yellow Archangel .... *Lamiastrum galeobdolon*
Yellow Bird's-nest .... *Monotropa hypopitys*
Yellow Centuary .... *Cicendia filiformis*
Yellow Glasswort .... *Salicornia fragilis*
Yellow Horned-poppy .... *Glaucium flavum*
Yellow Iris .... *Iris pseudacorus*
Yellow Loosestrife .... *Lysimachia vulgaris*
Yellow Oxytropis .... *Oxytropis campestris*
Yellow Saxifrage .... *Saxifraga aizoides*
Yellow Water-lily .... *Nuphar lutea*
Yellow Whitlowgrass .... *Draba aizoides*
Yellow-rattle .... *Rhinanthus minor*
Yellow-wort .... *Blackstonia perfoliata*
Yew .... *Taxus baccata*
Yorkshire-fog .... *Holcus lanatus*

Mosses and Liverworts

Alpine Silverwort .... *Anthelia julacea*
Bird's-foot Earwort .... *Scapania ornithopodioides*
Bitter Scalewort .... *Porella arboris-vitae*
Bristly Fringe-moss .... *Racomitrium heterostichum*
Broom Fork-moss .... *Dicranum scoparium*
Common Hair-cap .... *Polytrichum commune* var. *commune*
Common Tamarisk-moss .... *Thuidium Tamariscinum*
Compact Bog-moss .... *Sphagnum compactum*
Cow-horn Bog-moss .... *Sphagnum denticulatum*
Curled Hook-moss .... *Palustriella commutata*
Cypress-leaved Plait-moss .... *Hypnum cupressiforme*
Donn's Notchwort .... *Anastrophyllum donnianum*
Dwarf Neckera .... *Neckera pumila*
Feathery Bog-moss .... *Sphagnum cuspidatum*
Fountain Apple-moss .... *Philonotis fontana*
Fox-tail Feather-moss .... *Thamnobryum alopecurum*

Frizzled Crisp-moss .... *Tortella tortuosa*
Glittering Wood-moss .... *Hylocomium splendens*
Golden Bog-moss .... *Sphagnum pulchrum*
Greater Copperwort* .... *Cephaloziella nicholsonii*
Greater Water-moss .... *Fontinalis antipyretica*
Green Shield-moss .... *Buxbaumia viridis*
Hooked Scorpion-moss .... *Scorpidium scorpioides*
Imbricate Bog-moss .... *Sphagnum affine*
Juniper Prongwort .... *Herbertus aduncus* ssp. *hutchinsiae*
Lindberg's Bog-moss .... *Sphagnum lindbergii*
Magellanic Bog-moss .... *Sphagnum magellanicum*
Marsh Forklet-moss .... *Dichodontium palustre*
Mougeot's Yoke-moss .... *Amphidium mougeotii*
Mountain Thread-moss* .... *Pohlia wahlenbergii* var. *glacialis*
Neat Feather-moss .... *Pseudoscleropodium purum*
Northern Haircap .... *Polytrichastrum sexangulare*
Papillose Bog-moss .... *Sphagnum papillosum*
Purple Spoonwort .... *Pleurozia purpurea*
Red Bog-moss .... *Sphagnum capillifolium* ssp. *rubellum*
Red-stemmed Feather-moss .... *Pleurozium schreberi*
River Feather-moss .... *Brachythecium rivulare*
Rough Earwort .... *Scapania aspera*
Sand-hill Screw-moss .... *Syntrichia ruralis* ssp. *ruraliformis*
Smaller Lattice-moss .... *Cinclidotus fontinaloides*
Soft Bog-moss .... *Sphagnum tenellum*
Starke's Forkmoss .... *Kiaeria starkei*
Swan-necked Thyme-moss .... *Mnium hornum*
Tamarisk Scalewort .... *Frullania tamarisci*
Water Earwort .... *Scapania undulata*
Wood's Whipwort .... *Mastigophora woodsii*
Woolly Fringe-moss .... *Racomitrium lanuginosum*
Yellow Feather-moss .... *Homalothecium lutescens*
Yellow Starry Feather-moss .... *Campylium stellatum*

Fungi

Blue Tooth .... *Hydnellum caeruleum*
bracket fungi .... *Gandoderma* spp.
Chicken of the Woods .... *Laetiporus sulphureus*
earthtongues .... Geoglossaceae
fairy clubs .... Clavarioids
Fly Agaric .... *Amanita muscaria*
Hazel Gloves .... *Hypocreopsis rhododendri*
Nail Fungus .... *Poronia punctata*
Orange Tooth .... *Hydnellum aurantiacum*
pinkgills .... Entolomatceaeae
Southern Bracket Fungus .... *Ganoderma australe*
waxcaps .... *Hygrocybe* spp.

Lichens

Black Tar Lichen .... *Hydropunctaria maura*
Common Tree Lungwort .... *Lobaria pulmonaria*
cudbear lichens .... *Ochrolechia* spp.
Iceland Moss .... *Cetraria islandica* ssp. *islandica*
Octopus Suckers .... *Collema conglomeratum*
Orange Sea Lichen .... *Caloplaca marina*
reindeer lichens .... *Cladonia* spp.
Sea Ivory .... *Ramalina siliquosa*
Yellow Specklebelly .... *Pseudocyphellaria crocata*

Macro-algae

stoneworts .... *Chara* spp.

Seaweeds

Bladder Wrack .... *Fucus vesiculosus*
Bushy Rainbow Wrack .... *Cystoseira tamariscifolia*
Dulse .... *Palmaria palmata*
kelps .... *Laminaria* spp.
Oar Weed .... *Laminaria digitata*
Sea Lettuce .... *Ulva lactuca*
Spiral Wrack .... *Fucus spiralis*
Sugar Kelp .... *Saccharina latissima*
wracks .... Fucaceae

Invertebrates

Adonis Blue .... *Polyommatus bellargus*
Argent and Sable .... *Rheumaptera hastata*
Azure Hawker .... *Aeshna caerulea*
Barberry Carpet .... *Parelype berberata*
barnacles .... *Chthamalus* spp.
Beachcomber Beetle .... *Eurynebria complanata*
Beadlet Anemone .... *Actinia equina*
Beewolf .... *Philanthus triangulum*
Belted Beauty .... *Lycia zonaria*
Bilberry Bumblebee .... *Bombus monticola*
Bilberry Pug .... *Pasiphila debiliata*
Black Bog Ant .... *Formica picea*
Black Darter .... *Sympetrum danae*
Bog Bush-cricket .... *Metrioptera brachyptera*
Bog Sun-jumper Spider .... *Heliophanus dampfi*
Brown Argus .... *Aricia agestis*
Brown Hairstreak .... *Thecla betulae*
Brown-banded Carder Bee .... *Bombus humilis*
Bumblebee Robberfly .... *Laphria flava*
Chalkhill Blue .... *Polyommatus coridon*
Chequered Skipper .... *Carterocephalus palaemon*
Cliff Tiger Beetle .... *Cylindera germanica*
Common Blue Damselfly .... *Enallagma cyathigerum*
Common Field Grasshopper .... *Chorthippus brunneus*
Common Shore Crab .... *Carcinus maenas*
craneflies .... Tipulidae
Dark Crimson Underwing .... *Catocala sponsa*
Dark-green Fritillary .... *Argynnis aglaja*
digger wasps .... *Argogorytes* spp.
Dingy Skipper .... *Erynnis tages*
Dog Whelk .... *Nucella lapillus*
Duke of Burgundy .... *Hamearis lucina*
Dune Tiger Beetle .... *Cicindela maritima*
Emerald Damselfly .... *Lestes sponsa*
Emperor Moth .... *Saturnia pavonia*
Fairy Shrimp .... *Chirocephalus diaphanus*
Field Cricket .... *Gryllus campestris*
Fox Moth .... *Macrothylacia rubi*
Freshwater Pearl Mussel .... *Margaritifera margaritifera*
freshwater sponges .... Porifera
Gilkicker Weevil .... *Pachytychius haematocephalus*
Glanville Fritillary .... *Melitaea cinxia*
Glow-worm .... *Lampyris noctiluca*

Fishes

Pike .... *Esox lucius*
pipefish .... *Syngnathinae*
Powan .... *Coregonus clupeoides*
Rainbow Trout .... *Oncorhynchus mykiss*
Roach .... *Rutilus rutilus*
Rudd .... *Scardinius erythropthalmus*
Ruffe .... *Gymnocephalus cernua*
sandeels .... Ammodytidae
Sea-bass .... *Dicentrarchus labrax*
Tench .... *Tinca tinca*

Reptiles

Slow-worm .... *Anguis fragilis*
Smooth Snake .... *Coronella austriaca*
Sand Lizard .... *Lacerta agilis*
Grass Snake .... *Natrix natrix*
Adder .... *Vipera berus*
Common Lizard .... *Zootoca vivipara*

Amphibians

Common Toad .... *Bufo bufo*
Common Frog .... *Rana temporaria*
Great Crested Newt .... *Triturus cristatus*
Natterjack Toad .... *Epidalea calamita*
newts .... Urodeles

Birds

**Gill & Donsker & Rasmussen (2020) / IOC international
English name in square brackets where appropriate.**

Arctic Skua [Parasitic Jaeger] .... *Stercorarius parasiticus*
Avocet [Pied Avocet] .... *Recurvirostra avosetta*
Barn Owl [Western Barn Owl] .... *Tyto alba*
Barnacle Goose .... *Branta leucopsis*
Bean Goose [Tundra/Taiga Bean Goose] .... *Anser fabalis*
Bearded Tit [Bearded Reedling] .... *Panurus biarmicus*
Bewick's Swan [Tundra Swan] .... *Cygnus columbianus*
Bittern [Eurasian Bittern] .... *Botaurus stellaris*
Black Grouse .... *Lyrurus tetrix*
Black Guillemot .... *Cepphus grylle*
Black Redstart .... *Phoenicurus ochruros*
Black-tailed Godwit .... *Limosa limosa*
Black-throated Diver [Black-throated Loon] .... *Gavia arctica*
Black-winged Stilt .... *Himantopus himantopus*
Brambling .... *Fringilla montifringilla*
Brent Goose [Brant Goose] .... *Branta bernicla*
Bullfinch [Eurasian Bullfinch] .... *Pyrrhula pyrrhula*
Capercaillie [Western Capercaillie] .... *Tetrao urogallus*
Chough [Red-billed Chough] .... *Pyrrhocorax pyrrhocorax*
Cirl Bunting .... *Emberiza cirlus*
Common Sandpiper .... *Actitis hypoleucos*
Common Scoter .... *Melanitta nigra*
Cormorant [Great Cormorant] .... *Phalacrocorax carbo*
Corn Bunting .... *Emberiza calandra*
Corncrake [Corn Crake] .... *Crex crex*
Crane [Common Crane] .... *Grus grus*
Crested Tit [European Crested Tit] .... *Lophophanes cristatus*
Crossbill .... *Loxia curvirostra*

Curlew [Eurasian Curlew] .... *Numenius arquata*
Dalmatian Pelican .... *Pelecanus crispus*
Dartford Warbler .... *Sylvia undata*
Dipper [White-throated Dipper] .... *Cinclus cinclus*
Dotterel [Eurasian Dotterel] .... *Charadrius morinellus*
Dunlin .... *Calidris alpina*
Dunnock .... *Prunella modularis*
White-fronted Goose
    [Greater White-fronted Goose] .... *Anser albifrons*
Fieldfare .... *Turdus pilaris*
Firecrest [Common Firecrest] .... *Regulus ignicapillus*
Fulmar [Northern Fulmar] .... *Fulmarus glacialis*
Gadwall .... *Mareca strepera*
Gannet [Northern Gannet] .... *Morus bassanus*
Garden Warbler .... *Sylvia borin*
Garganey .... *Spatula querquedula*
Golden Eagle .... *Aquila chrysaetos*
Golden Plover [European Golden Plover] ...... *Pluvialis apricaria*
Goldeneye [Common Goldeneye] ...... *Bucephala clangula*
Goshawk [Northern Goshawk] .... *Accipiter gentilis*
Grasshopper Warbler
    [Common Grasshopper Warbler] .... *Locustella naevia*
Great Bustard .... *Otis tarda*
Great Crested Grebe .... *Podiceps cristatus*
Great Spotted Woodpecker .... *Dendrocopos major*
Green Woodpecker
    [European Green Woodpecker] .... *Picus viridis*
Greenshank [Common Greenshank] ...... *Tringa nebularia*
Grey Partridge .... *Perdix perdix*
Grey Wagtail .... *Motacilla cinerea*
Guillemot [Common Murre] .... *Uria aalge*
Hen Harrier .... *Circus cyaneus*
Herring Gull [European Herring Gull] ...... *Larus argentatus*
House Martin [Common House Martin] .... *Delichon urbica*
Kestrel [Common Kestrel] .... *Falco tinnunculus*
Kingfisher [Common Kingfisher] .... *Alcedo atthis*
Kittiwake [Black-legged Kittiwake] .... *Rissa tridactyla*
Knot [Red Knot] .... *Calidris canutus*
Lapwing [Northern Lapwing] .... *Vanellus vanellus*
Lesser Whitethroat .... *Sylvia curruca*
Lesser Spotted Woodpecker .... *Dryobates minor*
Linnet [Common Linnet] .... *Linaria cannabina*
Little Bittern .... *Ixobrychus minutus*
Little Grebe .... *Tachybaptus ruficollis*
Little Owl .... *Athene noctua*
Little Ringed Plover .... *Charadrius dubius*
Long-eared Owl .... *Asio otus*
Marsh Harrier [Western Marsh Harrier] .... *Circus aeruginosus*
Marsh Tit .... *Poecile palustris*
Meadow Pipit .... *Anthus pratensis*
Merlin .... *Falco columbarius*
Montagu's Harrier .... *Circus pygargus*
Nightingale [Common Nightingale] .... *Luscinia megarhynchos*
Nightjar [European Nightjar] .... *Caprimulgus europaeus*
Nuthatch .... *Sitta europaea*
Osprey [Western Osprey] .... *Pandion haliaetus*
Oystercatcher
    [Eurasian Oystercatcher] .... *Haematopus ostralegus*

Parrot Crossbill .... *Loxia pytyopsittacus*
Peregrine [Peregrine Falcon] .... *Falco peregrinus*
Pied Flycatcher
  [European Pied Flycatcher] .... *Ficedula hypoleuca*
Pink-footed Goose .... *Anser brachyrhyncus*
Pochard [Common Pochard] .... *Aythya ferina*
Ptarmigan [Rock Ptarmigan] .... *Lagopus mutus*
Puffin [Atlantic Puffin] .... *Fratercula arctica*
Purple Sandpiper .... *Calidris maritima*
Quail [Common Quail] .... *Coturnix coturnix*
Raven [Northern Raven] .... *Corvus corax*
Razorbill .... *Alca torda*
Red Grouse [Willow Ptarmigan] .... *Lagopus lagopus*
Red Kite .... *Milvus milvus*
Red-breasted Merganser .... *Mergus serrator*
Lesser Redpoll .... *Acanthis cabaret*
Redstart [Common Redstart] .... *Phoenicurus phoenicurus*
Red-throated Diver [Red-throated Loon] ..... *Gavia stellata*
Reed Bunting
  [Common Reed Bunting] .... *Emberiza schoeniclus*
Reed Warbler
  [Eurasian Reed Warbler] ..... *Acrocephalus scirpaceus*
Ring Ouzel .... *Turdus torquatus*
Ringed Plover [Common Ringed Plover] .... *Charadrius hiaticula*
Rock Pipit [Eurasian Rock Pipit] .... *Anthus petrosus*
Sand Martin .... *Riparia riparia*
Savi's Warbler .... *Locustella luscinioides*
Scottish Crossbill .... *Loxia scotica*
Sedge Warbler .... *Acrocephalus schoenobaenus*
Shag [European Shag] .... *Phalacrocorax aristotelis*
Short-eared Owl .... *Asio flammeus*
Siskin [Eurasian Siskin] .... *Spinus spinus*
Skylark [Eurasian Skylark] .... *Alauda arvensis*
Snipe [Common Snipe] .... *Gallinago gallinago*
Snow Bunting .... *Plectrophenax nivalis*
Spoonbill .... *Platalea leucorodia*
Spotted Crake .... *Porzana porzana*
Spotted Flycatcher .... *Muscicapa striata*
Starling [Common Starling] .... *Sturnus vulgaris*
Stone-curlew [Eurasian Stone-curlew] .... *Burhinus oedicnemus*
Stonechat
  [European Stonechat] ..... *Saxicola rubicola (torquatus)*
Storm Petrel .... *Hydrobates pelagicus*
Swallow [Barn Swallow] .... *Hirundo rustica*
Swift [Common Swift] .... *Apus apus*
Teal [Eurasian Teal] .... *Anas crecca*
Tree Pipit .... *Anthus trivialis*
Tree Sparrow [Eurasian Tree Sparrow] ..... *Passer montanus*
Tufted Duck .... *Aythya fuligula*
Turtle Dove [European Turtle Dove] .... *Streptopelia turtur*
Twite .... *Linaria flavirostris*
Water Rail .... *Rallus aquaticus*
Wheatear [Northern Wheatear] .... *Oenanthe oenanthe*
Whinchat .... *Saxicola rubetra*

White-tailed Eagle .... *Haliaeatus albicilla*
Whitethroat [Common Whitethroat] .... *Sylvia communis*
Whooper Swan .... *Cygnus cygnus*
Wigeon [Eurasian Wigeon] .... *Mareca penelope*
Willow Tit .... *Poecile montanus*
Willow Warbler .... *Phylloscopus trochilus*
Wood Warbler .... *Phylloscopus sibilatrix*
Woodlark .... *Lullula arborea*
Wren [Eurasian Wren] .... *Troglodytes troglodytes*
Yellow Wagtail [Western Yellow Wagtail] .... *Motacilla flava*
Yellowhammer .... *Emberiza citrinella*

Mammals

Badger .... *Meles meles*
Bank Vole .... *Myodes glareolus*
Barbastelle .... *Barbastella barbastellus*
Beaver [Eurasian Beaver] .... *Castor fiber*
Brown Hare .... *Lepus europaeus*
Brown Long-eared Bat .... *Plecotus auritus*
Chinese Water Deer .... *Hydropotes inermis*
Common Seal .... *Phoca vitulina*
Eurasian Elk .... *Alces alces*
Eurasian Lynx .... *Lynx lynx*
Fox .... *Vulpes vulpes*
Greater Horseshoe Bat .... *Rhinolophus ferrumequinum*
Grey Seal .... *Halichoerus grypus*
Grey Squirrel .... *Sciurus carolinensis*
Harvest Mouse .... *Micromys minutus*
Hazel Dormouse .... *Muscardinus avellanarius*
Hedgehog [European Hedgehog] .... *Erinaceus europaeus*
Irish Hare .... *Lepus timidus ssp. hibernicus*
Mink [American Mink} .... *Neovison vison*
Mountain Hare .... *Lepus timidus*
Natterer's Bat .... *Myotis nattereri*
Noctule .... *Nyctalus noctula*
Otter .... *Lutra lutra*
Pine Marten .... *Martes martes*
Polecat .... *Mustela putorius*
Red Deer .... *Cervus elaphus*
Red Squirrel .... *Sciurus vulgaris*
Reindeer .... *Rangifer tarandus*
Roe Deer .... *Capreolus capreolus*
Serotine .... *Eptesicus serotinus*
Spotted Hyena .... *Crocuta crocuta*
Stoat .... *Mustela erminea*
Tarpan .... *Equus ferus ferus*
Water Shrew .... *Neomys fodiens*
Water Vole .... *Arvicola terrestris*
Wild Boar .... *Sus scrofa*
Wolf .... *Canis lupus*
Woolly Mammoth .... *Mammuthus primigenius*
Woolly Rhinoceros .... *Coelodonta antiquitatis*

Photographic Credits

The production of this book would not have been possible without the help of the photographers whose images have been reproduced. In total, 914 images are featured, representing the work of 71 photographers. All photographs **apart from those taken by the authors** Sophie Lake, Durwyn Liley, Robert Still or Andy Swash are listed here, together with the photographer's initials used in the specific credits that follow:

Andy Acton [AA]; David Adam [DA]; Steve Aylward [SA]; Terry Bagley [TB]; John Bowler [JB]; Christophe Brochard (cbrochard.com) [CB]; Paul Brock [PB]; Laurie Campbell/SNH [LC/SNH]; Graham Catley [GC]; Channel Coast Observatory (channelcoast.org) [CCO]; Stella Clifford-Jones [SCJ]; Sandy Coppins [SC]; Greg and Yvonne Dean (WorldWildlifeImages.com) [G&YD]; Dorset County Museum [DCM]; Brendan Dunford (burrenbeo.com) [BD]; Guy Dutson [GD]; Peter Eeles/Butterfly Conservation [PE]; Rue Ekins [RE]; Knepp Estate [Knepp Est]; Steven Falk (flickr.com/photos/63075200@N07) [SF]; Rob Fuller [RF]; Bob Gibbons [BG]; Chris Gibson [CG]; Lorne Gill/SNH [LG/SNH]; Andy Harmer [AH]; Paul Harris [PH]; Hugh Harrop (hughharrop.com) [HH]; Hedgelink [H]; Hedgelink/Rob Walton [H/RW]; Roger Key [RK]; David Kjaer [DK]; Mark Lake [ML]; James Lowen (jameslowen.com) [JL]; John MacPherson (john-macpherson-photography.com) [JMac]; David Mardon [DM]; Tim Melling (flickr.com/photos/timmelling) [TM]; James Merryweather [JMe]; Peter Moore [PM]; Steve Moore [SM]; David Newland [DN]; Nick Owens [NO]; Dave Pickett [DP]; Gordon Rothero [GR]; RSPB [RSPB]; Dave Smallshire [DS]; Sue Smallshire [SS]; Richard Starling/The Broads Reed and Sedge Cutting Association [RS/TBRSCA]; David Tipling [DT]; Alan Watson Featherstone, Trees for Life [AWF].

Images by 14 other photographers have been reproduced under the terms of the Creative Commons Attribution 2.0 Generic license (CC BY 2.0), Attribution-ShareAlike 2.5 Generic license (CC BY-SA 2.5) or the Attribution-ShareAlike 3.0 Unported license (CC BY-SA 3.0), and one by another photographer is in the Public Domain. Images reproduced under a Creative Commons licence, or which are in the Public Domain, are indicated by "/CC" or "/PD" after the photographer's name, respectively, together with details of the relevant license. Finally, one image has been licensed from the photographic agency Alamy (alamy.com).

411

Map Credits

One of the key features of this book is the maps that provide an overview of the physical characteristics of Britain and Ireland and show the distribution of each habitat type. Many maps use data from a range of different sources and mapped at different resolutions. The following information summarizes the data sources and relevant copyright data.

The geology maps (*page 23*) are the same as in the first edition. Geology data are reproduced with the permission of the British Geological Survey. © NERC. All rights Reserved. The data for Ireland are Copyright Government of Ireland/ Geological Survey of Ireland.

Climate data (*page 27*) include gridded data from the Met Office. The data are © Crown Copyright (2009). The UK Climate Projections data have been made available by the Department for Environment, Food and Rural Affairs (Defra) and Department for Energy and Climate Change (DECC) under licence from the Met Office, Newcastle University, University of East Anglia and Proudman Oceanographic Laboratory. These organizations accept no responsibility for any inaccuracies or omissions in the data, nor for any loss or damage directly or indirectly caused to any person or body by reason of, or arising out of, any use of these data. Data for Ireland are from the MET ÉIREANN website and are © copyright Met Éireann.

The upland vegetation boundary (*page 26*) is drawn with reference to the 300 m contour and adapted from that in Averis, A., Averis, B., Birks, J., Horsfield, D., Thompson, D. & Yeo, M. (2004). *An Illustrated Guide To British Upland Vegetation*. JNCC, Peterborough, England and also from Bunce, R. G. H., Barr, C. J., Clarke, R. T., Howard, D. & Scott, A. (2007). ITE *Land Classification of Great Britain 2007*. NERC Environmental Information Data Centre.

SAC boundary data (*page 38*) are as supplied by the European Environment Agency. The data for the UK is © Natural England copyright. Contains Ordnance Survey data © Crown copyright and database right 2020.

The combined habitat map (*page 11*), habitat introduction maps (*pages 41, 121, 155, 199, 235* and *271*) and individual habitat maps (*pages 189, 327, 329, 333, 349, 369, 373, 375* and *379*) have been drawn using CORINE Land Cover (2018).

Maps on *pages 163, 169* and *193* are derived from CEH Landcover data, which are based on satellite data acquired during 2015. The data used are the dominant land classes for each 1 km square. Data are based upon LCM2015 © UKCEH 2017.

The Natural England Priority Habitat Inventory has been used in the maps on *pages 53, 131, 163, 169, 171, 175, 177, 183, 187, 195, 205, 209, 231, 249, 253, 257, 265, 329, 333, 343, 349* and *375*. This inventory replaced Natural England's earlier separate BAP habitat inventories. © Natural England copyright. Contains Ordnance Survey data © Crown copyright and database right 2020.

Irish Semi-natural Grassland Survey data 2007-2012 are used in the maps on *pages 169, 171, 175, 177, 183, 189*, and *193*. These data are made available by the Irish Government and are licenced under Creative Commons Attribution 4.0. For Ireland we have also drawn on the polygon data for individual Annex I habitats, generated as part of the 2013 reporting round. These data are the copyright of The Department of the Arts, Heritage and the Gaeltacht and are used in maps on *pages 57, 61, 63, 67, 79, 83, 87, 131, 141, 143, 149, 163, 169, 171, 175, 183, 187, 195, 205, 209, 212, 215, 225, 227, 231, 245, 249, 253, 257, 283, 285, 289, 329, 333, 339, 343, 349* and *353*.

Data for Scotland, used in the maps on *pages 53, 67, 79, 83, 87, 91, 97, 104, 117, 131, 141, 143, 149, 163, 169, 171, 175, 177, 183, 187, 189, 193, 195, 205, 209, 212, 215, 225, 227, 231, 249, 253, 257, 261, 265, 329, 333, 339, 343, 349* and *358*, are from the Habitat Map of Scotland (HabMoS). This contains SNH information licensed under the Open Government Licence v3.0.

Data from Wales (maps on *pages 53, 117, 131, 141, 143, 149, 163, 169, 171, 175, 189, 193, 209, 212, 215, 225, 227, 231, 249, 253, 257, 261, 329, 333, 343, 355, 358*) are from the Terrestrial Phase I Habitat Survey and the data for Coastal and Floodplain Grassland (map on *page 177*) were provided directly by Natural Resources Wales. All these maps contain Natural Resources Wales information © Natural Resources Wales and Database Right. All Rights Reserved. Contains Ordnance Survey Data. Ordnance Survey Licence number 100019741. Crown Copyright and Database Right.

Priority habitats data from Northern Ireland were used in the maps on *pages 53, 131, 163, 169, 171, 175, 177, 183, 187, 195, 205, 209, 231, 249, 253, 257* and *265*. There are separate databases for Woodland, Heathland, Fens, Peatland and Grassland. Provided by the Northern Ireland Environment Agency,they are used under an Open Government Licence.

For the UK and Ireland, we have shown the broad extent of various Annex I habitats in the maps on *pages 57, 61, 63, 67, 79, 83, 87, 131, 141, 143, 149, 163, 169, 171, 175, 183, 187, 195, 205, 209, 212, 215, 225, 227, 231, 245, 249, 253, 257, 283, 285, 289, 329, 333, 339, 343, 349* and *353*. These data are from the European Environment Agency, downloaded from EIONET. Detailed reports and accounts for each Annex I habitat accompany the data and provide further information on how the maps are derived.

Wood Pasture and Parkland for England (*page 73*) are from a provisional Wood Pasture and Parkland Inventory. © Natural England copyright. Contains Ordnance Survey data © Crown copyright and database right 2020.

The Valley Mire map (*page 261*) shows indicative locations across England as point data, these were provided by Ian Diack (Natural England).

Maps on *pages 271, 305, 307, 311* and *313* are derived from OpenStreetMap, © OpenStreetMap contributors.

The inset map of rivers on *page 272* contains Ordnance Survey Data. © Crown copyright and database right 2020. Turloughs (*page 291*) were mapped using the Environmental Protection Agency Turlough database. The Traditional Orchards map (*page 375*) includes survey data from the People's Trust for Endangered Species. The data for England are part of Natural England's Priority Habitat Inventory (see above). For Wales the data contains Natural Resources Wales information © Natural Resources Wales and database right.

Acknowledgements

There is a wealth of information about the habitats of Britain and Ireland. In the Further Information boxes for each habitat group we have listed key texts and sources that have particularly inspired us. We would like to acknowledge this work, without which the production of this book would not have been possible.

Many people have helped in the production of the first and second editions of this book and our sincere thanks go to them all. For information about habitats and places or access to sites, we thank: Isabel Alonso (Natural England), Steve Aylward (Suffolk Wildlife Trust), Jeremy Biggs (Freshwater Habitats Trust), Sandy Coppins, Alistair Crowle (Natural England), Iain Diack (Natural England), Mark Everard (Environment Agency), Digger and Lauren Jackson, Francisco Laborde, Richard Lindsay (University of East London), James Lowen, Lindsay Maskell (Centre for Ecology and Hydrology), Ed Mountford (Joint Nature Conservation Committee), Kenny Nelson (Scottish Natural Heritage), Colin Newlands (Natural England), Lisa Norton (Centre for Ecology and Hydrology), Matt O'Callaghan (University of Birmingham), Peter Quelch, the Randalls (Goodens Farm, Dorset), Phil Saunders (Footprint Ecology) and Ken Thompson (University of Sheffield).

A range of people helped us to source GIS data or assisted us in how to best use data and we extend our gratitude to: Lauren Alexander (People's Trust for Endangered Species), Dave Chambers (Joint Nature Conservation Committee), Katie Cruickshanks (Footprint Ecology), Iain Diack (Natural England), Peter Duffy (National Parks and Wildlife Service), Ian Denham (Natural England), David Edwards (Northern Ireland Environment Agency), Crispin Hayes (CW Hayes Associates), Michelle Lewis (Natural Resources Wales), Lisa Norton (Centre for Ecology and Hydrology), Ian Macleod (Forestry Commission), Antony Myers (British Geological Society), Daniel O'Connell (Ordnance Survey Ireland), Michael O'Neill (Environmental Protection Agency), Chris Panter (Footprint Ecology), Oliver Robertson (Centre for Ecology and Hydrology), Ray Scanlon (Geological Survey of Ireland), and Phillip Wyndham (Ordnance Survey). Copyright information and sources for map data are given on *page 413*.

We were very fortunate to be able to draw on the expertise and wide experience of a number of people who commented on drafts of the text: Malcolm Ausden (RSPB), Sandy Coppins, Rachel Hoskin (Natural England), Rob McGibbon (Footprint Ecology), Douglas Kite (Natural England), Miles King, Richard Lindsay (University of East London), Helen Read (Corporation of London), Peter Tinsley (Dorset Wildlife Trust) and Jim White (Footprint Ecology). In particular, we are grateful to the late John Underhill-Day (Footprint Ecology) for sharing the great breadth of his knowledge about British and Irish habitats and for his unstinting help and support. Gill Swash read through and commented on all sections of the book, and receives our wholehearted thanks. Our thanks also go to Chris Gibson and all others who provided comments and corrections on the first edition, which have strengthened the text of the second edition, and to Brian Clews for proof reading the final version. Any errors or omissions remain, of course, our own.

We are grateful to the photographers who allowed us to use their lovely images, which have greatly enhanced this book. They are listed on *page 411*. Particular thanks go to Graham Catley, Bob Gibbons, Lorne Gill, David Kjaer and the Scottish Natural Heritage image library, Mark Lake, James Lowen (jameslowen.com) and Andy and Gill Swash (WorldWildlifeImages.com). We are grateful to the following who helped us source images: Peter Brash (National Trust), Tom Brereton (MarineLife/Butterfly Conservation), Nigel Bourn (Butterfly Conservation), Keith Dover, Dave Foot, Andy Jukes, Paul Kirkland (Butterfly Conservation), Richard Lindsay (University of East London), Rob McGibbon (Footprint Ecology), Pam Moncur (Scottish Natural Heritage), Caroline Reid (Scottish Natural Heritage), Michael Szebor (RSPB) and Des Thompson (Scottish Natural Heritage).

Others provided help and support in a range of ways. We are grateful to Footprint Ecology for allowing us leave to work on this book and for the use of GIS. Many friends also provided support and encouragement, and our especial thanks go to Victoria Copley, Emma Foulger, Peter Fox, Tania Kaplan, Sarah Honour, Lisa Nicholson and Neil Wiffen.

Finally, a thank you to our families. Judy and Bill Lake were very generous with their time and energy. Mark Lake, Paddy Woodman and Mary Liley helped in an assortment of ways. Willoughby Liley and Tamsin Lake climbed mountains, ventured through bogs, traipsed across hillsides and escaped more or less unhurt from numerous escapades while our attention was elsewhere.

Index

Names in **bold** highlight the habitat types afforded a full account; other habitats are in regular text.
Bold numbers indicate the page where the main habitat account can be found.
Regular black text indicates other page(s) where the habitat is mentioned; *italicized black text* is used if the reference relates to a photograph.
Bold blue italicized figures highlight the main entry in the Habitat Correspondence Tables; *non-bold blue italicized* figures are used for other references in the Habitat Correspondence Tables.